# The Folklorist in the Marketplace

# The Folklorist in the Marketplace

Conversations at the Crossroads of
Vernacular Culture and Economics

Edited by
Willow G. Mullins
Puja Batra-Wells

Utah State University Press
*Logan*

© 2019 by University Press of Colorado

Published by Utah State University Press
An imprint of University Press of Colorado
245 Century Circle, Suite 202
Louisville, Colorado 80027

All rights reserved

 The University Press of Colorado is a proud member of the Association of University Presses

The University Press of Colorado is a cooperative publishing enterprise supported, in part, by Adams State University, Colorado State University, Fort Lewis College, Metropolitan State University of Denver, University of Colorado, University of Northern Colorado, University of Wyoming, Utah State University, and Western Colorado University.

ISBN: 978-1-60732-784-4 (paperback)
ISBN: 978-1-60732-785-1 (ebook)
https://doi.org/10.7330/9781607327851

Library of Congress Cataloging-in-Publication Data

Names: Mullins, Willow (Willow G.), editor. | Batra-Wells, Puja, editor.
Title: The folklorist in the marketplace : conversations at the crossroads of vernacular culture and economics / edited by Willow G. Mullins, Puja Batra-Wells.
Description: Logan : Utah State University Press, [2019] | Includes bibliographical references and index.
Identifiers: LCCN 2019020035 | ISBN 9781607327844 (pbk.) | ISBN 9781607327851 (ebook)
Subjects: LCSH: Folklore—Economic aspects. | Material culture—Economic aspects. | Markets—Folklore.
Classification: LCC GR873 .F65 2019 | DDC 398—dc23

LC record available at https://lccn.loc.gov/2019020035

Cover images, clockwise from top left: Detroit Steel Mill mural, Portsmouth, Ohio (photograph by Cassie Patterson); Pied-du-Courant prison, Montreal, Quebec (courtesy of Maison nationale des Patriotes); Tribute to Labor mural, Detroit Steel Mill, Portsmouth, Ohio (photograph by Cassie Patterson); hats for sale in Istanbul, Turkey (photograph by Domhnall Hegarty).

To all of the authors in folklore,
economics, and elsewhere who have
helped create this field of study

# Contents

*Acknowledgments* ix

Introduction
 *Willow G. Mullins and Puja Batra-Wells*   3

1   Folklore as a Networked Economy: Or, How a Recently-Invented-but-Traditional Artifact Reveals the Way Folkloric Production Has Always Worked
 *John Laudun*   26

2   Branding Unibroue: Selling Québécois Folklore through Beer
 *Julie M-A LeBlanc*   47

3   Market Forces and Marketplace Economics at the Smithsonian Folklife Festival
 *Halle M. Butvin and James I. Deutsch*   72

4   The Sweet Spot: An Epistemological Approach to the Economics of Sugarmaking in Vermont
 *Michael Lange*   92

5   Where the Creel Boats Go: The Politics of Sustainable Fisheries in a Small Orkney Community
 *Christofer Johnson*   109

6   The Economics of Curation and Representation: Dialogues in the Commemorative Landscape of Portsmouth, Ohio
 *Cassie Patterson*   129

7   An Ordered Mess: Folk Narratives and Practices in a Chinese Hui Muslim Market
 *Zhao Yuanhao*   155

8   Art/Work: Precarious Encounters and Vernacular Economic Remedies
    *Puja Batra-Wells*   174

9   From Vision to Implementation: Clashing Values of Economic Idealism and Solvency in Twin Oaks Community, 1967–1979
    *Rahima Schwenkbeck*   194

10  "Why the Sea Is Salty": Folktales as Sources of Grassroots Economics
    *Irene Sotiropoulou*   214

11  What Would Hermes Do? A Jungian Perspective on the Trickster and Business Ethics
    *William A. Ashton*   234

12  Folk Economies and the Artisan Workshop
    *Amy Shuman*   252

13  Consuming Authenticities: An Economics of Folklorists
    *Willow G. Mullins*   271

*About the Authors*   293
*Index*   297

# Acknowledgments

THIS BOOK WOULD NOT HAVE BEEN POSSIBLE WITHOUT the hard work and faith of a lot of people. In particular, we would like to thank the Folklore Studies program and Center for Folklore Studies at The Ohio State University, where many of the ideas that shaped this collection were first sparked, and the people there, including Amy Shuman and Dorothy Noyes, who have created such a rich environment for the study of folklore. Much thanks also goes to Elaine Lawless and Anand Prahlad at University of Missouri for their endless support and Kristin Schwain for helping tie together the folkloristic with the economic through material and visual culture. We couldn't be more grateful for the thoughtful comments of the readers and the conscientious shepherding of Rachael Levay and everyone else at USU Press. Thanks, too, to our families for putting up with us. Most of all, we would like to thank the scholars whose works appear here.

# The Folklorist in the Marketplace

# Introduction

Willow G. Mullins and Puja Batra-Wells

FOLKLORE SELLS. Companies from Etsy to IKEA have capitalized on cultural associations with the idea of "folklore"—a term in marketing meant to evoke the traditional, the exotic, the esoteric, the local, and the handmade. Folklore sells small. It sells in the shops that specialize in the handmade, from one person to another. One can see folklore for sale in the popularity of the "buy local" and "Slow Food" movements, intent on keeping craft and food production locally based and preserving traditional networks. But folklore also sells big. It sells in the mass market from corporations with thousands of employees and is bought in big box stores or consumed through mass media. Television and film capitalize on references to fairy tales and myths, from wholesale remakes of well-known stories (think of the many iterations of "Snow White" [Aarne-Thompson-Uther Classification of Folk Tales no. 709[1]]) to new formulations of the tropes of urban legends and wonder tales to the "Folkloric Charm" promised by a Behr Paints color swatch. And who buys and sells all of this folklore? Who are the actors in the folklore marketplace? The folk, of course.

It is by now commonplace among folklorists that everyone has folklore, that people engage in the exchange and coproduction of unofficial, artistic cultural meaning (Ben-Amos 1971; Brunvand 1986). Economists have argued for just as long, however, that everyone engages in economics, which reflects how people navigate their decisions about resources and scarcity (American Economic Association 2017). This collection starts with the premise that folklore and the folk themselves are deeply and productively engaged in economics, and further, that the economic worlds in which we all live shape our cultures, our lives, and our identities. Put simply, the folk are in the marketplace.

Economics has always been folklore's not-so-silent partner. Folklorists have a long history of pondering the economics of the folk and their relationship to the marketplace; recently, the 2017 Nobel Prize in Economics was granted to the founders of behavioral economics, which takes into account the direct influence of culture and psychology on economic actions, suggesting the importance of folklore to economists. Yet folklore and economics as a subfield has largely remained unarticulated, in part because of the constructs and institutional histories of each field.

At this moment, trade, technology, and geopolitics have led to a rapid increase in the global spread of cultural products, including media, knowledge, objects, and folkways. Accompanying that globalization have come fears, realized and not, of cultural appropriation, neocolonialism, and loss. Culture operates as a resource and a currency in the global marketplace. This movement of people and forms necessitates a new textual consideration of how folklore and economics interweave. Here, we hope to explore how the marketplace and folklore itself have always been integrally linked in ways both productive and subversive, in theory and on the ground, and what that means at this global, cultural, and economic moment. In order to create a more concise disciplinary history of folklore and economics and to provide the institutional background against which the current work is set, in the sections that follow, this introduction offers a tracing of the genealogy that has helped formed the field of folklore and economics.

Folklorists' ideas about the relationship between folklore and economics have tended to occur along three primary trajectories. First, at the macrolevel, folklorists have relied on socioeconomic status as a marker of folk status as a way to bound or propel the field, and, in a Marxist turn, they have considered the role of class in the production of folklore, particularly through labor lore. Second, scholars have invoked microlevel understandings of commodity and commodification, particularly in the study of material culture. This perspective has helped folklorists assess the relationship between folk artists, folklorists, and audiences and how practices and art forms may be influenced by consumers. A third, more theoretical but still microeconomic line of thought, has built on Mikhail Bakhtin's conceptualization of the marketplace as a center of village life (1965). In the marketplace, critical inversions of social status become possible and folk performance can take place.

Each of these trajectories has influenced how folklorists have constructed the folk both in relation and opposition to the marketplace, but they tell a partial story. Like the stage set of a play, these trajectories provide a background against which the chapters that follow are set, and like a stage set, they both give context to these discussions and influence how we understand them. But also like a stage set, these three specific trajectories are offered as not a whole story but a backdrop, an evocation of how economics and folklore have been explored by those before.

## MACROFOLKLORE: WHO ARE THE FOLK AND WHAT DO THEY DO?

Macroeconomics focuses on larger issues of economic systems—the who and the what of folklore. Class, large-scale labor, and the relationships of folk groups to these structures have tended fall within the scope of the macro. These studies have looked at the big picture in an attempt to discern where folklore flourishes, where the folk fit in society, and how society itself is organized and creates products, be they the output of factories or the folklore of the people who work in them. As Roger Abrahams has argued, however, it matters who counts as folk in what political context, because those constructions help determine what later counts as lore (1993, 389). Thus, we include in this macroeconomic approach to folklore the Marxist turn in folkloristics and the study of labor lore. These works have framed their studies from a larger class-based paradigm that allows them to reveal important relationships between work, lore, and resistance.

The earliest generations of folklorists tended to construct the subject of their study as outside of, or even in direct opposition to, market concerns. From Andrew Lang's "peasant class" (2015) to William Newell's four categories of people possessing folklore, found in the first issue of the *Journal of American Folklore* and focused entirely on those identified as outside of industrialized Euro-American society, class status,[2] or more precisely a lack thereof, has been understood as a criteria for folk status (1888, 3). In the earliest iteration of the term, the "folk" in folklore have been comprehended as residues of modernity—as anachronistic, illiterate people bound by their superstitions and irrational traditions, as "peasants and primitives" (Bauman 1992, 30–35).

This premise led to two instincts visible in the early scholarship of folklore. First, folklorists sought to salvage the vanishing "survivals" of authentic grassroots culture in the name of Romantic Nationalism and nostalgia. Folklore and its active bearers perhaps offered a refuge from the perceived stresses of the capitalist economy, and folk economies a potentially more holistic alternative to the homogeny of the industrial and mass produced. As Michael Taussig has argued, it can be difficult for a researcher to break out of the economic paradigm in which they themselves were raised, and precapitalist societies can "acquire the burden of having to satisfy our alienated longings for a lost Golden Age" (1980, 7). Second, folk production was ascribed to a lesser, imitative sphere, based on the argument that true folklore originated in the upper strata of society (cf. Naumann 1921). Many early collectors put folklore outside of modern modes of economic exchange by closely linking it with the domestic. The Grimms, for example, aligned folklore with women and the home, thus contrasting it to work and men, whose labor in the capitalist world made them less likely to possess folklore (Bendix 1997, 85). Both gestures, however, ultimately circumscribe the folk by relegating them to a subaltern class status.

The linking of the folk with precapitalism in the nineteenth century became more nuanced in the twentieth, as some researchers began to probe the class assumptions at work in this construction and ask how folk groups interacted with and resisted capitalist power structures (cf. Limón 1983). Marxist approaches to folklore studies arising in the first part of the twentieth century saw folklore's subject matter as offering potential for critique of the larger class system and capitalism itself (cf. Maurer 2006; Zinn 2015). Within this context, Antonio Gramsci's (1985) work on hegemony and the subaltern reoriented the structuring binary in folklore studies from traditional versus modern to dominant versus dominated (Crehan 2016). In a related theoretic shift in the Soviet bloc, beyond the formalist studies in the vein of Vladimir Propp (1968), the Marxist approach fostered an awareness of the burgeoning critical interventions in the study of developing nations as well as scholarship surrounding workers and working cultures (Tangherlini 1997).

As a class-oriented area of folklore developed, Western Marxism, following the theoretical trajectories of the Frankfurt School in particular, began to influence the discipline. Folklorists began to explore manifestations of cultural contestation, moments in which the folk resist or speak back to dominant ideological structures undergirded by capitalism. For example, the work of Américo Paredes challenged folklorists to more explicitly insert political imperatives into their praxis (1970). Similarly, José Limón argued in 1983 that folklorists could offer a critical reading of capitalism through folklore's context-oriented emphasis on performance. Limón noted the "inherently oppositional" qualities of folklore. He quotes Roger Abrahams that "all such performances may be displays of the possibility of hanging on to the use and value of things . . . in the face of those who would turn all of life into acts of consumption" (2012, 107). Similarly, looking into another genre, fairy tale scholar Jack Zipes interrogated the ideological underpinnings of fairy tales and the commodity fetishism associated with their mass-mediated adaptations (1979).

Building on the Marxist tradition, Stephen Gencarella more recently recommended that folklorists engage further with the realities of daily economic life (2011). Utilizing Max Horkheimer's concept of critical theory as a response to "bourgeois and capitalist ideology," Gencarella's larger project of critical folklore studies rests on a repositioning of critical capacity, putting the ethnographer into conversation with "everyday critics" (2011, 257 and 261). Interestingly, Gencarella and Limón both see the critical potential of folklore and the folk as a means to such understanding, but disagree with each other about the ends achieved by such interrogation. These Marxist critiques have provided much needed complexity to an understanding of how folklore and class intertwine. However, the danger remains that scholars focused on class may repeat a class-based bounding of the folk, this time in Marxist terms as the proletariat.

But folklorists are not only concerned with who counts as folk. If the folk were defined early on by where they resided in the socioeconomic system, then one way to identify the folk was to look to the common occupations associated with those lower classes. Studies of workers and labor cannot help but see the folkloric in the economic (cf. Green 1971, 1978, 1993, 2002). Workers' cultures were long perceived as a "degenerated form of peasant and craft cultures, that had emerged in the course of industrialization since most industrial workers were recruited from rural milieus" (Koch 2012). The early period of work-related studies, as a result, focused heavily on rural groups and occupations because of the folkloristic bias toward survivals (McCarl 1996, 1997).

Fleming Hemmersam's 1985 overview of worker lore studies shows four distinct approaches to the subject (as cited in Green 1997, 600). The first is the classic folkloristic and ethnological approach, which maintains the "antiquarian's ideological commitment to a peasant model of work" (cf. Nickerson 1974 and Jones 1984; see Hemmersam 1985, as cited in Green 1997, 600). The second is bourgeois research of worker culture; these studies, as seen in the work of Richard Dorson and Hennig Cohen, maintain that the increasingly standardized forms of urban experience have diminished and risk extinguishing the distinctiveness of working-class cultures. The third approach is explicitly socialist or communist and hypothesizes that working cultures are entirely defined by their antagonism to capitalist modes of production. This approach has a rich history in Europe and is represented contemporaneously in the work of Anders Björklund and Gösta Arvastson. Finally, the empirical approach has produced extensive collections of cultural artifacts related to work with little attention to their "social or ideological context"—research typified by the work of Wayland Hand and Horace Beck (Hemmersam 1985, as cited in Green 1997, 600).

Writing from different political contexts, European and American folklorists took different approaches to worker lore. Whereas in Europe, the study of occupational cultures was equally invested in the analysis of "work culture and labor ideology," under the influence of E. P. Thompson, parallel scholarship in the United States tended to emphasize the aesthetic and culturally expressive forms of the workplace (stories, songs, skills, customs, jokes), with less accent on the socio-economic-political contexts of their emergence (McCarl 1996, 597). One exception that would presage studies to come is George Korson's work collecting the folkways and lore of Pennsylvania coal mine workers (1927, 1938). Korson's ethnography balances between the descriptive and the analytic, which included identifying ideologically characteristic forms that expose miners' "resistance to capitalist exploitation," foreshadowing Paredes (Korson 1927, 599). It was only in the 1960s under the stewardship of Archie Green that the field of folkloristics reformulated the study of occupational folklore to account for both workers' cultural practices and their political and ideological conditions, as can be seen in the work of Jack Santino and Paula Johnson (Hemmersam 1985, as cited in Green 1997, 601; Johnson 1988; Santino 1990).

The biggest shift in folkloristic research into work, however, occurred at the turn of the twenty-first century in response to the cultural and economic reorganizations resulting from globalization and the technology and service-oriented worker regimes that have arisen in post-Fordist labor ideologies. As Gertraud Koch (2012) argues, these moves toward political economies of work have aligned folklore with more sociological perspectives that emphasize organizational forms and the distribution of societal resources (cf. Boutang 2007; Sennett 2006). Barbara Ehrenreich's ethnographic work on service-sector workers, for example, reveals the pressures and indignities of ever-increasing precarization, describing those who work without guarantees in an era with a shrinking social net and neoliberal imperatives (2001). Studies of knowledge work similarly reveal the ways in which the increasing flexibility of labor through freelancing and short-term contracting have led workers to lean on a "creative bricolage of practices" which efface the lines between work and leisure times (See McRobbie 2004; Ross 2010).

Referencing the extant class structure and the worker cultures it creates has helped folklorists locate both folklore and the folk's relationship to economics. Doing so, however, many early folklorists created an inverse relationship between class and culture. But this class-structured approach and its tendency toward essentialisms have not gone unquestioned (cf. Bendix 1997, 25; Clifford 1988, 162; Rosaldo 1989, 202). Turning the critical lens towards expertise and connoisseurship, for example, scholars have questioned how such thinking reinscribed extant class distinctions by limiting who possessed the ability to tell the real from the fake, a major concern for folklorists such as Richard Dorson. This move allowed folklorists and their audiences to separate themselves from the folk whose lore they studied as a result of the elite ability to identify what constituted art, or in this case folklore (Bendix 1997, 157), ultimately, as theorist Pierre Bourdieu argues, "[legitimating] social differences" (1984, xxx). Further, feminism, postcolonial criticism, and the Civil Rights Movement among others have each spurred their own critiques (cf. Behar and Gordon 1996; Prahlad 1999; Said 1979; Visweswaran 1994).

Despite such criticism and even as the definition of the "folk" exploded to include "any two people sharing at least one thing in common" (Dundes 1980, 2), a brief survey of published articles in folklore journals suggests that most folklorists continue to link folk-ness with the working class or with materials somehow perceived as outside of or even in direct opposition to capitalism. Refugees, evacuees, prisoners, global indigenous, and ethnic Others still make up the bulk of the subjects of articles; notably lacking are the middle class and the suburban[3] (cf. Ingram, Mullins, and Richardson 2019). Such a focus importantly does draw attention to folk groups who may otherwise be excluded from discourse through their alterity, but it might also create a gap by ignoring the economic relations and commentary between groups that Paredes and Limón sought to reveal.

The trajectory of macrofolklore has focused on the widest view, defining who the folk are within the larger class structure and using the overlay of class and occupation to further delineate what counts as folklore. Moving beyond early constructions, focusing on the macro level offers a way to reveal how folk groups participate in, respond to, and resist larger economic systems. Such a broad lens may be crucial in the current age of globalized capitalism. The macro shows how large economic networks can have impact for small, localized groups of people, and how those people can also send ripples of influence out into the globe.

## MICROFOLKLORE: FOLKLORE AS COMMODITY

Despite this engagement with large-scale social structures and macrolevel positioning of the folk and folklore, folklorists have more generally focused their attention on the micro, the individuals and small communities who make up those larger societies and live in relationship to those structures. Approaching the economic in folklore, many of these studies have tended to center on how folk products, both tangible and intangible, made within one folk tradition are commodified, used, and sold sometimes to people from other cultural backgrounds. Folk art and material culture have seemed natural places for folklorists to address these economic concerns, with a clear object offered in a clear market transaction that cannot be evaded but can be narrated (cf. de Certeau 1984). While much of this debate has taken place within the context of material culture studies, as our discussion here is also situated, it has posed important questions that extend to other genres.

Objects, commodities, and artifacts are repositories of material and semiotic significance and articulate power relations between individuals, groups and society writ large. Put bluntly, the folk make things, sell and exchange things, and consume and circulate things. Folklore's relationship with commodity has long been characterized by a tension between the pros and cons of capitalism. Concern over commoditization, with the decontextualization it implies, and the ways in which the marketplace potentially reinscribes socioeconomic hierarchies are balanced against seeing both process and space as potentially generative and empowering.

One could argue that folklorists have always been aware of folklore's sales potential, from Perrault and the Grimms on, but it has only been over the course of time that the complexities of folklore's economic value have been explored. Yet folklore as commodity or as used for commercial ends was generally seen as problematic through the mid-twentieth century. The use of "mass-mediated" and "commodified" as a negative defining characteristic, what folklore is *not*, typifies much of the writing in folklore from the nineteenth century to the twenty-first. Richard Dorson, notably, roots his definition of "fake lore" in commoditization—as those tales which have been decontextualized, stripped of everything folklorists might care about, specifically for the purposes of turning lore into commodity (1976). Part of the issue may reside in the field's historical investment in associating the folk with lower socioeconomic status. If the folk may not be of high status, their lore must also not hold economic value. Commodification, by contrast, revalues cultural products, giving them monetary value where they once held primarily cultural value. The belief that commodification poses a threat to authentic folklore, however, plays into the salvage narrative inherited from early twentieth-century folklore collection and has shown some tenacity in the field, despite critique (cf. Becker 1998; Kirshenblatt-Gimblett 1998).

Early material culture study seems to have largely evaded the question of commodification by tending to focus more on the object itself at the moment of its creation and those in charge of that creation, the makers, than on what happens to the object after it left the maker's hands. While there has been interest in the conditions that shape an object's production, this interest for scholars has remained pertinent only insofar as those conditions speak to the "physical properties and specific history" of the objects themselves (Sheumaker and Wajda 2008). American material culture study in particular has long emphasized the materialization of folk thought in artifacts and environments with specific interest in exemplary forms of folk art, craftsmanship, and vernacular production (Bronner 1996; Glassie 1968; Vlach 1991; Vlach and Upton 1986). As Barbara Kirshenblatt-Gimblett has pointed out, however, the focus on the thing and the maker leaves out much of an object's meaning, including the economic (1989).

The rise of context-oriented ethnography in the 1970s (cf. Bauman and Paredes 1972) drew attention to the larger cultural ecology in which folklore was performed. This watershed moment acknowledged the transaction between performer and audience, as a result opening up folklore studies to the possibilities of consumption as a form of agency and expression, effectively rehabilitating the commodity (Appadurai 1986; Miller 2006). By the end of the century, folklorists, predominantly working in material culture, assumed that folk things were up for sale and sought to understand the effects of such commoditization on the artist and culture rather than fight against the sale. Notably, Michael Owen Jones's *The Handmade Object and Its Maker* (1975) and Charles Briggs's *The Woodcarvers of Cordova, New Mexico* (1980), while still focused on specific makers of folk art, stand among the first works to deal bluntly with the market pressures placed on folk artists by both out-group and in-group consumers.

The difficulty arises, as Barbara Babcock has pointed out, when folk products and the folk themselves become commoditized. Tourist studies helped to draw attention to this problem. Tourism necessarily throws cultures into close contact, but with differing goals and differing levels of investment in local sustainability. Tourism scholars—such as Nelson Graburn (1976), Dean MacCannell ([1976] 1989), and John Urry (1990)—posited the tourist as a consumer, seeking in their touristic encounters those things they believe they lacked in modern life—the real, the natural, and the culturally marked. But these studies have tended to pay less attention to the reasons that a culture might choose to participate in touristic display. In many places, groups have made use of local identities and practices to celebrate their culture and push the local economy through tourism. Yet these touristic displays have caused tensions as well, as the ownership and responsibilities of public heritage come under debate (cf. Cantwell 1993; Guss 2001). Some of the most interesting of these conversations have also taken into account how folk groups bend to and manipulate economic pressures to further their art form to suit the group needs and the political moment (cf. Lee 2009).

In the 1980s and 1990s, these issues with cultural representation coupled with the crisis in ethnography (cf. Clifford and Marcus 1986) drew attention to the positionality of the ethnographer and the politics of cultural representation on a large scale. Addressing that issue of positionality, anthropologist Ruth Behar wrote in *Translated Woman* of her discomfort when the economic realities of her position relative to her informant Esperanza were brought home to her (1993). As they became aware of their own part in representation, folklorists complicated the discussion surrounding the commoditization of folklore and the folk themselves particularly in relation to festival and museum displays of folk culture (cf. Baron 2010; Bauman 1992; Cantwell 1993; Kirshenblatt-Gimblett 1998; Sommers 1995).

The brokerage model of folklore practice emerged to describe the role of folklorists working in cultural institutions as mediators, thus attempting to move away from what Deborah Root called the "necrophilic" tendencies of earlier museum display (cf. Appadurai 1986; Appadurai, Korom, and Mills 1991; Huyssen 1995; Karp 1991). Folklorists, such as Regina Bendix (1997), Frank Korom (see Appadurai, Korom, and Mills 1991; Korom 1999), and Richard Kurin (1997) employed economic metaphors for their work, positioning themselves and their institutions as brokers, mediating between the folk, who possessed culture, and the audience, who came to see it. Kurin contrasted such brokerage with what he termed "extractive" and "flea market" models of cultural representation, thus very clearly equating cultural products with commodities (1997, 18–19).

Yet, the 1990s also saw a rise in scholarship that attempted to find another metaphor beyond commodity for its subject. In contrast to Kurin and Korom, Mary Hufford's collection *Conserving Culture* (1994) also acknowledged the economic realities of folklore work but positioned folklore as resource rather than commodity. Hufford shifted the metaphor from brokerage to sustainability, weaving together narratives and goals in economics, ecology, historic preservation, and folklore. The authors in Hufford's collection provided their own critique of the emerging brokerage model, noting that cultural representation as commodity risks reification, a concern eloquently described by Robert Cantwell in *Ethnomimesis* (1993) and Dorothy Noyes in her article "Group" (1995). Others, including Barre Toelken (1995) from an ethical perspective and Dell Hymes (2003) from a pragmatic one, wondered if all culture could or should be represented.

These material culture studies demonstrated a microeconomic sensibility, exploring how a maker within a culture allocated their resources in terms of time, money, cultural capital, and creativity. At the same time that folklorists began to write about the social and economic systems that commoditized the folk and folklore, they questioned the results of that commodification, finally placing the micro and macro into conversation. Taking both micro and macro together, folklorists have raised real concerns about how cultural products, material or otherwise, could be commodified and detached from their originating culture and how such detachment can adversely affect that that culture. These fears have led to the involvement of folklorists in groups such as World Intellectual Property Organization and UNESCO, aimed at protecting cultural property from unfair use in a capitalist marketplace (Honko 1988; Noyes 2015).

## THE FOLKLORIST IN THE MARKETPLACE: WHERE FOLKLORE HAPPENS

Building on the assumption that the folk were already active in the marketplace, a third trajectory of economics and folklore has sought to describe the marketplace and economic transactions as part of folklife. The marketplace requires social interactions that are, by their nature, formulaic, but it also provides both literal and metaphoric space for artistic performance. Through these social interactions, people work out how they assign meaning and value; they negotiate how their lives intersect with others, culturally, materially, and economically.

In this reconfiguration of the marketplace, the works of cultural scholars such as Michael Owen Jones (1975), Charles Briggs (1980), and Babcock (1995) have proven crucial. Mikail Bakhtin posited the marketplace as a space for the negotiation of culture and tradition (1965). Weaving together Bakhtin's sense of conceptualization of the marketplace with performance theory, Deborah Kapchan's *Gender on the Market* uses the Moroccan marketplace as a field site for an investigation into women's folklore ([1996] 2010). However, unlike earlier studies, Kapchan describes the exchanges in that marketplace in folkloristic terms, as artistic, communicative, and traditional, marking the marketplace as a performative space.

While the marketplace may be space where internal cultural issues are worked out amidst the exchange of commodities, it has also been theorized as a cultural frontier, at the "crossing point between worlds" that bring together "marginalized outsiders and mobilized traders" (Abrahams n.d.). The marketplace is a contact zone and a space of hybridization and recontextualization (Pratt 1991). And it can simultaneously be a space of appropriation and exploitation that fetishizes the folk (Babcock 1995). Addressing some of these neocolonial concerns, Kimberley Lau's *New Age Capitalism* turns the folkloric lens fully onto the consumer (2000). Lau explores how the consumer might constitute their act of consumption as a conscious participation in a folk tradition, a tradition often quite distant from the consumer's own folk culture. Notably, Kapchan and Lau move the discussion of folklore and economics into the global present, drawing on postcolonial and neocolonial theory, and back into macroeconomics.

This last trajectory moves the discussion of folklore and economics into the space of the marketplace itself, defining that space as both a contact zone and generative, one that draws on, creates a venue for, and produces folklore. This approach points to the complexities of the social relationships at work in the marketplace. As Pratt has said of the contact zone, these are the "social spaces where cultures meet, clash, and grapple with each other" (1991, 34). Studying the marketplace has allowed folklorists to document the extent to which the folk are active agents in their economic lives, and the marketplace can serve as an important venue for the performance of folklore and the working out of cultural values. But looking at the marketplace also reveals the dangers of the power differentials at work and the commodification of a fuzzy "folkness" is a globalized capitalist society. To romanticize the marketplace, as Noyes warned, could be as dangerous an assumption as romanticizing the folk (1995).

As in economics itself, each of these trajectories has continued to hold sway and have value in the perspective it offers to the others. Further, these are not neat divisions. Rather, the history of folklore and economics has been one of rich discourse and nuanced complexity. These trajectories function here as the anchoring lines on a spider web: as each has been explored, it has pulled on the others; as each new study has added to the field, it has drawn connections between these lines, building a bigger and more complex web of discourse and understanding. Even Dorson eventually admitted the allure of a distinctive American folklore, while continuing to deride the mass-mediated "fakelore" often sold under that label (1959, [1977] 3–4).

Since the economic downturn of 2008, more folklore scholars have begun to interrogate the economics of the field and its subject matter, from a range of vantage points that show a distinct departure from earlier works. For example, in a presidential address to the Folklore society, Robert McDowell, assayed the role that folk beliefs played in bolstering the financial crisis of 2008. The belief in the infallibility of technology and mathematics, and financial beliefs about home buying ("the best investment anyone can make") and stock investments ("Buy whatever Warren Buffett is buying") represented a number of the unquestioned assumptions that led to the recession (2013). Alternatively, in her essay "Of Victims, Villains and Fairy Godmothers: Regnant Tales of Predatory Lending," Carolyn Grose (2009) analyzed stories that pushed against the default narrative of the victims of the subprime mortgage crisis as being irresponsible or unwitting. In "Fairy-Tale Economics: Scarcity, Risk and Choice," Dorothy Noyes (2011) traced the changes and innovations in the structure of fairy tales in response to variances in socioeconomic opportunities available to the working classes.

These newer studies have also drawn together the trajectories of folklore and economics, creating space for new approaches and intervening into some of the larger ongoing conversations in folklore studies itself. Some of the recent scholarship has sought to stretch the definition of folklore by viewing economic activity as a kind of "artistic practice" in itself. For example, Katherine Roberts (2012) deeply engages with the economics of land-tenure and resource management as an adaptive strategy in rural Appalachia. Roberts's critique of place studies develops from Debra Lattanzi Shutika's criticism that the legal and economic issues surrounding place have largely been ignored (2011, 409). Similarly, Timothy Austin (2012) describes theft as a folk practice in Mindanao, touching on how economic activity, or in this case the rejection of capitalist norms of exchange, may be encoded as both artistic and political folk production.

Other recent works explore the well-established tension between economic realities and the norms of social interaction. Greenhill and Magnusson (2010), for instance, probe the politics and polity of requesting cash wedding gifts. More subtly, John McDowell's work on *narcocorridos*, Mexican songs describing the narcotics trade and gang warfare, addresses how folklore can comment upon the ways in which economic structures shape communities (2012). Finally, William Ivey has probed the term "value" itself, with reference to divergent definitions of the term between folk groups, and how those definitions can affect how folklore is understood and used in public and governmental policy (2011). Ivey pairs the ideas of value and values, but in doing so subtly links and separates the economic and the ethical.

These three approaches to folklore and economics show not only the diversity of approach but also how folklorists interests have been honed from the macro to the micro to more holistic bridging of the two in their studies of the marketplace. Each approach provides perspective—the macro reveals the ontology of folklore and its relationship to class structures; the micro uncovers both the politics of commodification and the epistemology of that commodification as it relates to folklore; the marketplace lets us see how culture is produced, negotiated, and reproduced. At each level, meaning is made, power structures asserted and resisted, folklore and economics performed.

## WEAVING A WEB OF ECONOMICS AND FOLKLORE

Whoever they are and however we define them, the folk live in a global world in which they are economic actors. This book aims to further the study of folklore and economics. The authors of the chapters invoke all three of the approaches mentioned above, but they also query each, and allow new intersections to emerge to fit the global and technologized world. In order to maintain a holistic approach, while the book is loosely organized along the same three trajectories—macro, micro, and value in the marketplace—the chapters also blur these divisions and create bridges between them. In particular, the difference here between macro and micro draws on but varies somewhat from traditional economics. In economic theory, macroeconomics deals with class structures but centers more on how national economies work, and microeconomics focuses on supply and demand, individual decision-making about resource allocation, and specific products within the marketplace. However, because folklorists generally start with a narrower lens, what is macro to the folklorist—the economic functioning of a folk group—may count as micro to the economist. Here, then, the first chapters on the macro center on ideas of how the global and the local influence each other. The middle chapters take a more microapproach and look closely at how local groups navigate economic culture. The final chapters examine how folklore and economic activities are valued within folk groups. Themes centering on folklore as economic critique, performativity, commodification, and tourism weave through the chapters.

We have sought to include a multiplicity of disciplinary voices in the chapters that follow. By their very nature, folklore and economics lie at the nexus of disciplines, pulling together ideas, vocabulary, and practices from both and weaving them into a whole cloth. While we, as editors, and this introduction are firmly situated in folklore, we are pleased to include voices from business studies, economics, and psychology. If we believe, as we deeply do, that folklorists have something of value to say about the economic world, then we must also embrace the idea that economists and other scholars may have something of value to say about the folkloristic one. Above all, we hope that this work will serve as a testament to disciplinary diplomacy in the name of deeper conversations and stronger humanistic research. Because the authors here write from multiple disciplinary perspectives and paradigms, they also do not conform to a single genre: some chapters follow typical ethnographic style; others include creative approaches and metacommentary; others take a more philosophical tack. All are engaged in a discussion of how we culturally make meaning of ourselves as economic beings, through consumption and labor and through folklore, and what our folklore says about how we view these transactions. All start from an assumption that the folk are actively and thoughtfully engaged in the economy.

The first five chapters explore the economic relationship between the global and the local. Historically, the local has been the purview of folklore, what sets it apart from broader fields like cultural studies. In the global economy, however, the local is often already global in ways that can prove dynamic and productive. Further, this relationship works in both directions—a folk group may utilize globally sourced materials to produce a uniquely local product, and they may find their local product and its connection to a specific folk have value on the global market. In that larger market, folk culture can become a form of cultural sustainability and resistance against the pressures of globalization itself. The authors that begin this book, then, lay bare the assumption that the global and the local are necessarily a binary or that one can be separated easily from the other.

The first two chapters examine the ways in which the global is imbricated in the local and vice versa. In his chapter, 1, on Louisiana's crawfish boats, John Laudun reveals how folkloric forms have always incorporated elements from around the world, while responding to highly localized pressures and traditions. While in the Italian quarries and workshops that Amy Shuman describes in chapter 12, the local objects become globalized, the crawfish boats are local objects made of globally sourced materials and enmeshed in global economies of exchange. Laudun points to how the folklorists' paradigm has tended to guide them to focus on the locally contextualized object but not necessarily the global context that helped create it. Julie M-A. LeBlanc's work, chapter 2, reverses this flow from the local to the global. LeBlanc explores how brewer Unibroue's references to Québécois folktales on its labels have helped to safeguard a sense of local identification and pride even as the company moved into the global marketplace and was purchased by a larger, multinational corporation. Yet these symbols are read differently by different generations of Québécois, forcing a renegotiation of Québec's history and culture between not only emic and etic consumers but also members of the group.

Chapters 3, 4, and 5 continue to examine how local cultures are contextualized and valued as they are made available for consumption by outsiders. As folklore is commodified for outside audiences, folk groups may seek ways to express and sustain their own identities. The authors of these chapters move beyond tourism to consider how such identities can be honed and articulated in the global marketplace. In each of these chapters, local practices launched into a larger context help sustain culture, but in doing so they show how the location of cultural identification can shift. Academic critiques of offering culture as a commodity have centered on how those representations can be highly problematic depending on who is doing the commodification of what, how, and to what ends (cf. Barbara Kirshenblatt-Gimblett 1998; John Clifford 1997). However, such an assessment becomes more complicated when that cultural commodity has become a cornerstone of self-identity or the commodification is coming from within the community.

In chapter 3, James I. Deutsch and Halle M. Butvin move from the commercial to the cultural marketplace. Their chapter focuses on the role of the folklorist to address the competing needs and desires that arise between institutions, organizers, artisans, and the public in the touristic space, in particular during the Smithsonian's annual Folklife Festival on the National Mall. Here, labor itself can become "an object of touristic curiosity" (MacCannell [1976] 1989, 6). During the festival, traditional artisans' labor is the focus of the visitors' gaze, while the products that labor produces, sold in the Festival Marketplace, risk becoming detached from their producers. As Deutsch and Butvin describe, organizers and artisans must work in concert to keep the products for sale in the separate Festival Marketplace culturally contextualized and socially responsible within a festival and tourist environment.

Michael Lange's chapter 4 and Cristofer Johnson's chapter 5 suggest that while a culture-based origin story may add monetary value to a local product in the global marketplace, the value for the community may be in cultural sustainability. Lange describes how maple producers, who have historically sold their product using cultural iconography, may question whether they are selling Vermont or selling syrup and the ramifications of each. Faced with global reach, some of the Vermont identification is being dropped but the practices and group experience of producing maple remain strong. Where then is the traditional folklore located in the global marketing of maple? Focusing on the Orkney Islands, Johnson explores how some fishermen have similarly drawn on cultural knowledge to help maintain their livelihoods but transitioned their skills into running a fish hatchery. While the materiality of much of the fishermen's work remains the same, consisting of their interactions with the fish and sea, the hatchery requires a different kind of interaction between groups' members. As a result, the project has brought together diverse and historically at-odds groups within the islands. Set against the larger backdrop of the European Union, the hatchery becomes a source of pride, as it helps reclaim power and sustain the people both culturally and economically.

Lange's, Johnson's, and Cassie Patterson's chapters bridge between macrolevel concerns of global economies and local cultures and microlevel explorations of individual group responses to economic pressures. Turning more toward the micro, chapters 6 through 10 examine how folk groups—including towns, artists and artisans, and local communities—weigh choices within their economic and cultural lives, and use both economics and folklore as forms of resistance against economic structures. Cassie Patterson's chapter, 6, deals with the commodification of culture itself within the sphere of tourism, interrogating the economic and ethical stakes of displaying public heritage for outside consumption. Patterson delves into moral geographies, nonmonetary markets, and the economics of attention. Through ethnography, she analyzes a new set of murals in the town of Portsmouth, Ohio, and the tourism they have drawn. For Patterson, this discussion raises questions of the moral responsibilities of citizens to produce and promote public heritage and the usefulness of such cultural display as a mediation between the town and the world at large.

Bringing the lens even further in, Zhao Yuanhao and Puja Batra-Wells consider how individuals interact economically in their daily lives and make those lives and relationships work. In chapter 7, Zhao examines the deep structure and generative possibilities of a highly localized folk economy. Zhao's ethnography of a Hui marketplace in northern China proposes a quotidian and chaotic space of exchange, thus departing from the Bakhtinian carnivalesque market notable for its exceptionalism and liminality. While the Hui market may seem chaotic, the disorder belies a constantly negotiated order between government and people, different ethnic and religious groups, and individuals. The marketplace thus demonstrates economics and folklore in a conceptual and practical contact zone. Batra-Wells, in chapter 8, investigates the strategies visual artists use to monetize their artworks that must take into account valuations of their labor, their socially expected role as bohemians, and analysis of the influences of the art market and economy. Folklore's vernacular lens exposes how this group of artists both make and make do within their daily lives.

While the preceding chapters have shown folk groups utilizing the marketplace to preserve their livelihoods, such engagement in the marketplace can present challenges for groups who have chosen to identify themselves in opposition to it. The intentional community of Twin Oaks is also deeply and actively engaged in capitalism for their survival, an economic system to which they also stand in stated opposition (chapter 9). Writing in the tradition of critical folklore studies but from a business perspective, Rahima Schwenkbeck details the community's ambivalence regarding their own business practices. Built on utopian principles that eschew capitalism, Twin Oaks nonetheless became extremely successful making and selling hammocks, forcing the community to negotiate their relationships and positionality with each other, their labor, and the larger society and economy.

Schwenkbeck calls into question what happens when a community becomes victims of their own economic success and must weigh community and personal needs against the ideology by which they hope to live. Resistance to economic structures, however, can be overt or subtle.

While the artisan hammock makers feel the tension of needing to participate in the economy, Irene Sotiropoulou, in chapter 10, examines a community's use of folktales as critical commentary on the economy and mainstream economic values. Sotiropoulou uses a close reading of the Cretan tale "Why the Sea Is Salty" to describe an instance of how a folk group has chosen to define its own economics outside of or in opposition to mainstream capitalist ideas. Sotiropoulou looks to folktales, long analyzed in terms of the psychological and social content, to understand grassroots economics. Writing from a post-Marxist perspective and beginning with an autoethnography that exposes the Western and middle-class biases of economic study, Sotiropoulou argues for an economically savvy lower class who deploys folktales as a way to promote a more egalitarian system.

The previous chapters raise an important question: If capitalism, a system not without its faults, shapes the world economy at this juncture, then how do communities' values inform how they interact with and respond to capitalist structures and actions? How value is constructed and negotiated, what is valued and why, are the focus of the final chapters. Staying in cultural lore, William A. Ashton, in chapter 11, dives into the origin myth of Hermes and his dual role as trickster and god of the market. Ashton offers a psychological reading of the American corporate world through myth and archetype. Like studies in economic anthropology, such as Karen Ho's *Liquidated* (2009), Ashton turns an analytic lens on the American business community. In doing so, he offers a glimpse at the hegemonic economic values that the folk groups described in other chapters negotiate. Further, he raises the question of how the theories of folklore and deep analyses of the tropes of culture may guide, structure, or intervene in seemingly unrelated business practices. What, for instance, do the morals of folk tales and mythologies and the character of the trickster in particular, so often fixed in the making of bargains and the politics of exchange, offer us as we consider how we want our economy, both macro and micro, to work? What happens when we value the trickster in the economy?

Value, as Amy Shuman notes in chapter 12, can become a crucial metric in our attempts to understand the folk, folklore, and the marketplace. Shuman describes a group of artisans in the process of reassessing and reinterpreting the location of value—economic, material, cultural, knowledge-based, and environmental. Beginning with the artisans who quarry and work the marble of Pietrasanta, Italy, and the land through which they live, Shuman reveals how a folk economy incorporates a network of interrelated economies that work across several market levels and tie together several distinct technologies and folk groups in ways that challenge long-held academic distinctions between the modern and the traditional, the global and the local, art and craft.

If the previous chapters show how folklore and folk products can be discussed in economic terms, as both commodities and as critical interventions into capitalist systems, then we must ask anew where the folklorist fits in these folkloric exchanges. Folklorists have long been acknowledging their roles as culture brokers, but how else may they be implicated in systems of exchange as active participants in the marketplace? Willow G. Mullins, in chapter 13, considers the field of folklore's long investment in authenticity as a source of value. Reconsidering the metaphor of folklorist as culture broker in a globalized era of multicultural representation, Mullins suggests that if authenticity has become a commodity in itself, then folklorists may be among its most ardent consumers.

Folklore and economics have always been in conversation. That conversation, however, has often been dispersed. In an age of global media and global sourcing, folk arts online, and cultural sustainability, we see how our vernacular lives are intricately interwoven with the world economy. It may be more important than ever before to direct a folkloristic lens on economics and an economic one on folklore. Ultimately, we hope that this work will begin the creation of our own language of folklore and economics, a language we invite our readers to explore, to adapt, and to help remake, just as the folk in marketplace do.

## NOTES

1. See the Multilingual Folk Tale Database: http://www.mftd.org/index.php?action=atu.

2. Nineteenth-century Britain and the United States saw class as a highly structured system of social stratification, generally understood in terms of heredity—even in the non-aristocratic United States—social position, education, employment, and economic wealth.

3. Such studies do exist, but are few and far between. For some good examples of research that does address the middle class, see Dorst (1989) and Hathaway (2005).

## REFERENCES

Abrahams, Roger. 1993. After New Perspectives: Folklore Study in the Late Twentieth Century. *Theorizing Folklore: Toward New Perspectives on the Politics of Culture*, ed. Amy Shuman and Charles Briggs. Special issue, *Western Folklore* 52 (2/4): 379–400.

Abrahams, Roger. n.d. "The Winking Gods of the Marketplace." Ms.

American Economic Association. n.d. "What Is Economics?" *American Economic Association*. https://www.aeaweb.org/resources/students/what-is-economics.
Appadurai, Arjun, ed. 1986. *The Social Life of Things: Commodities in Cultural Perspective*. Cambridge: Cambridge University Press.
Appadurai, Arjun, Frank Korom, and Margaret Mills. 1991. *Gender, Genre, and Power in South Asian Expressive Traditions*. Philadelphia: University of Pennsylvania Press.
Austin, Timothy. 2012. "Takers Keepers, Losers Weepers: Theft as Customary Play in the Southern Philippines." *Journal of Folklore Research* 49 (3): 347–69. https://doi.org/10.2979/jfolkrese.49.3.347.
Babcock, Barbara. 1995. "Marketing Maria: The Tribal Artist in the Age of Mechanical Reproduction." In *Looking High and Low: Art and Cultural Identity*, ed. Brenda Jo Bright and Liza Bakewell. Tucson: University of Arizona Press.
Bakhtin, Mikhail. 1965. *Rabelais and His World*. Bloomington: University of Indiana Press.
Baron, Robert. 2010. "Sins of Objectification? Agency, Mediation, and Community Cultural Self-Determination in Public Folklore and Cultural Tourism Programming." *Journal of American Folklore* 123 (487): 63–91. https://doi.org/10.5406/jamerfolk.123.487.0063.
Bauman, Richard. 1972. "Differential Identity and the Social Base of Folklore." In *Towards New Perspectives in Folklore*, ed. Américo Paredes and Richard Bauman. Austin: University of Texas Press.
Bauman, Richard, and Américo Paredes. 1972. *Towards New Perspectives in Folklore*. Austin: University of Texas Press.
Becker, Jane. 1998. *Selling Tradition: Appalachia and the Construction of the American Folk*. Raleigh: University of North Carolina Press.
Behar, Ruth. 1993. Translated Woman: Crossing the Border with Esperanza's Story. Boston: Beacon.
Behar, Ruth, and Deborah A. Gordon. 1996. *Women Writing Culture*. Berkeley: University of California Press.
Ben-Amos, Dan. 1971. "Toward a Definition of Folklore in Context." *Journal of American Folklore* 84 (331): 3–15. doi:10.2307/539729.
Bendix, Regina. 1997. *In Search of Authenticity: The Formation of Folklore Studies*. Madison: University of Wisconsin Press.
Bourdieu, Pierre. 1984. *Distinction: A Social Critique of the Judgment of Taste*. Abingdon, UK: Routledge Kegan and Paul.
Boutang, Yann Moulier. 2007. *Cognitive Capitalism*. Cambridge: Polity Press.
Briggs, Charles. 1980. *The Woodcarvers of Cordova, New Mexico: Social Dimensions of an Artistic Revival*. Knoxville: University of Tennessee Press.
Bronner, Simon. 1985. *Chain Carvers: Old Men Crafting Meaning*. Lexington: University Press of Kentucky.
Brunvand, Jan. 1986. *The Study of American Folklore: An Introduction*. New York: W. W. Norton & Co.
Cantwell, Robert. 1993. *Ethnomimesis: Folklife and the Representation of Culture*. Chapel Hill: University of North Carolina Press.
Crehan, Kate. 2016. *Gramsci's Common Sense: Inequality and Its Narratives*. Durham, NC: Duke University Press.
Clifford, James. 1988. *The Predicament of Culture: Twentieth-Century Ethnography, Literature, and Art*. Cambridge, MA: Harvard University.
Clifford, James. 1997. *Routes*. Cambridge, MA: Harvard University Press.
Clifford, James, and George E. Marcus. 1986. *Writing Culture: The Politics and Poetics of Ethnography*. Berkeley: University of California Press.

de Certeau, Michel. 1984. *The Practice of Everyday Life*. Berkeley: University of California Press.
Dorson, Richard. [1959] 1977. *American Folklore*. Chicago: University of Chicago Press.
Dorson, Richard. 1976. *Folklore and Fakelore*. Cambridge, MA: Harvard University Press.
Dorst, John. 1989. *The Written Suburb: An American Site, An Ethnographic Dilemma*. Philadelphia: University of Pennsylvania Press.
Dundes, Alan. 1980. *Interpreting Folklore*. 12th ed. Bloomington: Indiana University Press.
Ehrenreich, Barbara. 2001. *Nickel and Dimed: On (Not) Getting by in America*. New York: Henry Holt Owl Books.
Gencarella, Stephen Olbrys. 2011. "Folk Criticism and the Art of Critical Folklore Studies." *Journal of American Folklore* 124 (494): 251–71. https://doi.org/10.5406/jamerfolk.124.494.0251.
Glassie, Henry. 1968. *Pattern in the Material Folk Culture of the Eastern United States*. Philadelphia: University of Pennsylvania Press.
Graburn, Nelson H. H. 1976. *Ethnic and Tourist Arts: Cultural Expressions from the Fourth World*. Berkeley: University of California Press.
Gramsci, Antonio. 1985. "Osservazioni sul folklore." In *Quaderni dal carcere*. Vol. 3. Turin: Einaudi.
Green, Archie. 1971. *Only a Miner: Studies in Recorded Coal Mining Songs*. Urbana: University of Illinois Press.
Green, Archie. 1978. "Industrial Lore: A Bibliographic-Semantic Query." In *Working Americans: Contemporary Approaches to Occupational Folklife*, ed. Robert H. Byington. Smithsonian Folklife Studies No. 3. Washington, DC: Smithsonian Institution Press.
Green, Archie. 1993. *Wobblies, Pile Butts and Other Heroes: Laborlore Explorations*. Urbana: University of Illinois Press.
Green, Archie. 2002. *Tin Men*. Urbana: University of Illinois Press.
Green, Thomas, ed. 1997. *Folklore: An Encyclopedia of Beliefs, Customs, Tales, Music, and Art*. Vol. 1. Santa Barbara, CA: ABC-CLIO Information Services.
Greenhill, Pauline, and K. Magnusson. 2010. "'Your Presence at Our Wedding Is Present Enough': Lies, Coding, Maintaining Personal Face, and the Cash Gift." *Journal of Folklore Research* 47 (3): 307–33.
Grose, Carolyn. 2009. "Of Victims, Villains and Fairy Godmothers: Regnant Tales of Predatory Lending" NYLS Clinical Research Institute Paper No. 08/09 #20. Available at SSRN: https://ssrn.com/abstract=1412784.
Guss, David. 2001. *The Festive State: Race, Ethnicity, and Nationalism as Cultural Performance*. Berkeley: University of California Press.
Hathaway, Rosemary V. 2005. "'Life in the TV': The Visual Nature of 9/11 Lore and Its Impact on Vernacular Response." *Journal of Folklore Research* 42 (1): 33–56.
Hemmersam, Fleming. 1985. "Worker Lore and Labor Lore." *ARV: Scandinavian Yearbook of Folklore* 41: 17–29.
Ho, Karen. 2009. *Liquidated: An Ethnography of Wall Street*. Durham, NC: Duke University Press.
Honko, Lauri. 1988. "Studies on Tradition and Cultural Identity: An Introduction." In *Tradition and Cultural Identity*, ed. Lauri Honko. Turku, Finland: Nordic Institute of Folklore.
Hufford, Mary, ed. 1994. *Conserving Culture: A New Discourse on Heritage*. Urbana: University of Illinois Press.
Huyssen, Andreas. 1995. *Twilight Memories: Marking Time in a Culture of Amnesia*. New York: Routledge.
Hymes, Dell. 2003. *Now I Know Only So Far: Essays in Ethnopoetics*. Lincoln: University of Nebraska Press.
Ingram, Shelley, Willow G. Mullins, and Todd Richardson. 2019. *Implied Nowhere: Absence in Folklore Studies*. Jackson: University of Mississippi Press.

Ivey, Bill. 2011. "Values and Value in Folklore (AFS Presidential Plenary Address, 2007)." *The Journal of American Folklore* 124 (491): 6–18. doi:10.5406/jamerfolk.124.491.0006.

Johnson, Paula, ed. 1988. *Working the Water: The Commercial Fisheries of Maryland's Pautuxent River.* Charlottesville: Calvert Marine Museum and University Press of Virginia.

Jones, Michael Owen. 1975. *The Handmade Object and Its Maker.* Berkeley: University of California Press.

Jones, Michael Owen. 1984. "Introduction: Works of Art, Art as Work, and the Arts of Working." *Western Folklore* 43 (3): 172–78.

Kapchan, Deborah. [1996] 2010. *Gender on the Marketplace: Moroccan Women and the Revoicing of Tradition.* Philadelphia: University of Pennsylvania Press.

Karp, Ivan. 1991. *Exhibiting Cultures: The Politics and Poetics of Museum Display.* Washington, DC: Smithsonian.

Kirshenblatt-Gimblett, Barbara. 1989. "Objects of Memory: Material Culture as Life Review." In *Folk Groups and Folklore Genres: A Reader*, ed. Elliott Oring. Logan: Utah State University Press.

Kirshenblatt-Gimblett, Barbara. 1998. *Destination Culture: Tourism, Museums, and Heritage.* Berkeley: University of California Press.

Koch, Gertraud. 2012. "Work and Professions." In *A Companion to Folklore*, ed. Regina Bendix and Galit Hasan-Rokem. Chichester, UK: Wiley Blackwell. https://doi.org/10.1002/9781118379936.

Korom, Frank. 1999. "Empowerment through Representation and Collaboration in Museum Exhibitions." *Journal of Folklore Research* 36 (2–3): 235–41.

Korson, George. 1927. *Songs and Ballads of the Anthracite Miners.* New York: Grafton Press.

Korson, George. 1938. *Minstrels of the Mine Patch.* Philadelphia: University of Pennsylvania Press.

Kurin, Richard. 1997. *Reflections of a Culture Broker: A View from the Smithsonian.* Washington, DC: Smithsonian Institution.

Lang, Andrew. 2015. "Modern Mythology." In *The Selected Works of Andrew Lang*. Vol. 1: *Anthropology: Fairy Tale, Folklore, the Origins of Religion, Psychical Research*, ed. Andrew Teverson, Alex Warwick, and Leigh Wilson. Edinburgh: Edinburgh University Press.

Lau, Kimberly J. 2000. *New Age Capitalism: Making Money East of Eden.* Philadelphia: University of Pennsylvania.

Lee, Tong Soon. 2009. *Chinese Street Opera in Singapore.* Urbana: University of Illinois Press.

Limón, José. 1983. "Western Marxism and Folklore: A Critical Introduction." *Journal of American Folklore* 96 (379): 34–52.

Limón, José. 2012. *Américo Paredes: Culture and Critique.* Austin: University of Texas Press.

MacCannell, Dean. [1989] 1976. *The Tourist: A New Theory of the Leisure Class.* New York: Schocken Books.

Maurer, Bill. 2006. "In the Matter of Marxism." In *Handbook of Material Culture*, ed. Chris Tilley, Webb Keane et al. London: Sage.

McCarl, Robert S. 1996. "Occupational Folklore." In *American Folklore: An Encyclopedia*, ed. J. H. Brunvard. New York: Garland.

McCarl, Robert S. 1997. "Occupational Folklore." In *Folklore: An Encyclopedia of Beliefs, Customs, Tales, Music and Art*, ed. Thomas Green. Santa Barbara: ABC-ClIO.

McDowell, John. 2012. "The Ballad of Narcomexico." *Journal of Folklore Research* 49 (3): 249–74.

McDowall, Robert. 2013. "The Folklore of Finance." *Folklore* 124 (3): 253–64.

McRobbie, Angela. 2004. "Making a Living as a Visual Artist in London's Small Scale Creative Economy." In *Cultural Industries and the Production of Culture*, ed. D. Power and A. J. Scott. New York: Routledge.

Miller, Daniel. 2006. "Consumption." In *Handbook of Material Culture*, ed. Chris Tilley, Webb Keane, et al. London: Sage.

Naumann, Hans. 1921. *Primitive Gemeinschaftskultur*. Jena, Germany: Diederich.

Newell, William. 1888. "On the Field and Work of a Journal of American Folk-Lore." *The Journal of American Folklore* 1 (1): 3–7. http://www.jstor.org/stable/532881.

Nickerson, Bruce. 1974. "Is There a Folk in the Factory?" *Journal of American Folklore* 87 (344): 133–39.

Noyes, Dorothy. 1995. "Group." In "Common Ground: Keywords for the Study of Expressive Culture." *Journal of American Folklore* 108 (430): 449–78.

Noyes, Dorothy. 2011. "Fairy-Tale Economics: Scarcity, Risk and Choice." Lecture, Western Michigan University, March 17.

Noyes, Dorothy. 2015. "From Cultural Forms to Policy Objects: Comparison in Scholarship and Policy." *Journal of Folklore Research* 52 (2–3): 299–313. https://doi.org/10.2979/jfolkrese.52.2-3.299.

Paredes, Américo. 1970. *Folktales of Mexico*. Chicago: University of Chicago Press.

Prahlad, Anand. 1999. "Guess Who's Coming to Dinner: Folklore, Folkloristics, and African American Literary Criticism." *African American Review* 33 (4): 565–75.

Pratt, Mary Louise. 1991. "Arts of the Contact Zone." *Profession*: 33–40. JSTOR 25595469.

Roberts, Katherine. 2012. "The Art of Staying Put: Managing Land and Minerals in Rural America." *Journal of American Folklore* 126 (502): 407–33.

Rosaldo, Renato. 1989. *Culture and Truth: The Remaking of Social Analysis*. Boston: Beacon Press.

Ross, Andrew. 2010. *Nice Work if You Can Get it: Life and Labor in Precarious Times*. New York: New York University Press.

Said, Edward. 1979. *Orientalism*. New York: Vintage Books.

Santino, Jack. 1990. "The Outlaw Emotions: Narrative Expressions on the Rules and Roles of Occupational Identity." *American Behavioral Scientist* 33 (3): 318–29.

Sennett, Richard. 2006. *The Culture of New Capitalism*. New Haven, CT: Yale University Press.

Sheumaker, Helen, and Shirley Teresa Wajda. 2008. *Material Culture in America: Understanding Everyday Life*. Santa Barbara: ABC-CLIO.

Shutika, Debra Lattanzi. 2011. *Beyond the Borderlands: Migration and Belonging in the United States and Mexico*. Berkeley: University of California Press.

Sommers, Laurie Kay. 1995. "Definitions of 'Folk' and 'Lore' in the Smithsonian Festival of American Folklife." *Journal of Folklore Research* 33: 227–31.

Tangherlini, Timothy. 1997. "Marxist Approach." In *Folklore: An Encyclopedia of Beliefs, Customs, Tales, Music and Art*, ed. Thomas Green. Santa Barbara: ABC-CIIO.

Toelken, Barre. 1995. "Fieldwork Enlightenment." *Parabola: The Magazine of Myth and Tradition* 20: 28–35.

Urry, John. 1990. *The Tourist Gaze*. London: SAGE.

Visweswaran, Kamala. 1994. *Fictions of Feminist Ethnography*. Minneapolis: University of Minnesota Press.

Vlach, John. 1991. *By the Work of Their Hands: Studies in Afro-American Folklife*. Charlottesville: University of Virginia Press.

Vlach, John, and Dell Upton. 1986. *Common Places: Readings in American Vernacular Architecture*. Athens: University of Georgia Press.

Zinn, Howard. 2015. *A People's History of the United States*. New York: Harper Perennial Modern Classics.

Zipes, Jack. 1979. *Breaking the Magic Spell: Radical Theories of Folk and Fairy Tales*. Austin: University of Texas Press.

# 1

# Folklore as a Networked Economy
*Or, How a Recently-Invented-but-Traditional Artifact Reveals the Way Folkloric Production Has Always Worked*

John Laudun

As Mullins and Batra-Well highlight in their introduction to this volume, folklorists have approached economics along some fairly well-worn paths: folk as a social class or category, folklore as artifacts to be produced and consumed, and the dynamics of folklore being best glimpsed within a marketplace of ideas and practices. All of these frameworks have, by and large, arisen as part of the field's own ongoing attempts to place itself within the larger history of the study of such things, especially as folklorists find themselves, as a result of economic opportunities and necessities—and sometimes it is difficult to tell such things apart—that split the field across a range of academic and public-sector institutional or organizational contexts. That is, folklorists themselves must compete in the marketplace of ideas, a competition that so often in the pages of our journals and books we frame as a losing proposition.

That we attempt to act as intermediaries for individuals and groups who are marginalized or misunderstood in some fashion has long been, thanks to our roots in the philological project, one of our core missions. That we obscure our own role in the fashioning of groups and margins is something the field has treated on occasion and will continue to examine as we move forward during what many concerned consider is a difficult economic moment both for folklorists and many of the folk.

The complexities, and nuances, of all this are something a number of folklorists have sought to understand (see Bauman and Briggs 2003, Bendix 1997). Because the valuation of artifacts carries obvious signs of economics, studies of material folk culture have often been iconic within folklore studies as sites where economic matters get addressed directly. Scholars of material folk culture have been quite good, I would argue, at following the transformation of what were craft activities, the making of stoneware pots or woven rugs or wooden household objects, into artisanal or artistic traditions. When combined with the transformations of the field with the turn toward performance, folklorists in general have provided detailed accounts of the life of artifacts, both material and verbal, as they are trafficked through various social spheres, be those spheres adjacent or distant. At the same time, we have been less interested in following the transformation of the craft tradition, as a kind of "mentifact," as it found new objects to create and produce.

In Louisiana, the crawfish boat is just such an object. Made of aluminum sheets and steel stock that arrive on flatbed trailers, held together by bolts made in distant factories and welds requiring vast amounts of electricity, and powered by small combustion engines driving complex hydraulic systems, the boats are about as modern as things get. Their diverse materials are a prism onto a global economy which otherwise seems so threatening to things folk. But the boats are made by hand by a handful of makers, all of whom have long ties to the landscape on which the boats work and with the people who work them: in some cases, the boats are made by the men who also operate them in a season that runs from some time in winter to early summer.

To get down to the brass tacks, to use a metallic metaphor, the crawfish boat must be understood in light of it having been, from the point of view of the economy within which it emerged, as a solution to a problem. That economy itself was, and is, fundamentally agricultural. The current context for American agriculture is one in which farmers face myriad complex networks that involve the manufacture of seeds, which now come with intellectual property regimes; the federal regulation, and support, of agriculture and agricultural lands both to protect the environment and to support food independence; and commodity price regimes and their diverse middle men (brokers, millers, distributors, wholesalers, food manufacturers); as well as the usual assortment of natural phenomenon that have always plagued farmers: droughts, storms, weeds, pests, and disease.

The crawfish boat arose in the middle of such things as an object that could harness immediate local interest, with the possible interest of more distant others in the future, as well as offer a "crop" outside the regulated economies of agricultural commodities such as rice and soybeans. (This also meant it was outside the protections of crop insurance or advanced bookings.) Understanding these economics is beyond the scope of this essay, which can offer only a sketch of such matters as they play out in the development of the form and the eventual manufacturing infrastructure. Put another way, a way perhaps more appealing to folklorists, farmers along the Western Gulf Coast Prairie are part of larger economic systems over which they have little to no control. Within such a context, however, the farmers in the Louisiana portion of the prairie developed an artifact, a machine (a text), which precisely addressed that context, drawing upon only their own ideas and experiences. The machine created additional spaces within the larger economy that gave farmers room to maneuver and, in some cases, to flourish. The machine itself was both part of, and an index of, this ongoing negotiation of economic space. In the process, it also created, quite literally, economic spaces for others, for example, fabricators, to develop, in some cases, businesses focused on the manufacture of the crawfish boat.

Economic spaces are, of course, abstractions, abstractions that reveal the necessary ideational nature of the subject at hand. Such spaces surely exist, but they exist only in the minds of the humans who move about within and across various groups that both they and we imagine as communities but might be better described as networks, with individuals making up nodes in a network that is always in motion, because people are always in motion, but which nevertheless instantiate dependably objective sets of relationships. Thus, the idea of clustering, central to network studies, is readily glimpsed on the rural landscape, as individuals transit between house and shop, between one site and another. They navigate that landscape, of course, by depending upon a network of ideas, which are held together through various discursive forms that emphasize narrative, locative, argumentative, or expository relationships. Like the individuals in whom they reside, these ideational networks are highly dynamic as they prove themselves to be useful and/or interesting, shaping actions in the world and in turn being shaped by those actions.

To understand folklore as a networked economy is to understand folklore as a collection of sociocultural networks whose connections scholars and scientists have only recently begun to trace. While much of that work has focused on rumors, legends, and news that make their way through online social networks, folklorists, and other ethnomethodologists (as Bruno Latour noted), can contribute to the larger inquiry by establishing that social networks have always been a part of the human experience of the world. Tracing such a network of ideas and people is a bit more complex in the field, but it can be done. By focusing on an artifact of relatively recent creation, but drawing upon obviously well-established networks of ideas as well as well-established lived, social networks, I hope to use the smallness of the subject to advantage, revealing how it draws upon concentric sets of ideas and individuals.

## A LARGER HISTORICAL CONTEXT

The overarching set of ideas, or context, for the crawfish boat is agricultural. The Western Gulf Coast Prairie has been transformed over the past three centuries from wild pasturage for small herds of buffalo to managed pasturage for cattle to a fairly productive agricultural region, which now, strangely enough, features aquaculture. Both the growing of rice and the raising of crawfish are made possible through careful terracing of what appears to be a flat landscape but is, in fact, one with rolls of sufficient gentleness to allow fields to be cut into pieces large enough to deploy machinery for harvest. That is, the Louisiana prairies are fundamentally dry but sourced well enough with water both above and below ground to allow for the pumping and holding of water in "paddies." The reason for flooding fields is to take advantage of rice's tolerance of water, enabling a fundamental form of weed control.

Rice first came to the Americas in 1685, when a severe Atlantic storm drove a brigantine bound from Madagascar to Europe into Charleston harbor. While the ship underwent repair, its captain passed along some seed rice to a local doctor, who in turn passed the seed along to some of his friends, who were able to grow the Madagascar rice, adding another crop to American agriculture.[1] When plantation owners found that some of their slaves knew how to grow rice, it wasn't long before demand for such slaves reached back to Africa. It is also quite possible that in the years that followed the eviction of the Acadians from the Canadian maritime provinces, some of the dispossessed would have witnessed these Carolinian plantations, with their complex networks of levees that took advantage of the ability of ocean tides, in raising the water level, to push fresh water into fields, where it could be held when the tide waned. Such a sight would, historian Carl Brasseaux (1992) has pointed out, certainly have reminded the Acadians of the similar structures they had built to reclaim land in the farms they had been forced to leave behind in what would become Nova Scotia.

In Louisiana, the city of New Orleans is founded in 1718 and the first slave ship arrives only one year later. A few records point to slaves with knowledge of rice being sought out, and the general sense is that rice was seen as a crop that could be grown where nothing else would. Its principle market was as fodder for slaves. The rest of the state's residents were much more focused on trying to grow wheat for bread or learning to master the many things one can make with the continent's own grain, corn.[2]

Rice remained an opportunistic crop for much of Louisiana's early history. Several observers noted its presence among Acadian farmers, especially among those who had moved away from the Mississippi River and its immediate tributaries to begin to populate the prairies west of the great Atchafalaya swamp. Among the prairies and bayous, small farmers planted patches of "providence" rice, broadcasting seed in low-lying spots—in coulees and ponds according to Lauren Post (1962)—where the grain might take advantage of its natural tolerance for standing water. While the supply was never great, it did cultivate, as it were, a taste for the grain that may have been as important as anything else, keeping it, as it did, rice growing an active part of the region, and thus an active part of the landscape.

Except for a brief moment immediately before and after the Civil War, rice was never subject to large-scale agricultural efforts.[3] The key to the transformation of the Louisiana prairies into an agricultural landscape was the completion of the Louisiana Western Railroad in 1881, bridging the gap that had existed since before the Civil War, when two lines had reached as far as Berwick from New Orleans and as far as Orange from Houston. The land through which the railroad ran had been, from the point of view of the powers that be, sparsely populated, filled mostly with grazing cattle. Several companies sprang up to fill this newly opened, and fertile, landscape, which was advertised as "free from protracted droughts which afflict Kansas and other prairies regions" (Dethloff 1988, 372). They bought up large chunks of land and then sold it in smaller chunks, often in quarter sections of 160 acres, to farmers who often came down in tours, sponsored by the companies or by the railroad (now the Southern Pacific), which was anxious to have the land settled and productive. In other words, the key to rice in Louisiana, now one of the iconic foods of the region, was the consolidation of a modern transportation infrastructure.

Thanks to the railroad, the population of the Louisiana prairies doubled in the last two decades of the nineteenth century, from 126,000 to 240,000. As historian Henry Dethloff noted, "Most of the new settlers were farmers from the North and Midwest lured by cheap land and driven by droughts and blizzards that beset the midwestern prairies in the 1880s and climaxed with the terrible winter of 1886–87" (Dethloff 1988, 374). These farmers were used to growing crops, such as wheat, which had never done well in the long hot, and humid, Louisiana summers, but it did not take them long to turn all the equipment they had brought with them—steam tractors, harrows, plows, and threshers—to the task of growing rice (Dethloff 1988, 375).

What they discovered was a landscape practically made not only for holding water but also for working with heavy equipment: under the Louisiana prairies lies an impervious clay pan subsoil that holds water the way cement does and supports heavy equipment, which would otherwise bog in deeper soils. Combined with a growing season that typically accommodates both a first crop and a ratoon crop and abundant rainfall, what had once been a small-scale agriculture intended for local consumption became an agricultural powerhouse whose output practically doubled decade after decade in its first forty years: 834,111 bushels in 1879 became 2,721,059 in 1889, then 6,213,397 in 1899, followed by 10,839,973 in 1909 and 16,011,607 in 1919.[4] The scope of the mechanization can be gleaned from equipment shipments during these years: the Southern Pacifica Railroad shipped 1 twine binder to southwest Louisiana in 1884, 200 in 1887, and 1,000 in 1890.

Reading histories of early efforts by the railroads and other private investment companies to settle the Louisiana prairies, you realize that the quarter sections of land that were being marketed to prospective buyers were being sold on the very basis of their mechanizability. It's not clear if the northern and European farmers necessarily expected such machines to be a part of the landscape or if it was part of the overall vision of progress being advertised, but steam tractors were regularly featured as plowing and cultivating in tours.

Contemporary memories of twentieth-century developments suggest that mechanization, or at least a desire to mechanize, is a significant part of farming practice.[5] While not that many farmers began with steam tractors, it remained a desire to have one. Most of the early agricultural machines were pulled by horses, be they gang plows or threshers or bailers. Self-binding reapers were drawn by rather large mule teams, with the machinery driven by a bull wheel that created the mechanical energy required to first cut the rice stalks, then push them onto a conveyor of some kind, then bind a group of stalks into a shock, which was then dropped to one side as part of the conveyance movement.[6] The shock, of course, dates back to antiquity and remained a part of agricultural practice until harvesting and threshing were combined into one machine, aptly named the *combine*, perhaps one of the greatest labor-saving devices ever invented.

Both the tractor and the combine did not really come into their own until the 1950s, a moment in which small gasoline-powered tractors became affordable and combines became self-propelled. The oldest farmers at work in the present have memories that date back to that time, and many of them have fond memories of their family's first tractor or combine. Until that moment, horses remained a significant part of farm life in south Louisiana, except on the largest or most profitable farms. The rise in productivity brought by the introduction of these machines, as well as improved varieties (known as cultivars) and synthetic herbicides, can be glimpsed in the history of rice yields: after the precipitous rise in the last two decades of the nineteenth century, yields hovered around 1,800 to 2,000 pounds per acre throughout the first half of the twentieth century. Only after the Second World War did rice production rise significantly, and then it did with pent-up ferocity, doubling to over 4,000 pounds per acre by the late 1960s. Further rises occurred in the 1980s and again in the late 1990s thanks to the development of cultivars, many of which were the product of the LSU AgCenter's Rice Research Station located in rice country itself, between the towns of Crowley and Rayne. (Such is their faith in technology, Louisiana rice farmers tax themselves in order to fund the research, and the relationship between the station faculty and staff and area farmers is quite open and warm.)

One should not imagine that the tractor, the combine, or other machines simply appear magically on the landscape and everything changes. Rather, they first appear in the fields of more prosperous, or more adventurous, farmers. Other farmers stop and stand at the edge of the fields, observe, wonder if it's worth the investment. There is a great deal of conversation in feed and seed stores, in hardware stores, at the mills, and at church. How is it? What's it like to work? Does it increase yields? Does it damage the land any? The questions are direct. These are men and women who have, thanks to mechanization, always worked alone or in small groups of two or three. As the years pressed on, they worked more and more acres, keeping the same amount of people per farm, resulting in fewer of them.[7]

## THE EMERGENCE OF THE CRAWFISH BOAT

As the machines they used became more capable of driving other machines, farmers began to seek out devices that solved particular problems. Sometimes they worked on their own, and sometimes they sought out the help of a local equipment repair shop. No matter the origin, if something worked it would soon find its way onto other farms, with variations the product of particular needs or ideas or experiences. Out of such moments were born PTO pumps, for moving water out of canals and ditches, and PTO ditchers, for creating the shallow, wall-less traces that allow water to drain out of near-level rice fields, as well as side plows and water levelers and a myriad other tools and machines.[8]

All of these things allow farmers to transform the gently sloping landscape of south Louisiana into a series of carefully calculated as-close-to-level-as-you-can-get rice fields that they maintain all year round by pulling levees up and then pulling them down, by carefully working inside flooded fields with giant tractors in order to make cuts as close to

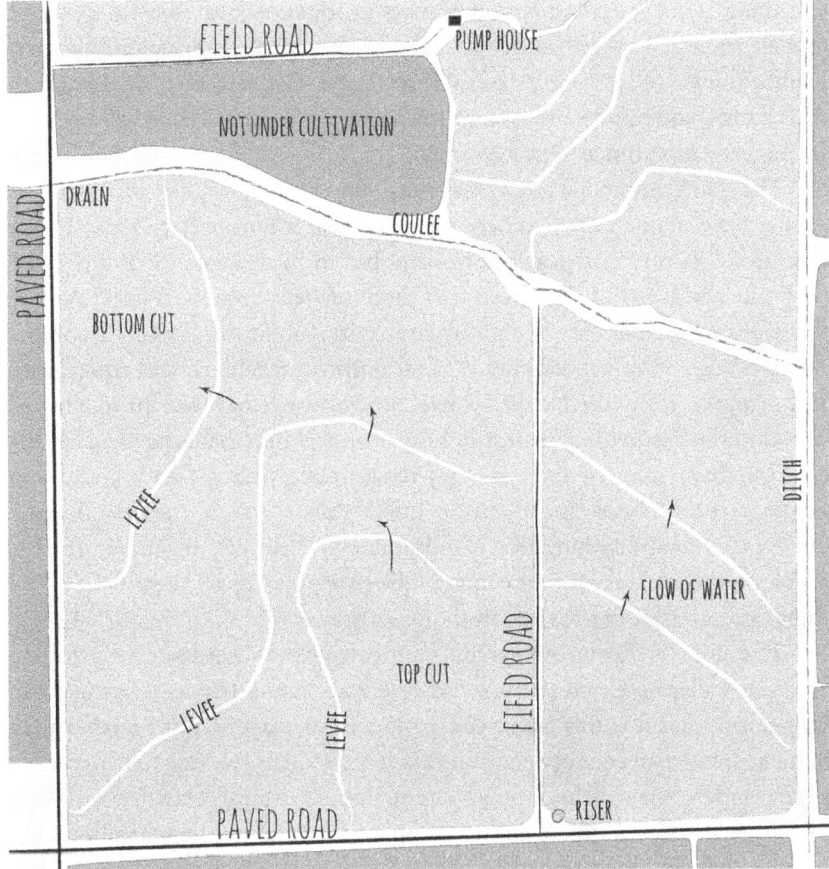

Figure 1.1. A plan of a rice field divided into cuts. Water is pumped into the top cut, or cuts, and then flows through the terraced levels via a series of gates, drains, or curtains to the bottom cut from which it drains into adjacent ditches, coulees, or bayous. While fields usually follow mapped survey boundaries, cut boundaries follow the land's topography.

level as you can get. There is never anything perfect. There is never anything complete, especially when confronted with both the uncertainty of cultivating living things while at the mercy of the randomness of the weather, a randomness redoubled by the greed of the commodity markets that are more than happy to punish mistakes and successes alike.

In the face of such forces, the ability to get a side plow made just for your tractor or a boat that works best in the kinds of fields you have seems a small affordance of security, a slight hedge against the many risks. It is no wonder then that the ties between farmers and fabricators are so strong. The men in the shops have, working as they do across farms, the knowledge of what can, or will, go wrong and right that wrong the next time they make that thing. They are not invested in mass production, and they do not have to wait to retool an entire manufacturing line. While robots and jigs may require weeks, or in some cases months, to be changed, men working with their hands, and minds, can change immediately. The next weld will be twice as long, the next brace, twice as thick.

The same immediacy, and the same knowledge, applies to repairs. A farmer comes into a shop in need of a repair. For him or her, it may be the first time this piece of gear has broken, but in most instances it is not the first time the fabricator has seen that piece of gear broken. A great deal of the gear that farmers use is built by large national, or international, companies who are, in effect, making general purpose machines and equipment. They cannot know the particular uses, and abuses, that their products will encounter in the fields. Farmers in Louisiana feel that that is particularly the case for them: a lot of the gear they use is made with the corn and wheat fields of the Midwest and Plains in mind. Rice is rough, they say. Its hull can wear almost anything down more quickly than any manufacturer has ever anticipated. It is up to the men in the shops nearby to know how to put things right, often improving on things as they go.

The ability to have your general-purpose gear customized or repaired to your particular needs creates a sense of collaboration between farmers and fabricators, and it is this larger sense of everyone being in it together that, in turn, created an economy within which individuals felt free to experiment rather widely when it became apparent that cultivating crawfish in fallow rice fields could not only be a nice supplement to traditional farm incomes but could in fact be a principle income. Catching crawfish was like returning to a previous moment in agriculture, when work and nature were the two dominant factors and not a commodity price index that really measured the minds of men in suits who worked in cities far from the hot sun and high humidity of the prairies.

A more detailed treatment of the years that precede the emergence of the crawfish boat would reveal the highly dynamic nature of the search for a solution that pursued almost every logical possibility, no matter how dead its end might be.[9] Many of the historical accounts I collected focused on the absurdity of the solutions before the arrival of the boat. Many of those stories focused on the image of a lone individual walking through a rice field with either five-gallon buckets in both hands or trailing a child's plastic splash pool behind him or her. In recalling the past in this way, tellers gently make fun of themselves, and, at the same time, the ludicrous nature of the image also emphasizes exactly how hard the work was, how much of it there was to do, and how crippling the available tools were felt to be.

The allure of a cash crop was too strong to wither before such physical vicissitudes, and as yields slowly but steadily increased farmers began to want to find ways to make the process more efficient. They wanted, as they noted, to automate the process, to give it more power. These were men, after all, who were comfortable with a wide variety of farm gear, and, just as important, most had some knowledge of and experience in making or modifying an implement in their own shops or equipment sheds. What happened next is not entirely clear. Memories in the present must reach back forty years and try to piece together, through reference to other events—often to when a child was born or to what grade they were in—that otherwise blend together as part of "life on a farm." There are few photographs available, even from the men who would become prominent as boat makers. Few farmers take pictures of their tractors, nor do they date when they first used them. The same is true for the crawfish boats.

More than once I have heard these early boats described as little more than "contraptions," as if that was all there were to say on the subject. Whatever the form of those first few proto-boats, they seem to have had the drive unit in the back, similar to the modern crawfish boat, and somehow managed to make their way through a field. Out of this initial period of experimentation emerged, in the very late seventies, the "tiller foot" boat. Like its predecessor, it was built on commercially available fishing boat hulls with the addition of a most extraordinary assemblage: the lower part of a garden rotary tiller driven by a five-horsepower engine separated by a long boom, made in place. At first one steered the machines with a tiller attached to the assembled drive unit, much like you would the outboard motor of a boat, but eventually someone adapted the power steering cylinder of a car so that steering could be handled more remotely. The tiller foot boats were used for a number of years, but eventually the fact that the drive units were assembled from such disparate parts meant the units were short lived: the transmission gears, often made of brass (which is more resistant to oxidation than steel but soft), were not intended for such intensive use and would typically fail within a year's time.

Interestingly, as farmers moved from pulling a boat or tub behind them to driving a powered boat, they realized they needed a better trap. Farmers had mostly been using a version of the pillow trap. Shaped like a pillow on your bed, the trap has two funnels for admitting crawfish at one end and is typically closed by folding the mesh over and keeping it closed with a clothes pin on the other end. As one farmer noted, however: "When we got away from pulling the boat to a mechanized boat, we moved to an open trap. You just couldn't move fast enough with the pillow traps. We started by making the traps look like a trash can. We made a circle out of expanded metal, put mesh on the bottom, sewed in two funnels, and left the top completely open. You would dump it just like a trash can." The trash can trap seems to have worked well enough that at least a few farmers remember using it for a number of years, but it would eventually be replaced by the design that is now the standard: the pyramid trap.

Designed for use in the long, wide, shallow, and flat bottoms of rice fields flooded with water, the pyramid trap is a mesh tetrahedron with a cylinder atop it.[10] Some stand about two feet high, and some are made a little taller: there are traps with extended chimneys that stand four and a half feet high. Each of the three bottom corners of the tetrahedron, or pyramid, has a funnel in it, allowing more crawfish to enter, and from more directions, netting a greater number of crawfish per bait.

Atop the trap is the chimney, which as aquacultural specialists Mark Shirley and Charles Lutz note, is an especially useful innovation, since it acts as a "combination collar and handle on the top of the trap, which prevents crawfish from climbing out while making the trap easier to grasp, lift and empty quickly" (2009, 2). The first cylinders were made out of six-inch PVC pipe, as many still are. While the first few chimneys were plain, and there are still a few in use, it did not take long for operators to realize that making them easier to grab from a moving boat would allow the work to go a lot more quickly, and someone discovered how easy it is to heat PVC enough to push a in one side of the top of cylinder to form a lip about one inch deep, just enough to catch it with fingers.[11]

The pyramid trap, as its description suggests, is not an easy trap to make. As both the traps and boats evolved, they both became simultaneously not only more efficient and more reliable but also more complex. They were less available to ordinary farmers with limited time to spend on building tools and machines. Gone were the days when, as one farmer put it, "three or four guys would get together and make a bunch of boats. Everyone would have one, and they would sell two or three. Everybody didn't make a boat, but it was a pretty small circle of who ended up with a boat you made." That is, the economics of trap- and boat-making changed.

Like other changes both past and present, the changes always have larger implications for the delicate, dynamic matrices of society and culture. In the case of the evolving ecosystem of crawfish production in rice fields, the change reflects larger trends to mechanize agriculture resulting in fewer farmers working in the fields. Today's three-hundred-horsepower tractors can level several hundred acres of fields in a day, if the work is not too demanding, and they can do it with greater precision and, in many cases,

Figure 1.2. A pyramid crawfish trap. Pyramid traps are distinct from other traps used in natural bodies of water because they are designed to sit on the flat bottoms of shallow rice fields. Integrated stakes keep traps from blowing over in strong winds or being knocked over by overly excited egrets.

with less wear and tear on the human sitting in the tractor cab who is also now protected from dust and insects. The American agricultural landscape has always been an individualized, and often lonely one, with the exception being harvest time, which is a relatively small portion of the year. It looms large in people's memories, however, and thus also in the larger imaginary that surrounds agriculture in general. Most farmers, however, readily remember the long hours spent plowing, driving around checking on fields, stacking materials in equipment sheds, and tucked underneath or around gear in order to repair or refine it.

The early years of the crawfish boat and the pyramid traps were something of a break from these larger trends. For older farmers, it felt more like the old days, when there were a lot more small farmers. In the case of the crawfish boat, there were a lot of people who were not themselves farmers but who had access to family land and could, in before- and after-work hours, fish fifteen or twenty acres. The increased number of individuals meant there was a lot of experimentation, some of which was simply because smaller operators did not have the desire, or the ability, to afford commercially made boats. The result was a lot of boats that resembled other boats in many ways but also bearing their makers' individual marks. Some boats, no doubt, manifested real insights, some of which were taken up by others. Other boats were less than inspirational but worked well enough to be kept running from year to year.

For folklorists, this economy sounds more like what interests us, one where abilities and interests are spread homogeneously through a community. It is important to keep in mind that like other kinds of artisanship, which I am using here to bridge the divide between notions of a craft and an artistic economy, there can be a widespread interest in a form without there necessarily being widespread ability in that form. Everyone can have something to say, which may or may not affect the nature of the form, but not everyone wants to participate actively. One of the very first makers of the crawfish boat found a friend and fellow farmer at his door with a check in his hand, telling him, "Make me a boat just like the one you made for yourself." Sometimes a folk economy is consumptive in nature, depending upon (relative) specialists to commoditize objects that circulate freely within the microeconomy of ideas and practices.

## COMMUNITIES AS NETWORKS

Both of the men, Ted Habetz and Maurice Benoit, who first demonstrated working models of what would become the modern crawfish boat—a boat whose mechanics were all run by hydraulics—noted that they had no intention of being in the boat-making business. Both men eventually succumbed to the requests, and the checks, being pressed upon them and entered into an artisanship that, ultimately, neither one particularly enjoyed pursuing. So they eventually left the business to others who had come along, some of whom remain to this day—Gerard Olinger and Kurt Venable—and others of whom took their turn being an active node in a network of makers and operators, fabricators, and farmers, who made various contributions to the boat's development.

It is important to remember when we examine an economy such as this one, which on its surface seems to be dominated by relatively few producers, that diversity lies in its depths. The ability to make useful things out of metal is diffused across the landscape, though perhaps not evenly. It is not uncharacteristic of farmers, at least in Louisiana, to be known for being very attentive to the money they spend, and so some are no doubt

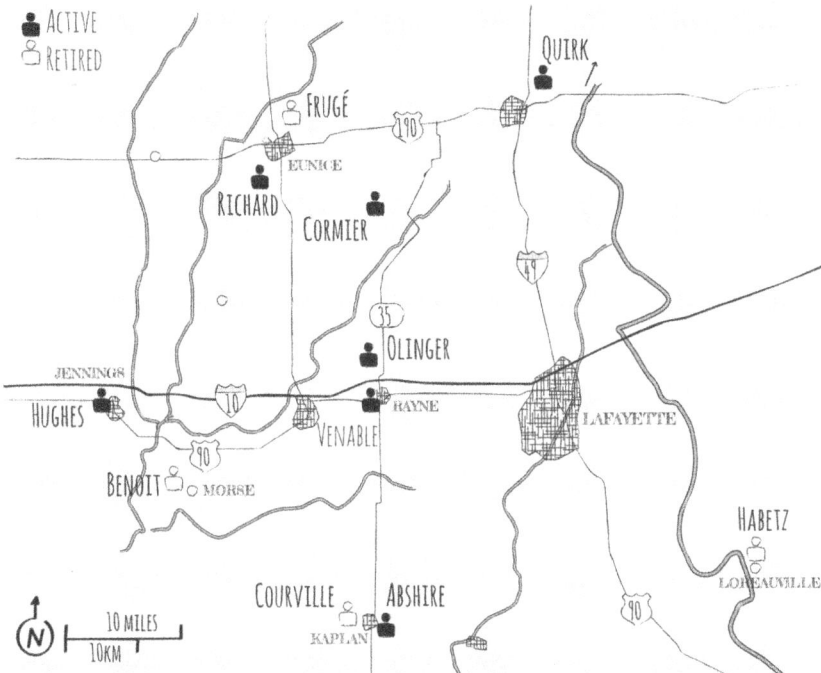

Figure 1.3. A map of active and inactive boat makers. Even now this map is outdated as some of the active makers have left the business and others have stepped forward, offering their own versions of boats. What the map does reveal is how spread out the makers are.

motivated to try making a boat out of a desire to save money. But there are others who enjoy trying their hand at making either because they are good at welding, they have a design or novelty they want to try, or they want a break from farming. All of these are reasons to try your own hand at making a boat. And the many different kinds of boats that I have glimpsed through thickets of grass or ivy are testimony to the widely available set of skills that many individuals in south Louisiana first encounter in agricultural shop in area high schools.[12]

But as the uses of the boats became more demanding—the drive units became more powerful and hulls became stronger and larger to withstand the crossings—the range of makers actively involved in the production of boats slowly constricted to a few individuals who possessed not only the skill set, but also the facilities and the economic wherewithal to make the new, substantially improved form of the boat. The modern "hydraulic boat," as it if sometimes called, is a far cry from the first boats, which were not much more than two commercially available items, a boat and a tiller, cobbled together. Such a transformation—from an assembly of widely available parts, and parts that were as easily had as the closest Sears—to a custom product requiring knowledge of two kinds of metal work, aluminum and steel, as well as an understanding of gear ratios and power distribution in hydraulic systems, meant that production that was once fairly evenly distributed across the landscape became centralized to a few nodes.

This particular form of distribution is not new, nor anything to be lamented. It represents a fairly old form of development of an industry, one dependent upon a variety of abilities focused on a particular artifact. Once upon a time, we called such a thing, the intertwining of skills and an object, "craft." The men who possessed the skills that led to particular kinds of products were known as craftsmen.

Craft, as ability and its application, is resurgent in contemporary discourse, both thanks to the maker movement but also to interesting introspections in the face of automation.[13] Folklorists have long taken craft as one of their central subjects, since craft is usually dependent upon a dense network, or, really, set of networks, that intertwine people, ideas, and practices. That is, craft foregrounds the role of culture in our lives. A craft is typically imagined as a set of skills organized around a particular product, be it a tangible object like a boat or a quilt or an intangible one like a legend or a song. In most instances, those skills are probably generally diffused across a group: lots of people sew or a good number can weld, and plenty of people tell jokes and countless others hum a tune while they do something else or to comfort themselves or a child.

Occasionally, however, someone has an especial affinity or ability for a task, or, at least, they apply themselves sufficiently that he or she comes in some way to be noted, marked, for being able to do a particular thing. Not everyone is asked to bake a dessert for a family gathering, and not everyone is consulted for advice about cars or computers. Rather, there are a handful of people within any particular family or community to which expertise has been attributed. To them, we bring our problems. From them, we anticipate solutions or, at least, a very nice slice of pie. These are the artists and craftsmen in our worlds. Too often we transmute their focus and their willingness to practice into something like a talent, a gift given from an ethereal realm as opposed to a hard-won ability that was perhaps, yes, driven by an as-yet-to-be-understood curiosity or desire.

Henry Glassie describes the larger phenomenon in articulating the way Turkish women assemble carpets of intricate design by doing nothing more than knotting together strings. The designs, of course, exist nowhere but in their heads, but how do the designs get there, and how does a woman know how to manifest that design through what amounts to a pixelated drawing, row by row, of a larger scheme? There is no sketch over which paints are applied. There is no plan lying on the floor by her side, occasionally drawing her attention. Instead, "a weaver is alone in concentration and part of a team at work" (1993, 51). Glassie observed that each act of a weaver "collects the whole of her biography," since she often grows up playing in the shadow of her mother weaving, first collecting scraps of yarn, getting a feel for the fiber and the colors involved, then making her first few knots and learning first techniques and then designs, finally making a carpet of her own while her mother, family, and friends look on (1993, 52–53). Craftsmanship, in many ways, refracts larger questions about human nature, of human as individuals and as part of a larger group, as Glassie mused, while watching the Turkish weavers: "To be human is to be alone and not alone, at once an individual and a member of society" (1993, 51).

Our farmers and fabricators who went on to become boat makers are no different. They are drawn to it because it represents an intellectual or technical challenge and/or because it represents an economic opportunity. The acumen they bring draws the attention of others. Many want a boat, but either lack the ability or the desire to make a boat for themselves. As we have seen, the initial experimentation was fairly diffuse, with, as an older fabricator once remarked, "all kinds of fellows making all kinds of jackleg contraptions." But refinement quickly concentrated around a handful of makers, some of whom are still making boats with having moved on to other pursuits. Even the reasons for getting out of the business of building boats are diverse: for some, interest in building boats waned; for others, it was no longer as profitable as it once was. For at least one, retirement called, the next stage in a life already richly lived.

This is a terribly important point that cannot be made often enough: any community seen from the outside, from an initial glance, appears homogeneous to the untrained, unfamiliar eye. One equipment shed on a farm or one welding shop at the end of a gravel drive looks like another when seen from a car traveling too fast on a country road. But the similarity ends there, with the superficial, with the snapshot, with the windshield. Once you are out of the car and into the shed or shop and you have spent some time watching people work and listening to them talk, the differences become apparent. Personality and experience always matter, and they are always different.

## A NETWORKED ECONOMY

Understanding of the economics of the crawfish boat emerges out of a consideration of its form and manufacture. The current moment has a

Figure 1.4. A crawfish boat parked next to a field. This particular boat was built by Kurt Venable of Rayne. Venable's boats are distinguished by having their forward wheels housed inside the hull of the boat and by the red Z-shaped steel drive unit, which steers the boat at the point of the wheel. Other boats either swing the entire drive unit or are hinged at some midpoint.

relatively small number of makers actively building boats, but a brief history of the boat's development reveals that not only were others part of the network of ideas, but that their movement was itself guided by economics. Just as important as the individuals involved are the ideas in play and how they play out, which are here guided both by local culture and the lack of intellectual property regimes. There are, for example, no patents on any part of the crawfish boat. This is not because the men who make them are not fierce competitors, nor is it because they are unaware of intellectual property laws or contemporary trends in patents and copyrights. In addition to his boat business, Kurt Venable mills a variety of custom parts for other manufacturers using his own CAM system. Gerard Olinger orders parts from his shop in the middle of Roberts Cove via his satellite service. Both of them are fully aware of the full force of the contemporary legal apparatus surrounding technology. On more than one occasion, Olinger has remarked that local fabricators always fill niches perceived as too small or unprofitable by large manufacturers. Both of these men, and any of the others, are fully capable of pursuing the legal steps necessary to mark some facet or another of the crawfish boat as belonging exclusively to him.

And yet no one does. As far as each maker is concerned, their reputations as builders, and the reputations of their boats—obviously, the two are intertwined—are well known throughout the community. Venable prides himself on making the strongest hulls, Richard on flexible hulls, Olinger on dual-wheel drives. Each has also borrowed ideas from the others. Such borrowing is not always from direct observation but can often be in the form of indirect reporting: a farmer admires something on another farmer's boat and then requests that a maker add that to his own boat. Sometimes the addition catches on more broadly; sometimes the logic of the addition or emendation is obvious to the maker in a way that leads to further innovation.

Creativity draws from the deep well of common knowledge and individual experience. Farming, like any other domain, presents a series of problems to be solved, but how those problems are solved is largely determined by how they are framed or understood, and that understanding is itself a function of individual and collective experiences that are constantly being negotiated not only in terms of content but also in terms of context. Thus, the framework for any solution, and thus the solution itself, is really a function of which individuals within a community are involved, which individuals have contributed, and who has accepted their contribution.

If that sounds a lot like a network, that's because it is. And thinking of individuals as nodes with differential experiences and desires forces us to think of each individual in a community as someone not only with particular abilities and self-perceived roles—only a farmer, a farmer who occasionally fabricates something when he or she needs it, a farmer who actively fabricates for himself or herself and others, a fabricator who farms, or strictly a fabricator—but also in term of personal proclivities. For example, one fabricator is a tinker by personality, another is a born competitor and must win in whatever domain he enters, and yet another is a raconteur of exceptional abilities. Together they make up not a homogeneous community but rather a network of individuals who, through their presence, maintain a network of ideas, and concomitant practices, that have evolved over time. (Those ideas are, of course, situated in a value matrix that has remained fairly stable for at least three decades, and it is reasonable to assume the stability extends further back in time.)

Such an approach highlights what Bruno Latour describes as the fundamental properties of an "actor network." Latour himself once described actor-network theory (often abbreviated as ANT) as "simply another way to be faithful to the insights of ethnomethodology" (1999, 19). While much of ANT has been focused on studies of science and technology in large industrial or organizational contexts, its orientation toward a rich understanding of the relationships between competence, texts, contexts, economics, and individuals makes its application within folklore studies a fairly straightforward proposition, which should not be surprising given its roots in semiotics, anthropology (particularly Douglas 1966), the genealogy of knowledge (Foucault 1977), and the sociology of science and technology awoken by Kuhn's *Structure of Scientific Revolutions* (1962). Some may find the confusing—or confused or, perhaps better, simply fused—nature of actants in ANT to be frustrating, but much of it seems to be simply another way of reflecting within a theoretical framework the idea that people are shaped by ideas and ideas shaped by people. In many ways, ANT is the social construction of reality in a sociological garb.

Its utility, to my mind, for folklore studies is as a possible bridge between the kinds of network studies already taking place, which tend to focus on networks of like objects—of texts, of computers, of cells—and the studies that have begun to emerge of networks of diverse nodes and relationships. These are the networks that constitute things such as ecologies, when we deal with the natural world, and economies, when we deal with the social world of humans, wherein valuation is simply a part of a larger collection of exchanges that are always already ongoing. If we take those same sets of interests and examine a network of individuals, ideas, and objects that reveal both simultaneous invention and diffuse experimentation embedded in the social and economic matrix that is at the heart of modern American farming, we find ourselves with an artifact such as the crawfish boat, an artifact born of modernity, but realizing a number of traditional ideas. Tracing out these various ideas reveals the artifact, be it a story or a boat, to be more than simply a thing in itself. It always expresses something about the individual who made it and the individual who uses it. When those two individuals are part of a larger group with shared ideas, a larger network, the artifact cannot help but express something of that culture as well as the landscape on which the group resides and the artifact operates. It is the peculiar charm of the crawfish boat that its destiny was to be born of an ambiguous landscape. Its mobility no matter the circumstance allows us a glimpse into how creativity has been practiced in a particular place at a particular moment in time. Perhaps no more, but certainly no less.

## NOTES

1. Babineaux's 1967 thesis, "A History of the Rice Industry of Southwestern Louisiana," remains one of the central references for people interested in the early economics of rice farming.

2. Indeed, the first accounts of gumbo are of the dish being eaten not over rice but over corn meal mush, or "coush coush," as it came to be known. (The grain is American; its preparation as a mush is European; and its name is African, taken, scholars believe, from its resemblance to couscous.)

3. For about twenty years, between the 1850s and the 1870s, there was a moment in which the availability of steam power to pump water into fields and a depressed market for sugar made rice agriculture an interesting proposition for river plantation owners. But, like the Carolinian planters, they too suffered from the loss of enslaved labor after the Civil

War, and given the higher costs of planting, when you actually had to pay people to work for you, it only took a few years of restored profitability in the sugar market to return them to raising cane.

4. These figures are from the United States Bureau of the Census, United States Census (Department of Agriculture, Washington, DC), 3:759, as noted in Dethloff (1988).

5. Perhaps as important as the mechanization was the introduction and diffusion of the idea of forming companies in order to achieve larger goals. One of the first instances of this, after the land companies themselves, was the creation of an alternate system of mills as a response to the oppressive pricing of the New Orleans mills—the latter of which found themselves obsolete within a decade. Another instance, this time in response to the droughts of the mid-1890s, was the development of a number of canal companies. Canals acted not only as means of conveying water from a source, such as a bayou (usually by pumping), but also as reservoirs, holding water until it was needed. Some canal companies offered more than water: they would give farmers land and seed as well in return for a share of the crop. An advertisement by the Vermilion Development Company read: "To any party having working-stock we will build a house and pasture. Any amount of land required will be furnished . . . The seed required will be advanced, same to be returned after harvest. A complete pumping outfit will be rented at cost for the purpose of irrigating the rice field. We pay our share of threshing and furnish our share of sacks. We ask as our share one-fourth of the total crop." Such a successful engine, technology, and economic cooperation—for inputs such as water as well as outputs in terms of milling—drove land values from fifty cents to ten dollars within a decade, which in turn drove farmers into eastern Texas and, later, southern Arkansas, developing those areas as rice producers.

6. It should be noted that the term "bull wheel" is a later appellation, used first in the oil field and later applied to all such mechanisms. The first bull wheels, however, appeared on farm implements: Cyrus McCormick's 1834 reaper featured a bull wheel, which remains an important part of agricultural machinery until small gasoline engines became more widely available in the 1920s.

7. Even the need for day laborers, once a space and time within which blacks and whites worked together, slowly wore away, and only while in town will white farmers encounter black city dwellers, and they will have little in common, little to discuss.

8. Tools and machines are locally distinguished, for the most part, by whether or not a device is self-powered. In general, if a device requires external power, then it is a tool. A hammer is a tool, but so is a side plow. A crawfish boat is a machine. A PTO ditcher has a spinning heard that throws the dirt clear of the ditch it makes, but the device itself is attached to a tractor and driven by the power-takeoff: the effect is a hybrid conceptual space, with the ditcher sometimes called a machine but usually called a tool. Thus, tools and machines are as much mentifacts as artifacts.

9. As Malcolm Comeaux (1985) observes, a larger history of boats in Louisiana reveals that the flat bottoms of pirogues and chalands had long dominated the inland waterways, especially when the boats were used as platforms for trapping and fishing in swamps, marshes, and bayous. I add that the putt-putt and mudboat were, respectively, early and late twentieth-century responses to needs to power through the confused landscape of south Louisiana (Laudun 2016).

10. I have heard the cylinder referred to as the throat, akin to the throat of a combine; as a spout, akin to a bottle; and as a chimney, which is the same word often used to describe the tall muddy tubes crawfish make when they burrow on land.

11. This design has been solidified in the cast-plastic tops that are now widely used and are sold separately, either for those wishing to make their own traps or those needing to replace a failed top.

12. Maurice Benoit was at one point in time teaching agricultural shop classes and remembers working with students on drawings for boats as a way to expose them to drafting.

13. Sennett offers an extended meditation on craftsmanship in the era of CAD in *The Craftsman*. Sennett's treatment is compelling but is weakened by his jumping to antiquity to collect up craftsman when they are probably thousands of such men and women in Sennett's hometown of New Haven, Connecticut, if he would but look in small shops and equipment sheds. Matthew Crawford writes about the nature of work in such a small shop in *Shop Class as Soulcraft* (2009), a belletristic examination of the nature of work and the relationship between body and mind not unlike George Sturt's *The Wheelwright's Shop* ([1923] 1963) from a century earlier. For those interested, Latour has also written on this topic (1986).

# REFERENCES

Babineaux, Lawson P., Jr. 1967. "A History of the Rice Industry of Southwestern Louisiana." MA thesis, Lafayette: University of Southwestern Louisiana. http://ereserves.mcneese.edu/depts/archive/fTBooks/babineaux.htm.

Bauman, Richard, and Charles Briggs. 2003. *Voices of Modernity: Language Ideologies and the Politics of Inequality* (Studies in the Social and Cultural Foundations of Language). Cambridge: Cambridge University Press.

Bendix. 1997. *In Search of Authenticity: The Formation of Folklore Studies*. Madison: University of Wisconsin Press.

Brasseaux, Carl. 1992. *Acadian to Cajun: Transformation of a People, 1803–1877*. Jackson: University Press of Mississippi.

Comeaux, Malcolm. 1985. "Folk Boats of Louisiana." In *Louisiana Folklife: A Guide to the State*, ed. Nicholas R. Spitzer. Baton Rouge: Louisiana Folklife Program / Louisiana Department of Culture, Recreation, and Tourism.

Crawford, Matthew B. 2009. *Shop Class as Soulcraft: An Inquiry Into the Value of Work*. New York: Penguin Press.

Dethloff, Henry C. 1988. *A History of the American Rice Industry, 1685–1985*. College Station: Texas A&M University Press.

Douglas, Mary. 1966. *Purity and Danger*. New York: Routledge.

Foucault, Michel. 1977. *Discipline and Punish: The Birth of the Prison*. New York: Vantage.

Glassie, Henry. 1993. *Turkish Traditional Art Today*. Bloomington: Indiana University Press.

Kuhn, Thomas S. 1962. *The Structure of Scientific Revolutions*. Chicago: University of Chicago Press.

Laudun, John. 2016. *The Amazing Crawfish Boat*. Jackson: University Press of Mississippi.

Latour, Bruno. 1986. "Visualization and Cognition: Thinking with Eyes and Hands." *Knowledge and Society: Studies in the Sociology of Culture Past and Present* 6: 1–40.

Latour, Bruno. 1999. "On Recalling ANT." In *Actor-Network Theory and After*, ed. Law and Hassard. Oxford: Blackwell Publishers.

Post, Lauren. 1962. *Cajun Sketches from the Prairies of Southwest Louisiana*. Baton Rouge: Louisiana State University Press.

Sennett, Richard. 2008. *The Craftsman*. New Haven, CT: Yale University Press.

Shirley, Mark, and C. Greg Lutz. 2009. "Crawfish Trap Design and Construction." SRAC Publication No. 2404. Baton Rouge: LSU AgCenter Research and Extension.

Sturt, George. [1923] 1963. *The Wheelwright's Shop*. Cambridge: Cambridge University Press.

# 2

# Branding Unibroue
*Selling Québécois Folklore through Beer*

Julie M-A LeBlanc, PhD

> *In Western developed societies culture is profoundly connected to and dependent on consumption. Without consumer goods, modern, developed societies would lose key instruments for the reproduction, representation, and manipulation of their culture.*
>
> —McCracken, *Culture and Consumption*

MORE THAN TWENTY-FIVE YEARS after this statement was made by anthropologist Grant McCracken on Western consumer society, it still rings true and is particularly important in branding. In the brewing industry, using cultural codes to convey messages to target markets is pervasive—beer labeling and advertisements are carefully crafted to ensure brand loyalty. While large-scale brewers focus on global markets to sell their products, microbrewers and craft-brewers master the art of appealing to smaller, local, and regional markets by using specific shared cultural traits and recognizable elements of culture and folklore to sell "terroir" products.

In Canada, and particularly in Québec, one microbrewery is known as a trailblazer, using folk narratives, heroes, and romantic history to sell their beers. Unibroue (2017) became synonymous with regional folklore, and its consumers quickly connected with the product as their own. Unibroue's legacy is largely due to a successful marketing mix of product quality and positive effects of cultural appropriation. The microbrewery prides itself on explicitly extracting regional folklore to attract and retain consumer loyalty. However, using folklore to sell products comes at a price: authenticity in displaying one's folklore and the impacts of folklore redistribution are arguably controversial. Discourse surrounding the misuse of folklore—the perception and interpretation of a group's shared culture—how it is exploited, reshaped or created as "fakelore," has been debated by folklorists largely since the late twentieth century (Denby 1971; Dorson 1969; Dundes 1963).

There has been considerable interest in the matter of using folklore for branding over the years. Authorities on nostalgia, rebuilding nations via commercializing culture, the market surrounding heritage and its display—such as historian and geographer David Lowenthal (1985), cultural historian Robert Hewison (1987), and folklorist Barbara Kirshenblatt-Gimblett (1998)—were particularly groundbreaking on the matter. Studies by folklorists and marketers on the commodification of folklore into "Folklure" or using folklore in advertising and the marketing of tradition (Brewer 1994; Denby 1971; MacGregor 1981, 1992, 1995, 2003) have drawn attention since at least the 1950s to the aspects of culture being used to sell products. However, I define "folklore branding" as identity based on an item or element of folklore that people recognize and utilize through products. Anthropologists and consumer studies experts have looked at this phenomenon through the lens of nation branding and using culture to brand products (Campbell 1997; Dávila 2001; Goodwin, Ackerman, and Kiron 1997; Vannoy 2009) but no substantial combination of the commercial discipline and its methodology within folkloristics (other than combining media, popular culture, and minor genre research) has been particularly examined.

In 2003, I began to study the impact and role of commercialization as well as the transmission of folklore by focusing on a Québécois microbrewery, Unibroue (figure 2.1), and comparing it with other Canadian and international breweries. My observations and analyses, based on extensive fieldwork with more than 150 participants, suggest a case for the unconventional medium of commercialized folklore as a means of promoting or safeguarding folklore. It was during the fieldwork process that I was able to delve into Unibroue's use of the folk narratives, beliefs, and traditions of Québec as they are explicitly portrayed in their beer labeling.

Legends such as the "Chasse-Galerie" (also known as "Witch/Flying Canoe") showcasing the Devil as an enabler sealing a pact with lonesome and isolated lumberjacks wishing to visit their loved ones by flying the night skies on New Year's eve, and supernatural trickster characters such as the ephemeral feux-follets ("willow wisps"), are examples of Unibroue's folk selection prominently displayed on labels.

By adapting consumer studies and folkloristics in cultural and political appropriation, brands and regional identity, I facilitated discussions with participants on multinational mergers and local ties to regional breweries. Early in the process of this research I conducted interviews and focus groups with Québécois, non-Québécois, Unibroue consumers and nonconsumers,

Figure 2.1. Unibroue logo prior to the Sleeman purchase, Chambly, QC brewery (photograph taken by Julie M-A LeBlanc in April, 2003).

brewery representatives and market analysts, beer aficionados and beer experts. I interviewed brewpub owners and craft brewers and participated in a private home-brewing event to understand the interest in beer-making. I also conducted an online survey to reach an international crowd interested in answering various demographic and knowledge questions on political and marketed identities found in brewery advertisements and publicity campaigns (LeBlanc 2005–6). The contribution of each participant provided me with a sample of individuals covering a broad range of socioeconomic backgrounds. The overall sample totals sixty female participants and ninety-two male participants aged between younger than eighteen to older than eighty and originating from Canada (British Columbia, Alberta, Northwest Territories, Ontario, Québec, Newfoundland), the United States, Costa Rica, Ireland, Sweden, Finland, Greece, Romania, Bulgaria, France, and the Czech Republic. The eighteen- to thirty-year-old male bracket was the most represented in my study.

Three goals were set in this research: (1) tracing elements of Québec's legendary culture exploited through a commercialized product; (2) understanding their representations, connotations, and denotations; and (3), determining what constitutes meaning and interpretation. I used a quantitative/objective data-gathering and qualitative/subjective narrative approach to the collection of information to discuss what items of folklore are used, why they are used, who are using them, and to whom they are transmitted. Furthermore, I traced the dynamic correlation between the selection of folk narratives in beer labels and the regionalist perspectives of local folklore through form and medium. The denotative and connotative reflections of cultural representation as well as the relationship between signifier and signified in relation to images, their polysemic nature, and their (de)construction were examined. I found cultural codes within the transmitted folk items in beer labels that serve as resonant signifiers. The intertextuality of beer labels, folklore selection process, research outcomes, intermingled signs, interpretative study, and poststructuralist notions apply to the pattern relationship between identity, signs, and meanings connected to the images found on beer labels, as manifest uses of folklore. I approached the content and structure of this study with a representative and interpretative lens providing critical analyses of socioeconomic factors related to marketing folklore. This includes a study of products and events, negative/positive reinforcements of the use of folklore in the marketplace, romantic nationalism and heritage as major influences in product advertisement, and the selection process of folklore items for target market sales. The outcomes of this study have provided insight on how target markets for marketing strategies are representative of specific folk groups that respond to identity and ideology branding.

## ABOUT UNIBROUE

Created in 1991, from a financially strained brewing company by the name of Massawippi Brewery Inc., Unibroue saw its first production of popularly praised crafted beers in that year. The founders of Unibroue, entrepreneurs André Dion and Serge Racine, produced and marketed their beers toward young professionals by including parts of Québec's folklore in their campaigns and on their beer labels. The labels were created in memory of vibrant traditions as well as heroes and historical periods that marked Québec and its people. Their trademark logo, a crested "U" adorned with devilish wings, reminds one of the Devil, a favorite Québécois legend figure. Unibroue, along with other microbreweries, knew that to make its products more marketable, it needed to include a clever appeal that often called upon cultural traits. Beer specialist Sylvain Daignault writes about this marketing tactic adopted by larger brewers when trying their hand in creating folkloric labels to attract microbrewery consumers (2004, 111). Labatt's Celtique and Molson's La Rousse were supposed to evoke microbrewery-like labels and taste to compete with small-scale brewers (Daignault 2004, 111). Daignault writes:

> Il est curieux de constater que plusieurs microbrasseries ont adopté pour leurs produits des noms et des étiquettes qui incitent les gens à plonger dans le passé et le folklore. Pensons simplement à *La Maudite*, à *La Blanche*

*de Chambly*, à *La Bolduc* (Unibroue), à la *Titanic* (Les Brasseurs R.J.) ou à la *Barbeau* (Broue Chope). (Daignault 2004, 111–12)

[It is curious to state that many microbreweries chose names and labels for their products inciting people to immerse themselves in the past and folklore. We should be reminded of *Maudite*, *Blanche de Chambly*, *Bolduc* (Unibroue), *Titanic* (Les Brasseurs R.J.) or *Barbeau* (Broue Chope)].

Among the younger body of Québécois participants for my research, the distinct uses of folklore in Québécois microbrewery labeling is part of their culture and how they feel they are represented as a people. For English Canadians, Molson's "I am Canadian" slogan of the mid-1990s served that more conglomerate description of cultural appropriation and mass "national" identity—in other words, English Canadians identified with the slogan as part of what it means to be Canadian. I queried whether or not a large brewer in Québec, such as Molson, could use the same cultural markers associated with microbrewers to reach a larger population. To answer this, I made the distinction between micro- and macrofolklore, that is, folklore studied from a small and specific group versus that which ties large sums of population under a general and recognizable category. I then pondered: what happens when a small-scale microbrewer, say, Unibroue, is purchased by a larger small-scale brewer, say, Sleeman, and when that brewer is then purchased by a multinational business say, Sapporo? The concept of identity and cultural appropriation is not as clear considering the merge from regional product to multinational and non-Canadian companies.

When Sleeman (figure 2.2) first purchased Unibroue in 2004, articles and blogs from Unibroue lovers and proud Québécois immediately expressed concern about the future of the company in the hands of an Ontarian "outsider" (Lanouette 2004).

There were similar reactions in Ontario when that province's beloved Sleeman brewery was bought by the Japanese company Sapporo on August 11, 2006. The reaction reflected how consumers were affected by the representational and ownership aspect of this brewery and whether or not it would continue to deliver its "local pride." Ironically, even a small-scale brewer can appeal globally and merge with other companies without its consumers necessarily knowing about it, such as the case with Alexander Keith's. This "Proudly brewed in Nova Scotia. Since 1820" brewery is owned by InBev, a Belgian company that merged with Canada's Labatt and Brazil's AmBev in 2005 (Ambev 2015).

When smaller local companies merge with larger global conglomerates, there are perceived disadvantages: just as culture is used to sell products, it

Figure 2.2. Sleeman/Unibroue headquarters, Lachine, QC brewery (photograph taken by Julie M-A LeBlanc in March, 2005).

may ultimately backfire in the marketing process if a small-scale brewery owned by a large-scale brewery knows that its clientele identifies itself with the small-scale "locally owned, brewed, and operated" image. It is obviously not in the company's best interest to reveal their association with the "global market." In dealing with such a situation, however, advantages exist for both the consumer and the producer because the producer may feel the need to emphasize local culture as part of the product and, at the same time, promote local events.

This culturally engaging business behavior is often publicized on the brewers' websites and through their active promotional funding of local beer and food events (e.g., Festival des Bières et Saveurs de Chambly, or the Outaouais Brewfest). Using folklore to sell a product may bring the producer closer to its consumer and may influence the producer in being involved locally or regionally. This model of business and marketing behavior can be applied to how the government foresees promoting and safeguarding traditions. By recognizing what the market (or folk group) wants and transmits to each other, public policies may be developed to benefit the local as much as the global.

It is through this optic that I chose to examine how meaning, intertextuality, and folk knowledge are used, made, and transmitted by a commercialized product. As one of my participants, André St-Georges, put it:

> Ben, Unibroue c'parce-que quand tu penses à la bière, veut, veut pas, tu dis ben, quand, quand tu penses à Unibroue, pardon, tu penses pas juste à la bière. Habituellement moi j'pense pas juste à la bière, j'pense à qu'chose d'ici. C'est *très* Québécois Unibroue pis il l'évoque. Justement on va en parler des étiquettes, ça évoque toute quequ'chose d'ici, très spécifiquement . . . C'est clair que ça puise dans le folklore. (LeBlanc 2003a; ellipsis added)

> [Well, Unibroue it's because when you think of beer, like it or not, you say to yourself well, when, when you think of Unibroue, sorry, you don't simply think of it as beer. Normally for me I think it's not just beer, I think it's something from here. Unibroue is *very* Québécois and they evoke this. In fact, we'll be speaking of labels, that all evokes something from here, more specifically . . . For sure it draws on folklore.]

## FOLKLORE AND BEER IN ADVERTISEMENTS

Folklorist Sheila Douglas writes, "the purpose of advertising [is] to sell the product and the advertiser will use as a means to this end, anything that will help him to do this" (1987, 11). Furthermore, as stated by advertising expert Elizabeth Williamson (1980), "advertising is probably the most pervasive form of popular culture" (1980, 3). Indeed, from its origins to selling a product, or service, advertising is increasingly a part of everyday life and of mass culture. Williamson's historiography of advertising culture illustrates the interest marketers and scholars have in psychoanalyzing the effects of advertisements on consumers (1980, 14).

Since the early twentieth century, theorists have been studying the impacts that advertisements have over populations from micro- and macro-perspectives. The 1950s marked the beginnings of this analytical venture, but the 1970s also revealed new theoretical interests in the matter (Williamson 1980, 14). Advertising became increasingly studied in the media and in socioeconomic fora (15). Folklorists and anthropologists also viewed the growing trend of advertisement being tied to folklore and folklorism at this period (Douglas 1987; Dundes 1963; Sullenberger 1974). Psychiatrist J. A. C. Brown's ([1963] 1968) historical glance at advertising reveals how the 1880s changed the face of print and mass-targets in advertisements (169). Folklorist Linda Dégh's (1994) "Magic for Sale: Märchen and Legend in TV Advertising" examined advertisements as tales or legends because of their ostensive nature. The Keebler elves, Pillsbury Dough Boy (strangely resembling a witch's golem), and the Jolly Green Giant (Sullenberger 1974) are symbols of "magical" beings that appear in folktales and legends. As for the beer market, having fluctuated since the end of the 1960s, it still holds a particularly high place in advertising. Its political and cultural implications have perhaps made beer advertisements even more of a priority in selling the product.

The cultural importance of advertisements is highlighted in cultural studies expert Judith Williamson's 1978 *Decoding Advertisements: Ideology and Meaning in Advertising*. Williamson writes, "[advertisements] are ubiquitous, an inevitable part of everyone's lives: even if you do not read a newspaper or watch television, the images posted over our urban surroundings are inescapable" (11). Moreover, they are strategically designed "to attract the attention of people with suitable demographics and the proper psychographics—values and lifestyles—for some product or service" (Berger 2004, 4). Concerning the microbrewing industry in Québec, representational advertisements are key in attracting consumers because of the apparent identity factors.

The relationship between producer and consumer, how consumers decode advertisements and labels, what folklore is selected and rejected for the use of marketing are all important factors to examine in the redistribution of folklore. The commercialized product becomes a conduit of folklore in the consumer community. What was coined as "folklure" by folklorist Priscilla Denby in the 1970s continues to be a trend in advertisement culture and is certainly a main marketing tactic for Unibroue. However, what makes Unibroue stand out in particular is not only its use of folklore to sell a product but in its contribution toward the general folk repertoire in Québec. This folklore branding is not only integral to the way in which Unibroue markets its beers but also vital in how people choose to be represented through a product, how they identify and engage with it. By targeting regional lore as part of its marketing strategy, Unibroue piqued international interest while promoting folklore in Québec.

## IDENTITY AND FOLK IMAGE

During focus groups, discussions moved toward esoteric and exoteric (insider/outsider) perspectives of Québécois history and culture and the relevance of using certain aspects of folklore to sell regional products. These commodified aspects of Québécois culture have been the subject of many scholars and literary artists since the twentieth century. The internal colonial gaze of the Québécois by English Canadians is especially exploited in advertisements and promotional campaigns for both macro- and microbrewing industries. By colonial gaze, I mean the same stereotypical image perpetuated in tourism as it was once described by poet and writer Northrop Frye in *The Bush Garden* (1971):

> The French are on the whole the worse off by this arrangement, which has made Quebec into a cute tourist resort full of ye quainte junke made by real peasants, all of whom go to church and say their prayers like the children they are, and love their land and tell folk tales and sing ballads just as the fashionable novelists in the cities say they do. True, I have never met a French Canadian who likes to be thought of as an animated antique, nor do I expect to: yet the sentimental haze in which the European author [Louis Hémon] of Maria Chapdelaine saw the country is still quite seriously accepted by Canadians, English and French alike, as authentic. (Frye [1971] 1995, 135; O'Grady and Staines 2003, 30)

French culturalist Peter van Lent criticized this passage in "La Vie de l'Habitant: Quebec's Folk Culture of Survival" (1985). Van Lent wrote about this phenomenon in the 1980s and how Québec was both victim and abuser of the mass-marketed "fake handicrafts to exporting would-be 'folksingers' who are in reality chansonniers from Montreal's counterculture" (van Lent 1985, 330).

These areas of criticism were in fact part of the way in which Québec's folk culture developed and how the Québécois identified themselves with it, and van Lent illustrates this via the "typical Quebecker" Jos Ferrand (more commonly known as Jos Montferrand) caricatured on television by a "huge bearded woodsman . . . who poured maple syrup on the pea soup that he guzzled by the gallon" (van Lent 1985, 339). Van Lent's description of this caricature as a response to the "repression" felt by the French Canadians in Québec was part of an identity reaffirmation and that the "popularization of the Quebec folk image . . . provide[s] the province with an identity, the one thing that all Canadians seem to need most" (van Lent 1985, 339). This trend was perpetuated in the mid-1980s, postreferendum nationalism and cultural identity statements recurrent in ethnological, folklore, and political science debates.

While van Lent focused on the stereotyped image of the "habitant" in Québec, folklorist Janet McNaughton (1985) examined the birth of folklore studies in Québec as it was strongly tied to French Canadian nationalism. Indeed, the notion of defining a culture, "distinct" from Canada as it was popularly referred to in politics, was—and still is—important in Québec.

The province was shifting from the Quiet Revolution's heritage toward a future that would be constantly reminiscing about the oppression lived by its ancestors from the fallen Patriotes to the two failed independence referenda. These images continued to shape the nationalist debate in Québec but were also very much present in the popular forum, exploited for the mass media and in advertisements. Using these sentiments and shared items of folklore to reengage and capture the emotional identity of a people is exactly what local producers of goods have done over the past few decades to sell their "home-grown" and "home-brewed" products. Consumers identify with products that claim representational qualities, and the impacts of commodified folklore can be measured.

What is perceived as regional folklore, what is selected and consequently produced by a company, be it a microbrewery or other, becomes an element of folklore itself as it is transmitted to a group and regenerated through variant forms. This is parallel to cultural anthropologist Hermann Bausinger's and folklorist Elke Dettmer's statements about the relationships between folklorism and folklore (Bausinger 1990, 128; Dettmer 1991, 170).

Selected folklore, that is relaunched and transmitted as part of a group's identity, promotes local folk heroes and legends. This appeals to consumers at large but the cultural codes are specifically understood by those "in-the-know" who see how these marketing trends perpetuate an interpretation of a group's folklore and sense of belonging. The cultural codes interpreted are one of the most important outcomes of the commercialized products. Marketers know that it is important to fully understand their target market. Their approach in learning about target markets is similar to folkloristics in doing research and defining a "folk group." In "Ethnic Groups and Ethnic Folklore," folklorist Elliott Oring (1986) writes: "Groups, indeed all categories, result from perceiving some similarity within a broader population of individual elements. Groups exist only if they are recognized and some claim is made for their existence (if only by the members themselves)" (24–25). In comparison with marketing research and target/niche markets/consumers, the American Marketing Association (AMA) defines groups in a similar way: "Marketing research is the function that links the consumer, customer, and public to the marketer through information—information used to identify and define marketing opportunities and problems; generate, refine, and evaluate marketing actions; monitor marketing performance; and improve understanding of marketing as a process. Marketing research specifies the information required to address these issues, designs the method for collecting information, manages and implements the data collection process, analyzes the results, and communicates the findings and their implications" (American Marketing Association 2004). Furthermore, marketing holds into account folk groups and branding as part of defining identities. As anthropologist Marianne Lien, in her 2000 article "Imagined Cuisines: 'Nation' and 'Market' as Organising Structures in Norwegian Food Marketing," explored further: "Marketing is a system of knowledge which marketing professionals will frequently consult when they make their decisions. In this sense, marketing is an applied branch of the discipline of economics . . . marketing is local practice. As a system of knowledge, marketing is only influential to the extent that it is taken into account by its practitioners in day-to-day decisions" (155). The way folk groups respond to ideological branding, that is, branding appealing to a specific market, is representative of what constitutes their identity within that specific group and what bonds them together. When a microbrewer uses elements of local or regional folklore to sell a product, it evokes specific cultural codes that are picked up by the said folk groups (or target market). These codes are important for the producer because they communicate with their consumers. The codes are usable forms of folklore similar to what folklorist and anthropologist Teri Brewer wrote about in the 1994 issue of *Folklore in Use* on "The Marketing of Tradition." Brewer argued that "folkloristics is not just about ways of approaching the description of tradition or the evolution of tradition . . . rather it should give us ways to approach an understanding of the *uses* of traditions and therefore a more explicit take on cultural politics" (Brewer 1994, 9). This statement grazes the immense potential of how one can study folkloristics through nonconventional mediums and how these mediums may also serve as case examples of ways to promote and, at times, even safeguard culture and traditions. An additional argument would be to question whether or not a government may use the mechanisms of market economy to promote the survival of culture. Indirectly, the market economy can be a cultural promoter. The commercialized product inadvertently contributes to the safeguarding of intangible cultural heritage, serving as a reminder of local heroes, legends, and historical events that live through a different, contemporary medium.

In the case of Unibroue, the company's labeling is a solid example of folklore in use. Roughly a dozen of these labels consciously use Québécois legendary themes that portray and incorporate issues of cultural and political identity. Unibroue, like other companies who use folklore to sell goods, redistributes selective perceptions of what constitutes a provincial, regional or local folklore.

As folklorist Lutz Röhrich ([1978] 1980) stated in "Folklore and Advertising": "Man lives by his symbols, many of which have been formed in the past. Where can one locate better symbols of man's heritage that are readily recognized as such—at least unconsciously—than in folklore?" (115). Using cultural codes, these items that convey messages to its group, microbreweries are able to appeal to a smaller and more local market while telling the said group's story. The product reflects a part of local folklore, a part of the shared cultural traits that may unify the consumers. The process of folklore in use, the perceived cultural representations of particular groups and the interaction between the commercial producer and its political market, becomes a form of popular metanarrative and (perhaps boldly) metafolklore. To frame this study in the context of its time and place and of the people it communicates to, it becomes revealed that cultural codes not only have multiple meanings but also lead the way toward an interactive and dynamic example of how the traditional may coexist with the contemporary in a commercial and political climate.

## HOW TO SELL QUÉBÉCOIS FOLKLORE THROUGH BEER

The potential traps in using folklore to sell products are in the "misuses" of folklore, because the consumer's perception of the product and its supposed representational aspect are highly valued in the marketing process. Folk notions and explicit uses of legends in Unibroue's marketing campaigns makes the company one of, if not *the*, most long-standing and recognizable microbreweries out of the growing microbrewery scene in Québec.[1] Andrée Marcil, Unibroue's public relations officer at the time of the interview (2003), confirmed for me that the choice of labels and the association of legends were explicitly used as a marketing tool. When asked how Unibroue chose the names and legends to be placed on the labels, Marcil answered that there are no folklorists hired to do research on the collection of potential legends to exploit in the market. She noted: "nous connaissons cependant suffisamment notre histoire pour savoir (où) y puiser" (we sufficiently understand our history to know where to look) (LeBlanc 2003b). When asked about the selection process and whether the company chooses particular versions of legends, Marcil referred to the primary concerns of the brewery in creating a label reflecting the recipe and how some legends appear to fit the recipe description. Although there may be a great repertoire of legends to select from in Québécois folklore, Unibroue did not deliberately pick a legend to then create a beer; the beer recipe came first and the name and label, second.

McCracken notes, the directors that make the selection process are aware that it must reflect "cultural categories and principles" to attract consumers toward the product in meaning and context (1988, 78–79). This aspect of knowing or recognizing the symbols that would attract consumers is essential for Unibroue, and its success was largely based on this marketing mix and quality of the product offered.

In 2004, Sleeman bought Unibroue for $36.5 million and absorbed the Québécois microbrewery's $5.5 million debt (Sleeman Breweries Ltd. 2004). One year prior to the purchase, Unibroue was boasting an increase in sales and international market distribution (Business Wire 2004). The company was clearly prepping for an upcoming sale.

In 2005, after the Sleeman purchase, Sleeman moved its Sleeman/Unibroue headquarters in Lachine (QC) and started producing Sleeman Silver Creek in the Chambly plant. John Sleeman marketed his beers under the copy of "family recipe," claiming generations of brewmasters in the family (Fennell 1996, 27). When Tom Fennell published his article featuring Sleeman beers in 1996, there was no foreseeable link between Sleeman and Unibroue at the time, though both were equally successful in their respective provinces. The piece published in *MacLean's* sought to promote craft breweries in the country. Fennell writes:

> His (Sleeman's) timing could hardly be better. The so-called craft beer and microbrewing sector, spiced with exotic brands . . . now accounts for about three percent of the Canadian beer market. But at a time when overall sales of alcoholic beverages are stagnant because of the aging population and increased health concerns, the specialty beer market—dominated by premium beers aimed primarily at well-paid men in their 30s—is expanding by an estimated 25 per cent a year. In response, the giants of the Canadian beer industry, Molson Inc. and Labatt Breweries Ltd., have launched a string of competing products. And now, even some major distillers are trying to break into the business. Last week, Seagram Co. of Montreal began test-marketing several new ales and lagers across the United States, under the brand name Devil Mountain. (26)

This was a pivotal time for microbrewers to garnish their portfolios and prepare for multinational mergers. In addition to benefitting from the Québécois market in brewing and selling their own Sleeman brand through the Unibroue plant, Sleeman/Unibroue was boasting their increase in production. As John Sleeman stated in their 2004 fourth quarter reports: "We are pleased with our progress in achieving our strategic and financial goals this year. Our premium brands continue to generate increased sales and margins and we delivered strong growth in revenue, net income and core volume," said John Sleeman, Chairman & CEO. "The Unibroue integration was completed in the quarter as planned. The integration has provided a positive impact on our operations and our relationships with our customers. We are confident that the integration of that business into our premium portfolio will generate increased revenue and positive returns" (Market Wired 2005). This clearly helped in making Sleeman/Unibroue interesting as a purchase for Sapporo in 2006, after which time the sense of local was lost to an international perspective, but the Unibroue products themselves continued to appeal to the collective folklore of Québec.

Even after Sleeman's purchase of Unibroue in 2004, the nature of the selection process for beer names remained the same creative process and no collecting was made from a folkloristic point of view (LeBlanc 2005). This reinforced what Andrée Marcil had told me previously in 2003. However, the assistant director of branding in 2005, Stéphane Berranger, did point out that there were moments where the creative process was not done in-house with marketing experts; rather, it "happened by chance" through stories shared by owners and shareholders of the original Unibroue company (LeBlanc 2005). This was certainly the case with the Eau Bénite beer. According to Stéphane, Robert Charlebois (previous shareholder, product promoter, and well-known Québécois folksinger) was at a costume party promoting the beer and mistook two real nuns for costumed laywomen. He insisted they drink the beer even with the "Devil" on it by telling them it was like "Holy Water," emphasizing the colloquial *eau bénite* to let the "nuns" know this was a harmless drink (LeBlanc 2005; figure 2.3).

The motifs of selling one's soul to the Devil and the problems in distinguishing between good and evil are recurring themes in Unibroue's legend selection process. These themes are suggestive of what Brewer terms "marketable tradition," that is, "what some agents of change . . . perceive as the *unique* and *externally presentable* cultural heritage of those societies, the acceptable face of the past . . . and those aspects of it which are not too private to share with outsiders" (Brewer 1994, 6). The Devil in Québécois culture is a perfect antagonist in legendary narratives to explain the historically significant Catholic mores of its society. With the eighteen- to twenty-five-year-old focus group, the discussion led to how the Devil may not represent the same image for them as it did and still does for their parents. The image depicted on the labels was perceived as nonthreatening, inoffensive, and almost mocking, whereas those I interviewed who were above the age of fifty held reservations toward the use of a Devil on a beer label, regardless of its representation in a French Canadian narrative. The word choice for naming the beer, however, held more meaning for the older generation of interviewees than the younger

Figure 2.3. "Eau Bénite" beer label (photograph taken by Julie M-A LeBlanc, personal collection).

Figure 2.4. Maudite beer label (label image courtesy of Unibroue).

ones. *Maudite* or *maudit* (meaning "damned" or "damn") holds a strong meaning as an expletive for older generations, a binding, damning oath, in contrast to younger generations, who generally view the term in derision (figure 2.4).

The specific legend alluded to above is the "Chasse-Galerie." This legend recalls a pact between lumberjacks and the Devil so the men may reunite with their loved ones during the holidays. Restrictions are placed in

Figure 2.5. The "1837" beer label, Unibroue (label image courtesy of Unibroue).

exchange for one night of dancing and singing. While some versions have the men damned for eternity to fly the skies in their canoe because they broke their contract with the Devil, other versions highlight how one crew member duped the Devil by invoking God or coming into contact with a holy object, thus freeing the crew from the Devil's bond.

Unibroue also borrows periods and heroes from popular history in Québec. For example, the beer 1837 (which is no longer brewed)[2] depicts a view of the year that marks the political movements and future executions of many Patriotes in Québec—rebels who fought against British colonial powers in Lower Canada for self-governance and economic autonomy (figure 2.5).

A well-known image that has been used on the Patriotes' tricolor flag is artist Henri Julien's interpretation of the Patriotes (figure 2.6). One hundred and sixty years after the Patriotes rebellion and shortly after its European introduction at the international beer industry's marketing show, Eurobière 1997, the "1837" beer campaign was launched in Québec for the Québécois market from the Governor's Mansion in Montréal, a provincial heritage residence previously occupied by the Pied-du-Courant Prison governor and currently owned by the provincial liquor board, the Société des alcools du Québec (SAQ). The site was highly symbolic as it was the prison where Patriotes were executed (figures 2.7–2.8).

During the beer-launching ceremony, the company commemorated the anniversary of the Patriotes' uprising. As claimed on the label, the beer was

Figure 2.6. "Un vieux de '37'" Patriote drawing by Henri Julien (image taken from Library and Archives Canada [2017b], Acc. No. 1932-266).

"brewed in honour of past heroes who gave their life for country and freedom . . ." (Unibroue).

Looking at the versions and short legend descriptions on the Unibroue labels, one sees what seems to be an insider's perspective of Québécois folklore, an emic corpus. What is found on the label may represent the brewing company's particular versions of legends known by staff or available through popular media transmission. The selection process of historical events, insiders' perceptions, and repertoire of folklore also feeds back to consumers and is redistributed to the folk from which it came.

There is also a natural variety of folklore in transmission that occurs. Folklorist and anthropologist Herbert Halpert writes: "Where the legend-making process is alive we get infinite variety that cannot, or rather should not, be standardized. Indeed, if in any area you find only one unchanging version of a legend told by many informants, you may begin to suspect either an extremely dominant informant, or what is more probable, the influence of print. It is well known that if a competent author weaves a pattern out of a mixture of legends from one region, and his published version becomes popular and 'feeds back' to the original area, it may often replace other versions" (1971, 48–49). Because "there is no 'right' version for a folklore item" (47), it is possible to analyze the labels as particular versions

Figure 2.7. Pied-du-Courant prison, Montréal, QC (photo credit: Maison nationale des Patriotes).

themselves. The "traditional" versions that we see in books, collected and selected for publication, are from a particular exclusive body of informants. Versions selected by participants in focus groups, group sessions and individually vacillate between the perceived "traditional" version and that which is packaged and labeled in a product.

In Unibroue's case, the versions produced are "cherry-picked" by the brewing company to sell their product. This is an explicit use of "folklure," a projection of what one would consider traditional images into a product (Denby 1971, 117). Although "folklure" aims to sell products by using folklore, whether the folklore per se is of pure invention or of some rooted tradition, Unibroue has managed to portray Québec's oral traditions with little or no invention save for the occasional out-of-the-ordinary "theme" beer such as the Éphémère, portraying a fairy. The recipe for the Éphémère used to change every so often, hence the "flighty" depiction of a fairy, toying with the playful trickster theme found in the *feux-follets* (willow wisps) legends and belief in Québec (Bergeron 1988, 126–27; Fowke 1976, 58–64). Using what is perceived to be folklore and cultural traits to attract consumers has and continues to be an effective advertising strategy. The danger lies in how these perceptions of self and "other" are constructed in advertisements and whether or not ethnic marketing is a cultural diversity enabler.

Figure 2.8. "Execution of rebels in front of the Montreal Gaol"; drawing by Henri Julien (image taken from Library and Archives Canada [2017a], Acc. No. 1989-466-61).

## SENSE OF SELF AND "OTHER"

Anthropologist Arlene Dávila's investigations of Latino-inspired and -focused advertisements reveal the making and breaking of stereotypes. Some clichés and cultural misconceptions of a people within a nation may empower minorities into having their voices heard in the consumer market, in ads and the products targeted toward them, thus creating popular discrimination (Dávila 2001, 68, 86–87, 88–152; Fiske [1989] 2007, 129–58).[3] As advertising and marketing specialist Kim Sheehan writes: "If people in the target audience relate positively to a stereotypical portrayal, the portrayal may help sell the product. If people in the target audience create opinions about groups of people other than the group that they are in, and these opinions put the stereotyped group into a negative light, a stereotyped portrayal could be problematic" (2004, 83). In the same way that, as Dávila writes, Spanish television networks politically engaged Hispanics (Dávila 2001, 153–80), French in Québec is prioritized and even though Unibroue is no longer Québécois owned and operated, the beers all kept their French labels, connotations, symbolism, and meaning.

Ethnic marketers are faced with selling images of a cultural group positively and building on feedback from the target consumer group;

ethnic marketing is, after all, "politicized" (Dávila 2001, 240): "In marketing discourse, 'consumers' must prove their value and advertising worthiness through behavior, attitudes, and consumption. Of concern is whether this discourse promotes a 'politics of worthiness' and the assumption that people are only entitled to visibility, rights, or services from society after they have proved their marketability and social worth" (237). For businesses focusing on "ethnic markets" or ethnic niches, meaning submarkets of people with a perceived cultural difference from the received standard culture, the marketer must look at how cultures may be exploited in a way that would profit the business while creating loyalty with this target market. In the brewing industry, trends in advertising have used elements of interest, such as sports, to reach ethnic markets. In much the same way that the brewing industry in Canada focused on hockey in advertisements, the brewing industry in the United States wanting to target the Hispanic market, consumer studies specialist Tanya Vannoy notes, used soccer in advertisements in addition to advertising American Football in Spanish via NFLatino.com (Vannoy 2009, 7–8). But, Vannoy writes, expanding the approaches in marketing to ethnic niches is particularly important in the cultural sense, and the brewing industry would gain significantly in using "culturally relevant" messages (18). This is noteworthy when using folklore to sell a product as it is the same process as advertising.

Advertisements depend on imagery and symbolism as well as poetic implications to sell a product and have the purpose of fulfilling their duty as informer of a product or service's existence and function in society, but they may easily fall in the pattern of selling "the sizzle and not the steak." This pattern was voiced by Labatt when the company admitted, "We didn't sell beer . . . We just told a picturesque historical story" (Heron 2003, 319).

Beer product image and its essence are both marketed through various themes, tastes, and styles. Representation of a product and knowing to whom it speaks is vital to its success. As consumer specialists Michael R. Solomon, Judith L. Zaichkowski, and Rosemary Polegato note in *Consumer Behaviour: Buying, Having and Being*, "advertisers often place great emphasis on vivid and creative illustrations or photography" to "deliver big impact" (2002, 261). The image, with or without a brief narrative, is then crucial for branding identity.

David Novitz's (1997) "Art, Narrative, and Human Nature" illustrates how image is tied to narrative and the way in which we represent ourselves tells a story that "shape(s) and convey(s) our sense of self . . . there is an intimate connection between the ways in which people construe themselves and the ways in which they are likely to behave" (143, 146). Unibroue uses elements of what constructs Québec's folklore and culture and narrates it through their products. To the extent they are successful, consuming Unibroue is like consuming a part of Québec's culture. The fact that it is advertised through beer makes it all the more interesting because of the subculture it penetrates: that of all beer aficionados who may or may not share traits with Québec. Beer as a product has become a source of inspiration for food and culture publications, chemists, and general amateurs over the years. Many beer lovers and drinkers of the world may tap into the internet to visit sites dedicated to the drink.

For example, the online magazine *BièreMAG* an international magazine published in Chambly hosting both European (mostly Belgium) and Canadian editors and chroniclers (Théodore 1999), published in the fall 1999 issue an article by beer amateur Pierre Théodore "(P.T.) DE LA BROUE" (punningly "mad-for-brew") about labels and the "real" essence of beer. Throughout his article, mentions of "folklore" and "Devils" quickly captured my attention; however, I found particularly useful one remark:

> Les étiquettes des bières sont trop souvent des projets de marketing visant les faibles de ce monde; elles les incitent à consommer un produit pour ce qu'il représente socialement, parce qu'il répond à la quête d'identité de la masse: ces étiquettes ne sont pas à l'image de leur goût véritable, de leurs qualités et de leur singularité. (Théodore 1999, 27)
>
> [Often enough, the beer labels are marketing products targeting the weaker individuals of this world; they attempt to consume a product for its social representation because it answers to the quest for mass identity: these labels are not representative images of their real tastes, qualities and uniqueness].

Although Théodore's personal reflection, shared by many craft beer consumers, may seem to blame the corporate beer market and the vulnerable beer consumer, it is also possible to examine a deeper meaning to the application of folklore on beer labels. The cultural context of advertising is phenomenal with beer labeling. It appeals to masses and target markets, it reaches out to match the product with the consumer through identity markers and though it may be questionable whether the marketing of the product is actually of the product itself, it is consumed by those to whom it appeals largely because of its visual or colloquial meaning. The use of the bottle and label as a signified object, and the legend portrayed as signifier, transmit versions of legends and act as catalysts for discussion among groups.

Finally, a brewing company using folkloric elements in their labels intends not simply to attract a large variety of beer drinkers but also to choose a subject matter dear to the population such as folk legends, and to exploit it in a way that will ensure the product's survival. The images used to sell beer and the brief description of legends on the labels attract those who know legends and those who can associate them to collective memories or what they have heard of in the recent past. The beer label as a legend transmitter is perceived differently in the generational groups interviewed. In general, Unibroue has strategically chosen specific legends applied on beer labels and in their campaigns that could potentially reach a large body of consumers. The selected local history, legends, and heroes from Québec illustrate a collected sense of familiarity with the items of folklore used in the microbrewery's marketing strategy. Unibroue managed to capture the soul of a people and charm its consumers. As stated by folklorist Alan Dundes (1963) in "Advertising and Folklore" and perfectly in keeping with Unibroue and Québec, "within the geographical and cultural area in which a given advertisement is disseminated, chances are that the folklore based upon this advertisement will thrive" (150). The Québécois microbrewing industry is a perfect laboratory for examining the use of legends, local heroic protagonists, popular strong-man narratives, recognizable Québécois supernatural characters, and more explicitly political legendary moments in Québec's history. These beer labels play the role of active and passive bearers or catalysts of folk knowledge and are recognizable versions of legends themselves. By examining the interdependence created by outside uses of folk items and their outcome in marketing and its targeted public, discussions about cultural and political identities and ideologies, collective representations through images, and their selection process are pivotal in the assessment of the use of folklore to sell beer. Unibroue has made this its core marketing strategy—a legacy that, out of the numerous microbreweries that have appeared in the Québécois landscape for the past two decades, continues to stand out.

## NOTES

This work developed from my PhD dissertation, "Marketing Traditional and Contemporary Folklore: How Microbreweries and Community Events Process Local Legends and Folklore in Québec" (2015), deposited at Memorial University of Newfoundland.

1. Since its inception, Unibroue's founding member and previous owner, André Dion, advocated extensively to safeguard the microbrewing industry in Québec. In 2001, when appearing at the Standing Committee on Finance at Parliament, Dion provided evidence

of the microbrewing industry in Québec and how Unibroue exported "30% of its production worldwide" but was faced with the realities of surtaxes and excise duties that impacted the industry's success in Québec (Parliament of Canada 2001). Only one third of Québec's microbreweries survived that period, including Unibroue (Parliament of Canada 2001). As stated by the former president and chief executive officer of the Brewers Association of Canada, Sandy Morrison: "I think André Dion in Chambly has made an incredible contribution to that community and the area around there with the development of Unibroue and what he's brought to that community" (Parliament of Canada 2001, n.p.). Consumers recognized this contribution and passion for promoting local economy as much as the province's lore. Unibroue quickly became a microbrewing leader in Québec, and its legacy impacted the creation of more than 150 microbrewers in the province.

2. Unibroue's website no longer displays this beer (see Unibroue.com). While it has been erased from their promotional archives, the bottle and label continue to circulate among collectors (either at microbrewery events or sold online).

3. Popular discrimination is defined by Fiske as follows: "The people discriminate among the products of the culture industries, choosing some and rejecting others in a process that often takes the industry by surprise, for it is driven by the social conditions of the people at least as much as by the characteristics of the text" (Fiske [1989] 2007, 129).

## REFERENCES

Ambev. 2017. "History." *Overview*. Accessed October 17, 2017. http://ri.ambev.com.br/conteudo_en.asp?idioma=1&conta=44&tipo=43355.

American Marketing Association. 2004. "Definition of Marketing." AMA.org. Accessed July 10, 2019. https://www.ama.org/AboutAMA/Pages/Definition-of-Marketing.aspx.

Bausinger, Hermann. 1990. *Folk Culture in a World of Technology*. Trans. Elke Dettmer. Bloomington: Indiana University Press.

Berger, Arthur Asa. 2004. *Ads, Fads, and Consumer Culture: Advertising's Impact on American Character and Society*. 2nd ed. Lanham, MD: Rowman and Littlefield.

Bergeron, Bertrand. 1988. *Au royaume de la légende*. Chicoutimi: JCL.

Brewer, Teri. 1994. "Preface: The Marketing of Tradition." Special theme issue. *Folklore in Use: Applications in the Real World* 2 (1): 1–11.

Brown, J. A. C. [1963] 1968. *Techniques of Persuasion: From Propaganda to Brainwashing*. Middlesex, UK: Penguin.

Business Wire. 2004. "Sleeman Reports Third Quarter Results: Unibroue Acquisition Contributes to 14% Revenue Increase." Accessed October 17, 2017. http://www.thefreelibrary.com/Sleeman+Reports+Third+Quarter+Results+-+Unibroue+Acquisition . . .-a0124072954.

Campbell, Colin. 1997. "Consumption: The New Wave of Research in the Humanities and Social Sciences" In *The Consumer Society*, ed. Neva R. Goodwin, Frank Ackerman, and David Kiron. Washington, DC: Island Press.

Daignault, Sylvain. 2004. *Histoire de la bière au Québec*. Montréal: Éditions Trait d'Union.

Dávila, Arlene. 2001. *Latinos Inc*. Berkeley: University of California Press.

Dégh, Linda. 1994. "Magic for Sale: Märchen and Legend in TV Advertising." In *American Folklore and the Mass Media*. Bloomington and Indianapolis: Indiana University Press.

Denby, Priscilla. 1971. "Folklore in the Mass Media." *Folklore Forum* 4 (September 5): 113–25.

Dettmer, Elke. 1991. "Folklorism in Newfoundland." *Studies in Newfoundland Folklore: Community and Process*, ed. Gerald Thomas and J. D. A. Widdowson. St. John's: Breakwater.

Dorson, Richard M. 1969. "Fakelore." *Zeitschrift für Volkskunde: Halbjahresschrift der Deutschen Gesellschaft für Volkskunde* 65: 56–64.

Douglas, Sheila. 1987. "The Folklore of Television Advertising." *Forum* 19: 11.

Dundes, Alan, ed. 1963. "Advertising and Folklore." *New York Folklore Quarterly* 19 (2): 143–51.

Fennell, Tom. 1996. "No Small Beer." *MacLean's*, June 17, 26–27.

Fiske, John. [1989] 2007. *Understanding Popular Culture*. London: Routledge.

Fowke, Edith. 1976. "Légendes." In *Folklore of Canada*, ed. Edith Fowke, 58–64. Toronto: McClelland and Stewart.

Frye, Northrop. [1971] 1995. *The Bush Garden: Essays on the Canadian Imagination*. Introduction by Linda Hutcheon. Concord: House of Anansi.

Goodwin, Neva R., Frank Ackerman, and David Kiron, eds. 1997. *The Consumer Society*. Washington, DC: Island Press.

Goodwin, Neva R. 1997. "Volume Introduction." In *The Consumer Society*, ed. Neva R. Goodwin, Frank Ackerman, and David Kiron. Washington, DC: Island Press.

Halpert, Herbert. 1971. "Definition and Variation in Folk Legend." *American Folk Legend: A Symposium*, ed. Wayland D. Hand. Berkeley.: University of California Press.

Heron, Craig. 2003. *Booze: A Distilled History*. Toronto: Between the Lines.

Hewison, Robert. 1987. *The Heritage Industry: Britain in a Climate of Decline*. London: Methuen.

Kirshenblatt-Gimblett, Barbara. 1998. *Destination Culture: Tourism, Museums, and Heritage*. Berkeley: University of California Press.

Lanouette, Jean-Paul. 2004. "Mise en bière d'Unibroue." *Soreltracy.com*. Accessed October 17, 2017. http://www.soreltracy.com/liter/2004/avril/23av.htm.

LeBlanc, Julie M-A. 2003a. *Focus Group Interview, Gatineau, QC*. Pts. 1 and 2. CD. MUNFLA 2005-124. April 21.

LeBlanc, Julie M-A. 2003b. *Questionnaire (online) for Andrée Marcil, Unibroue*. CD. MUNFLA 2015-035. March.

LeBlanc, Julie M-A. 2005. *Interview with Stéphane Berranger, Lachine, QC*. CD. MUNFLA 2005–124. March 16.

LeBlanc, Julie M-A. 2005–6. *Beer and Folklore Survey (Online)*. MUNFLA 2015-035.

Library and Archives Canada. 2017a. *1839-02-15 Execution of Rebels in Front of the Montreal Gaol*. Drawing by Henri Julien, 1852–1908, LAC, Acc. No. 1989-466-61. Accessed October 17, 2017. http://collectionscanada.gc.ca/pam_archives/index.php?fuseaction=genitem.displayItem&rec_nbr=2933808&lang=eng.

Library and Archives Canada. 2017b. *1839-02-15 Un Vieux de "37."* Drawing by Henri Julien, 1852–1908. LAC, Acc. No. 1989-466-61. Accessed October 17, 2017. http://collectionscanada.gc.ca/pam_archives/index.php?fuseaction=genitem.displayItem&rec_nbr=2924336&lang=eng.

Lien, Marianne. 2000. "Imagined Cuisines: 'Nation' and 'Market' as Organising Structures in Norwegian Food Marketing." *Commercial Cultures: Economies, Practices, Spaces*, ed. Peter Jackson, Michelle Lowe, Daniel Miller, and Frank Mort, 153–73. Oxford, New York: Berg.

Lowenthal, David. 1985. *The Past Is a Foreign Country*. Cambridge: Cambridge University Press.

MacGregor, Robert M. 1981. "Implications of Ethnic Labels on Product Packages." *Proceedings of the Annual Conference of the Atlantic Schools of Business Marketing Section*, ed. Erdener Kaynak. Saint John: University of New Brunswick.

MacGregor, Robert M. 1992. "The Golliwog: Innocent Doll to Symbol of Racism." *Advertising and Popular Culture: Studies in Variety and Versatility*, ed. Sammy R. Danna. Wisconsin: Popular Press.

MacGregor, Robert M. 1995. "Québec's Killer Beer: Dark T(ale)." *Contemporary Legend* 5: 101–14.

MacGregor, Robert M. 2003. "I Am Canadian: National Identity in Beer Commercials." *Journal of Popular Culture* 37 (2): 276–86.

Market Wired. 2005. "Sleeman Reports Fourth Quarter and Fiscal 2004 and Senior Management Addition." Accessed October 17, 2017. http://www.marketwire.com/press-release/sleeman-reports-fourth-quarter-and-fiscal-2004-and-senior-management-addition-534057.htm.

McCracken, Grant. 1988. *Culture and Consumption: New Approaches to the Symbolic Character of Consumer Goods and Activities*. Bloomington: Indiana University Press.

McNaughton, Janet. 1985. "French-Canadian Nationalism and the Beginnings of Folklore Studies in Quebec." *Canadian Folklore Canadien* 17 (1–2): 129–47.

Novitz, David. 1997. "Art, Narrative, and Human Nature." *Memory, Identity, Community: The Idea of Narrative in the Human Sciences*, ed. Lewis P. Hinchman and Sandra K. Hinchman. Albany: State University of New York Press.

O'Grady, Jean, and David Staines, eds. 2003. *Northrop Frye on Canada: Collected Works of Northrop Frye*. Toronto: University of Toronto Press.

Oring, Elliott. 1986. "Ethnic Groups and Ethnic Folklore." *Folk Groups and Folklore Genres: An Introduction*, ed. Elliott Oring. Logan: Utah State University Press.

Parliament of Canada. 2001. "Standing Committee on Finance." Accessed October 17, 2017. http://www.parl.gc.ca/HousePublications/Publication.aspx?DocId=1041084&Language=E&Mode=1.

Röhrich, Lutz. 1980. "Folklore and Advertising." *Folklore Studies in the Twentieth Century: Proceedings of the Centenary Conference of the Folklore Society*, ed. Venetia J. Newall. Woodbridge, Suffolk: Brewer.

Sheehan, Kim. 2004. *Controversies in Contemporary Advertising*. London: Thousand Oaks.

Sleeman Breweries Ltd. 2004. "Sleeman offre d'acheter Unibroue afin de poursuivre son expansion au Canada." Press Release, April 20, 2004.

Solomon, Michael R, Judith L. Zaichkowski, and Rosemary Polegato. 2002. *Consumer Behaviour: Buying, Having and Being*. 2nd Canadian ed. Toronto: Prentice-Hall.

Sullenberger, Tom E. 1974. "Ajax Meets the Jolly Green Giant: Some Observations on the Use of Folklore and Myth in American Mass Marketing." *Journal of American Folklore* 87 (343): 53–65.

Théodore, Pierre. 1999. "L'étiquette n'est que le pâle reflet de ce que souhaite devenir une vraie bière." *BièreMAG* 25 (Fall): 5 and 27. Accessed October 17, 2017. http://www.bieremag.com/PDF/bm25-m02.pdf.

Unibroue. 2017. Accessed October 17, 2017. https://www.unibroue.com/en/.

van Lent, Peter. 1985. "La Vie de l'Habitant: Quebec's Folk Culture of Survival." In *Explorations in Canadian Folklore*, ed. Edith Fowke and Carole H. Carpenter, 329–39. Toronto: McClelland and Stewart.

Vannoy, Tanya. 2009. *Trends in Marketing Beer to Hispanics*. Phoenix Marketing International, Multicultural Practice.

Williamson, Elizabeth. 1980. "Advertising" in *Handbooks of American Popular Culture*, ed. M. Thomas Ingle. Vol. 2. Westport, CT: Greenwood Press.

Williamson, Judith. 1978. *Decoding Advertisements: Ideology and Meaning in Advertising*. London: Marion Boyars.

# 3

# Market Forces and Marketplace Economics at the Smithsonian Folklife Festival

Halle M. Butvin and James I. Deutsch

WHEN THE SMITHSONIAN INSTITUTION'S Festival of American Folklife began on the National Mall of the United States in 1967, it sought to represent a very broad cross-section of American folk culture. Previous folk festivals—such as the Mountain Dance and Folk Festival (established in 1928), the National Folk Festival (established in 1934), and the Newport Folk Festival (established in 1959)—had focused primarily on music, but the Smithsonian event aimed to highlight the full range of cultural expressions: from music, song, and dance to foodways, storytelling, arts, and crafts. Indeed, demonstrating at that first Folklife Festival were more than fifty craftspeople: basket makers, carvers of wood and ivory, doll makers, needleworkers, potters, silversmiths, weavers, and others, many of whom had their handmade items for sale in the Festival Marketplace. By providing festival visitors with ample opportunities not only to observe the craft process, but also to purchase traditional crafts, festival planners hoped not only to serve those members of the public who valued and appreciated hand-crafted items, but also the artisans and tradition-bearers who were investing their knowledge and skills in the production of those items.

Fifty years later, the Smithsonian Folklife Festival, produced by the Smithsonian Center for Folklife and Cultural Heritage, still highlights traditional artisans and their handiwork, and it still offers visitors the opportunities to purchase those items in the Folklife Festival Marketplace, where items produced by festival participants are sold. But the festival is also implementing new models for the twenty-first century for not only its own physical Marketplace tent, but also the broader market for folk and traditional arts. The Festival Marketplace mirrors what artisans experience all over the world—from Peruvian weavers to Maasai beaders—as they navigate constantly shifting market forces. Festival planners regard both the marketplace and the wider market as beneficial tools for cultural exchange by celebrating what traditional communities produce and, in that same process, enhancing cultural diversity, cultural sustainability, and mutual understanding.

This chapter has several goals: to provide historical background on the Folklife Festival's sale of crafts; to review the current context for artisans in the global marketplace; and to explore the festival's ongoing relationship with artisans and tradition-bearers, particularly as the festival attempts to connect artisan-participants to wider consumer markets. Primary sources will include archival records and documents, contemporary newspaper accounts, and interviews with contemporary artisans and buyers.

The origins of the Festival of American Folklife—which changed its name in 1998 to the Smithsonian Folklife Festival—may be traced to S. Dillon Ripley, the Smithsonian secretary from 1964 to 1984, who wanted to make the Smithsonian Institution more relevant (a key word in the 1960s) and also make the National Mall more lively. Ripley and James Morris, head of what was then the Smithsonian Division of Performing Arts, hired Ralph Rinzler to help produce the Smithsonian event. As the Newport Folk Festival's director of field research, Rinzler had conducted fieldwork in many traditional communities and knew that their crafts traditions were as important as musical performances in conveying the folklife and identities of those communities. As one historian has explained, "Although Rinzler came to the Smithsonian to escape the overly commercial atmosphere of Newport, he did not entirely abandon commerce at the Smithsonian festival. He recognized that connecting traditional artists and craftspeople with markets for their work was an excellent way of ensuring the persistence of their traditions" (Walker 2013, 108). Ripley shared Rinzler's belief in the importance of artifacts; in the very first printed program book for the festival, which appeared in 1968 (there was no printed program in 1967), Ripley was quoted as follows: "Objects are documents to be read as much as the printed page. Many people and all children need to touch objects, assess their texture, not simply read about them, in order to learn . . . we have need for objects. Through them the truth is seeking us out" ("Smithsonian Museum Shops—Showcase for Crafts" 1968, 39).[1]

## CRAFT SALES DURING THE EARLY YEARS OF THE FOLKLIFE FESTIVAL

Looking back at the earliest years of the Folklife Festival reinforces the perception that many of the details and arrangements were improvised—made up by Morris, Rinzler, and others in the process of producing the event. After all, there had never before been a festival of this sort on the National Mall. Details about the 1967 event are particularly scarce and conflicting, in part because no program was printed. For instance, according to one history, "The first Festival was held July 1–4 in two tents—one for crafts and one for sales—a music stage, and a performance area on the terrace of the Museum of History and Technology" (now the National Museum of American History) (Kurin 1998, 116). This corresponds with one article in the *Washington Post*, which spoke approvingly of the craftspeople, who were "demonstrating their technical skills on the Mall from 11 a.m. to 5 p.m." and whose "handiwork . . . will be on sale daily from 9 a.m. to 7 p.m." ("Good News" 1967, G8). However, according to a daily schedule of Washington-area events that was published in the *Washington Post* on each of the four Festival days, those crafts sales would be taking place not inside a tent, but rather inside the Arts and Industries Building, directly adjacent to the Smithsonian Castle ("Events Today" 1967, D13).

Crafts sales taking place inside the Arts and Industries Building might suggest their being managed by one of the Smithsonian stores. However, according to James Morris's memoir, he and other organizers of the 1967 Folklife Festival had "wanted to sell crafts to Festival visitors but the museum shops were reluctant to leave the museum and move onto the Mall. Instead [they] hired Roger Paige, a young college student, rented a U-Haul truck and sent him on a buying trip to several southern and Appalachian crafters. The crafts sold well and opened the way for continued craft sales in the museum shops" (Morris 2011, 47). No references to Paige or to this buying trip can be found in the festival archives, but one of Rinzler's files confirms the predominance of crafts—particularly pottery, baskets, cornshuck dolls, and quilts—from the southern and Appalachian states being sold at the 1967 festival (Untitled inventory 1968).

Roger Paige went on to become the executive director of the Kentucky Arts Council in Frankfort, executive director of the Lexington (Kentucky) Children's Museum, and an assistant professor of arts administration at the University of Kentucky in Lexington. When reached by phone in 2016, Paige could not recall many of the details of craft sales from fifty years earlier, but he had vivid memories of his road trip to Appalachia to purchase crafts for the festival. "Jim [Morris] had first given me a van to pick things up in, a nine-passenger van, and that was a government vehicle. I never did know if he completely misunderstood the volume of stuff. I filled that van up with pottery, and it would not move. It just sat there, and I called in and told him" (Paige 2016). To replace the government van, Morris rented a U-Haul truck, which according to Paige was "three or four times bigger than what the van would carry." By the time that Paige had picked up all the crafts, "it was full" "It was packed like the way movers packed . . . I don't know if this was stuff on consignment or if we purchased it. You know Jim, he's a smooth talker" (2016). Paige does not recall crafts being sold at the 1967 Folklife Festival inside the Arts and Industries Building. But he does "remember a big tent full of stuff, and all displayed very nicely. I don't remember where that tent was. It may have been in front of the Castle" (2016).

Regardless of where the crafts were actually sold, business was brisk at the first festival. According to a report for the year, total craft sales were $8,559.05, which is roughly equivalent to $63,000 in 2016 dollars ("Smithsonian Museum Shops—Report for Mall Festival" 1967).[2] At the following year's festival in 1968, craft sales nearly tripled, with total sales receipts at $23,020.65 (or $164,000 in 2016 dollars, which calculates to $32,800 per day of the five-day festival) ("Smithsonian Museum Shops: Report for Mall Festival" 1968). These impressive sales figures are confirmed by other archival documents. For instance, in preparing for the 1968 festival, Rinzler wrote to C. E. Cornelison of Bybee Pottery in Bybee, Kentucky, as follows: "As you well remember, the Smithsonian Museum Shops succeeded in obtaining about $1,000.00 worth of Bybee Pottery for our Smithsonian Festival of American Folklife last summer. Had we succeeded in securing a complete order, we could have sold out the entire shipment over the July 4th weekend. During the Festival last summer attendance was estimated by the National Park Service at 431,000 over the four-day period and sales were in the neighborhood of $8,560.00. Pottery sales accounted for approximately 50% of that total. We would like to increase our orders for this year by 200% and look forward to the time when you will be able to meet the demands that admirers of your ware are making" (Rinzler 1968).

Cornelison was not one of the actual participants at the Festival in 1967 or 1968, but Rinzler included his work because he believed that "Bybee is the only traditional pottery in our nation with roots firmly planted in tradition [producing] the sturdy, simple ware characteristic of grass roots American pottery" (Rinzler 1968). Moreover, in his work as festival director, Rinzler was particularly sensitive to ensuring that crafts vendors at the festival would be treated fairly. When David R. Short, a Smithsonian contract administrator, wrote to Ernestine Potter, the festival's participant coordinator, to propose raising the Smithsonian's share of gross sales to 20 percent, Rinzler scrawled, "Seems high!" on the memo and then added by way of explanation, "Books, crafts, records are educational materials sold at FAF as a service rather than income source for us. The vendors are small operators with *little margin* of profit" (Short 1974; emphasis in original).

Looking through the files of correspondence and memoranda from the festival's early years, the impression is that Rinzler and others were seeking to strike a delicate balance among the various needs of craft demonstrators, craft vendors, sales managers, the buying public, and the Smithsonian. For instance, in 1973, festival staff tried combining book sales in the same space as craft and record sales. The results were disastrous, at least from the perspective of Lillian Krelove, the cofounder of Legacy Books, which was one of the leading distributors of books about folklore. As Krelove complained to David Short two weeks after the 1973 FAF ended: "If part of your need is to make money from sales, we expect to be treated a little better than third-class operations. The records were warping in the sun, many books were ruined in the rain, all because our sales accomodations [*sic*] were incidental and thoughtless. It took us three days to discover who controlled the post-hole digger so we could put up one post and attach a tent flap to provide some shade and reasonable comfort for browsers and buyers. Nobody knew anything in the administration tent. We were told to 'go find somebody in charge'" (Krelove 1973). In response, Sarah Lewis, a member of the festival's production team, wrote to James Morris, explaining that "from the very beginning, Mrs. Krelove was a difficult person." Nevertheless, Lewis acknowledged that "some of Mrs. Krelove's complaints are well taken." "It seems that there must be a better manner in which to handle record and book sales in the future . . . Last year when sales were small and only Rounder [Records] was involved we could do things on an informal basis and get away with it. But our Festival has expanded far beyond that type of arrangement" (Lewis 1973). For these first several years of operation, festival planners such as Morris and Rinzler were experimenting with different methods and modes of presentation, trying to determine the best way to proceed. Some attempts seemed to fail, such as the sale of books in 1973; but by and large the festival succeeded on all fronts, including the sale of crafts. Visitors kept coming in large numbers, the reviews in the press were positive, and the craftspeople themselves "frequently viewed the festival as an opportunity to expand markets for their work and gain national recognition as skilled tradition bearers" (Walker 2013, 108).

## CRITIQUES AND CHALLENGES OF FOLKLIFE FESTIVAL CRAFT SALES

In some ways, the festival was indeed becoming a victim of its own success, particularly as it moved toward the unprecedented (and never again equaled) twelve-week Folklife Festival to mark the bicentennial of the United States in 1976. To prepare for this event, Rinzler and Morris commissioned a dozen observers—largely prominent folklorists from outside the Smithsonian—to evaluate the 1974 festival. One of those evaluators was Bess Lomax Hawes, a professor of anthropology at California State University Northridge who in 1977 became the director of the Folk Arts Program at the National Endowment for the Arts. In her report to the Smithsonian, Hawes commented directly on the growing size: "I was enormously impressed by the Festival. It is too big, but I don't see anything to do about that; it is on the verge of being an absolute stunner" (Hawes 1974). Addressing the issue of craft sales and the need for accompanying educational materials, Hawes advised: "People ought to have more to take home. It's crucial, it seems to me, for festival-goers to go away not just with a string of beads from the Native Americans or a corn-shuck doll from the Mississippi folks, but with some stimulating and concrete information which they can go over later and which will suggest ways to help satisfy some of the curiosity hopefully developed during their festival attendance" (1974). Further constructive criticism of the festival's efforts to promote crafts sales was offered by Rayna Green, who served as the workshop coordinator for the Native Americans program at the 1974 festival and who later became director of the American Indian Program at the Smithsonian's National Museum of American History. Green observed:

> There was little tourist garbage made in Hong Kong. BUT, I do not like the presence of the craft sales tent in the area because it evokes that trading post/commercial idea. If we are going to have it, let it be smaller and let it sell only things by the craftspeople at the festival or by the craftspeople from the groups we chose to participate. I don't like the Indian crafts all lumped together, no matter what group they come from. And what we sell could serve as much of an education function as the presentations if they came from the areas and peoples represented. Moreover, this serves as an incentive to the peoples chose to participate as well as their relatives and neighbors who can't come by offering them a legitimate market for what they do. (1974).

More than forty years have passed since Hawes and Green wrote their evaluations of the festival and its craft sales. Yet, in many ways, the festival and its marketplace are still a work in progress, as festival organizers seek to balance not only the needs of craft demonstrators, craft vendors, sales managers, and the buying public, but also the National Park Service, which manages the National Mall where the Folklife Festival takes place. As Rinzler explained in a June 30, 1970, letter to prospective crafts demonstrators, "Under ordinary conditions, commercial sales of any kind are forbidden by law unless covered by a special permit. The crafts sales tent is the only area of the Festival where crafts sales are provided for in our permit. Crafts cannot legally be sold on any other part of the Festival grounds" (Rinzler 1970). In 1995, the National Park Service removed even the option of a special permit by initiating a general ban on all sales—making exceptions only for books, newspapers, leaflets, pamphlets, buttons, and bumper stickers. As a result, the Folklife Festival has had to find space on Smithsonian land for the sale of crafts. To this day, the Festival Marketplace takes place at various locations that are adjacent to the National Mall, but physically situated on Smithsonian property.

One advantage of not selling on the actual site of the festival itself is that it "removes the question of commodification from the main Festival presentation, so that, when visitors approach a craftsperson on the Mall, they are less inclined to ask 'how much does that cost,' and prompted to ask questions more like 'how'd you learn to make that,' 'why do you do that,' and so on" (Kurin 1998, 88). However, the disadvantage is that the distance between the festival marketplace and the crafts demonstrations areas may be too vast for some visitors to navigate, especially amidst the heat and humidity of a typical Washington, DC, summer.

During the many years between the 1976 Folklife Festival and the present, the Smithsonian has tried different approaches, but always seeking a Marketplace that would (a) provide income for festival participants (and the festival itself), (b) deliver quality crafts for visitors eager to take something home from the festival, and (c) properly honor the artisans and their traditions. To this end, in early 2014 the Smithsonian hired several new staff members (including one of this chapter's coauthors) whose mandate was to look closely at the most current trends and to demonstrate best practices in artisan sourcing for the Festival Marketplace. The remainder of this chapter explores some of major issues and challenges faced by one of these new staff members.

## THE ARTISAN EXPERIENCE: TO THE FESTIVAL AND BACK

For artisans, participation in the Folklife Festival is in many ways an ideal commercial environment. During demonstrations on the festival site, artisan-participants share their traditions, process, and personal narrative with a captive audience of hundreds of thousands of visitors who then clamor for the opportunity to purchase their products in the marketplace. For many artisan-participants, this experience is far from the reality to which they return. Historically, artisans have also worked as designers, creating products based on local aesthetic and sociocultural requirements of their client. The rapid changes brought on by both urbanization and globalization have largely isolated artisans, as local clients turn toward cheaper, foreign-made alternatives and artisans lack knowledge of and access to unknown urban and foreign niche markets. This isolation has contributed to the loss of traditional knowledge as artisans turn to agriculture and other trades to earn a living. Further, as young people flock to urban centers in search of new opportunity, artisans are less likely to continue the long tradition of passing on this knowledge through family or apprenticeship. Traditions passed down and evolved over thousands of years can be lost in the length of one generation.

According to UNESCO: "Crafts have never been purely an artistic or aesthetic undertaking, supposedly existing in a bubble of creativity uncontaminated by material interests. Crafts are very much an economic activity. In most traditional societies, design evolved somewhere in the interaction between the artisan and the patron or commissioner; a professional designer as a middleman between the artisan and the client did not exist. In traditional contexts, the artisan was usually familiar with the aesthetic and sociocultural requirements of the client and designed an appropriate object accordingly" (2005, 3). From hiring stone carvers for architectural detail on a church to the production of needlework for a bride's dowry, the end product makes a visual statement about cultural identity, simultaneously bridging and differentiating groups. The quality of craft elevates individual artisans within a group, and as trade increases between groups, distinctive traditions accumulate value across cultures.

For example, in early twentieth-century western Armenia, women learned needlework from their mothers, creating intricate lace, bedding, and towels for their personal dowry and at times designing and selling pieces to other members of the community. As western Armenians fled to Syria in the early twentieth century, wealthy families in Aleppo often hired young Armenian women to create needlework pieces for their daughter's dowries, recognizing the excellence of craftsmanship. This production and commercial exchange also enabled these young women to preserve knowledge of the tradition while earning a livelihood as they found their way as refugees in a new country (Grigoryan 2016). The relationship between commercial exchange and craft production has always evolved, but globalization has both disrupted and accelerated these processes at an unprecedented rate. Many artisans today are located in rural communities and continue to practice traditional skills and traditional technology while trying to compete with mass production of products with a similar look and feel. This dynamic makes it incredibly challenging for artisans to compete, and this increasing "disenfranchisement has moved them further from their markets, both literally and figuratively" (UNESCO 2005, 4).

Despite these challenges, the development of the fair-trade sourcing movement, changes in the American retail landscape, and the emergence of an artisan support sector bring new opportunities for commercial exchange between craft producers and consumers. The Festival Marketplace has an important role to play in this changing environment. Taking note of these changes and the opportunities they bring, festival planners and the marketplace team increasingly view the event as a catalytic moment for artisan-participants to connect with broader markets and expand their understanding of consumer demand. Decades of experience working with artisan-participants on presentation and sale of their products in the marketplace has emphasized the critical importance of market access for the sustainability of craft traditions.

## MARKET ACCESS FOR ARTISANS: OPTIONS IN A GLOBALIZED WORLD

### The Fair Trade Movement

While on a trip to Puerto Rico in 1946, Edna Ruth Byler was inspired to create solutions for the extreme poverty she witnessed during her visit. In purchasing crafts from impoverished artisans, she imagined the potential sale of craft products in the US market as a means to improve livelihoods and ultimately alleviate poverty. Her grassroots effort, started by selling handcrafted products out of the trunk of her car, evolved into Ten Thousand Villages, a retail enterprise providing market access for craft producers ("History" n.d.). In 1949, Sales Exchange for Refugee Rehabilitation and Vocation (SERRV) International began sourcing products from artisans in Europe as a way to help refugees recover economically and socially from World War II ("About Us" n.d.). Ten Thousand Villages and SERRV were among the first to set up what became known as artisan supply chains, embracing the principles of fair wage, gender equality, long-term relationships, concern for the environment, democratic decision making, safe working conditions, respect for culture, and prohibition of child exploitation. Their efforts provided a bridge for artisans to begin accessing the newly evolving global market. Over time, their principles formed the foundation of the fair trade movement, defined by the World Fair Trade Organization (WFTO) as a trade partnership based on dialogue, transparency, and respect that seeks greater equity in international trade and contributes to sustainable development by offering better trading conditions to, and securing the rights of, marginalized producers and workers. Fair trade organizations, backed by consumers, are engaged actively in supporting producers, in awareness raising, and in campaigning for changes in the rules and practice of conventional international trade ("Definition of Fair Trade" n.d.). For hundreds of thousands of craft producers around the world, the fair trade movement has provided new links to global markets. However, while influential and impactful for the producing individuals, communities, and craft enterprises, historically fair trade has represented only a tiny niche and counternarrative in the expansive environment of global retail market.

## The Changing American Retail Landscape

The global retail market in the twentieth century quickly shifted in response to advances in transportation and logistics and changing consumer demand. "At the center of the creation of the new economy and culture was a revolution in the production of industrial and agricultural goods and the advent of the profit-driven corporation" (Leach 1993, 16). By the early 1900s, dry goods stores were replaced by the ubiquitous department store, which provided consumers with an "ever-increasing variety" of product—all under one roof.

In the 1960s, as the Folklife Festival was exploring the relationship between craft demonstrations and commercial exchange in its production planning, mass global travel and tourism took root. Increased travel provided new opportunities for cultural exchange, and craft producers experienced new opportunities for direct exchange as tourists purchased souvenir crafts. While increases in global travel and exposure to handmade artisan craft inspired a "global" aesthetic in home accessories and textiles, sourcing directly from artisans was difficult and prices were often too high in an environment where consumers increasingly demanded cheap goods. The oil crisis of the 1970s kicked off a dramatic increase in demand for lower prices. Shopping malls, strip malls, and mass retailers emerged, offering even greater product variety. Finally, between 1970 and 1990, value players and club stores entered the scene, offering rock-bottom retail prices. With price was often the determining value for consumers, commoditization and private label production created homogeneity within product choices and across the country (Leibowitz 2013).

The combination of the contraction of the global economy that kicked off the recession in 2008 and the internet-based democratized flow of information once again dramatically changed the retail landscape. Power is shifting away from corporate retailers as everyday consumers are forcing transparency into the process. Faced with contracted earnings and savings, millennial consumers are spending much less and showing greater discernment with their purchases. They are increasingly holding retailers accountable for their actions, providing real-time, influential feedback through social networking channels (KPMG 2009). At the same time, the Maker Movement, styled on the Arts and Crafts movement of the late nineteenth century, is building interest in do-it-yourself (DIY) projects and handmade items (Morin 2013). Etsy Inc., an online marketplace for handmade goods and crafts, was valued at $4 billion when it went public in 2015 (Dimri 2015). Retailers are taking note of these changes in consumer behavior and attitudes, introducing unprecedented transparency into their supply chains, and beginning to experiment with sourcing handmade craft products from artisans. The increasing engagement of artisans in the global retail market prompted the need for a definition. In 1997, the UNESCO/ITC International Symposium on Crafts and International Markets defined artisanal product as "those produced by artisans, either completely by hand, tools or even mechanical means as long as the direct manual contribution of the artisan remains the most substantial component of the finished product. These are produced without restriction in terms of quantity and using raw materials from sustainable resources. The special nature of artisanal products is derived from their distinctive features which can be utilitarian, aesthetic, artistic, creative, culturally attached and socially symbolic and significant" (UNESCO 2005, 2). This definition itself serves as a mark, recognizing the added market value of handmade artisan goods.

## Linking Artisans to Markets

Given the existing but narrowing gap in communications and geography between most artisans today and the modern consumer, a burgeoning artisan support sector has developed to serve as a bridge, mediator, and translator. The goals of this sector range from pure economic development—seeing artisan craft as a means to employ rural and marginalized groups—to cultural sustainability. As Patrick Ela, former director of the Los Angeles Craft and Folk Art Museum once pointed out, "craftspeople create because they need to create; like all of us, they must eat. To overlook the inescapable need for economic development as well as technical and artistic development would be naïve" (UNESCO 2005, vi). From an economic perspective, investment in the artisan craft sector has been seen for years by the development community as a means to increase incomes—and social and economic integration—for women, especially, and for rural, impoverished, and marginalized groups around the world. Ten Thousand Villages and SERRV, both initially operated as nonprofit 501c3 entities, were among the first to see the value in connecting craft production to the global market to build stronger local economies. Recent research has sought to quantify the value of the artisan sector, and preliminary reports suggest that in the developing world, engagement in craft production as an economic activity—job creation—is second only to agriculture (Aspen Institute n.d.). Donors have funded artisan support programs with increasing frequency in the last twenty years, recognizing craft traditions as the community asset most easily linked to markets for increased incomes. The fair trade movement, while serving important functions in both the social and economic advancement of artisans, has also served as an important branding tool to connect artisans to new retail opportunities. The movement hopes to leverage consumer awareness about workers' rights and the renewed interest in handmade goods to bring increased market access to organized artisan groups. External, primarily Western groups have also organized to provide support to artisans, accessing donor resources to bridge the widened gap between rural artisans and their mostly urban (and global) clientele. Combining design and business development expertise, groups such as Aid to Artisans helped artisans to understand the ever-evolving interests of global markets, linking traditional skills and technologies with mainstream Western aesthetics.

### Buyer Attitudes and Their Role in Sustaining Cultural Process and Product

There are three major ways that the global retail trade is currently engaging with artisans. The first is a combination of corporate social responsibility and public relations—using artisan products and stories to benefit from the growing consumer interest in both transparency and handmade product. In these efforts, authenticity of product is central, as the story behind the product serves the buyer's primary goal of enticing consumers with the story behind the artisan. However, most of these buying relationships are short term. The second, far less common, is a shift in business strategy to incorporate artisans into the supply chain as part of a product matrix incorporating artisan product with mass-produced goods. In this approach, the buyer may mix current design trends and color palettes with traditional skills, preserving the process but in many cases distancing the traditional design from the process itself. The third, building on the fair trade movement, is a buyer relationship based on dialogue and focused on both sustainability of craft traditions and increased livelihoods for artisan producers. In this section we will explore cases of each of these examples, considering some of the benefits and drawbacks of these approaches with regard to cultural sustainability.

Artisan product sourcing as corporate social responsibility or an effort to enhance public relations often leverages consumer awareness of world events. These types of exchange are often one-off and managed through either a corporate social responsibility office or public relations team for a large brand. They can be extremely effective in introducing artisan product to new audiences, but it is important to manage expectations when engaging in this type of buying relationship. However, when these efforts are successful, they can alter a retailer's sourcing strategy. Macy's Rwanda Path to Peace initiative is a good example of an exchange that has had lasting effects for both the retailer and for Rwandan artisans. As noted in a *Business Wire* article introducing the tenth season of Rwandan baskets to be sold in Macy's stores nationwide: "Macy's Rwanda Path to Peace program was one of the first-ever 'trade-not-aid' efforts and is the longest-enduring, impacting thousands of women throughout the country of Rwanda," according to Willa Shalit, cofounder of the program (Thomas 2015). "This important initiative, in partnership with the Rwandan weavers' cooperative, Gahaya Links, has enabled women in Rwanda to take care of essential human needs, send their children to school, buy health insurance and malaria nets, and help rebuild their communities. We are so grateful to Macy's and its customers who have responded with open hearts, so that Americans can directly support peace and prosperity from one continent to another" (n.p.).

This initiative, started ten years after the Rwandan genocide, was built on consumer awareness of the issue and a consumer desire to "do something." The longevity and broad awareness of the initiative—via Macy's reach of almost 800 retail locations—has introduced Rwandan basketry to the American consumer, which paved the way for many smaller retail businesses to engage Rwandan artisans in the development and export of Rwandan baskets. Other examples of this type of engagement include Kate Spade / Bloomingdales sourcing earrings from Turquoise Mountain, an artisan enterprise reviving traditional craft in Kabul, Afghanistan; Hallmark's introduction of the Bogolan (mud cloth) tote from Mali, which paved the way for duty-free exports of products made from Mali's traditional textiles; and J.Crew's inclusion of Fibre Tibet scarves made from cashmere wool collected by Tibetan nomads in its holiday 2015 collection.

Most of these exchanges are one-offs, but through their expansive market reach can play an important role in introducing consumers to handmade artisan products. Given the reach of the participating retailers, the scale required for an artisan to participate in a program such as this can cause disruptive change. On one hand, the initiative created new demand for a product, as in the Macy's Rwandan basket example. The local partner, Gahaya Links, was able to capitalize on this demand and build additional relationships to help create a sustained demand for the artisans producing basketry. For other, less-well-organized artisan groups, the expertise and financial requirements to scale production can be a distraction—especially when the authentic product being marketed succumbs to fast-paced trends and is no longer relevant to consumers.

The second approach is far less common, but holds great promise for the direction of artisan engagement with major retailers. In 2010, when Jim Brett took the helm at West Elm, the company was closing doors. Consumers were not engaging with the product line of home goods. "It was all machine-made, all very clean and simple, and all very soulless," Brett explained. "I wanted to bring personality and soul and handmade into the business" (Lozanova 2015). Over the last five years, West Elm has humanized its products, and its relationships throughout the supply chain—entering uncharted territory in the process. West Elm's Impact Sourcing Program began as a collaboration between the company's design team and artisan groups. Brett explained how his travels informed this shift in strategy: "I found my greatest inspiration while traveling through India—where I came to truly understand the soulfulness of craft. Even more than a country's culinary traditions, craft represents cultural heritage to me, a fascinating blend of local resources, both material and imaginative. I never tire of trying to capture the essence of each journey by bringing home just the right handcraft. It's hard to tell what my life would be like—or certainly what my home would look like—without these meaningful mementos of my travels" (Lozanova 2015). When Brett joined the brand, he saw the potential to use West Elm's design process to preserve traditional techniques and employ crafters around the world. West Elm's model integrates artisans into the supply chain, building long-term relationships that help address many of the challenges faced by artisans as they attempt to scale up. The company's designers work closely with artisans on product development, echoing the old artisan-patron relationship, but emphasizing the needs for consistency and production growth. West Elm's commitment to this approach is company-wide and fully integrated into its business processes.

The third approach is an offshoot of the model started by Ten Thousand Villages and SERRV. Artisan sourcing is part of the core mission and vision for these groups, which often operate as nonprofits or social enterprise models. Their market access is not as broad as the large retail partners described above, but they consider cultural sustainability—sustaining craft traditions in part through increased revenue for artisans—as an integral part of their business model. Their sourcing is informed by local conditions, allowing for flexibility in production scale and product design. For example, Global Goods Partners, a nonprofit social enterprise, sources exclusively from artisans. Their sourcing strategy seeks to identify authentic product, which Global Goods Partners defines as produced by a locally organized group and made with locally sourced materials using techniques specific to local culture. "Handmade" is the foundation on which the Global Goods Partners brand is built, but authenticity of craft tradition is only one of several considerations on which they evaluate prospective partnerships. "We are realists and know that to expand the market for our partners' products, we have to adapt to the fickle and ever-changing market place in which we operate. For example, we recognize that the range of textiles produced in Rwanda may require our partner there to buy fabric in India; that Khamak, the indigenous form of embroidery in Afghanistan, will sell more when applied to jewelry than to traditional table linen; and that the brilliant colors used in traditional Guatemala weavings need to be toned down for the American marketplace" (Shifrin 2016).

Ten Thousand Villages' approach is still in line with how the enterprise began seventy years ago, focusing on dialogue, connection to culture, transparency, and an effort to stay on the learning curve. Kathleen Campbell, director of retail and public relations for Ten Thousand Villages describes this process as a back-and-forth: "Dialogue doesn't dismiss quality standards and production and shipping deadlines. It means that information is moving in both directions to help make artisan groups and the buyer sustainable. Customers want to be able to recognize that a product is made by hand. They want to see that the glass is hand blown and that no two of the same item are exactly the same—as long as the quality outstanding" (2016). However, even for Ten Thousand Villages, customers expect high quality and for products to reflect current trends. Rather than sustaining the traditions themselves, Ten Thousand Villages sees the design work as a way to provide economic independence for families and communities so that they can determine for themselves how to define and preserve their own culture (n.d.).

### Artisan Perspectives on Evolving Role of Commercial Exchange

When analyzing feedback from artisans on their view of the global retail market and their engagement in commercial exchange, two perspectives are evident. The first is that access to new markets provides an opportunity to showcase artisan skills. Cultural pride is inherent when a patron from another culture appreciates one's own craft traditions. This was the case with trade between communities along the Silk Road thousands of years ago, and it is the case today on the floor of Artisan Resource, a sourcing platform connecting artisans and buyers at the NYNOW international gift show.

Nilda Callanuapa, founder of the Center for Traditional Textiles in Cuzco, Peru, and a participant in the 2015 Smithsonian Folklife Festival program featuring Peru, describes authenticity thus: "[The] art or textile processed using the materials available in our region (wool, fibers of animals, natural sources of materials), techniques that we inherit from our ancestors, done by hand of weavers of the region following the meaning, uses and values that we have learned or we have been touch. The textiles represent a living culture with identity of a region, culture, community and so on. It has story of the weaver or community. It is so important for me because the products will be unique and that has story of our culture. That authenticity is what will make a difference from other cheap products" (Callanuapa 2016). She sees Peruvian textiles—with little variation on the traditional designs—as differentiated from other products precisely because of their authenticity. Manos Preciosas, a company based in Antigua, Guatemala, is a producer and exporter of Mayan and Guatemalan artisan-made products. Manos Preciosas' founder Irma Yolanda Zuleta says that "each village has their own design and colors, such as pyramid and sun patterns based on traditional Mayan designs. Authenticity means bringing a piece of our people in our products" (Zuleta 2016). This commitment to traditional designs and palettes means that artisans such Nilda and Irma actively set the terms for their commercial engagement, especially for buyers who wish to influence design and product development to meet consumer demand.

The second perspective views adaptation and product development for new markets as a requisite for cultural sustainability. For Muna Siddiqui, a Pakistani mosaic artist and owner of the Craft Company, based in Karachi, Pakistan, the goal is drawing on culture and fashionable ideas, adding a little heritage and history [to create] original crafts that can be recognized for their historic origin yet are modern. Your product has to be functional and mean more to your customer in the context of today. It should be authentic to its origin of culture and history but should make sense to the customer. We achieve this by utilizing cultural icons and imagery on our products. Whether the products are mosaic or carved or painted or even embroidered textile they are distinctly from Pakistan in appearance and the materials they are made from are sourced from Pakistan too. Of course, this is all in context to our motto of creating products that keep the art and craft of Pakistan alive. (Siddiqui 2016)

Similarly, for Ana Maria Torres of Fundación Hilo Sagrado (FHS; Foundation of the Sacred Thread), process takes precedence. The foundation is an NGO focused on supporting women of the Wayuu tribe in the mineral-rich department of La Guajira in rural northeastern Colombia through training and capacity-building workshops. "Due to climate change, the Wayuu have been forced to migrate as their safety is endangered by armed groups. The traditional way of weaving is no longer passed from generation to generation. The company aims to rescue traditional skills by conducting workshops and creating sustainable handicraft production centers. A majority of the women they work with are illiterate and communicate visually through woven patterns. These patterns are a reflection of their thought and are synonymous with a way of writing" (Torres 2016). For FHS, the sustainability of the weaving process itself supersedes the requirement to adhere to specific patterns, styles, or palettes.

## OPPORTUNITIES AND RISKS

Most artisans see connections to new markets as an opportunity. Cultural sustainability cannot be divorced from economic contexts, as craft sales equate to livelihood for most artisans around the world. With changing dynamics in local communities, the marketing and sale of their crafts for tourists and for export is at times the best and only opportunity to earn a living. During the 2014 Smithsonian Folklife Festival program featuring Kenya, festival planners met with Ali, a dhow maker from Lamu. He came to the festival to demonstrate this centuries-old craft of boat building, spending two weeks refurbishing the *Lamu*, an old dhow in need of repair. The iconic dhow is a symbol of the Swahili coast, both to local populations and to the tourists who visit Kenya and Tanzania. However, given the flood of inexpensive fiberglass speed boats—both cheaper and faster—Ali is no longer making dhows for local customers. His family has shifted their efforts into agriculture, hoping to earn enough to send their children to school. It is likely that the tradition of dhow making, at least in this particular community, will not survive market forces.

Links to the global market can be a stimulant for the continuity, revival, and evolution of traditional craft, but they do not come without challenges. While communication technology continues to improve at an exponential pace, most artisans are still isolated from consumers. The artisan-support sector and engaging retailers can help close this divide, but large retailers will need to take patient approaches to artisan sourcing. If access to global markets is going to work for artisans, then there is a great deal of work to be done in shifting the supply chain to understand the inherent challenges. Achieving scale may not be a sustainable outcome for artisans, and scarcity would need to be seen as an added value, not a problem. Consumer interest in cultural sustainability would need to prove a lasting trend—not just a temporary, postrecession rejection of the current speed of global trade.

## EVOLVING APPROACH AT THE FOLKLIFE FESTIVAL

Looking forward, Folklife Festival director Sabrina Lynn Motley has stated the belief that the long-term success of the festival relies on continued and deep engagement with artisan-participants. Here, the marketplace will play an increasingly important role beyond simple commercial exchange. This work is amplified by the Center for Folklife and Cultural Heritage's commitment to cultural sustainability, adopted in the 2014 strategic plan, asserting that its "work goes beyond documentation and affirmation. The Center works to increase the visibility and vitality of culture bearers, artists, and traditions and to promote cultural expression as essential to human well-being and community health. We will build on our foundational work with individuals and communities to preserve and elevate cultural practices including those that improve and sustain local economies" (Smithsonian Center for Folklife and Cultural Heritage 2014, 11).

For many artisan-participants, the marketplace serves as an orientation to the US market. By maintaining an active knowledge of the retail trade, staff are better able to ensure that the festival and the marketplace can be an effective catalytic moment. The documentation work completed as part of the prefestival research can become an important tool for artisans and their communities. It can serve the dual role of preventing the irreparable loss of craft traditions, as well the basis for protection of intellectual property. Festival planners and marketplace staff walk participants through the process of international sale and export—a process that can be extremely burdensome for artisans not already exposed to international markets. The marketplace keeps running data on what sells, and works closely with participants to evaluate their own product lines to choose items appropriate for the festival audience, and it helps artisans to understand the pricing involved. In some cases, staff also provide design assistance and suggestions in which items might be slightly adapted for increased likelihood of sale—for example, helping a Chinese kite maker to design a frame so that his tiny, intricate kites could be seen, and purchased, as an art piece; or working with a Kenyan silversmith to create rings made with broken shards of pottery, and identifying a specific color range to increase marketability; or licensing more expensive art pieces to make greeting card sets, instantly making the craft more accessible to price-conscious festival visitors. In these ways, the marketplace acts as both a retailer (in outright purchasing of product from artisans) and as an artisan support organization (providing advice and training to assist artisans in product development, export process, and market linkages). As we continue to change and adapt the processes of the festival and engagement with artisan-participants, the marketplace can serve as a model for engagement.

## NOTES

1. No author is credited for this article, which may have been written by Rinzler himself.
2. Conversion to 2016 dollars, according to http://www.calculator.net/inflation-calculator.html.

## REFERENCES

"About Us." n.d. *SERRV International*. Accessed August 31, 2016. http://www.serrv.org/category/about-us.

Aspen Institute. n.d. "The Alliance for Artisan Enterprise: Bringing Artisan Enterprise to Scale." Accessed August 31, 2017. www.aspeninstitute.org/content/uploads/files/content/images/Alliance for Artisan Enterprise Concept Note_0.pdf.

Callanuapa, Nilda. 2016. Interview by Halle M. Butvin, January 27.

Campbell, Kathleen. 2016. Interview by Halle M. Butvin, January 24.

"Definition of Fair Trade." n.d. *World Fair Trade Organization*. Accessed August 31, 2016. http://wfto.com/fair-trade/definition-fair-trade.

Dimri, Neha. 2015. "Crafts Website Company Etsy Valued at $4 billion in Market Debut." Reuters Technology News. April 16. Accessed August 31, 2016. http://www.reuters.com/article/us-etsyinc-ipo-idUSKBN0N71T420150416.

"Events Today." 1967. *Washington Post*, July 2, D13.

"Good News from 3 Museums." 1967. *Washington Post*, July 2, G8.

Green, Rayna. 1974. "Evaluation of the Festival of American Folklife, 1974." Smithsonian Folklife Festival–Division of Performing Arts (hereafter, SFF-DPA), Box 14, file FAF 74 Evaluation, Ralph Rinzler Folklife Archives and Collections, Smithsonian Institution, Washington, DC (hereafter, RRFAC).

Grigoryan, Silva. 2016. Interview with Halle M. Butvin, February 16.

Hawes, Bess Lomax. "Official Observer's Report," August 30, 1974, SFF-DPA, Box 14, file FAF 74 Evaluation, RRFAC.
"History." n.d. *Ten Thousand Villages*. Accessed August 31, 2016. http://www.tenthousandvillages.com/about-history.
KPMG. 2009. "The Evolution of Retailing: Reinventing the Customer Experience." Accessed August 31, 2016. www.kpmg.com/CN/en/IssuesAndInsights/ArticlesPublications/Documents/Evolution-retailing-o-200912.pdf.
Krelove, Lillian. 1973. To David R. Short, July 19. SFF-DPA, Box 14, file Craft Sales 74 FAF, RRFAC.
Kurin, Richard. 1998. *Smithsonian Folklife Festival: Culture of, by, and for the People*. Washington, DC: Smithsonian Institution.
Leach, William. 1993. *Land of Desire: Merchants, Power and the Rise of a New American Culture*. New York: Pantheon Books.
Leibowitz, Josh. 2013. "How Did We Get Here? A Short History of Retail." June 7. August 31, 2016. https://www.linkedin.com/pulse/20130607115409-12921524-how-did-we-get-here-a-short-history-of-retail.
Lewis, Sarah. 1973. To Jim Morris, "Book and Record Sellers at the Festival, 1973," August 3. SFF-DPA, Box 14, file Sales, RRFAC.
Lozanova, Sarah. 2015. "West Elm Shifts Strategy toward Fair Trade." October 23. Accessed August 31, 2016. http://www.triplepundit.com/special/future-of-fair-trade/west-elm-makes-the-bold-decision-to-shift-business-strategy.
Morin, Brit. 2013. "What Is the Maker Movement and Why Should You Care?" *Huffington Post*, May 2. Accessed August 31, 2016. http://www.huffingtonpost.com/brit-morin/what-is-the-maker-movemen_b_3201977.html.
Morris, James. 2011. *Smithsonian Impresario: A Memoir*. Charleston, SC: n.p.
Paige, Roger. 2016. Interview by James I. Deutsch and Katherine L. Kennedy, March 10.
Rinzler, Ralph. 1968. To C. E. Cornelison, February 1. SFF-DPA, Box 8, file Craft Orders '69, RRFAC.
Rinzler, Ralph. 1970. To "Dear Friends." SFF-DPA, Box 9, file Craft Sales 1970, RRFAC.
Shifrin, Joan. 2016. Interview with Halle M. Butvin, January 26.
Short, David R. 1974. To Ernestine Potter, "Concessionaire Agreements," March 21. SFF-DPA, Box 14, file Craft Sales 74 FAF, RRFAC.
Siddiqui, Muna. 2016. Interview by Halle M. Butvin, January 25.
Smithsonian Center for Folklife and Cultural Heritage. 2014. *Strategic Plan, 2014–2018*. Washington, DC: Smithsonian Center for Folklife and Cultural Heritage.
"Smithsonian Museum Shops: Report for Mall Festival, July 1–July 4, 1967." 1967. SFF-DPA, Box 8, file Craft Orders '69, RRFAC.
"Smithsonian Museum Shops: Report for Mall Festival, July 4–July 8, 1968." 1968. SFF-DPA, Box 8, file Craft Orders '69, RRFAC.
"Smithsonian Museum Shops—Showcase for Crafts." 1968. In *Festival of American Folklife 1968*, ed. Ruri Sakai, 39. Washington, DC: Smithsonian Institution, 1968.
Thomas, Holly. 2015. "Macy's Commemorates 10 Years of Rwanda Path to Peace Initiative." October 21. Accessed August 31, 2016. http://www.businesswire.com/news/home/20151021006583/en/Macy%E2%80%99s-Commemorates-10-Years-Rwanda-Path-Peace.
Torres, Ana Maria. 2016. Interview by Halle M. Butvin, February 10.
UNESCO. 2005. *Designers Meet Artisans: A Practical Guide*. New Delhi: Craft Revival Trust.
Untitled inventory. 1968. SFF-DPA, Box 8, file Festival '68, Sales Crafts, RRFAC.
Walker, William S. 2013. *A Living Exhibition: The Smithsonian and the Transformation of the Universal Museum*. Amherst: University of Massachusetts Press.
Zuleta, Irma Yolanda. 2016. Interview with Halle M. Butvin, February 10.

# 4

## The Sweet Spot
*An Epistemological Approach to the Economics of Sugarmaking in Vermont*

Michael Lange

> *You sugar because you have to, it's in your blood, you just love it that much. But then you have to sugar because you've got that cash outlay in the sugarhouse and the evaporator and the tubing and the marketing to get the customers to a place like this.*
>
> —anonymous interview, May 27, 2010

SUGARMAKING, OR SUGARING, is the process of making maple syrup and its derivative products from the sugary sap of any of several species of maple trees (primarily genus *Acer*). At its core, sugaring involves simply the removal of water from the sap, leaving a thicker fluid with a much higher sugar content. This fluid syrup is sometimes called simply "maple," a term that encompasses all the products, such as syrup, maple sugar, maple candy, and so forth. People have been removing water from maple sap for millennia in the area that is now the northeastern bit of North America (Thomas, Jackson, and Guthrie 1999), and the knowledge of sugaring has been passed from person to person in formal and informal education processes since its beginning.

Various changes in technique and technology have been introduced (Farrell 2013; Lange 2012), but the basic process of water removal has remained the one constant and necessary aspect of sugaring. In its simplest current form, sap is collected from holes drilled into the trees. That sap is brought to the sugarhouse, where it is boiled down to the necessary consistency in a device called an evaporator, basically a big pan over a big heat source. Various means of collecting and moving the sap (buckets hung on the sides of trees, plastic tubing systems that pipe the sap to centralized locations, vacuum pressure systems), fueling the fire (oil, wood, steam), and enhancing the quality and economy of the process (bubble injectors, reverse osmosis) can all be particular to the sugarmaker, but the sap coming out of a tree and being boiled down to a final syrup consistency are constant. That simplicity of sap and heat, which runs through all narratives of sugarmaking, contains many different, individualized processes to get from the tree to the shelf.

Maple sugaring has long been an important and meaningful activity in what is now Vermont, although, like many activities that are thought of as folk, the importance and meanings of maple are not often considered from an economic standpoint. The economics of maple sugaring are, at one level, just another set of meanings assigned to syrup, negotiated and agreed upon just like any other set of meanings that are created and exist within cultural contexts. What are some of those cultural meanings that are understood as economic? In the current chapter, I explore two kinds of economic meanings of the many that occur in any cultural activity. I examine some of the key differences between the actual production of maple syrup and the stories that are told about maple as part of its marketing. Then, I discuss how these narratives shape the use value and exchange value of syrup, ultimately drawing together the economics of maple and the narrative construction of those economics. There is not a single story of making maple syrup that is universally told. Elements do recur, no matter whose sugarhouse or farm stand you visit for a quart, but each sugarmaker has an individual take on sugaring's meaning to them, just as each has an individualized version of the tapping and boiling process. It is this intense personal quality that forms the basis of maple's story. No matter where you get your syrup, you are getting the syrup from *someone*—often an individual, or a family, or, at worst, an anonymized figure—still an individual—on a label with the word "Vermont" prominently attached. The idea and the story of maple are that it was made by someone, *a particular* someone, and that buying the syrup provides access to a portable version of that someone. Exploring how and why these connections are made and meanings assigned is the purpose of this chapter.

To explore this question, I have conducted ethnographic fieldwork with sugarmakers across Vermont, starting in 2008 and continuing through the present. My fieldwork has included working with sugarmakers with various sized operations, from 10 taps in their backyard up through 70,000+ taps spread across miles of hillside, and I have spoken with sugarmakers from every county in the state, as well as others working in related areas, such as academic research, government oversight, and marketing. My work here is based on this ongoing ethnography. More recently, I have been giving talks throughout the state, sponsored by the Vermont Humanities Council, discussing with audiences the ways in which maple is meaningful to them. These talks continue to reinforce the economic importance of sugaring to Vermont, as audience members tell me anecdotes of past and present, wherein syrup pays the property taxes, or generates the first income of the calendar year on a farm, or supplements the household income by supplying quarts and gallons to neighbors up and down the road.

As I discuss elsewhere (Lange 2017), maple has become a commodity in Vermont because it is *considered* a commodity, when the meaning of commodity (an item or substance with economic value) is assigned to it. Economists and others can talk about commodity pricing and various other measures that may differentiate a single ear of corn, for example, from commodity corn, as in Michael Pollan's *Omnivore's Dilemma* (2006, 25–28). Corn is understandable in two different forms, as discrete pieces of a plant and as an undifferentiated mass of valuable stuff—"corn-the-food" and "corn-the-commodity" (2006, 58). The transformation is one of twenty ears of corn to twenty tons of corn. The change is partly predicated on scale (no one goes to the grocery store to buy 20,000 ears of corn, and no grain elevator loads in a mere bushel), and it is partly shaped by grammar (corn shifts from being a countable noun, five ears of corn, to being a mass noun, some tons of corn). But syrup works a little differently, and commodity is not determined by amounts or measures. From the outset, syrup is understood as a mass, so the transition is not negotiated along the axis of countable-to-mass-noun. Instead, commodification happens when a mass of syrup transforms from being identifiably from one sugarmaker or sugarhouse, and becomes part of an undifferentiated collection of syrup. When the individual sugarmaker's identity is removed from syrup, it is replaced with the identity of commodity. In so doing, the syrup itself is not changed; it doesn't suddenly transform from one thing to another. Rather, commodification changes the way the syrup is considered and thought about and the meanings that are assigned and assignable to it. It is in this crucial moment that economics and folklore meet. It is fairly easy to see normal folkloric concepts such as traditionality and identity in sugaring, and it is easy to see the dollars and cents of maple syrup, but there is not a gulf between these two understandings. My fieldwork has demonstrated amply that there is no authentic maple that is somehow internal to Vermont and that is somehow violated by becoming a bought-and-sold product. For many Vermonters, the buying and selling of maple are as authentic and fundamental a part of their identity as the tapping of a tree or the roar of a wood fire.

Whether they are making syrup for themselves or selling to neighbors or bulk packers to send around the world, sugarmakers always consider the syrup to be an economic thing. Where and to whom it is sold means less than where and how it is made. Production of maple syrup is always understood to be local, and localness is very important to the economic meaning of maple. Making maple syrup is a sort of distillation process, but the thing being distilled is Vermontiness. Sugaring only occurs in this one part of the world (southeast Canada and northeast United States), so there is a sense that the process belongs to that location and the sugarmakers who live there. The syrup is a commodity, but the syrup is representational of the place where it is made, in this case, Vermont. Because there is such a strong connection between the syrup and the place, and such a strong connection between the place and the people who live there, the syrup becomes representational of the identity of Vermont and Vermonters. The process is similar to what Keith Basso explains among the Cibecue Apache of Arizona, who "describe the land [. . . and] take steps to constitute it in relation to themselves" (1996, 40). In the Apache process of narrating their landscape, they construct explicit connections between themselves, their land, and their shared identity. Because the syrup takes on the identity of the people who make it, sugarmakers themselves become a bit commodified as the syrup get commodified.

These two meanings are linked, to the point of becoming nearly the same, by the narrative that sells maple. The marketing of syrup for a long time has relied on what Amy Trubek calls an "Elysian dream" of Vermont's people and landscape (2008, 221–22). Rustic images of horses and buckets root sugaring in Vermont, and that narrative makes maple appealing as a product. Consumers want to buy a bit of the clean, green, and serene chunk of Earth that is Vermont, and they do so by buying, and buying into, the story that is told about maple syrup production.

Maple syrup does not remain local in its identity *in spite of* commodification; that very localness is part and parcel of the commodification and commodity that results. Because production remains local, locality is part of the commodity: "I love to see the branding of Vermont and the movement toward buying local and consuming more food close to home, and that's true, that would have benefits all over the world. But my rationale for maple is that since it is only made in seventeen states and provinces, except for those, we're local to the world" (interview, June 13, 2011). Even though maple is made in a particular place, that particularity of place can be made part of the economic meaning that maple carries to other parts of the world. The phrase "local to the world" may seem odd, even contradictory, at first glance. However, this person is expressing in their own words the concept of the "glocal," the intersection of local and global identity: "The term 'glocal' is meant to imply that in the global age it is difficult to find much, if anything, that is not influenced in some way by the global (as well as the local). Culinary traditions that were once uniquely local now incorporate global products" (Ritzer and Galli 2013, 58). George Ritzer and Anya Galli are talking about the fact that few culinary items are the product solely of one geographic location, so Peruvian corn tortillas may be made authentically with mass-produced shortening from the United States. The incorporation of an international ingredient does not harm a sense of authenticity if the idea of glocality is allowed. The local and global exist naturally and expectedly with one another. The global product in the case of maple syrup is not an ingredient or additive (indeed, pure maple has no additives), but an awareness of the global market. Even the smaller-scale sugarmakers I have visited have spoken to me about the growth of the maple industry as far afield as China, Australia, and Japan. A sugarmaker who sells syrup only within a fifteen-mile radius still often knows what is happening globally in the industry. In a glocal conception, the idea of maple as locally oriented is not violated by sugarmakers being acutely aware of international markets.

Maple is economically viable as a commodity outside of the locale of its production because it carries a bit of that locale with it. The localness gets commodified, so anywhere syrup goes, some sense of localness goes with it, making it local to the world, no matter where it hits the shelves. "That is a big part, I think, of the marketing plan, is a lot of syrup that's sold over there [Asia, Europe] goes along with a little information packet on the bottle or can, whatever it seems to be marketed in. And it's a little explanation of how and where it's produced, and I think it really helps the marketing end of it" (interview, July 21, 2010). When Vermont exports syrup, it also exports the localness. Both get commodified with a narrative explanation of where and what—where the bottle comes from, what is inside it, and how those two things are intimately tied together.

The tying of Vermont and syrup together in this way is not always a comfortable process for sugarmakers. As one source commented, "Vermont does have an identity, they call it a Vermont brand. I hate that word 'brand' because 'brand,' I think of Aunt Jemima's a brand, Philip Morris is a brand" (interview, June 7, 2010). This man is troubled by the branding that occurs when syrup is taken to other places, thereby taking Vermont to other places. It is interesting that the first two examples he comes up with for what he sees as the distasteful concept of brand are Aunt Jemima and Philip Morris. Aunt Jemima is, of course, a brand of corn-syrup-based pancake syrup, which is presented as representative of branding in a negative sense. The implication that this sugarmaker is making is that a brand is artificial, more corporate, more commoditized, and therefore less worthy of respect. To equate Vermont maple with Aunt Jemima is something close to heresy for sugarmakers, so when this man sees the branding of Vermont as approaching the Aunt Jemima end of a spectrum, his discomfort is clear. The large, corporate, and industrialized product Aunt Jemima is the anathema of the small, local, and handcrafted purity of real maple syrup. Aunt Jemima is made by a large, faceless operation somewhere, with corporate headquarters in an office building. Real maple syrup is made by the family up the road, with a tin money box laying open in their garage. Trust in what (and who) you know is key in creating a feeling of safety and comfort in maple as a product. The fact that the next example given by this man is a cigarette company makes even more obvious the distasteful nature of such branding for him. Aunt Jemima and Philip Morris are, in this construction, both huge, distant, corporate machines that make something unhealthy. To subject Vermont maple to the same branding treatment appropriate for those products is problematic.

The branding of maple, and by association the branding of Vermont, is slowly changing for other reasons as well. As syrup is being sold more widely across the world, the idea of Vermont is carrying less and less meaning. Within the United States and Canada, the term "Vermont" means something. What it means may not be consistent, or even at times accurate, but it conveys a definite meaning. In Australia or Malaysia, those meanings become decidedly less distinct and therefore less meaningful. Some sugarmakers are purposefully changing the graphics on their labels to respond to the widened maple market. One sugarmaker in the Northeast Kingdom (the northeastern part of Vermont, centered on Orleans, Caledonia, and Essex Counties) has based her design language around a stylized tree shape. It is not even obviously a maple tree, simply a tree. Her bottles carry branding that focuses not on a particular locale, but on a more generalized sense of nature and of the natural, clean qualities of the syrup. Of importance, her decisions about the design of her syrup containers started with an analysis of authenticity—she delved into what her understanding of her story as a sugarmaker was, who she wanted to be. That analysis created a narrative of her sugaring operation, which then led very naturally to the imagery on her bottles.

The links among land, syrup, nature, and sugarmaker can take varying forms, but the links are always present. Being a sugarmaker and being a farmer are still closely associated in Vermont, regardless of whether the person sugaring also farms in other ways or not. There is a certain logical flow to these connections, given the prudent and practical stereotype of Vermonters. Farmers as a lot are nothing if not economically practical. From the earliest days of agriculture, a farmer had to be fluent with a wide range of processes that all depended on one another, with an eye toward generating some product at the end. The sheer number of knowledge areas that come into play when one farms is staggering to the uninformed and still humbling to those who know. Having to coordinate so many interrelated processes tends to make farmers a fairly practical bunch, with a focus on the task and an eye on the economic bottom line. Because maple is understood as part of the agricultural world in Vermont, many of the same ways of farmers' thinking can be associated with sugaring. One source summed up what is necessary to sugar, "There's an awful lot of knowledge you need in order to make all that [sugaring] equipment work for you. It doesn't come with a lot of good instructions" (interview, June 15, 2011).

Operating sugaring equipment requires knowledge drawing on the realms of plumbing, electric, mechanics, fluid dynamics, basic physics and chemistry, and a host of other areas. None of that will come as a surprise to anyone who has done any farming, where such combinations of knowledge bases are the norm, rather than the exception. Paying attention to the numbers, maximizing output, and balancing many different inputs have always been aspects of sugaring, as with almost all forms of agriculture.

The practical, pragmatic mindset of the farmer very easily informs the general understanding of sugaring so that even the most romantic notions of the old ways and keeping heritage alive that maple evokes are layered with a knowledge that what comes out of the tree eventually goes into a bottle, often onto a shelf with a price tag attached. Maximizing profit, even for the smaller scale of production, is often a priority over other considerations: "You know the old joke about finding the mice. Sometimes you find [dead] mice in your buckets on the trees, and the old thing goes that over in New Hampshire, they just look the other way and take the mouse out and keep the sap. But here in Vermont, we like to wring the mouse out first" (October 23, 2010). The joke here is partially on the thriftiness of Vermonters, who are known to be able to pinch a penny paper thin. However, also contained in this joke is a recognition of how important economic meanings are and have long been in sugaring. It is easy enough to romanticize the old ways and think of economics as a relatively new addition (intrusion?) into sugaring, but the joke above has been around a while. It's not a joke about mice in the vacuum-driven sap receiver—it's about mice in the buckets. Economic meanings are not an intrusion into the heritage of maple; they are a part of that heritage, and they make the narrative that sells the syrup.

Sugarmakers are constantly balancing various sets of numbers in order to maximize their efficiency: cords of wood or gallons of oil burned, number of taps set, gallons per tap, percentage to which sap is concentrated in a reverse osmosis (RO) machine, acres of woods and yards of tubing, inches of pressure in their vacuum system. Each of these numbers represents some portion of the complicated dance that coaxes the sap from the tree and into an evaporator. Before the sap ever comes to a boil, it has been commodified umpteen ways to maximize the output of syrup at the end. Many sugarmakers are constantly tweaking their system, upping the vacuum one season, lowering the RO percentage another, in order to find the sweetest of the sweet spots, wherein they are making the most syrup they can, at the most economical rate, off the trees they are tapping. The constant push and pull of the various numbers is reflected in technological changes as well. Reverse osmosis machines were brought into sugaring to increase the percentage of sugar in the sap before setting it on the heat, allowing less fuel to be used to boil the sap down to the required percentage to be legally called syrup.

Interestingly, in sugaring, RO machines are used in a manner opposite of what they generally are employed to do. In just one more example of sugarmakers tweaking numbers and maximizing output through innovative means, the process of RO separates water from particulate contaminants suspended in the water by running the water through a filter membrane under pressure. So, running liquid through a reverse osmosis machine generates two products: purified water (permeate) and a slurry containing the contaminants (concentrate). Usually, the goal of reverse osmosis is to remove the particulates (pollutants, salt, etc.) from the water. However, sugarmakers want to remove the *water*, leaving the particulate sugar in suspension. Purified water is the waste product of RO in sugaring, although many sugarmakers put that purified water to some use. Because the process of RO puts a lot of heat into the water, several sugaring operations use the hot, purified water to wash their equipment. In so doing, they are tweaking one more number in the complex of commodified systems by not having to use water and cleanser from the store. For those who wash with permeate, the trees provide not only the maple that comes out of the evaporator but the means to scrub them down after a boil. Such tweaks and maximizations are designed to make sugaring as profitable as possible.

A basic understanding of economics says that profit ultimately comes from a difference between use value (the intrinsic value of an item based on the costs of its creation) and exchange value (the amount of value one can get for the item in an exchange process). Karl Marx touched upon this process up in the first chapter of *Capital*, when he calls commodities "social things whose qualities are at the same time perceptible and imperceptible by the senses" (qtd. in Heilbroner 1996, 166). The value of a thing is not merely its mechanical or practical value, but its perceived values, understood in a particular *social* context. The use value of maple is pretty easily calculated, by taking into account the cost of the material input (the land and trees, the tubing, the releasers and tanks, the evaporator, the fuel, etc.) and then adding in the labor costs (the time and effort to check the lines, move the sap, run the boil, filter and bottle, etc.). The balance of all these numbers is the constant tweaking game that every sugarmaker plays, trying to maximize her or his output to achieve the lowest use value for a set amount of syrup. The use value of maple is not fixed, but fluctuates within a fairly bounded range based on each sugarmaker's operation.

So, if that is the origin of syrup's use value, from where does maple derive its exchange value? What makes it a commodity in a financially sustainable sense, with profit potential? Adam Smith, in his *Theory of Moral Sentiments*, discusses the making of exchange value at the perceptual level by invoking ideas of sympathy and vanity (Heilbroner 1996. 58–73). Where Smith restricts these perceptions to the realm of desire (the desire to be perceived a certain way, or to desire that which we perceive in others), he is scraping against the realities of exchange values of commodities—that they are shaped not by what a thing *is*, but by what we *want it to be*. Maple consumers construct ideas about what they want maple to be, what they want it to represent, through the construction of narratives about maple, and through the use of narratives of maple that they are provided, through the marketing and packaging, for example.

When looking at the retailing of maple, common images appear and reappear. On older syrup bottles, sugaring operation websites, and brochures, images of the sugarhouse and stands of maple trees are no surprise, but very often outside the sugarhouse in a red-checked coat is a man,[1] and hanging from the trees are buckets. Horse-drawn sledges are common as well, and smoke rising from the sugarhouse suggests a wood fire. These tropes evoke an old-timey narrative of sugaring, with what is perceived as a low level of technology,[2] and with a process dripping (literally) with tradition. The images themselves attempt to convey a simpler way of life, thereby placing maple syrup into a "way we were" narrative frame. Regardless of whether any individual sugarmaker (or any individual consumer) ever was that way, the tropes evoked on the standard labels try to create a shared connection to a fictive past, when things were simpler, better, and more pure. Maple syrup, with its one ingredient and simple recipe—take sap, boil—makes for an easy vehicle for such tropes.

The containers that carry these tropes are pretty standardized, with the vast majority coming from a small number of companies. Sugarhill Containers, a division of Hillside Plastics out of Massachusetts, makes many of the plastic containers that receive Vermont syrup (as well as syrup made in other parts of the sugaring world), and their imagery often includes the tropes of the red-checked coat, horse, and bucket, though trends in branding are changing. A common type of bottle itself, though made of injection-molded plastic, is shaped to resemble an old earthenware jug, again connecting to old-timey imagery. Sugarhill is by no means alone in evoking these tropes, but as one of the largest manufacturers and distributors of the maple containers, they have helped write a script that many others now follow. However, as mentioned earlier, some sugarmakers are removing the old-timey imagery and evoking other tropes, such as cleanliness or naturalness. The Vermont Maple Sugarmakers' Association itself is phasing out one of its iconic branding images, an outline map of the state with a tap in the side, dripping into a bucket. This image, which speaks directly of maple dripping from the core of Vermont, is viewed as problematic in foreign markets, where the outline map doesn't communicate much and Vermontiness means little. The new iconography is based around natural images of trees, leaves, and mountains, which are images that communicate more broadly.

The fact that few of the sugarmakers who package their syrup in those wholesale jars from Sugarhill actually collect on buckets and that fewer still use a horse team to draw their syrup to the sugarhouse matters little. It is not the process itself that is important to maple's economic meaning; it is the *narrative* that spans the gap between the use value and the exchange value of syrup. People pay a premium for the story of maple. By pointing out the importance of the narrative, I am not diminishing the importance of what's in the jar. If the syrup in the jar is not a top-quality product, all the fancy labeling in the world won't bring a customer back for more, and the same is true for fancy stories. However, the narrative's importance in the commodification of maple cannot be underestimated. Vermont is very protective of that narrative, as demonstrated by Vermont's two US senators and lone congressional representative taking action to prevent the Log Cabin brand of artificial pancake syrup, from co-opting tropes of the branding (*VTDigger* 2011). Ambiguous labeling and a syrup bottle shape that was too similar to the Sugarhill-type standard for real maple showed the makers of artificial maple attempting to evoke the same narrative, to get consumers to attach the old-timey, traditional story to their products. The story is what gets a price per gallon from the use value, which is just the cost of production, up to the exchange value, which is what the customer is willing to pay.

The exchange value of a bottle of syrup can be influenced by many things. The narrative of production that is told by the labeling can up the price, but so can the narrative of acquiring the syrup. The sugarmaker (via other entities such as Sugarhill and the Vermont Maple Sugarmakers' Association) crafts the former narrative with the images of buckets, horses, mountains, or trees. But the narrative of acquisition is made by the consumer, and it is made at the moment of purchase. Sugarmakers can influence how these acquisition narratives are made, of course. How a sugarmaker markets their syrup can be shaped by how they operate, but how they operate can also be shaped by how they market. One sugarmaker in the southern part of the state was describing his operation to me:

> A sugarhouse like the one we're sitting in here now has no business belonging here from a production standpoint. It belongs at the lowest point of the sugarbush, especially back when they had horses, because you fill a tank up with sap, you want to go downhill and if you have pipeline, downhill, everything's downhill. The sugarhouse belongs down in the sugarbush at the lowest point. And [—] was one of the first guys—he actually hooked onto his sugarhouse with his tractor and pulled it up beside the road. And the reason he did that was because at that time, the roads were starting to improve and cars and tourists and roadside stands, that whole thing was starting up and [—] was looking to sell his syrup so, anyways, so that's all true. (interview, June 9, 2011)

This sugarmaker is making the connection between production and marketing, between use value and exchange value. His operation sells primarily on the roadside, to a customer base that is driving through Vermont and wants to stop at the road for some maple syrup. In order to do so, he has located his sugarhouse in a spot that is illogical. His sugarhouse, as well as that of the other sugarmaker discussed in his story, were placed up a hill, away from the natural point of production. Sap, like all liquids, flows downhill, so the use value of having the sugarhouse in as low a spot as possible has been sacrificed for greater roadside visibility, for the sake of increased exchange value. Having the sugarhouse easily accessible to the passing tourist doesn't make the syrup more accessible—jugs of syrup can be put by the side of the road without much trouble. Having the sugarhouse there where the cars can see it, where the visitors can enter it, makes the *narrative* of maple more easily accessible. The experience of being inside the sugarhouse makes the story of acquiring syrup more special, more meaningful. Clearly, the story is worth something, as prices for maple have generally risen over time, and the customer base is constantly increasing.

The visit to the sugarhouse translates directly into the economic meaning of dollars for syrup. A visit to a sugarhouse, especially when it is in operation, is such a powerful part of the process that some sugarmakers will go to great lengths to make sure it happens: "There was times I'd boil water out there to make steam, and be able to talk about it" (interview, July 20, 2010). The experience of the sugarhouse, with the raging boil over the heat and steam dripping from the rafters and running down the walls, is so important that this sugarmaker has been known to fake it, for the sake of giving tourists something closer to a real experience. The reality of such an experience is certainly open to question, though, as the steam created by running regular water through the evaporator does not have that evocative perfume of maple sap that invades your clothing and your nostrils for days. And the notion of boiling at a time of year outside of regular sugaring can undermine some of the realities of sugaring's seasonality. But, at least for this sugarmaker, the power of the experience trumps those considerations. He boiled *something* to put on a show, because the show has such impact for visitors, and that impact helps create the narrative that he talks about.

The show becomes part of the tourists' narrative of acquisition, while the story this sugarmaker tells is one of syrup production, even if the story is a little fudged by boiling water instead of sap. The show and the narrative help turn syrup into dollars, "It is suggested that tourists cultivate meaning attached to objects, service and experience at the level of exchange, not at the level of production" (Cleave 2013, 159). The visitor seeing the boil, regardless of *what* is being boiled, is more likely to translate the experience of the sugarhouse in action into the purchase of some syrup, thereby negotiating the meaning at the level of exchange. The line is admittedly blurry in this instance, as the level of production and the level of exchange are close to one another. Indeed, that is one of the charms of maple. Its production is easily accessible to the consumer because it takes place in and among people and their everyday lives, as opposed to having been created in a factory in some nameless industrial estate. There is something powerful about being able to watch a product being made, and knowing the maker. Anonymity is not an option in a sugarhouse, whereas a factory is predicated on excluding the public and forces anonymity between maker and consumer, creating a Marxian "fantastic form of relation" (Heilbroner 1996, 166) between a consumer and the item they consume. By abstracting a product from its means of production, the commodity becomes a thing unto itself, without a sense of being connected to the people who made it. This analysis ignores that the people working in the factories on the industrial estates are, in fact, people living everyday lives as well, but the physical proximity of production and product available for exchange conveys an access and intimacy of meaning that often translates into a visitor buying some syrup. The product is not fantastical or mystical; indeed it is very much the known-ness of the process that makes maple syrup appealing as a consumer product. Knowing the process by seeing it unfold increases the exchange value of a bottle of syrup. An economic meaning is grafted onto the experience of visiting the sugarhouse the moment that happens.

Both narratives, of maple production and maple acquisition, have played a role in the making of syrup's exchange value. The story of the red-checked coat, horse, and bucket has become commodified itself, as is made clear by how standardized that story has become on the containers. The story of the sugarhouse visit is made more available to the consumer and potential consumer by shaping the sugarhouse to meet the consumer where they are, in this case literally, by placing the house on the roadside. The experience becomes both the performance and the source of authenticity (Kirshenblatt-Gimblett 1998). The story sells because there is a mystique behind the syrup's production, even for those who might be expected to be in the know: "Yeah, it's surprising how many people we get during maple season are Vermonters or from New Hampshire, Massachusetts, that really don't get it, don't understand the process, don't understand the different grades, you know, what makes the different grades" (interview, June 9, 2011). Having the sugarhouse immediately available to the consumer allows her or him to explore sugaring and gain a little knowledge in addition to a little syrup. Because there is an unknown there, learning about the production process makes the narrative of acquisition more satisfying to the consumer. As much as a factory can be anonymous, the story of making can be opaque, but in a sugarhouse neither is the case. A sugarhouse at the bottom of the hill, far from the road, will not provide that part of the story, but one that has been dragged right up next to the road can, becoming a commodified version of "living history" that visitors can access (Dicks 2003. 122).

The commodification of all the different narratives moves the price from use value to exchange value, based on the desire of the customer to buy not just syrup, but *Vermont* syrup. The story about the sugarhouse perched at the top of the hill by the road becomes more meaningful when the sugarmaker telling it explains that his customer base is largely tourists driving up into Vermont from the south, Connecticut and Massachusetts. They are outsiders stopping by his place to get some syrup on their way to see fall colors or to ski. The primary goal of his customers is to get a little

Vermont, not to get syrup. They are leaving their home to visit Vermont. Buying some maple on the way fits right into the plan. Vermont trades itself on being a clean, green, and serene place, with a lifestyle that is rooted in tradition and authenticity, and the state is conscious of, and protective of, those meanings: "You look at the Vermont special food industry today, people just look at Vermont as being, right or wrong, something solid, something genuine. It's amazing how many companies from outside the state try to come in here, want to produce something one way or another, be able to utilize the name 'Vermont,' and it's a big discussion in the specialty food industry" (interview, June 7, 2010). The economic meaning of the state's name is protected by those who oversee the specialty food industry because they know that the name carries along other meanings, meanings of "something solid, something genuine."

"Genuine" in this context is synonymous with authentic, and authenticity is part of what makes Vermont and maple a commodity. Authenticity is, of course, a slippery concept in the social sciences, as explored by Regina Bendix (1997) and Nelson Graburn (1983). When people drive into Vermont to take a piece of it home, they want something authentically, genuinely Vermonty, and that means clean and green. The name of the place serves as a container for that cleanliness and greenness, so to bear the name Vermont on the bottle implies an authentic version of the state—clean and green. Because Vermonters, and sugarmakers in particular, have a vested interest in protecting that bridge of authenticity between the place-name and the sense of clean and green, quite a bit of attention is placed in keeping the name unsullied by inauthenticity. Many sugarmakers talked with me about the necessity of keeping maple, and maple's reputation, protected because of the economic importance of maple to the state. Hearing about this kind of economic protectionism put me in mind of one of some earlier fieldwork I had done in an island group just north of mainland Scotland:

> Some years ago, there was a guy [who] had requested financial assistance from the Islands Council [the local governmental authority] to help to start another jewelry industry, and he was going to call it what was it . . . 'something-something Orkney Jewelry,' almost suggesting it was exclusively his prerogative, this 'Orkney Jewelry.' He would get the grant only if he changed its name because he had just settled here a few months, and he tried to get the exclusive name 'Orkney Jewelry.' [. . .  The Council] couldn't actually stop him doing the name, but they could give him no assistance, and clearly it was quite crucial for the start of his business, this assistance. So, he had the choice, either change the name or do without assistance. (Lange 2007, 249–50).

In both cases, Orkney and Vermont, there is a protectionist attitude on the part of authorities to the place's name. It is interesting to note also that in both interviews, the speaker makes known that the entity claiming the name is in some measure an outsider. In the case of Orkney, it is a man who had only lived in the islands for a few months, while in Vermont, it is companies coming into the state from outside. There is something about using the state's name to sell a product that raises flags. The flags are not about the commodification of the name, but about the name being applied authentically—either by someone with a properly authentic claim to it, or by what is understood as a proper, authentic version of the place. As one person put it, "The connection of Vermont to maple really works extremely well, and there's a heritage of Vermont supporting maple, and the purity and authenticity of the product, and the quality of the product" (interview, June 13, 2011). Here, the speaker is extolling Vermont's connection to maple, but the justifications being made are interesting. Why is the state's claim to maple valid? Part of the justification is Vermont's history of supporting and protecting maple, which aligns nicely with the narrative of heritage meanings, but also with the purity and authenticity *of the product*, the quality *of the product*. The implication is that Vermont does maple right, and that it has done so for a long, long time. The authenticity, heritage, purity, and so on, that are parts of Vermont's identity are here being given explicit economic meaning by being attached to the product of maple syrup. This speaker takes the discussion that connects the state's reputation to maple a step or two further. The purity is not a thing of Vermont that gets transferred to the syrup—it is a quality of the syrup itself. Vermont and maple become almost interchangeable in this construction, and the tropes of authenticity, heritage, and so forth are just as easily applied to the state as a place as they are to the syrup as a product, a sellable commodity.

A sense of authenticity adds value to the commodity of maple, and it raises the exchange value significantly because people want to buy into (and then literally buy) the story of the old-timer boiling sap that he collected from buckets and dumped into a barrel on his horse-drawn sledge before hauling it to the sugarhouse. Earlier, I discussed how sugarmakers commodified their own identity and put it into the bottle right along with the syrup. That process only works economically if someone is willing to buy their syrup mixed with a story. That's where authenticity comes into play. Visitors to the state want something that is authentically Vermonty, and maple has been positioned not just as authentically Vermonty, but as paradigmatically Vermont. In this way, the narrative of maple becomes part of the commodification process of maple. Even beyond that, though, the narrative itself becomes commodified. The previous standardization of the tropes that make the narrative is stunning, though as Vermont is reacting to the widening marketplace, more individualization is entering into the system, and the tropes that are becoming the new standard are telling a slightly different story. In the older (but still widely used) story, a man in a red-checked coat is drawing syrup to the sugarhouse nestled deep in a woods, boiling over a wood fire, and using buckets and a horse team. In the newer narrative, maple syrup comes from a comparatively undifferentiated place of trees and mountains, with nature and calm cleanliness at the fore.

In a way, the Marxian fantastical relation discussed earlier becomes more possible with this shift in the marketing. The individual in the red-checked coat (generic form of an individual that it is), who stood in for the direct human relation that a consumer assumed themselves to have with the sugarmaker when buying a quart of syrup, is now replaced with an abstracted idea of maple production as coming from a standardized place of mountains and trees. The new labeling norms, as they take more hold in the constantly evolving Vermont maple industry, are reacting to the economic realities of trying to sell syrup in more distant and more varied markets. The lens of economics continues to be useful in understanding how the shifts in marketing are inclusive of, and dependent on, shifts in narrative construction of the identities of the syrup, the people and places that make it, and of Vermont itself.

Maple has many different economic meanings. It is a commodity in the most basic sense of the word, and it gets commoditized in many different ways, along all parts of its process. The very fact that the word "maple" describes both a product (or, more accurately, a set of products) and a process indicates how many different economic meanings can be made with maple. Because sugaring has long been an activity with economic aspects, making economic meanings with it has been a norm far into the past. Most important here is the intense interactions among narrative, identity, and economic meanings. Narrative and identity have been the province of folklore for a very, very long time, while economics is traditionally not seen as part of folklore's wheelhouse. As this chapter indicates, though, economics is simply a set of meanings. As such, economics is negotiated on a cultural level, through narratives and meaning-making processes. As the example of maple in Vermont demonstrates, folklore and economics aren't really separate categories in the first place.

## NOTES

My interviewees are cited by their interview date, in order to anonymize them.

1. The imagery is nearly always male. Female figures are not absent from maple containers, but they are very seldom depicted. On the infrequent occasions when they do appear, they are always in the company of men, usually in red-checked coats.

2. Such an interpretation relies on a very limited definition of technology, of course. To think of plastic tubing and vacuum systems as technology and buckets as not technology, or to put them on a spectrum from more technological to less technological, is a very chauvinistic and self-centered mindset. If Marshall McLuhan taught us nothing else, he showed us that technology is a thing with which people can make more or less meaning but is not usefully differentiated as more or less validly technological.

## REFERENCES

Basso, Keith. 1996. *Wisdom Sits in Places*. Albuquerque: University of New Mexico Press.
Bendix, Regina. 1997. *In Search of Authenticity*. Madison: University of Wisconsin Press.
Cleave, Paul. 2013. "Sugar in Tourism: 'Wrapped in Devonshire Sunshine.'" In *Sugar Heritage and Tourism in Transition*, ed. Lee Jolliffe. Toronto: Channel View Publications.
Dicks, Bella. 2003. *Culture on Display: The Production of Contemporary Visitability*. Maidenhead, England: Open University Press.
Farrell, Michael. 2013. *The Sugarmaker's Companion: An Integrated Approach to Producing Syrup from Maple, Birch, and Walnut Trees*. White River Junction, VT: Chelsea Green Publishing.
Graburn, Nelson. 1983. "The Anthropology of Tourism." *Annals of Tourism Research* 10 (1): 9–33.
Heilbroner, Robert. 1996. *Teachings from the Worldly Philosophy*. New York: Norton.
Johnston, Josée, and Shyon Baumann. 2010. *Foodies: Democracy and Distinction in the Gourmet Food Landscape*. New York: Routledge.
Kirshenblatt-Gimblett, Barbara. 1998. *Destination Culture: Tourism, Museums, and Heritage*. Berkeley: University of California Press.
Lange, Michael A. 2007. *The Norwegian Scots*. Lampeter, Wales: Edwin Mellen Press.
Lange, Michael A. 2012. "Sweet Bedfellows: Continuity, Change, and Terroir in Maple Syrup." *Digest* 1 (1) (Fall). http://digest.champlain.edu/vol1/article1_3.html.
Lange, Michael A. 2017. *Meanings of Maple*. Fayetteville: University of Arkansas Press.
Pollan, Michael. 2006. *The Omnivore's Dilemma*. New York: Penguin Press.
Ritzer, George, and Anya Galli. 2013. "Food and Drink: The Declining Importance of Cultural Context?" In *Food and Drink: The Cultural Context*, ed. Donald Sloan. Oxford: Goodfellow Publishers.
Thomas, Matthew, Kelly Jackson, and Marcus Guthrie. 1999. *An Archaeological Overview of Native American Maple Sugaring and Historic Sugarbushes of the Lac du Flambeau Band of Lake Superior Chippewa Indians*. State Historical Society of Wisconsin, Lad du Flambeau Tribal Historic Preservation Office, and George W. Brown Jr. Ojibwe Museum and Cultural Center. Report for Planning Grant #55-98-13157-2.
Trubek, Amy. 2008. *The Taste of Place*. Berkeley: University of California Press.
*VTDigger*. 2011. "Welch Takes Issue with Log Cabin's 'all natural syrup.'" March 19. Accessed June 25, 2018. https://vtdigger.org/2011/03/20/welch-takes-issue-with-log-cabins-all-natural-syrup/.

# 5

# Where the Creel Boats Go
*The Politics of Sustainable Fisheries in a Small Orkney Community*

Christofer Johnson

I can see the big draggers have stirred up the bay
Leaving lobster traps smashed on the bottom
Can they think it don't pay to respect the old ways
That Make and Break men have not forgotten?
        —Stan Rogers, "Make and Break Harbor"

IT IS HARDLY AN ORIGINAL ARGUMENT that the current state of the world's commercial fisheries is dire. One need look no further than the tragic collapse of the herring and cod fisheries during the latter portion of the last century to see the wide-ranging impact of fishery collapse. There are devastating immediate consequences as jobs are eliminated, families uprooted, and an entire traditional way of life jeopardized. Further, the ecological ramifications reach far into the future, wreaking untold havoc for years to come. Needless to say, ecosystems are delicate constructions, and the removal or acute reduction of an entire species, or multiple species, carries the risk of a series of cascading, catastrophic ecological events.

    John Briggs defines a state of fishery collapse as meaning "the population has become so low that the species no longer plays an effective role in the ecosystem" (2008, 180). In the case of some species, there is some small hope of recovery should harvests be limited and carefully managed, but in others it is already too late to take reparative action. As Briggs notes, "the populations of all the noted Atlantic species [of commercially fished populations] are so low that they cannot or should not be harvested and it may not be possible for them to recover their former abundance in the foreseeable future" (182). By the year 2048, he states, trends observed in the erosion of marine biodiversity in the North Atlantic "predict the global collapse of all currently fished taxa" (180).

With that being said, total cessation of commercial fishing is neither economically nor politically viable. A sustainable middle ground is needed—an approach that balances the needs of the fishing industry, government regulatory requirements, and the people who live and work in small fishing communities. Such an approach would need to not only be effective at ensuring resource conservation, but would need to balance conservation efforts with a relatively low participation threshold. It must be both environmentally and commercially friendly, operating at low or no cost to either the industry or the taxpayer and able to produce marked and measurable results.

In the Orkney Islands such an initiative has taken the form of a self-sustaining lobster hatchery meant to help mitigate the impact of lobster fishing on the local ecology. This hatchery serves the dual purpose of helping to maintain the fishery health by making real annual contributions to the juvenile breeding lobster population, as well as serving as a bulwark against outside forces placing increasing pressure on small-scale commercial fishers. By taking firm action to maintain the health of the lobster fishery, Orcadians reliant upon the small-scale fishing trade, directly and indirectly, help to support the continued viability of small-scale commercial fishing as a way of life. This activity, in turn, helps to ensure that a major structuring force in the island community remains intact and communities remain stable, if only for a little while longer. The hatchery is, in short, a resilient response to the encroaching forces of globalization.

The origin of the lobster Hatchery project in Orkney is interesting for a number of reasons—not least because it evolved out of a grassroots approach to sustainability. Amid an uncertain economic future as climate change and depleting oil stocks threaten the economic and social stability of the Orkney and Shetland Islands, a small group of local fishers from the villages of Holm and St. Margaret's Hope began a do-it-yourself project aimed at making small-scale commercial lobster fishing viable in the long term. Although initially quite small, the Lamb Holm Lobster Hatchery project quickly grew from an amateur operation into a sophisticated union of the public and private sectors, striking a delicate balance between the health of the environment and profit. The Hatchery project sought to occupy the middle ground of long-term sustainability for both the health of the European lobster fishery and the local fishing industry by providing a boost to the local lobster population, however indirectly. The Hatchery has emerged as a powerful institution largely through this unprecedented state of cooperation among traditionally opposing parties and gains a great deal of significance in the way that it combines the strengths and contributions of each interest group into an institution that transcends the sum of its parts.

In the view of local fishers, as well as other members of the Orcadian community, the Lamb Holm Lobster Hatchery is valuable in that it allows Orkney fishers to take a more direct and official kind of ownership of the process of fisheries management. The role of the hatchery is not merely to create a sustainable model for the industry, but also to grant the fishers themselves a sense of control. For one of my informants, Willie, this role takes the form of a symbolic stand against globalization and the elimination of traditional small-scale commercial fishing in the face of rampant corporatization. The hatchery represents a grassroots-led move toward wresting control from outside, disconnected institutions and relocating power where it belongs—in the hands of those whose lives are intimately connected with Orkney's natural resources. For John, another informant, it is a physical manifestation of Orcadian commonsense attitudes. Eminently practical, he cites the unpredictability of oil prices and declining overall barrels produced as evidence that Orkney must take a more active role in cultivating and preserving its other natural resources. Perhaps nothing can be done about the Shetland oil reserves, but certainly fishers and the local community can take steps to preserve small-scale commercial fishing as a way of life and a viable occupational culture.

Although initially a primitive grassroots operation, the Lamb Holm Lobster Hatchery quickly gained traction, and from 1995 through 2005 produced steadily increasing crops of juvenile lobsters to be released back into the Orkney lobster fishery. After the hatchery proved itself to be a viable approach to sustainable practice, its funding and operations were taken over by the Orkney Council and the local UK Inshore Fisheries governing body (under the name "Orkney Sustainable Fisheries") in 2006 (Orkney Islands Council, Economic Review 2012). The council moved to increase production from the respectable 6,000 juveniles released in 2006 to current levels of approximately 100,000 specimens each season (Orkney Lobster Hatchery 2015).

This "intense connectedness between plants and supply, coupled with processors' personal links with their communities, translates into great social familiarity between fishers and buyers" (Apostle and Barrett 1992c, 262). The recognition of the importance of the hatchery on the part of the industry is what is truly remarkable here, as is the largely successful way in which these diverse interests have come together to make huge inroads in sustainable management and fishing practices (Orkney Sustainable Fisheries

2015). The success of this partnership, I suspect, is also partially responsible for other sustainable measures the Orkney Council is currently involved in—most notably an attempt to harvest Orkney's ample wave-energy in a cost-effective way.

In this circular, self-contained system a new balance emerges. Lobster fishing is allowed to continue in a profitable way for small-scale commercial fishers, helping to keep the interference of large corporations in the commercial lobster fishing trade to a minimum, while also ensuring a steady and reliable revenue stream for First Purchaser and industry partners into the foreseeable future. Additionally, the hatchery, the site of sustainable practice, becomes self-sustaining through revenue generated by lobster sales. In keeping the Orkney Lobster Fishery healthy and stable, small-scale commercial fishing is able to remain economically viable, ensuring continued industry profits, leading to continued industry and government investment, leading to expanded juvenile crops, and back around to a healthy and stable fishery. The system is destined to eventually reach a point of maximum growth, but that is almost immaterial. What is important here is preservation and continuation in a way that is both environmentally and commercially friendly, allowing for traditional practice to continue in a way that is largely compatible with a globalized world itself highly skeptical of the local and the traditional.

What the hatchery represents is an emergent cultural hybrid form, a combination of the traditional with the eminently modern. It is a breakthrough of traditional knowledge and interests into the global realities of commercial fishing and capitalism. It is a manifestation of an isolated island community's resilient response to ever-encroaching modernity and representative of an effort to keep a traditional way of life viable in an ever-more-uncertain world. On the one hand, the drive to protect the small-scale commercial fishing industry, and by extension small-scale commercial fishers themselves, comes from a place we might easily identify as "traditional." This is the conservative drive to keep things the same, to achieve a state of social and economic stability that never veers too far right or left of center. As it once was, so shall it ever be. It is a world that is contained, easily (at least on the surface) delineated by boundaries, and relatively impermeable.

The friendly Orcadian attitude toward sustainable practices is not unique in the North Atlantic: the Scandinavian countries have tried their hands at sustainable initiatives for decades; however it seldom takes such an involved form. One notable exception is in the case of the US state of Maine, where coastal fishing communities have been involved in sustainable practices since at least the late 1980s (Acheson 1988, 136). Part of this drive is philosophical, and part is practical—that is, fishers throughout the North Atlantic tend to both view their work in agrarian terms and also see the practical benefits of resource conservation. As James Acheson argues, "where fishermen exercise control of territories, they act to conserve the resource" (qtd. in Durrenberger and Palsson 1987, 514).

One of the ways that fishermen exert control over territory is through controlling access—determining who is allowed to participate in the industry and who is ultimately excluded. Paul Durrenberger and Gisli Palsson, citing James Acheson's work with Maine Lobstermen (broadly), note that on the American side of the North Atlantic the practice of perimeter defense strategies often takes the form of an active move to restrict access by both legal and illegal means. "If the people involved can organize for territorial defense, they can keep others out, but if they cannot or do not, then they lose the area to others" (Durrenberger and Palsson 1987, 510). Acheson himself notes that the reason that Maine's territories continue to be fished primarily by small-scale, traditional operators is their willingness to stake out and defend their traditional fishing territories. "Men fishing the island areas have been willing to mount a spirited defense of their areas, despite the smaller number of gang members. It is common knowledge that anyone who attempts to fish in the area around Monhegan, Green Island, or Criehaven will meet with coordinated resistance from the island men" (Acheson 1988, 82).

In the case of Orkney, the local Inshore Fisheries agency simply restricts licenses to British fishers (with a very few exceptions) with boats registered in Orkney. There are also more informal social controls that fishermen can exercise to control access. Access to social networks in the home community and among other fishermen, denial of important local fishing knowledge to new fishermen from outside the community, informal access to local fish purchasers, hostility to those not from traditional fishing families, and even the always effective "shunning" are effective social controls on fisheries access.

Stevie Hutchinson spoke to me at length about the challenges he faced upon entering the crab and lobster fishing world. What began as friendly competition eventually developed into open hostility after Stevie purchased a catamaran-style fishing boat for running creel pots. This broke a social taboo, and to many of the other fishermen seemed to signal that Stevie was flaunting his wealth and difference—cardinal sins in Orcadian culture. As a result, the other fishermen docking at Tingwall Pier moved to socially isolate him, refusing to speak to him when they crossed paths and allowing the small community rumor mill to do its work. Legally he was free to fish and sell his catch, but social isolation can take its toll. After the catamaran sprang a leak after only around two years in service and went down, Stevie decided to cash it in and left the fishing trade (Hutchinson 2017).

That said, in both Maine and Orkney (and I would suspect in most other North Sea fisheries), when legal options aimed at restricting access are exhausted, illegal action may also be taken. This can take the form of intimidation, destruction of tackle, refusal to purchase catches, and other action aimed at driving the offending party from the fishery. Several of my informants were more than willing to talk about sabotaged gear, damaged hulls, and other questionable strategies—always, of course, with the recorder turned off.

As Acheson hints in his descriptions of nucleated and perimeter defense models, and as Durrenberger and Palsson elaborate upon, much of the world of the fishery is predicated upon a sense of ownership (be it communal or bounded in some way). The ownership I speak of here is, of course, twofold—physical and what I will call, for lack of a better phrase, spiritual. First there is the physical and material ownership of the fishery and fish stocks. By practice and force of tradition, in some cases stretching back for hundreds of years, many of the fishers I spoke to make a claim to not only responsibility for fish stocks, and therefore to traditional and small-scale commercial fishing as an occupational culture and a way of life, but also to the right of harvest—the right of the one who has sown the seeds to reap the grain. This type of ownership shares much with the notion of the Commons, or of a collective ownership of resources. Access is controlled in several ways, among them simple secrecy, or not making public the knowledge necessary to successfully fish for a given stock in a given location (Durrenberger and Palsson 1987, 510).

The second type of ownership I speak of is spiritual. Its power lies in a deep psychosocial connection to the land, the sea, and all of Orkney's natural resources. It is a different kind of ownership, one that eschews logical connection in favor of emotional and psychological pull. Spiritual ownership is situated firmly within the realm of identity, where people begin to form notions of themselves through the nature of the work they perform. For the fishers I spoke to, a deep sense of connectedness to the ocean and to fishing as a way of life underlay many of our conversations. I of course do not mean to say that fishers spoke to me of fishing with any kind of undue reverence, but rather that there was always an acknowledgment, stated or unstated, that hard work and toil in some way formed the basis for individual identity. This was especially true of some of the older fishers I spoke to, including a semiretired man by the name of Dennis.

At the time of my initial fieldwork, Dennis was eighty-three and had spent more than sixty years of his life reliant upon the ocean for his work in some way or another. "As a young man I worked the ferries, the boat called Hamnavoe tha' goes between Thurso and Stromness. She was known by a different name then, not the bloody Hamnavoe. She was the 'Rolly Polly Ola'" (Dennis 2014). Later in life he began fishing on the side, taking work as a deckhand with friends and acquaintances and pitching in in an as-needed capacity. He currently works with a man named Magnus out of Herston, a small enclave of English retirees from the mainland.

Of all of my informants, it was Dennis who invoked blood imagery most often in conversation as a way of describing his connection to Orkney and her natural resources. It is in the blood, it gets in your blood, it seeps into your blood, it was in my father's blood—all of these are gestures at a powerful sense of connection and almost hereditary ownership that is difficult to adequately put into words. It is an assertion of ownership by spiritual and psychological connection—a way of saying that one can only take part in the "ownership" of natural resources by developing a deeply personal connection to them, often a connection rooted in how one conceptualizes one's self as a person. This, too, is a way of managing exclusivity, especially as one can only develop such a bond through close personal contact and over many years.

What the case of Orkney represents is a community resiliency response. Presented with the mandate to globalize—to obey limits on catch sizes and restrictions on species landings, to move away from subsistence practices, and to enter into the global capitalist extraction mechanism—the community has chosen not to resist, but to endure. Subsistence fishing may be at an end, but small-scale commercial fishing operations may be still be maintained and nurtured, leaving more power in local hands and keeping corporate influence at arm's length. Fishers may be forced to participate in the global capitalist market, but there is no reason that fishing needs to be structured in a way that leads to the collapse of fish stocks. Rather, a balance may be struck that both takes the needs of industry into consideration and also ensures that small-scale commercial fishing may remain a viable industry well into the future. By blending traditional forms with the drives of the increasingly global, it is possible to retain some degree of local agency.

Dorothy Noyes notes in "Compromised Concepts in Rising Waters" that "fostering resilience has become a central concern of infrastructural and organizational design as well as of the new-style environmentalism, which given the massive pushback against state regulation, is focusing on communal self-organization and response (drawing on entrepreneurial innovations as resources)" (2016, 12–13). This is precisely the response that has taken root in Orkney's Lamb Holm Lobster Hatchery. Where state regulation in the Nordic and Mediterranean fisheries has failed spectacularly, the local has reasserted itself in Orkney as the rightful steward of natural resources—responding to the outside world's demand for product through self-organization and microsteps in service of community endurance. The demands of global capitalism cannot be ignored, but they can be moderated, and, through self-organization and careful planning, the damage can be mitigated.

Resilience theory, Noyes notes, "posits that disturbance is inevitable" and that "gradual phase shift is likely to transform even the most resilient systems into new configurations" (2016, 12). Fishing as a way of life has persisted in the Orkney Islands for millennia, with evidence from Neolithic sites throughout the islands pointing toward fishing activity going back at least 6,000 years. Although practices have changed throughout the centuries, as subsistence practice evolved to meet the demands of regional, and later national and international, markets, fishing as an occupational culture and a structuring force in island life has remained a constant. By changing the emphasis from resource exploitation to long-term sustainability, Orcadian fishers are merely adapting otherwise traditional practices into a new configuration to meet new demands.

That is not to say that Orkney's specific model is applicable, practical, or even desirable in other contexts. The first major issue that arises when implementing sustainable practices is overcoming cost and overhead. Noyes argues that sustainability is often viewed with skepticism by the business world because "in the short term, it's too expensive. In the long term, it's too cheap. By contrast, there is much money to be made in managing the problems we cannot be bothered to fix" (2016, 10). Acheson noted these same kinds of skeptical attitudes in Maine in the 1980s, stating, "Certainly Maine fishermen distrust the government and do not want massive intervention in their affairs. But as economic problems in the industry appear to worsen, there is a growing recognition that something must be done and that only the government can do it" (Acheson 1988, 136). Much resistance was sidestepped in Orkney because of the close involvement of the local Council and UK Inshore Fisheries governing body, but at other times, in other places, the issue looms large.

The second major obstacle is the prevalence of national fisheries governing bodies that may not be quite as sensitive to local ecological needs as those connected more directly to the specific demands of a locale. Norway, for example, has been largely unsuccessful in managing their fish stocks because overbroad national policy, though designed with sustainability as the end goal and oriented correctly in spirit, has been clunky in practice. The overabundance of regulation, designed to promote fishery health, has exponentially increased operating costs (McDonald and Kucera 2007, 289)—pushing small-scale commercial operators out of business and making it only economically viable for large-scale, vertically integrated corporate actors to operate in the Nordic fisheries (Durrenberger and Palsson 1987, 514). These large-scale commercial entities often operate at a distance from the traditional site of fishing occupational practice and as a result tend to be less sensitive to the needs of the local specific (ecological and cultural).

The third major challenge to promoting a sustainability program in the vein of the lobster hatchery is the community dynamics on the ground. This situation in Orkney is unique in the global industrialized world, as small-scale commercial fishing forms the backbone of not only economic activity but also community structure. Nearly all local businesses are tied to small-scale commercial fishing in some way, with a few specific exceptions centered on catering to tourists and the oil industry. As such, the environment is ripe for cooperative projects such as the hatchery that promote fishery health and make it possible for small-scale commercial fishing to remain economically viable in the long term.

For Orcadians tied to the fishing industry, the hatchery represents an assertion of this drive to resiliency—responsibility and deep personal connectedness to the land and the tradition of small-scale fishing. One of my informants, a man by the name of Willie, describes his support for the hatchery in this way. "It's a way of giving back a little, you know? You take from the sea—some lobster, some crab, a fish or two—but you don't ever really give anything back. The hatchery does that, and it's all the better it doesn't cost anything" (Willie 2014). William Kittredge, in his essay "Owning It All," describes views such as Willie's as "personal mythologies," which are used to define us both as individuals and as smaller actors within a larger community. "The majority of agricultural people," he argues, "if you press them hard enough, even though most of them despise sentimental abstractions, will admit they are trying to create a good place and to live as part of that goodness, in the kind of connection which with fine reason we call *rootedness*" (2001, 148).

Although Kittredge waxes poetic here, he is nevertheless not far from the mark. I would complicate his generalization of "agricultural people," however, and argue that many would indeed willingly make use of "sentimental abstraction" given the correct social context. They might not necessarily equate the goals of raising a family in a safe, wholesome community with a quality tied directly to land or work, but the connections still exist. It is not uncommon to hear from agricultural workers that they are seeking a better way of life, a simpler way of life, a closer relationship with their families, the community, or the land. It is likewise not unusual to hear work discussed as being hard but good for the soul in some way that defies conventional explanation. Willie, for example, frequently spoke about his connection to the land and its ability to shape those who dwell within it. An Orkney man, he asserts, is rooted in the good land, fed by the fickle sea, and shaped by the wild winds. These are certainly sentimental abstractions, and though any given individual interviewed may have slightly varying views on any portion of the above, the same essential qualities are being gestured at. As Kittredge notes, we are all reaching for some kind of goodness and seeking to take part in that goodness ourselves.

That is not to say that all perspectives on identity must necessarily align. It is not quite as simple as saying, "we are fishers because we have always been fishers," but rather something a bit more nuanced. Regardless of whom I interviewed in the Orkney Islands, the same theme seemed to crop up. As Bob Gibbon, another of my informants, puts it: "Me personally, I work for the government. In the Agricultural Department. Now, in terms of what I do, I wouldn't really define that as being me. I wouldn't introduce myself and say, 'Hello, I'm a civil servant.' I would say 'Hello, I'm a musician,' or, 'hello, I'm a farmer.' Or 'Hello, I'm a dad.' That's the three main things I do outside of work, and to be honest they take a much higher priority in defining who I am" (Gibbon 2014). Often to be found in flannel, jeans, and work boots, Bob fits the very portrait of a rural agricultural worker. When he is not found playing the fiddle at Stromness and Kirkwall pubs, Bob works his own land with his wife, Dr. Sarah-Jane Gibbon, and serves part time as an agricultural officer for the Orkney Council. His personal philosophy is that someone's identity should be located in her or his hobbies—the things one chooses to do, rather than the work that one must do. Social identity, in Gibbon's view, is rooted in process and action—performance within the context of the community (Bauman 1971, 33–34).

Adding a further dimension to this mix is the unique historical situation of the islands. Although the larger towns of Kirkwall and Stromness are relatively modern (Kirkwall more so than Stromness), much of the archipelago did not receive electricity until the latter half of the twentieth century. Sarah-Jane Gibbon, a professor of archaeology at the local Orkney College and lifetime resident of the Orkney mainland, argues that understanding this particular moment in history is central to understanding the trajectory of Orkney's culture into the contemporary period (Gibbon

2014). Being so isolated, and being so insular (in the most literal way possible) helped to ingrain traditional forms as a valuable source of stability well into the present day. If Orkney's culture is, as Bob Gibbon asserts, "not a culture of sittin' around watchin' tele" (Gibbon 2014), a culture mired in the loneliness, isolation, and disconnectedness of a modern teleconnected world, then it must follow that, in his view, that Orcadian culture is rooted in action and community.

Willie and Bob, like the agrarians Kittredge is concerned with, envision themselves as honest workers, deeply connected (*rooted*) to the land and the sea.

> Many of us like to imagine ourselves as honest yeomen who sweat and work in the woods or the mines or the fields for a living. And many of us are. We live in a real family, a work-centered society, and we like to see ourselves as people with the good luck and sense to live in a place where some vestige of the natural world still exists in working order. Many of us hold that natural world as sacred to some degree, just as it is in our myth. Lately, more and more of us are coming to understand our society . . . as an exploited colony, threatened by greedy outsiders who want to take our sacred place away from us, or at least to strip and degrade it. (Kittredge 2001, 153)

It is important to note here that Willie considers himself to be, quintessentially, a fisherman. His father, Magnus the Elder, was a fisherman. His brother, Magnus Junior, is a fisherman, and he is a fisherman. As far back as anyone in his family can remember, they have always been farmers and fishers, working to eke a living out of Orkney's wind-blasted coast. "My dad fished and my brother fishes. My granddad fished, and his dad fished, too" (Willie 2014). His family has also traditionally worked the land, bringing up sheep, cattle, and oats. This would make Willie a fairly prototypical example of a North Atlantic fisherman.

All of this is a roundabout way of saying that Willie is a man who sees himself as closely connected to the land and to the sea and who tends to be skeptical of outsiders who may not share that connection. It is also to illustrate how heavily invested he is in the continued viability of the fishing industry both in terms of the economic opportunities it provides and the vital role it plays in shaping his own identity. Within this context, the lobster hatchery and other sustainable projects perhaps represent a chance to "do" something about the sad state of the world's fisheries—to make some kind of tangible contribution to the continued health of fisheries and of small-scale commercial fishing as an occupation.

Although certainly taking more from the ocean than "some lobster, some crab, [and] a fish or two," Willie's approach to sustainability is nevertheless informed through this worldview. In a very powerful, almost spiritual way he sees his life and the life of the fishery as being deeply interconnected. Willie sees himself, more or less, as a responsible conservator of the sea and its resources. The lobster fishery, to his mind in a very real way, belongs to him—and he to it.

In viewing himself as being somehow connected to the land, the sea, and its resources in an almost mystical way, giving back and working to preserve that resource becomes not an onerous task, but an act of reciprocity. It is a way of symbolically giving back, recognizing the importance of the natural world in a gesture of almost-worship. By supporting sustainable initiatives such as the hatchery, Willie is able to reify his connection to the environment.

When I asked Willie if and how the hatchery has impacted his work, the answer I received is that, at least to his mind, it hasn't. Catches, he says, are still relatively small and if anything feel like they are shrinking. In real numbers, on our two trips out to sea Willie pulled in around 250 pounds of lobster and 300 pounds of brown crab each trip. Asking how representative this was, I was told that it was low, but normal for the summer. The hatchery, then, might be said to hold more of a symbolic power for Willie than anything else—it is a representative step in the right direction and has the affective power to appeal to Willie's sense of identity.

I use "symbolic power" here to highlight the way that Willie views the hatchery. Even if the hatchery seems to have no direct impact on his daily life, Willie nevertheless recognizes its importance to the community in standing against the "wrong" kind of fisheries management. Support for the hatchery encapsulates more than a desire to be more sustainable, or to better manage fish stocks like one would a crop or a herd on land. It speaks to a desire to do things the right way, a desire to at least do something in the face of a shifting global climate—both political and ecological—and the very real possibility that small-scale commercial fishing, as with other forms of traditional and household industry, could very well be in its winter years. It is about laying claim to a particular kind of narrative, that of the responsible steward who stands in contrast to that of ravager, pillager, and exploiter—those who would use fish stocks with wild abandon in pursuit of ever-greater profit and pay little heed to the long-term viability of the fishery as a whole.

Of course beyond this, one of the most important things for Willie is that the hatchery is essentially self-funding. By instituting a levy on each lobster sold through local merchants and earmarking these funds for the hatchery, the project becomes at least partially self-sustaining and allows for the council to visibly support an ecologically sustainable initiative without having to divert financial resources from elsewhere. It also imposes a minimal additional burden on the fishers themselves with clear and tangible results—in this case large crops of lobster reintroduced to the fishery each year.

Cost is important to Willie's operation because it is by its nature small-scale. Generally speaking, the largest costs to small-scale commercial fishers are linked to vessel size. Larger boats may lead to increased holding capacity, longer overall range, and options to diversify catch throughout the year, but they also lead to increased maintenance costs and overhead. Because of this, "most vessels over 95 feet [tend to be] vertically integrated into the land-based operations of fish processors" and larger corporate operations (Apostle and Barrett 1992b, 162). Willie operates a forty-foot lobster boat, which, while above the average for the UK fleet, is still relatively small compared to the average fishing boat size across Europe (McGlade 2002, 364). Stephen Kasperski and Daniel Holland note that "smaller vessels (those less than 50 feet in length) tend to be less diversified than larger vessels," which limits a fisherman's ability to diversify their fishing revenues (2013, 2077). He is therefore limited to fishing for European lobster, European brown crab, and velvet crab with little room to seek other fish stocks.

His vessel is further served by a crew of only two: Willie and his deckhand, John. John is a young man in his early twenties and a resident of the village of St. Margaret's Hope. Although they work together to man the vessel, one gets the sense that Willie views himself as almost a paternal figure for John. In many ways, work on the boat is patterned on patriarchal and family structures, with John acting as the youth learning as much as he can from the older, more experienced Willie. Such patterns in employment have been noted in small fishing communities throughout the North Atlantic, with these community ties tending toward reproducing older, more traditional approaches to labor. This orientation furthers the goal of establishing close community ties to particular trades and allows workers such as John additional nonmonetary benefits, for instance, flexible hours, variable job tasks, and a personal stake in their work. These relationships also tend to be "non-hierarchical and fraternal. While not lacking in conflicts, they reflect long-standing personal and familial ties between owner-tradespeople and both the industry and other workers" (Apostle and Barrett 1992a, 27–28).

This tendency toward informal, nonhierarchical structures extends well beyond the microcosm of the fishing boat and reaches into the social systems within traditional fishing communities such as St. Margaret's Hope. Ayse Uskul contends that "members of farming and fishing communities, which emphasize harmonious social interdependence, [exhibit] greater holistic tendencies" (Uskul, Kitayama, and Nisbett 2008, 8552) than those in other communities, which prize independence. In other words, the emphasis is on "us" over "me." As I was told many times in the islands, when one lives on an island one learns to rely upon one's neighbors. Living too independently is impractical and provides no social protection for the lean years (which, after all, must inevitably come in any sustainable cycle).

Uskul further argues that "dominant forms of ecocultural activity of a community influence the degree of social interdependence of the community as a whole. All members of the community are, therefore, likely to be cognitively shaped regardless of whether they directly engage in the economic activities at issue" (Uskul, Kitayama, and Nisbett 2008, 8555). In communities such as these, the impulse toward pure independence in a classically Liberal sense is made impractical and the needs of the individual and the particular are in many ways made subject to the communal and the holistic. Interdependent social systems, such as those commonly found in traditional and small-scale commercial fishing communities, use "the holistic mode of thought because the individual must pay attention to a broad range of social cues. Attention to the social field also entails greater attention to the physical field" (8552).

Operating from the position that the primary form of economic activity in a small community tends to impact and shape social interactions on all levels, it is then not surprising that support for sustainable initiatives has achieved such a wide base of support. From this perspective, fish stocks are a community resource—a shared property and a shared responsibility. Taking the next step from government protectionist regulation to active, communal, personal efforts at conservation is then all but a given. What better way to support the larger communal good than to work together to preserve a shared heritage, a communal font of identity and economic stability.

If we were to envision commercial fishing on a continuum from small-scale to industrial in scope—or traditional to modern/globalized—Willie's operation would fall squarely on the traditional/small-scale side (Apostle and Barrett 1992a, 25). There is a certain advantage to the small scale. Apostle and Barrett note that often "fish prices bear no relationship to supply and demand," and instead exist on a sliding scale about a fixed mean (Apostle and Barrett 1992b, 153). Small-scale, local catches, such as "artisan" products, can be infused with additional value. When coupled with a close relationship between producers and merchants, this gives the fisher greater latitude to make individual decisions about catch size and the frequency of fishing trips.

Understanding this, it is then perhaps surprising to learn that John's perspective on the hatchery and on sustainability projects in general diverges from that of other Orkney fishers. "It's about keeping the tradition alive. Orcadians have always fished, and they always will" (John 2014). As a fisher, John resides on the opposite end of the spectrum from Willie. First and most important, John does not own his own boat, nor does he have to worry as much about the increasing overhead costs associated with fishing. Instead, he sails with Willie and approaches lobster and crab fishing as more of a job than a vocation. His interest is in bringing in a large enough catch to pay the bills and to ensure that Willie, his employer and partner, is able to stay solvent. It would be entirely accurate to say that at least at this stage in his career, John is not tied to the sea in the same way that Willie is and that fishing as an occupation is not as fundamental to his identity.

Strangely enough, however, it was John who first directed my attention to the hatchery project and its implications for the fishing trade in terms of long-term sustainability. For him it is not as much about giving back to the sea or taking a symbolic stance against global fisheries depletion, but rather making an effort to protect the natural environment and Orkney's natural resources: "The oil can't last forever, you know? What are we going to do when Shetland dries up and [the refinery on] Flotta shuts down?" (John 2014)

I feel it is important to note here that John is not particularly inclined to hop on to any ecological initiative for the sake of being sustainable. He is, for example, opposed wholeheartedly to what he sees as outside involvement in the form of EU Commercial Fisheries Policy (CFP). The EU CFP sets limits on catch sizes and regulates national catch apportionment according to the tenets of the Esbjerg Declaration of 1997. While not necessarily opposed to the overall goals of the Esbjerg Declaration, which defines the primary goals of North Sea Fisheries management to promote "sustainable, sound and healthy ecosystems, maintain biodiversity and ensure sustainable exploitation of the living resources in order to achieve economically viable fisheries" (McGlade 2002, 372), John nevertheless sees it as an extragovernmental overreach. Although John is well intentioned, I find problematic his argument that the CFP and other Europe-based approaches intrude unnecessarily into local and UK matters and have a generally negative impact on small communities and commercial fishing as a trade.

Presented in this way, with particular emphasis on local cooperation and the important role that the Orkney Fishermen's Society plays in drafting and implementing policy, sustainable approaches transform from outside interference into insider experience—it is regulation by fishers, for fishers, with the intent to preserve fishing as a way of life for years to come. Self-regulation and wide participation in this way allow for fishers to become personally invested in preserving fishery health, to take ownership of fish stocks and responsibility for proper management. In the words of Stewart Crichton, former head of the Orkney Fishermen's Society and current head of Orkney Sustainable fisheries, "Orkney Fishermen's Society takes the view that the marine environment is going to come under increased pressure from other potential users including marine energy, aquaculture, and marine protected areas—and that all these may have an impact on the traditional inshore fisheries of the area. By having industry-driven local science, we are better placed to make management decisions, decisions which could help secure the vital future of our industry" (Orkney Fishermen's Society 2016).

The way that the independent attitudes of Orcadian fishers collide with the interests of the Orkney community, Orkney Council, local merchants, and the wider fishing industry reveals the emergent qualities of the Lamb Holm Lobster Hatchery. Although initially and in many ways yet a cooperative project, the hatchery has begun to transcend the bounds of its constituent support structures, taking on a life and cultural force of its own. It is supported by industry, but not beholden to it. It is managed by government, but not shackled by it. It is constituted of local political and social expressions of power, and yet also constitutive of them. The hatchery has transcended the bounds of mere sustainability project and has grown to take on a greater significance both locally and internationally. It has transformed from a local side project, to an industry- and government-backed experiment, to a model for not only sustainable initiatives, but also community cooperation and sustainable *attitudes* throughout the EU.

This last is especially important when one takes into account the rampant overtaxation of resources and fishery collapse in the region. As long as commercial demand and inefficient, unsustainable fishing practices continue to tax fisheries to—and over—the brink of economic viability, decline and collapse remain inevitable. Although the economic impact of global fisheries collapse cannot be understated, the human impact would likewise be devastating.

Most immediately this would take the form of the disappearance of small-scale commercial fishing as a way of life. Already endangered as an occupation in many parts of the world, and especially in the North Atlantic region, continued excess stress on fisheries spells an absolute end to the traditional small-scale commercial fisher. Complicating and speeding the process is the growing power of corporate commercial fishing operations. As shifting regulatory measures and shrinking catches increase overhead and decrease potential for profit, small business owners and traditional fishers are being pushed out of the market. When it comes to marshaling vast quantities of capital, the corporate model is simply a force that small-scale fishers cannot compete with.

With all of that in mind, we must then ask why any of this is important at all. In an era in which the value of the local is suspect, and its long-term viability uncertain, why should we spend any time at all concerning ourselves with the survival of what appears to be an obsolete way of life centered on a fading economic model? This is a question that goes back to the root of folklore. Alan Dundes notes that the folk have traditionally (particularly in the nineteenth century) been marked as rural, and in the study of folklore "rural is implicitly compared with urban. The folk were rural because they could be contrasted with city dwellers" (1980, 2). Although Dundes pushes back against this classification, and the association of "the folk" with lower-stratum and implicitly lesser social importance, the question of why we study these groups on the fringes—the small-scale, the rural, the fading—remains.

First and foremost, the local and the small scale are important to study because the resilient responses developed in small, isolated places such as the Orkney Islands not only are illuminating culturally, but also hold promise for potential replication elsewhere. The lobster hatchery, for example, is a resilient response to encroaching globalization that holds promise for striking a sustainable balance between full capitulation to the domination of the globalized world and maintaining a traditional way of life. In part because of their geographic, economic, social, and political isolation, small communities have been forced to become creative in finding solutions to the sustainability and survival questions—finding a way to cling to life in the face of encroaching globalization and globalizing projects.

What this leaves behind is a community and an occupation stuck in a state of flux. Bulwarks against projects of outside domination may have been temporarily reinforced, but exerting one's presence in a resilient way often comes at the expense of reinforcing a kind of essentialist view of the local while leaving the question of long-term economic viability largely unanswered—the site of activity and practice relegated to heritage (Noyes 2014, 82–83). Although resilient responses have been developed in part to deal with the problem of outside domination, the fact nevertheless remains that the very thing being preserved is itself in the process of becoming outmoded. Small-scale commercial fishing has either died out or is in the process of dying out in many parts of the world because the practice itself is a relic, a ruin, an anachronistic survival from a collective island past (Slyomovics 1998, 30). It is an occupational fragment from a former era reaching into the present and the future. But it is a fragment that we can still learn from.

I am not arguing that the Lamb Holm Lobster Hatchery is the sole contributing factor in maintaining the health of Orkney's lobster fishery. That would be overly reductive, and there are many other factors at play besides. It is my argument, however, that a unique combination of community engagement with sustainable initiatives, the continued presence of small-scale commercial fishing as both a traditional occupation and a viable economic pursuit, the continued cultural importance of fishing in towns and villages throughout the archipelago, the relatively low capital investment threshold for successful lobster farming, and a friendly council governing environment have come together in the form of the Lamb Holm Lobster Hatchery to manifest something both emergent and inspiring. Despite its obvious unsuitability as a blanket model for universal application, the situation in Orkney nevertheless poses intriguing questions and offers useful models that have the potential to be successfully replicated elsewhere.

Founded as the Lamb Holm Lobster Hatchery was, through the unique confluence of occasionally conflicting interests, it has since reached beyond these interests and transcended the boundaries of any single interest group. Seeking the middle way of long-term sustainability for the Orcadian marine environment and the shellfish industry, the hatchery has succeeded in become a cultural force all its own. Bringing together the competing interests of the government, the private sector, small-scale commercial fishers, local communities, conservationists, and capitalists alike, the hatchery is a testament to the good that can be accomplished when interest groups demonstrate a willingness to cooperate and to combine their individual strengths. It is further a testament to the power of the transformative moment, when the interests of individual constituent parts become subjugated to the need of the holistic collective, and balance and stability are prized over short-term profit. This is where the emergent qualities of the Lamb Holm Lobster Hatchery can be found—the moment when the whole transcends the simple sum of its parts and takes on a greater significance. The specific layout, design, or goals of the hatchery may not be applicable in all places at all times, but the emphasis on a balance that seeks to reconcile competing interests in the name of stability and continued viability make the example of the hatchery notable and well worth following.

## POSTSCRIPT

A brief note here to conclude: Since conducting my initial field work in the Orkney Islands in 2014, the lobster hatchery has fallen on difficult times. Faced with a declining interest from industry due to a lack of provable impact on profits (again, pointing to Noyes, it seems that the too-high cost on the front end and the too-low cost on the back end of sustainable projects have left businesses with little motivation to pursue sustainable options in the present moment) and coupled with the loss of a crop of juveniles to a malfunctioning filter, the hatchery shut its doors at the beginning of 2017. Martin Fouls, a local fishermen, active member of the Orkney Fishermen's Society, and director of Orkney Sustainable Fisheries, asserts that this setback will likely be temporary. His hope is to have the hatchery back up and running in some form or another within the next few years, hopefully with a dedicated sponsor. The benefit this time around is that the former hatchery's members already have the equipment and experience. All that is required is the capital. This is the heart of resilience—the ability to roll with the punches, to endure, and to persevere even in the face of overwhelming odds. The battle may be lost before it begins, but that doesn't mean that nothing can be gained from the fight.

## REFERENCES

Acheson, James. 1988. *The Lobster Gangs of Maine*. Hanover, NH: University Press of New England.

Apostle, Richard, and Gene Barrett. 1992a. "Captains and Buyers." In *Emptying Their Nets: Small Capital and Rural Industrialization in the Nova Scotia Fishing Industry*, ed. Richard Apostle et al. Toronto: University of Toronto Press.

Apostle, Richard, and Gene Barrett. 1992b. "Communities and Their Social Economy." In *Emptying Their Nets: Small Capital and Rural Industrialization in the Nova Scotia Fishing Industry*, ed. Richard Apostle et al. Toronto: University of Toronto Press.

Apostle, Richard, and Gene Barrett. 1992c. "A Theoretical Overview." In *Emptying Their Nets: Small Capital and Rural Industrialization in the Nova Scotia Fishing Industry*, ed. Richard Apostle et al. Toronto: University of Toronto Press.

Bauman, Richard. 1971. "Differential Identity and the Social Base of Folklore." *Journal of American Folklore* 84 (331): 31–41.

Briggs, John C. 2008. "The North Atlantic Ocean: Need for Proactive Management." *Fisheries* 33 (4): 180–85.

Dennis. 2014. "Dennis." Orkney Field Notes.

Dundes, Alan. 1980. "Who Are the Folk?" In *Interpreting Folklore*. Bloomington: Indiana University Press.

Durrenberger, Paul E., and Gisli Palsson. 1987. "Ownership at Sea: Fishing Territories and Access to Sea Resources." *American Ethnologist* 14 (3): 508–22.

Gibbon, Robert. 2014. "Robert Gibbon," May 31. Tape recording. Kirkwall, Orkney.

Gibbon, Sarah-Jane. 2014. "Sarah-Jane Gibbon," May 15. Orkney Field notes. Kirkwall, Orkney.

Hutchinson, Stevie. 2017. "Stevie Hutchinson," June 20. Tape recording. Finstown.
John. 2014. "John—Fishing Trip." Orkney Field Notes.
Kasperski, Stephen, and Daniel S. Holland. 2013. "Income Diversification and Risk for Fishermen." *PNAS* 110 (6): 2076–81.
Kittredge, William. 2001. "Owning It All." In *The New Agrarianism: Land, Culture, and the Community of Life*, ed. Eric T. Freyfogle. Washington, DC: Island Press.
McDonald, Mary Anne, and Kristen L. Kucera. 2007. "Understanding Non-Industrialized Workers' Approaches to Safety: How do Commercial Fishermen 'Stay Safe?'" *Journal of Safety Research* 38 (3): 289–97.
McGlade, Jacqueline M. 2002. "The North Sea Large Marine Ecosystem." In *Large Marine Ecosystems of the North Atlantic: Changing States and Sustainability*, ed. Kenneth Sherman and Hein Skjoldal. Amsterdam: Elsevier.
Noyes, Dorothy. 2014. "Heritage, Legacy, Zombie: How to Bury the Undead Past." In *Cultural Heritage in Transit*, ed. Deborah Kapchan. Philadelphia: University of Pennsylvania Press.
Noyes, Dorothy. 2016a. "Compromised Concepts in Rising Waters: Making the Folk Resilient." *Humble Theory: Folklore's Grasp on Social Life*. Bloomington: Indiana University Press.
Noyes, Dorothy. 2016b. "Group." *Humble Theory: Folklore's Grasp on Social Life*. Bloomington: Indiana University Press.
Orkney Fishermen's Society. 2016. "Orkney Fishermen's Society." https://www.orkney foodanddrink.com/orkney-fishermens-society.
Orkney Islands Council. 2012. "Orkney Economic Review, 2012–2013." *Development and Infrastructure Services*, Orkney Islands Council. School Place: Kirkwall. http://www.orkney.gov.uk/Files/Business-and-Trade/Economic_Review/Orkney_Economic_Review_2012-13.pdf.
Orkney Lobster Hatchery. 2015. "Orkney Lobster Hatchery: About." http://orkneylobster hatchery.co.uk/.
Orkney Sustainable Fisheries. 2015. "Lamb Holm Lobster Hatchery." http://www.orkney sustainablefisheries.co.uk/?page_id=245.
Rogers, Stan. 1977. "Make and Break Harbour." *Fogarty's Cove*, Track 11. Barn Swallow Records.
Slyomovics, Susan. 1998. "Sequence and Simultaneity: Dada Colonialism in Ein Houd." In *The Object of Memory: Arab and Jew Narrate the Palestinian Village*. Philadelphia: University of Pennsylvania Press.
Uskul, Ayse K., Shinobu Kitayama, and Richard E. Nisbett. 2008. "Ecocultural Basis of Cognition: Farmers and Fishermen Are More Holistic than Herders." *PNAS* 105 (25): 8552–56.
Willie. 2014. "Willie—Fishing Trip." Orkney Field Notes.

# 6

## The Economics of Curation and Representation
*Dialogues in the Commemorative Landscape of Portsmouth, Ohio*

Cassie Patterson

On October 4, 2014, Stephanie Wright was volunteering at the Portsmouth Farmers Market on the Roy Rogers Esplanade, handing out tickets for Healthy Bucks, a free program that encourages families to visit farmers' markets. That day, I was in town to host the Murals Story Booth, which aimed to capture residents' reflections about what the Portsmouth Floodwall Murals, a local citizen-run revitalization project in the small postindustrial city in southern Ohio, meant to them. Stephanie only had a few minutes to talk between customers:

> When I used to work at American Cab Company there would be workers who would come in from out of town who would do various jobs around town, construction and different things, and they would want to know what there was around Portsmouth because they would be from bigger towns, and so they always just thought this was a boring town and there was nothing to do. And I said, "Oh, there's lots to do." And so I would tell them about the 1810 House and the Stone House and different things . . . but our biggest achievement is our floodwall and the murals . . . I was supposed to charge for everywhere I took 'em but I would pay to take 'em down there myself.
>
> And I would drive 'em down by the murals and I would give 'em my own little self-guided tour explaining about the history of Portsmouth and Scioto County as we drove by . . . [s]o that they understood that this was a piece of our history, this was something that we were *extremely* proud of, so that they understood that Portsmouth isn't just this little town, little hick town somewhere, a little dot on the map at the bottom of Ohio that nobody ever talks about . . . And it's not just the murals, it's everything . . . it's a wonderful town, and it's got a lot of history.

DOI: 10.7330/9781607327851.c006

Stephanie later added that the murals are a "gateway" to the city—"what people start at before they go look at all the rest of the history of Portsmouth." Her response, as well as the other interviews I collected that day, served as a turning point in my research on the Portsmouth Floodwall Murals. Prior to speaking with Stephanie, my work had focused on understanding the Floodwall Murals as a semi-grassroots heritage tourism project,[1] which aims to serve both as a source of economic revitalization and community cohesion.

I had been analyzing the formal features of mural images as well as the organizational structure of Portsmouth Murals Inc. (PMI), the governing body of the project.[2] However, that day I was struck by the ways that residents redirected my question about what the murals project meant to them by telling me how they contributed to the murals project (through storytelling, one-off tours, contributing ideas to the muralist, considering the economic impact of the project, etc.) and what outcomes they desired or expected from the murals project (such as community and economic connectivity, and appreciation for local history and culture). As Mandy Hart, then executive director of the Center for Appalachian Philanthropy, put it, while the murals had done a good job of bringing visitors to the area, "I think there needs to be a strategic plan around the murals to help utilize the asset and the tool . . . collectively as part of a strong economic development plan for the community" (Mohl, Hart, and Hart 2014). Thus, residents shifted the focus of my questions so that *they*, rather than the murals project alone, were instrumental in curating personal and local history and strategizing revitalization opportunities, since they were personally invested in shaping visitors' understanding of the past, present, and future of the city. Interviewees positioned themselves as curators of the local commemorative landscape, which included but also ultimately extended beyond the Portsmouth Floodwall Murals project.

Since my initial interview with Stephanie a few years ago, I have undertaken ongoing fieldwork[3] that has allowed me to further explore Portsmouth's extensive commemorative landscape, noting the ways that residents engage questions of curation and representation. While I am still learning many of the logistics and histories of each of the individual commemorative displays in Portsmouth and their relationships to one another, the abundance of projects (especially along the Ohio River and in nearby neighborhoods) invites analysis of their formations and meanings. For example, in 2016, Maureen Cadogan, executive director of the Scioto County Homeless Shelter, showed me a carved granite bench commemorating the Underground Railroad and introduced me to unmarked homes that may have sheltered runaway slaves. Maureen's tour encouraged me not only to think more deeply about the ways that my own positioning (both as a newcomer to the area and as someone who had primarily interacted with white residents up until that point) impacted my analysis, but also to consider the relative visibility of different sites of memory and commemoration. Indeed, there are some sites to which I do not, and may never, have access.

In 2017, I noted several other instances of commemoration: a mural located at Shawnee State Lodge depicting Native Americans scanning the valley from Raven Rock, a natural overhang from which Native Americans scouted invading settlers; Facebook posts by locals announcing the restoration and reopening of McKinley Memorial Pool, an integrated swimming pool built in 1966; bricks and stars embedded in the walkway on top of a hill overlooking the Ohio River at the Ulysses S. Grant Bridge; a concrete area under the same bridge covered with graffiti; and the Facebook page for a local reunion of the African American neighborhood where people identify friends and family, post stories, and share memories. I wondered how these differently visible, sustained, and oriented commemorations and markings related to one another and what they said about the politics of representation in a small postindustrial city.

James Connolly observes, in the introduction to *After the Factory: Reinventing America's Industrial Small Cities* (Connolly 2010), "Every smaller post-industrial city faces this same challenge—to remake itself into something new" (11). As the magnitude of the Floodwall Murals project and a host of other local commemorative projects demonstrate, image (re)construction and management are deeply intertwined with economic revitalization initiatives, and yet also open up larger conversations about the intersection of local narratives, politics, and public representation. Indeed, Setha M. Low argues in her essay "Cultural Conservation of Place" that "many of the most bitter fights over cultural conservation in communities are about the dialectic between the past and the future control of culture" (1994, 74). Low explains how the pressure to revitalize communities in economic transition can generate a host of "placeless" middle-class experiences that privilege those already in power rather than spaces and experiences that serve a diverse local population (68–74). Low's essay encouraged me to explore the ways that locals engage aspects of power and representation in the revitalization projects in their city, paying particular attention to both subtle and overt modes of critique. Although the murals can serve as a gateway for deeper engagement with local history and politics, this engagement requires an investment of time and energy from both the curator and the visitor.

Residents' work to manage local and larger-than-local representations of Portsmouth leads me to ask,[4] in what ways do residents and projects conducting activity around, behind, between, and beyond the Portsmouth Floodwall Murals use, shape, and respond to their commemorative landscape? What are the means and forms of (counter)representation, dialogue, and critique? I provide examples to show how residents leverage their knowledge, resources, (volunteer) labor, money, and energy to (re)shape the commemorative landscape. Investigating the commemorative dialogues that occur through various inscriptions on the local landscape provides insight into the struggle for representational space and power in a small postindustrial city.

## MORAL GEOGRAPHIES OF COMMEMORATION

The ways that people respond to landscapes and how people position themselves in relation to the landscape form what folklorist and sociolinguist Gabriella Modan calls a "moral geography." In her book *Turf Wars: Discourse, Diversity, and the Politics of Place*, Modan defines moral geography as "an interweaving of a moral framework with a geographical territory" through which "community members create alignments and oppositions among people and places" that are then assessed according to community values (2007, 90). The concept is adapted from Jane Hill's original coining of the term in her chapter "The Voices of Don Gabriel: Responsibility and Self in a Modern Mexicano Narrative" in *The Dialogic Emergence of Culture* (1995). Hill's chapter explored the ways that Don Gabriel's narrative about his son's murder and the recovery of his body mapped values onto the physical landscape. Modan expands Hill's use of the term to include the dialogic relationship between people and places, such that evaluations of places simultaneously construct speakers' own identity alongside assessments of others. Inevitably, she argues, because people have many facets that link their identities to their place of residence, "community members talk about the neighborhood in multiple and sometimes conflicting ways" (Modan 2007, 92). This complex "stance-taking," or the process by which community members articulate their alignments, builds on Goffman's notion of footing;[5] the process encompasses not only the ways that people position themselves but also how they position others in relation to place (Modan 2007, 297). Modan emphasizes that positioning (or stance-taking) is dynamic, emergent, and relational and that it relates to places as well as people (Modan 2007, 297).

Folklorists Barbara Kirshenblatt-Gimblett and Michael Dylan Foster both emphasize the intentionality of such positionings in the construction of heritage tourism sites. The authors describe heritage sites as locations of complex, contingent cultural and economic exchanges between heritage producers and heritage consumers. Kirshenblatt-Gimblett notes the ways that heritage "interfaces" indicate a "crisis in memory" that are the second life of the things they represent (Kirshenblatt-Gimblett 1995, 371), and Foster conceptualizes these representations in terms of an "*economic system*," a "dynamic cycle of production and consumption" that allows us to "consider how local resources . . . are managed by a community" (Foster 2013, 312; emphasis in original). Especially relevant is the way that these authors shift the conversation about heritage tourism away from claims about cultural authenticity and toward conscious cultural production and consumption to leverage local resources toward engaging the global economy.

Scholars of social memory and heritage have been particularly interested in the ways that these conscious cultural productions engage the past to articulate a vision of the present and the future. They focus critical attention on the dynamic relationship between the economics, spatial and temporal referents, and cultural dynamics of official and vernacular commemorative practices. Guy Beiner's *Remembering the Year of the French* (2007) thoroughly details the ways that French support of the 1798 uprisings have eluded historical documentation yet remain deeply embedded in social memory, the vernacular landscape, folklore, and recent commemoration practices. "Social memory" is defined as "representations of traditional bodies of knowledge" while social remembrance (or *remembrance*) is the "dynamic processes of reproduction" (Beiner 2007, 28). "Folklore accounts, which reflect how historical events were interpreted locally," he argues, "are not only apposite sources for [analyses of the dialogue between metanarratives and micronarratives] but can also, by exhibiting indications of instances when 'official' versions of history filtered into popular discourses, accommodate a history of reception" (11). Beiner's interest in analyzing folk reception calls to mind Alessandro Portelli's analysis of "the cultural construction of the event" as articulated in *The Battle of Valle Giulia: Oral History and the Art of Dialogue* (1997), in which he outlines a way of analyzing vernacular understandings of places and events in relation to the ways they are recorded or remembered within institutional, communal, or personal social referents (91–113, 102). Elaborating the ways in which memories are narrated and translated into commemorative forms provides the basis for describing systems of power that govern representation. In some instances, as Ray Cashman argues in his essay on commemorative practices in rural Northern Ireland, sites are significant precisely because of what is no longer present or visible (2008).

Expanding scholars' attention to include a range of communicative devices that form dialogues within the commemorative landscape generates questions about how aspects of local identity and values inform moral geographies of places such as Portsmouth. In *Walls of Empowerment: Chicana/o Indigenist Murals of California*, Guisela Latorre highlights the dialectic relationship between muraling traditions in Los Angeles and Mexico in which a "relational yet conflictive and oppositional dialogue" emerged as Chicanas/os borrowed from Mexican Indigenism in order to reclaim "a culture and a history traditionally commodified by Western powers of colonization" (2008, 13). Jack Santino, in his analysis of conflict and public display in Northern Ireland in *Signs of War and Peace*, refers to this dialogue as *assemblage*, "the juxtaposition of elements that can be and often are displayed as discrete units in order to modify, strengthen, or otherwise develop a symbolic public statement" (50–51). Latorre and Santino emphasize the ways in which relationships between multiple commemorative efforts within a local landscape reveal how they are in dialogue with specific histories as well as with one another—how they borrow from or critique one another, and how different forms of commemoration provide opportunities for articulations of identity and values to surface. Further, these dialogues point to the power structures that enable or curtail individual creations, as well as the ways in which representations speak to multiple audiences.

Local commemorative sites form a moral geography of commemoration that offers differing conceptions and representations of place, creating a "commemorative dialogue" within the landscape. The form, content, and longevity of any of these representations are impacted by the physical, economic, and social structures that can hinder or assist the maintenance of the representation. Throughout this chapter, I argue that residents use narratives, tours, physical structures, graffiti, websites, and social media—each with their own location, audience, platform, organizational structure, and content—to form a network of dialogues within the commemorative landscape in Portsmouth, Ohio.

## PORTSMOUTH, OHIO, AND THE PORTSMOUTH FLOODWALL MURALS

Portsmouth, the seat of Scioto County, is located at the southern border of the state near the confluence of the Scioto and Ohio Rivers. Portsmouth is a little over a hundred miles east of Cincinnati and a little less than a hundred miles south of Columbus; thus, some residents drive to either city for work or shopping, traveling more than four hours a day. Southern Scioto

County is across the river from Lewis and Greenup Counties in Kentucky, and crossing state boundaries is common, with some people crossing the river daily for work. According to the US Census Bureau, in 2010, the city of Portsmouth was reported to have a population of 20,226 residents, and Scioto County had 79,499. Within Scioto County, African Americans make up 2.6 percent of the population, Hispanic and Latino residents make up 1.3 percent, and American Indians and Alaska Natives account for 0.5 percent of the population. Scioto County's nineteenth- and twentieth-century economies were sustained by a mix of extractive industry (timber, sandstone, coal, iron ore) and agriculture (livestock as well as crops, including grains, milk, and vegetables). Transportation of these materials was facilitated by the Ohio River and the railroad (Vastine 1986, 53–56; Willard et al. 1916, 120–25). As in many other postindustrial Midwestern cities in the so-called rust belt, manufacturing declined significantly during the latter half of the twentieth century, devastating the economy.[6] Portsmouth and Scioto County have engaged in a number of commemorative, economic, and social initiatives to mitigate this decline.

## THE PORTSMOUTH FLOODWALL MURALS

In the early 1990s, a handful of residents in Portsmouth initiated a public project that would grow to include over sixty mural images and an audio driving tour. Fifty-six of these murals are painted on a twenty-foot-tall floodwall along the Ohio River. The US Army Corps of Engineers built the wall between 1940 and 1950 to protect the city after multiple floods had devastated it since the late 1790s (Horr, McClellan, and Dafford 2003, vi). Bob Morton, president of Portsmouth Murals Inc. (PMI), local historian, and former AAA motor coach tour guide and club president, wrote articles in two separate editions of *AAA Today* about the original idea for the murals and how the project was launched (Morton 1996a, 1996b).

Pooling the artistic talents of muralist Robert Dafford (who, in signing on, committed to the life of the project), a AAA seed loan, donations from members of the small mural committee, and 501(c)(3) tax-exempt status from the Portsmouth Area Community Exhibits, the mural project became a reality (Morton 1996a, 5). Local business owners and corporate chains pitched in to provide Dafford lodging and meals during his summer residencies (Morton 1996a, 7). In 1993, speaker of the Ohio House of Representatives, Vern Riffe, committed $115,000 over two years for the mural project. Numerous donations from locals, including in-kind donations, and heftier sums from fundraisers, such as revenue from the sale of mural calendars sold at Kroger (which raised $30,134), kept the project going. Morton estimated that the total cost of the murals project was around $370,000 in 1996. Today, PMI maintains the murals project by hosting a fundraising banquet each year featuring famous sports stars from the city.

The Portsmouth Floodwall Murals transformed a large, gray concrete wall into a tourist destination. The tagline for the murals, "2,000 years of history, 2,000 feet of art," emphasizes the vastness of time and space the mural project covers. Stretching from east to west, the panels are mostly arranged chronologically, starting with the ancient Adena and Hopewell cultures, whose descendants, the Shawnee, inhabited the area for several centuries before being forcibly removed in the nineteenth century. Henry Massie's plan for the city and the early founders in the 1800s are shown alongside major industries. Next are murals showing Portsmouth's men fighting in the battle of Gettysburg, the sixteen founding churches in the city that still stand today, and the old train station and market square.

Murals depicting life in Portsmouth in the twentieth century include depictions of industries such as shoe and shoelace manufacturing, steel production, gray iron casting, and uranium enrichment; major local figures such as Roy Rogers, Clarence Carter, Carl Ackerman, Vern Riffe, and Shakespearean actress Julia Marlowe; local sports events and figures, such as Branch Rickey, and an homage to local baseball stars (who are invited back each year for the annual fundraising banquet); transportation innovations such as streetcars, the Greyhound bus station, and railroads; and commemorations of the 1937 flood. A few murals, such as the one dedicated to organized labor, "Tour of the Scioto River Valley," and the Kroger mural, dot the city landscape beyond the floodwall itself.

The Portsmouth Floodwall Murals project is an extensive undertaking that has been maintained for over fifteen years and to which additional murals are being added today. In 2013, John and Nathan Lorentz produced *Beyond These Walls: Building Community through Public Art*, a documentary that describes the murals project as a dual economic revitalization and community-building project (Lorentz et al. 2013). Some residents feel deeply connected to and represented by the murals, while others feel excluded, misrepresented, or left out of the decision-making process.

Although the Portsmouth Floodwall Murals are a semi-grassroots endeavor, they serve as a metanarrative in the area because they make up a large-scale tourist destination that maintains consistent financial and structural support. As a metanarrative, the murals strike a problematic and uncritical nostalgic tone that I attribute to (1) the perspective and experiences of PMI Board members (overwhelmingly older white males with access to social capital), (2) PMI's assumptions about the kind of tourist who would visit Portsmouth to view the murals (perhaps not dissimilar to their own demographics) and, thus, the kind of representation that could generate income for the city, and (3) a desire to recuperate a particular set of values that supply a vision for the city's future while also continuing to generate funds for the continuation of the murals project. Cashman has argued that some expressions of "critical nostalgia" allow community members to pause to evaluate rapid and radical changes that have taken place in an area and to critically articulate desirable values (such as cooperation and personal agency) that have been lost in such transitions (Cashman 2006). The Portsmouth Floodwall Murals present a complex case in which residents disagree about the nostalgic process and the values expressed in its commemorative outcomes. That is, some community members (PMI, for instance) may consider the project to be an act of critical nostalgia while others consider the depictions of history and culture to be uncritical and dismissive of the experience of groups with less power.[7] Considering the ways in which conflict is represented (or omitted) in the murals provides insight into this dynamic.

The murals evoke a generally nostalgic tone, sometimes obscuring the interconnected social and economic shifts to which they respond—or, perhaps, situating these shifts among the multiple devastations the area and its residents have experienced. The ways that the Portsmouth Floodwall Murals obscure conflict in favor of celebration points to the potential difficulties of translating a complex and conflicted historical past into a heritage tourism site. In some cases, conflict is recast or sidelined, while in others it is avoided completely. In some cases, conflict is suggested to exist just outside of the mural panel. Periodization and romanticization of traumatic events also work to carve out a story of the past that appears peaceful, natural, and benign. There are no murals, for instance, depicting local worker strikes in 1914, 1936, 1956–57, or 1978, and the dates on *Steel Industry* function as periodization rather than condemnation for the largely unmediated impacts of deindustrialization.

Instead, labor is commemorated in *Tribute to Labor*, a panel located just around the corner from the main floodwall, which lists the charter date of various occupational unions and features images of men working in their respective fields, rather than depicting strikes or the picket line.[8]

Writing about the ways that such problematic depictions of economic history subdue and avoid conflict, Michael Frisch, in "De-, Re-, and Post-Industrialization: Industrial Heritage as Contested Memorial Terrain," examines the roles that various groups play in planning public heritage

Figure 6.1. *Steel Industry*, which indicates that steel was produced from 1870 to 1980. Photo by the author.

commemorations, noting that the outcomes of such negotiations impact the communities they depict. Frisch considers how categories such as "rust belt" came to signal a "profoundly naturalized and historicized" notion of national economic, political, and historical progress (1998, 247). Frisch argues that the ways in which postindustrial spaces are commemorated take on special significance because they engage narratives of progress in ways that obscure the choices (and responsibilities) of actual companies, owners, and boards. Heritage tourism sites engage these naturalized and historicized processes in ways that "sentimentalize the past, that distance it and its dynamics from contemporary choices and options" (Frisch 1998, 247).

Although Frisch focuses on the ways that economic decisions are obscured in this passage, his argument can be extended to include questions

Figure 6.2. Section of *Tribute to Labor* mural. Photo by the author.

about the representation of groups and experiences that are marginalized, obscured, and even misrepresented throughout in the murals project. The killing of Shawnee chief Tecumseh and the subsequent settlement of the area are depicted as a peaceful transition, with White settlers lounging in the foreground or looking peacefully up at Tecumseh's spirit, while the Shawnee walk west into the distant sunset. Similarly, the souvenir photobook sold in the Visitor's Bureau titles the mural *1810 House* rather than addressing the violence of displacement. It describes the scene as Tecumseh "overlooking the *migration* of his people westward, out of the Ohio River Valley" (Horr, McClellan, and Dafford 2003, 10; emphasis added). Tecumseh had, in fact, created a pan-Indian movement that included multitribal solidarity and a band of skilled warriors to counter the divide-and-conquer strategies of the United States government that threatened the livelihoods of Native American tribes throughout the Northwest Territory (Calloway 2007, 126–54).

Even *Civil War*, the mural dedicated to the Portsmouth men of the First Ohio Light Artillery, Battery L, who fought at the Battle of Gettysburg, lacks any depiction of an opponent or the ravages of war, and the local activities of the Underground Railroad are painted on the bottom frame—rather than as the centerpiece—of the Civil War mural.

Low explains that "processes of cultural hegemony (that is the preeminence of one cultural group's ideas and values over another) maintain the control of middle-class, white values over the very definitions of what can

Figure 6.3. *1810 House* mural and the rewriting of the history of Tecumseh and Native American removal. Photo by the author.

Figure 6.4. *Civil War* mural. Photo by the author.

be considered a relevant group with the power to give its own meanings to local environments" (1994, 68). Although the history of Scioto County is indeed saturated with historical, economic, social events, movements, and relationships, they are not equally engaged and commemorated across group experiences. The scenes in these murals portray a perspective that is unwilling to engage disturbing social issues in ways that could be off-putting to the kind of tourist who wants to reminisce about "the good old days."

Figure 6.5. Close-up of the Underground Railroad scene in the *Civil War* mural. Photo by the author.

Accessing commemorative dialogues within the local landscape—analyzing the responses to the large-scale narrative of the murals—provides insight into the ways that residents relate to the Portsmouth Floodwall Murals and construct their own meaningful connections to the local landscape and to the past. Interestingly, dialogue, conflict, and critique are inscribed behind, around, and beyond the large-scale murals project, often avoiding direct confrontation, but nevertheless making important representational claims. More important, they employ creative ways of engaging citizens in community gathering, restoration projects, and place-making that represent conflict as an integral part of the city's past and present.

## DIALOGUES WITHIN THE COMMEMORATIVE LANDSCAPE

The existence of representational projects that are proximate to the Floodwall Murals as well as placed throughout the city, engaging both physical and digital modalities, speaks to residents' desires to articulate experiences, perspectives, and histories that are not included within the Floodwall Murals project. Not only do these articulations present arguments in themselves, but the conversations that surround their production and maintenance provide opportunities for residents to engage in dialogue about local racial, economic and community issues. I offer examples of how residents have enacted more inclusive and egalitarian processes and representations. Examining the relative governance, representational strategies, and meanings of these commemorative projects, and the dialogues and divergences they present, provides insight into the strategies that individuals and groups employ through commemorative projects that operate outside the representational power of the nonprofit governing board, PMI, in Portsmouth, Ohio.

## Portsmouth Floodwall Stars and the Desire for Democratic Commemoration

If you look to Portsmouth from the Kentucky side of the Ohio River, you'll see a long stretch of the floodwall painted blue with white lettering and red trim. The center of the wall states in big white letters, "Welcome to Portsmouth 1803–2003," and along either side of the sign are individual, perfectly aligned large white stars. Underneath each star is the name of a notable local written in capital letters, with professions listed underneath the names. While some stars are still blank, the majority of them contain, in black, a signature and the date of signature in the middle of each assigned star.

The Floodwall Stars project was initiated by then Mayor Frank Gerlach shortly after the Floodwall Murals project began and continued over the course of four mayoral terms before being passed over to the city manager, and, most recently, to the Visitors Bureau. The Floodwall Stars focus on individuals who have contributed to Portsmouth and gained national acclaim, typically through their profession.[9] They also offer a more democratic commemorative process because any resident can nominate someone to be considered for a star, the judging process is outlined in a public document, and a rotating committee judges the nominations. The nomination packet, which can be obtained at the Visitor's Bureau, outlines the nomination procedure. Eligible nominees are those over eighteen who "have brought recognition or have made outstanding contributions to the quality of life in and/or development of Scioto County, Ohio or Greenup or Lewis County, Kentucky." Nominators are asked to specify the "field of endeavor" to which the nominee contributed, such as arts, business, professional, public affairs, voluntary service. The selection committee chooses up to three inductees each year, and any nominee who was not chosen in the year of her or his nomination is automatically nominated the following year. Reminders about nominating individuals for a star are published in the *Portsmouth Daily Times*. Each year, local media notify residents that nominations are open, and submissions for the Stars are received between January 2 and May 31 and then awarded at the annual River Days event held on the Thursday before Labor Day.

Because the Stars are maintained with public funds and engage a more transparent nomination process, there are different opportunities for voicing discontent about the Stars project. Maintaining the Floodwall Stars has been an expensive and sometimes contested practice, as evidenced by former city councilman Harald Daub's August 11, 2007, *Portsmouth Daily Times* letter to the editor in response to an announcement that the city would "start repairing the stars . . . at a cost of $15,000" (A001).[10] Citing other projects the city

Figure 6.6. Portsmouth Floodwall Stars facing Kentucky along the Ohio River. Photo by the author.

had not been able to fund recently, Daub complained that improving the Floodwall Stars was "the latest waste of our tax dollars" (A004).

The almost contemporaneous development of the Floodwall Murals and the Floodwall Stars signals a desire for a more democratic system of individual recognition that speaks to local as well as larger-than-local audiences, yet it also raises questions about the role of this kind of commemoration in the larger revitalization project. Further, the two projects' different strategies of governance (nonprofit board versus public entity) and representation (individual images painted in a realist style versus a series of stars with a template of formulaic stars) reveal their different financial structures and commemorative ethic.

### Reopening McKinley Pool: Complex Commemorations of Racial Inequality

On June 10, 2017, McKinley pool reopened as Portsmouth's only swimming pool. Reopening the pool was a significant local event because it represented a commitment to remembering the legacy of racism, segregation, and interracial solidarity in Portsmouth. Andrew Feight's essay "Eugene McKinley Memorial Pool and the End of Jim Crow in Portsmouth, Ohio," written for his local geohistory website and app, *Scioto Historical*,[11] describes the way that young Eugene McKinley drowned while swimming in a sand and gravel pit on June 9, 1961. At the time of McKinley's death, the only pool in the city, Dreamland, was segregated. In her MA thesis, "Forgotten: Scioto County's Lost Black History," Rebecca D. Jenkins critiques Portsmouth's Floodwall Murals for their depiction of African Americans sitting on the lawn of Dreamland pool in the *Remembrance Scrapbook* mural because it does not accurately represent the struggle for racial equality that occurred at the site but rather paints an inaccurate picture of interracial harmony (2015, 31–33). Feight explains that, following McKinley's death, both black and white residents banded together to create a new integrated pool that would be located in the North End, the traditionally African American neighborhood, even forming a nonprofit organization called the Community Recreational Society (CRS), which was unable to raise enough funds to construct the pool.

Meanwhile, the Civil Rights Act passed in 1964, but it did not govern private clubs such as the Terrace Club, where Dreamland was located. On July 17, 1964, Charles Stanley Smith, Eugene Collins, Curt Gentry, Roy Burns, Jessee Baggette, two juveniles, and Collin's and Gentry's mothers (serving at witnesses) staged a wade-in at Dreamland. "At 1pm, the appointed time, when the pool was packed and everyone was enjoying the sun and water, Smith, Gentry, Burns, Baggette, and two juvenile aged African American boys (who go unnamed in the newspaper accounts) approached the entrance. They asked for admission and were denied. As planned, they placed their 60-cent guest membership fee on the counter, hopped over the turn-styles, and made their way to the pool" (Feight n.d.b). Although the lifeguard on duty insisted that everyone get out of the pool, the protesters stayed in the water and "some of the younger white swimmers jumped back in the pool in a show of solidarity" (Feight n.d.b). Charges were dropped against the protesters and Dreamland was legally desegregated in 1965, but, with "the opening of McKinley Pool in 1966, the two pools allowed for the continuance of a form of de facto segregation in Portsmouth . . . supported by continued racism and the legacies of red-lined residential neighborhoods" (Feight n.d.b). Both pools eventually closed, and Dreamland was eventually paved over and made into a parking lot, but Feight describes the reopening of McKinley Memorial Pool on June 10, 2017, as "a tribute to those members of the community who stood up for justice and equality, those residents, white and black, who helped bring segregation to its end in the city."[12]

Feight, Jenkins, and others who describe McKinley's death and the activism that it sparked offer up a corrective to the image painted on the

*Remembrance Scrapbook* mural by directly engaging both the racial conflict (enacted through law as well as custom) and interracial collaboration that resulted in the desegregation of Dreamland as well as the eventual construction and reopening of McKinley Memorial Pool (Conley 2017; Feight n.d.b; Jenkins 2015; McKinley Pool GoFundMe webpage ["Help Fix Portsmouth's McKinley Pool" 2017]; Thompson 2017). Documentation of the efforts of local black and white residents on the GoFundMe campaign for the pool opening show numerous volunteers who offered their time to create "a place in the sun for everyone." While racial inequalities in Portsmouth are deeply rooted and still impact daily life for African American residents, the commemorative dialogues produced by the reopening of McKinley Memorial Pool provide an opportunity to engage aspects of the past that are filled with conflict and injustice.

### CADOGAN'S TOUR, STOUT'S UNDERGROUND RAILROAD BENCH, AND COMPETING NOTIONS OF FREEDOM

In November 2016, I met Maureen Cadogan—a local activist, storyteller, and community archivist—who regularly participates in and leads events and activities in the North End, the historically African American neighborhood in Portsmouth.[13] Maureen took me for a short tour of Front Street (where the murals are prominently displayed). In addition to showing me a house that was believed to have harbored African Americans who were fleeing slavery in Kentucky, she pointed out a granite bench that is located directly across from the *Twentieth Century Armed Forces* mural, part of the Portsmouth Floodwall Mural series.

The bench features the poem "A Struggle to Be Free," written by local poet Walter Stout. The poem describes a male African American slave who learns of the Underground Railroad and seeks freedom in Portsmouth: "If he ever got the chance he would surely go / To this place called Portsmouth in the state of Ohio" (Stout 2004). The slave's journey is detailed, with "cuts and bruises" being "added to his whipping scars" as he made his way north toward the river. When he finally arrived at the Ohio River, "he fell upon his knee" and exclaimed, "Oh thank you God for all your help. I have a chance to be free, free, free" (Stout 2004)![14] "A Struggle to Be Free" is one of several benches that were authored, commissioned, and donated to the city by Walter Stout, who passed away in July 2017. Stout's benches, which are placed around Portsmouth and McDermott, tackle a range of ethical topics (Concerned Citizens Group Roundtable 2007).

Figure 6.7. Granite Underground Railroad bench with poem by Walter Stout. Photo by the author for the Ohio Field Schools Collection at the Folklore Archives of the Center for Folklore Studies at Ohio State University: OFS(S)20161120-22CP1.

Stout's 3,000-pound tribute to the Underground Railroad sits directly across from the Portsmouth Floodwall Murals and thus calls into question the notion of freedom being offered up by the image. The *Twentieth Century Armed Forces* mural has the words "For Freedom" written in large lettering across the top. It depicts six branches of the military and lists the "five horrific wars of the twentieth century" (Horr, McClellan, and Dafford 2003, 46). The mural shows individual service members in uniform, standing between stone columns. Since the mural honors twentieth-century veterans, the Civil War and the Underground Railroad are not depicted as one of the wars that were waged "for freedom." The *Civil War* mural does not mention the Underground Railroad on the mural itself (the corners of the image honor Portsmouth soldiers at various battles, and the Battle at Gettysburg takes up the majority of the panel), and the attending commemorative booklet has just one identifying sentence confirming that the image at the bottom of the frame is of that dangerous passage. It reads, "The Underground Railroad (bottom) delivers runaway slaves from the South to freedom" (Horr, McClellan, and Dafford 1993, 16).

Here, periodization and marginalization define freedom as abstract military service and exclude the specificity of the Underground Railroad from

*The Economics of Curation and Representation* 147

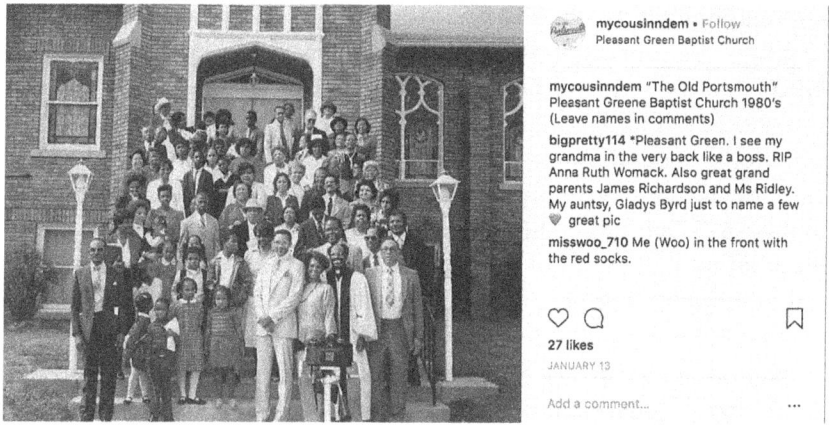

Figure 6.8. Screenshot of @mycousinndem Instagram feed from January 13, 2018, illustrating how people identify friends and family members from the North End.

the mural. The Underground Railroad bench calls attention to the temporal and representational gap that erases the conflict of the Civil War and the struggle for freedom by African Americans both locally and throughout the United States.

### Cultivating Social Memory through Collaborative Remembering on Facebook and Instagram

While the Underground Railroad bench engages the physical landscape,[15] digital commemorations also provide content for commemorative dialogue. The North End Super Reunion Facebook Page and the @mycousinndem Instagram account create a communicative network of intergenerational, interracial, and inter-neighborhood social memory.

The North End Super Reunion Facebook page (the social media page for the quadrennial neighborhood reunion) serves as a space for current and former residents to share images and reflections about people, places, and events in and from the North End. In the months leading up to the reunion, page administrators posted "throwback Thursday" and "flashback Friday" photos so that current and former residents could identify members of the community and comment about their memories of growing up in the neighborhood. The images, comments, and the Super Reunion itself intentionally create opportunities for collaborative remembering that links North End community members to one another. Similarly, an anonymously hosted Instagram account started in January 2018, @mycousinndem, features photographs of "The Old Portsmouth" and provides another digital venue for members of the North End to consider the past as it relates to the present and future of the city.

Guy Beiner explains that "social remembering" or "remembrance" is a practice "commonly shared by a community" in which "members of a society draw and contribute to a communal body of cultural knowledge relating to the past" (2007, 28). Multiple authorship and "issues of multiple receptions" of memories and knowledge characterize the "dynamic synthesis" at play in the process of constructing social memory (28). Engaging in the processes of remembrance keeps the connections among people alive by cultivating social memory. Keeping the wider community invested—especially those who no longer live in the neighborhood—is important because residents and the Fourteenth Street Community Center (a primary gathering space that coordinates after-school activities, educational programs, fundraisers, and other important community events) rely on donations and fundraisers to sustain life-changing community programs, especially those aimed at struggling families and youth. The ability to fund and implement essential community programs relies upon a common cause and connection that must be continually cultivated in and beyond the immediate neighborhood.

Both the North End Super Reunion Facebook page and the @mycousinndem Instagram account encourage local and beyond-local participation with those connected to the Portsmouth area by asking followers to identify and comment about individuals and places within the photos. Important and significant, this work is primarily if not entirely carried out on a volunteer basis and is often accomplished either using free social media platforms or with local funds through community fundraising.

### Graffiti and Public Art as Critiques of Representational Power

Of course, not all aspects of the commemorative landscape are officially sanctioned by a board or are attached to a social media account. Graffiti painted or etched along the floodwall provides another expressive dimension to the city's commemorative landscape. In the image that follows, which I found one day by walking along the bank of the river, a local artist had painted an image of a mother and child.

The woman, positioned ahead of the child, is walking forward with her eyes closed, her thin legs bent at the knee. Her bulbous dress sways slightly behind her. The woman's right arm stretches behind her as she pulls the boy along with her. The child, wearing a black shirt, slouches slightly in resistance to her grasp, bowing his legs. One of his eyes is x'd out, and his mouth is agape,

Figure 6.9. Painting by anonymous artist and graffiti etched with rock along the lower portion of the floodwall, with the Floodwall Stars behind. The artist's signature has been intentionally covered. Photo by the author.

with drool dripping out of it. The movement and relationship depicted in the image are expressive of the familiar tension of intergenerational conflict, of youth feeling dragged and deadened by the constrained path of the previous generation. There are, in fact, numerous examples of intergenerational cooperation in Portsmouth, most of which are carried out on an individual level. However, the artist is commenting specifically on the inability of some young entrepreneurs and artists to gain access to routes of representational power within the city and the constraints that are put on creative expression.

A couple of other paintings by the same artist had been profiled in the *Portsmouth Daily Times* in summer of 2011 (Dumas 2011). The article, "Graffiti, the Other Murals," provides cursory information about the graffiti artwork, stating, "while coming nowhere near the caliber of the floodwall murals, [they] are interesting in their own right." Heather Dumas, staff writer for the paper, describes the images as "cave paintings done in spray paint" that have a "certain urban-primitive type charm" (n.p.). Members of the PMI board and others who are involved with the Floodwall Murals project have cited the fact that the murals have not been defaced as evidence of community buy-in to the project. Dumas's deference toward the artistic merits of the Floodwall Murals, as well as the presence of visible

Figure 6.10. "Our wall" spray-painted in white at the far west end of the Floodwall Stars. Photo by the author.

inscriptions around the murals, is perhaps an indication of the economies and politics of representation in Portsmouth. While residents clearly want to engage the representational landscape on their own terms, they are hesitant to do so through direct confrontation (an ethic echoed in the Floodwall Murals themselves). Rather, representations that elaborate the commemorative landscape and form dialogues with more official tourist sites appear to be acceptable forms of critique. The most direct critique I have seen was along the floodwall in December 2017: someone had spray-painted the words "our wall" in white on the far west side of the Floodwall Stars, where there is a lot of unmarked floodwall space.

While defacing the treasured and protected Floodwall Murals may be too risky, young residents remain committed to making their mark on the representational landscape, claiming creative and representational space for public art and commentary.

## CONCLUSION

Throughout this chapter, I have explained how residents' multiple contributions to and curations of the local landscape serve as ways for them to respond to the metanarrative of the Portsmouth Floodwall Murals, thus engaging in alternative and critical forms of remembrance. The commemorative dialogues between the murals and other physical and digital commemoration projects raise important questions about the stakes of selection and representation in local heritage revitalization projects, especially in terms of the ways that local conflict and politics are depicted. Relative funding models (state funds vs. volunteer labor, e.g.) further highlight the disparities between different groups' access to the power and resources needed to sustain the representations they value. The landscape reveals the politics of its construction, with particular projects surfacing to be able to exhibit sentiments that demand articulation at the local and larger-than-local level. In Portsmouth, critical commemorative representations such as the reopening of McKinley Memorial Pool receive much less attention from tourists (and, in fact, may be largely invisible to them), but are nevertheless at the heart of community solidarity efforts. Critical representations that engage commemorative dialogue form crucial moments in social memory that serve to connect like-minded community members to one another and consider alternative conceptions and representations of people and place.

I have investigated the ways in which residents and local nonprofit organizations create and engage the moral geography of Portsmouth by positioning themselves as curators of the physical and digital commemorative landscape. While the Floodwall Murals orient themselves toward the tourist in order to articulate the significance of the area, seeking to engage the heritage tourism for revitalization, Stephanie Wright's taxi tour, the Floodwall Stars, the reopening of McKinley Memorial Pool, Maureen Cadogan's Underground Railroad tour, Stout's granite bench, the North End Super Reunion Facebook page and @mycousinndem Instagram account, and a young artist's generational commentary position themselves in response to local and larger-than-local politics of representation. These examples reveal the ways that the economics of landscape interpretation, expression, and infrastructure impact but do not necessarily limit the proliferation of representations in Portsmouth.

## NOTES

1. I use "semi-grassroots" here because though it is carried out at the local level, the governing board is made up primarily of white, male city elites and because funding for the murals project has been garnered from both state-level as well as local fundraising sources. Further, the overall budget for the Portsmouth Floodwall Murals far exceeds those that have been raised by the other projects I examine later in this chapter.

2. In previous conference papers, I focused on the ways in which the 2,000-year history presented in the murals project extends the spatiotemporal significance of the small

postindustrial city to contextualize its current economic struggle as one of the many ways that the city has remained resilient despite economic change. I argued that this historical lengthening—as well as techniques of framing, mirroring, and incorporating images of local residents in the design—resists the dominant rust-belt narrative of the region by emphasizing the ways that the city has a history of coming together to reinvent itself.

3. Continued fieldwork from 2016 to the present has been sustained through the Ohio Field School initiative carried out by the Center for Folklore Studies at Ohio State University. The Ohio Field School project is generously supported by the Columbus Foundation.

4. In "Dismantling Local Culture," Shuman argues that the local is "always part of a larger-than-local context" (Shuman 1993, 345).

5. Goffman defines footing as "a change in the alignment we take up to ourselves and the others present as expressed in the way we manage the production of reception of an utterance" (1981, 10).

6. For more information about deindustrialization in the United States, see Bluestone and Harrison 1982; for more information about strategies for and challenges to revitalization, see Connolly 2010; for creative responses to and a reclaiming of the "rust belt" label, see Piiparinen and Trubek 2012; and *Belt Magazine*.

7. This is not a critique of Cashman's argument for considerations of instances of critical nostalgia, but rather a way to point out that at least in this context, the heritage product under consideration is in alignment with the values of some residents while it is out of alignment with others.

8. I have heard that there's a strong local sentiment that the unions destroyed Portsmouth throughout the twentieth century by driving away business, as the city developed a reputation for being a tough union area.

9. While the majority of the individuals on the stars are not also on the murals, there are some instances of overlap.

10. The city shouldered $10,000 of the $15,000 expense, with $4,000 being contributed by the Scioto Foundation and $1,000 by the Glockner Foundation.

11. Since 2013, Dr. Andrew Feight, professor of American and Digital History at Shawnee State University, has been publishing, along with his students, historical essays in the area on his website sciotohistorical.org and accompanying app (Feight 2013). Feight uses Curatescape, a free, open-source website and app platform that maps stories onto specific places using geolocation tools. Feight's project includes several essays on local African American history.

12. The pool's reopening is recorded in Conley 2017.

13. Three years after having met Ms. Cadogan, two students from my Ohio Field School service learning class of 2019 (at The Ohio State University) worked with Maureen Cadogan to digitize her family history. Their digital gallery can be viewed at https://cfs.osu.edu/archives/collections/ohio-field-schools/family-history-maureen-cadogan.

14. Stout's poem is overly optimistic about life in the 1830s and the prospects of his protagonist, as the city enacted the "Black Laws" that very same year. Feight explains that "eighty African American residents of the city were expelled under the threat of enforcement of Ohio 'Black Laws,'" which "stipulated that all African-American residents were to register with their county clerk, providing their free status" (Feight n.d.a).

15. While recent fieldwork made me aware of the Underground Railroad bench and the social media presence of the North End, I am still in the early stages of research on this topic. My findings and interpretations are thus preliminary and admittedly cursory.

# REFERENCES

Beiner, Guy. 2007. *Remembering the Year of the French: Irish Folk History and Social Memory.* Madison: University of Wisconsin Press.

Belt Magazine. http://beltmag.com/.

Bluestone, Barry, and Bennett Harrison. 1982. *The Deindustrialization of America: Plant Closings, Community Abandonment, and the Dismantling of Basic Industry.* New York: Basic Books.

Calloway, Colin G. 2007. *The Shawnees and the War for America.* New York: Penguin Books.

Cashman, Ray. 2006. "Critical Nostalgia and Material Culture in Northern Ireland." *Journal of American Folklore* 119 (472): 137–60.

Cashman, Ray. 2008. "Visions of Irish Nationalism." *Journal of Folklore Research* 45 (3): 361–81.

Concerned Citizens Group Roundtable. 2007. "One Man, Making a Difference. Walter Stout." *Runboard.com.* May 12. http://www.runboard.com/bccgforum.f1.t423.

Conley, Ciara. 2017. "McKinley Pool Opens: A Place in the Sun for Everyone." *Portsmouth Daily Times* (Portsmouth, OH), June 15. http://www.portsmouth-dailytimes.com/news/16732/mckinley-pool-opens.

Connolly, James J. 2010. *After the Factory: Reinventing America's Industrial Small Cities.* Lanham, MD: Lexington Books.

Daub, Harald. 2007. "Letter to the Editor: Painting the Floodwall Stars Is a Waste of City Money." *Portsmouth Daily Times* (Portsmouth, OH), August 11.

Dumas, Heather. 2011. "Graffiti, the Other Murals." *Portsmouth Daily Times* (Portsmouth, OH), June 7.

Feight, Andrew Lee. n.d.a "Black Friday: Enforcing Ohio's 'Black Laws' in Portsmouth, Ohio: The Origins of the African-American Community of Huston Hollow." *Scioto Historical.* Accessed August 4, 2018. http://sciotohistorical.org/items/show/108.

Feight, Andrew Lee. n.d.b "Eugene McKinley Memorial Pool and the End of Jim Crow in Portsmouth, Ohio." *Scioto Historical.* Accessed July 19, 2019. http://sciotohistorical.org/items/show/117.

Folklore Archives, Center for Folklore Studies, Ohio State University. Ohio Field Schools. OFS(S)20161120–22CP.

Foster, M. D. 2013. "Inviting the Uninvited Guest: Ritual, Festival, Tourism, and the Namahage of Japan." *Journal of American Folklore* 126 (501): 302–34.

Frisch, Michael. 1998. "De-, Re-, and Post-Industrialization: Industrial Heritage as Contested Memorial Terrain. (Point Park Revisited: Legacies and New Perspectives on Applied Folklore)." *Journal of Folklore Research* 35 (3): 241–49.

Goffman, Erving. 1981. "Footing." In *In Forms of Talk*, 124–59. Philadelphia: University of Pennsylvania Press.

"Help Fix Portsmouth's McKinley Pool." 2017. www.gofundme.com. May 25. https://www.gofundme.com/help-fix-portsmouths-mckinley-pool.

Hill, Jane H. 1995. "The Voices of Don Gabriel: Responsibility and Self in a Modern Mexicano Narrative." In *The Dialogic Emergence of Culture*, ed. Dennis Tedlock and Bruce Mannheim. Urbana: University of Illinois Press.

Horr, Charles H., John McClellan, and Robert Dafford. 2003. *Floodwall Murals: Portsmouth, Ohio: 2000 Years of History, 2000 Feet of Art.* Portsmouth, Ohio: Portsmouth Mural Products.

Jenkins, Rebecca. 2015. "Forgotten: Scioto County's Lost Black History." MA thesis, Bowling Green State University, Bowling Green, Ohio.

Kirshenblatt-Gimblett, Barbara. 1995. "Theorizing Heritage." *Ethno-Musicology* 39 (3): 367–80.

Latorre, Guisela. 2008. *Walls of Empowerment: Chicana/o Indigenist Murals of California.* Austin: University of Texas Press.
Lorentz, Nathan, John H. Lorentz, Mikael Jacobson, Paul Cracchiolo, Fino Roverato, Erik Dunham, and Robert Dafford. 2013. *Beyond These Walls: Building Community through Public Art.* http://www.floodwallfilm.org. Portsmouth, OH: Lorentz Productions.
Low, Setha M. 1994. "Cultural Conservation of Place." In *Conserving Culture: A New Discourse on Heritage*, ed. Mary Hufford. Urbana: University of Illinois Press.
Modan, Gabriella G. 2007. *Turf Wars: Discourse, Diversity, and the Politics of Place.* Malden, MA: Blackwell.
Mohl, Robert, Mandy Hart, and Nevada Hart. 2014. Interview for the Murals Story Booth, interview by Cassie Patterson, October 4.
Morton, Robert. 1996a. "The Floodwall Murals: How It All Began." *AAA Today* (AAA South Central Ohio) (Winter): 4–7.
Morton, Robert. 1996b. "The Floodwall Murals: How It All Began—Part Two." *AAA Today* (AAA South Central Ohio) (Summer): 4–7.
Piiparinen, Richey, and Anne Trubek. 2012. *Rust Belt Chic: The Cleveland Anthology.* Cleveland: Rust Belt Chic Press.
Portelli, A. 1997. *The Battle of Valle Giulia: Oral History and the Art of Dialogue.* Madison: University of Wisconsin Press.
Santino, Jack. 2001. *Signs of War and Peace: Social Conflict and the Use of Public Symbols in Northern Ireland.* New York: Palgrave.
Shuman, Amy. 1993. "Dismantling Local Culture." *Western Folklore* 52 (2/4): 345–64.
Stout, Walter. 2004. "A Struggle to Be Free" (granite bench). Portsmouth, OH. May 5.
Thompson, Frank. 2017. "'Wade in the Water': The Story of Dreamland Integration." *All Things Wildly Considered.* February 4. http://allthingswildlyconsidered.blogspot.com/2017/02/wade-in-water-story-of-dreamland.html.
US Census Bureau. 2017. "QuickFacts: Scioto County, Ohio." Accessed December 15. https://www.census.gov/quickfacts/fact/table/sciotocountyohio/PST045216.
Vastine, Roy E. 1986. *Scioto, a County History.* Portsmouth, Ohio: Knauff Graphics.
Willard, Eugene B., D. W. Williams, George Ott Newman, and Charles Boardman Taylor. 1916. *A Standard History of the Hanging Rock Iron Region of Ohio: An Authentic Narrative of the Past, with an Extended Survey of the Industrial and Commercial Development.* Chicago: Lewis Pub.
Wright, Stephanie 2014. Interview for the Murals Story Booth by Cassie Patterson, October 4.

# 7

# An Ordered Mess
*Folk Narratives and Practices in a Chinese Hui Muslim Market*

Zhao Yuanhao

IN THIS CHAPTER I look at narratives from an ethnic village market in Shandong Province, China, and people's everyday experiences in it, to discuss the relationship between order and disorder in the market as a social space. I suggest a dialectic and dialogic relation of market orders and transgressions.

On a hot summer day in 2013, I stepped for the first time into the marketplace affiliated with the H Village. The villagers are Hui, a Muslim minority officially recognized by the Chinese government. The market is called "The Great Three and Eight Market" (*san ba da ji* in the local dialect). It obtains its name from its opening dates: lunar month days whose single digit is 3 or 8.[1] The market occupies the main street running north-south in the east part of the village,[2] with narrow alleys extending from it to the east or west. Shops lining the street are run by villagers and are partially converted from households. People, not only Hui, but also Han (the majority Chinese) from adjacent villages or places further away, such as the SW City,[3] gather here on market days.

The first impression that the marketplace gives me is that it is a mess. Beside shops, there are pushcarts, three-wheeled motorcycles, peddlers with shoulder-poles. and goods spread on sheets on the ground. Everything a Hui (or a non-Hui) needs to maintain his/her everyday life, from cradle to grave, could be found here: beef and lamb slaughtered right on the street; chickens cooing in overloaded cages and fish munching water for oxygen in shallow barrels; tea leaves in cans and packs on shelves; snacks of alluring artificial colors neatly stored in cardboard-cells; vegetables in piles with mud on them; hand tools, toys, clothes, and bedding displayed on the ground beside boards inscribed with Quranic verses. Public bathrooms, shadowy showrooms, food stalls and restaurants, midwife services, and tombstone workshops are open side by side. To render its label of "Hui [Muslim] market" problematic, one can even find blood tofu and liquor stores in the market.[4] This chapter reads through the market's chaotic surface and decode the logics underpinning market practices, to argue for an orderliness of the market.

## A MAP OF THIS RESEARCH AND ITS ARGUMENT

Activities in the marketplace should not be "considered unifaceted" (Bateson 1987, 65) and reduced to economics. As Henri Lefebvre has argued: "The social relation between individuals and products (and works) embodies modalities and various aspects which can be distinguished by analysis. It cannot be reduced to the economic study of the process of production and circulation (or as vulgar economics has it: distribution). It involves a sociology and even a psychology. It has ideological, cultural and even ethical aspects which the economist may glimpse but which he is unable to grasp" (2014, 119).

Many scholars—including folklorists, ethnographers, and anthropologists—have all made their contribution to describing the marketplace as a "contact zone" (Pratt 1991) of different ideas and activities—an economic and cultural phenomenon where dense communications and performances of people's quotidian life are observed (cf. Bauman 2004; Black 2012; Kapchan 1996; Liu 2012). Others have positioned their focus on the transgressing role of marketplaces, such as the market analyzed by Mikhail Bakhtin (1984) as an extraterritorial space of carnivalesque and authority-challenging encounters with the folk, Jean-Christophe Agnew's (1986) description of the market as a threshold phenomenon, and Peter Stallybrass and Allon White's (1986) analysis of carnivals and market-like events as sites of not only challenging authorities, but also sometimes confirming established social values.

Following these scholars, and by looking at various permutations of expressive culture in the Hui market, I offer a description of different networks of relationships in it. I hope to read "a complex political, economic, geographic, and cultural story [that] lies behind those piles of tomatoes or jackfruit" (Jordan 2011, 70), to code and decode the market in my field site as a rich and complex social space, as a "social morphology" or network of relationships (Lefebvre 1991, 94), and simultaneously an "actant,"[5] a symbolic power that enacts various effects in these networks in the social relations that happen in and around it.[6] Despite its seemingly chaotic appearance and accommodation for transgressive activities, I argue that the market is ironically in a state of orderliness, not in the physical sense of the word, but rather in a balance achieved by tolerating some transgressions while excluding others. This argument is of course not only limited to my market, but could be expanded to other open-air markets in China with careful examination of their own spatiotemporal specificities.

I verify my argument by looking at negotiations between the actants in social spaces or networks of relations that impose upon, penetrate with, and interact with one another in the market. I relay a tour of the marketplace from the time it was established to the current date. I rely on both my own observations obtained from fieldwork in the market and my collaborators' narratives.

My path of reasoning in this chapter is: disorder—order—problematized order—ordered disorder. To realize this I divide this chapter into four sections. The first section focuses on the formation of the market as a new order that was delivered by disorder and conflicts. The second section's dialogues address some of the transgressive trading activities tolerated within the market, to problematize the idea of orderliness presented in the first section. The third section provides a contour of the market's migration and refusal of migration in order to demonstrate how the political and economic struggles produce, organize, or fail to organize the market. In the final section, I question the idea of transgression and disorganization and demonstrate that though transgressions are part of market order, it also conforms to limits and a certain organization; otherwise the order turns into crisis.

## THE FORMATION OF THE MARKET

*Before the market was set up, an old man came from the West, with a shoulder-pole [carrying goods for peddling]. He passed the Han villages, he didn't stop, [but] when he arrived at our village, he put down the pole and said, "Business could be done here."*

—"Prophecy of a Mysterious Old Man," Summer 2014, narrated by Mr. Jun

The moral of this story is that opening the market was legitimized by a mysterious power. As my friend and collaborator Jun explains that the old man was foretelling the location of the Three and Eight Market—that it should be in the H Village—as he said, "business could be done here," only *here*, not in other places. Legitimating narratives are not rare in Hui folktales to explain their ancestors' arrival in China from the "West" (cf. Li and Luckert 1994, 240–41), but ones specifically addressing the arrival at a marketplace are not usual.

In the folktale, the mysterious old man came from the West. This seemingly innocent movement actually accommodates more than one reading, though my collaborator did not clearly suggest so. First, the picture here could be larger than local: here "West" could be understood as the direction from which Islam came into China. In fact, many Hui people believe that their ancestors are from the West (from Xiyu). The mysterious old man in this setting becomes a bearded Sheikh (in my imagination), a helper sent by Allah from the Hui's spiritual homeland to establish the marketplace and grant it a heavenly legitimacy. Second, this narrative could probably be more local and related to the Baba (Muslim Sufi Saint) worshiping custom that is observed in the village. There is a Baba's shrine lying on the nearby hillside, which is also *west* to the village and is still frequented by many villagers. In this reading, the old man is a local Sufi master, who has the ability to perform saintly deeds and make prophecies. Moreover, the presence of a mysterious old man, many times described as a vendor alerting a catastrophe, exists in Han folk belief too. Mr. Jun's narrative conveniently avoids mentioning the ethnicity of the old man.[7] Therefore, if the connotations regarding the "West" or foreign traits of the mysterious old man are played down, a Han market frequenter could also appreciate this narrative.

This narrative tries to propagate a mystery that both Hui and Han can understand to legitimate the market's location. More important, the market power calls for a new order, in which, as the mysterious old man says, "business could be done." However, legends depicting a peaceful and mysterious initiation of the market are not dominant: most local narratives intend to present a piece of history, in which the new order was never granted by a mysterious power, nor was the right of running a market conveniently bestowed onto the Hui by an old man: rather, the right was won. A larger number of narratives suggest that the marketplace is painfully delivered by *disorder*: fights between Hui and Han.

## Fighting for the Market: A New Order Delivered by Disorder

None of my collaborators could give an exact time for when the market was first started, but it is agreed that it was started before the Second Sino-Japanese War (i.e., before the 1930s). Back then, due to a less dense population, the demand and produce of individual villages could only support one market in that area of five or six villages. As a result, the right to run a local periodic market elicited conflicts between rival villages, as whoever controlled the market would be dominating the networks of exchange, thus the social resources; and a marketplace will expand the scope of the local social networks, in that it brings flows of people and currency and thus prosperity to its village.

H village was in such a position. There were several villages around it inhabited by the Han people. Hui and Han both foresaw the benefit of their village becoming the location of the marketplace. But there was one overwhelming reason for the Hui to desperately demand the right to run a market in their own village: when frequenting a market, they did not want to see pork, which happens to be the main type of meat consumed by the Han. Conflict was thus inevitable, and the Han and Hui decided to settle the dispute by force. My friend Old Man Mal used to narrate the story of winning the market so vividly that every time I heard it, I felt the winds from the brandishing of cold weapons. I chose two versions of this narrative to present here. Old Man Mal recalled back to some seventy years ago not without longing and nostalgia,

> That was the first time I saw a seven-segmented chain whip[8] . . . All the Hui even from the City Pass made the battle. . . . They loaded their carts with hundreds of ash-wood batons and joined us[9] . . . They [people of Han villages] were scared and said, "no, we don't want to fight, we quit." . . . The great market became ours, and those people in other [Han] villages only dare to run their own markets secretly, some did the "ghost markets"[10] ("How the Hui periodic market in H Village was established," summer 2013, by Mr. Mal).

And from other collaborators, too:

> Carts of batons were [for a fight that happened] later. But that fight for the market . . . You mean Big Din, right? He was tall, like taller than 1.8 meters (5.9 feet), . . . he came to the front [of the group] and smashed a rock on his head . . . then they [the Han] were silenced . . . ("How Big Din helped win the market," Summer 2014, by Mr. Rud and Mr. Hes).

Other versions also mention Hui fighters descending from hills like Areses, rallying along the pathways to Han villages, and frightening the latter to surrender. We can see that the narrators disagree about certain details such as when the carts of batons were loaded. Was it in the first or the second battle with the Han?[11] Nonetheless, their narratives serve equally well as a lens through which my collaborators' attitude toward the market, their Han neighbors, and also themselves in a specific time and place is magnified. At least in this chapter, variations do not influence my analysis.

Let's return to the battle. The fight was of course a mess: a chaotic, armed conflict between two groups. But the purpose of this disorder, as mentioned, was to bring a new order of resource distribution to the local and new modes to the interethnic contact as well. Here the market, even before its formation, started to behave as a symbolic and agentic power, a force driving different parties to negotiate their space, if we consider armed conflict as an extreme form of negotiation. Hui and Han were not in such close contact in everyday life previously, that is to say, although they lived close to each other, they inhabited their respective villages. The market, however, demanded a new order, in which all the villagers from different ethnic groups could assemble and do business. As a "threshold phenomenon" (a phenomenon driving people to cross social boundaries; see Agnew 1986, 24), it forced the two groups to cross historic barriers, a thin line of peaceful but separate coexistence, to enter a contact zone that though marked by fierce physical conflicts at the beginning is broad and profound enough for them to experience new relationships and even expect more from those relationships. The result is at once dividing and merging. Although the Hui clearly defined their right to run the market and over the space, the losing party, the Han, did not completely lose the market: they continued to occupy it in many senses, because the marketplace is, after all, a public sphere. Old Man Mal mentioned the "ghost markets," but this does not deny the fact that the Great Market hosted and still hosts both ethnic groups. In years following up to the present, the Great Three and Eight Market would serve as the major source of food and extra income for not only the Hui who manage the market but also the Han living in nearby regions. No restraints, according to my observation, are set for Han people for frequenting the market or selling their produce and other goods in the market except for pork. That is to say, a "Hui's" market does not accommodate only the Hui, but also the Han, shoppers and vendors alike. Hui and Han share the market; therefore they likewise share a public space that offers more relationships and richer lived experiences than an ethnically "homogeneous" space could, with the awareness that any ethnic group is a social construction and thus not really homogeneous. Disorder (fights) also offers chances for establishing a new order of interethnic coexisting and sharing.

### The Order Reiterated in Street Fights

Insightful readers may have already noticed that neither of the two narratives about Hui-Han fights over the right to run the market ends with the actual application of violence: Hui only demonstrated martial power, and Han were left an opportunity of surrendering without fighting with their rival, the Hui. The market in the narratives is thus a space for negotiation on the basis of a martial morale in which power is demonstrated with mercy.

However, violence is not always for mere display, sometimes market order, or an order of a wider scope, was reiterated by application of violence. My collaborators were not reluctant to show me their fathers' more "violent" side. There are narratives in which we find severe results brought by Hui-Han conflicts, such as the one that I will present here: "My uncle, Chiang, saw in their [the Han] Buddhist temple . . . a statue of our 'fourth master' kneeling down to a cow,[12] . . . He [Chiang] was mad, he rallied the Hui people from the City Pass to fight with the Han, . . . [T]hey fought their way to the market, and smashed every [Han's] stall they run into" ("How Uncle Chiang became mad and beat the Han," in Summer 2014, by Mr. Rud; Mr. Hes was present too).

My collaborators believe that the Hui's violence was triggered by the Han's deed: they erected a statue of the mosque's fourth master kneeling down to a cow. It positioned the Hui (the fourth master) in the Han's belief system in order to say that the former should express penitence for the karma generated by their slaughtering cows for beef. This deed, if juxtaposed with Mal's discussion of the "ghost market," may lead to a conclusion that they are both fragments of a continuous idea: that of the great division between "us" and "other." In the narrative cited earlier, Old Man Mal told me that the Han had to run "ghost markets;" thus the Hui's right over the Great Three and Eight Market becomes a force of othering and dehumanization for the Han (i.e., the Han as "ghosts"). The Han's erection of the statue in the Buddhist temple is in dialogue with the market, in that by placing a representative of the Hui, the fourth master, in a position lower than a cow, the Han took their revenge and dehumanized the Hui in turn or at least degraded their humanity.

However, as I demonstrate, this conflict was not only a negotiation between us and other or different belief systems,[13] but a more profound negotiation of social relations and local dominance. I include this narrative because the fight was directed to the market (the Han's stalls were smashed), though the trigger of conflict was not related to the market at all. The market as a social space is therefore connected with other social spaces, in this case the temple, and they interact and influence one another, to impose or suggest a social order in a wider scope and a layered way.

The Hui are a minority, so we could argue that they are subalterns living in a social margin. However, after they won their "spatial struggle" (Yang 2004) over the marketplace, the Hui and their village became a center, at least among neighboring villages, because the marketplace is a locally crucial node where people, money, goods, and ideas gather and are redistributed.

Not only were they horizontally central through the marketplace, the Hui also became vertically, or hierarchically, dominant rule makers who started to claim their right not merely in the market context but in other social spaces. Disagreements in beliefs were negotiated in the market through approval or disapproval of commercial activities. The market thus engages with the whole mixed-ethnic community and its social spaces (such as the temple) beyond trades and business. As G. William Skinner suggests, "The market itself then constitutes one focus of social structure within the marketing community" (1964, 38).

This last narrative as well further suggests that the marketplace is the major space for Hui and Han to converge and make conversation, while simultaneously showing that the market is a crucial social and economic resource to the locals despite (socially constructed) ethnic differences. But the Hui was in a higher position in the balance of power to manage, attribute, or deprive resources. Besides, the market—as a public space that links the most local population together—behaved as a network in which news spreads fast. When Uncle Chiang smashed the Han's stalls, this activity would have been a powerful way to warn the Han "whose market it is" and make the warning spread in the "marketing community" widely and quickly.

From mess (fights) to order (market), the Hui seem to have won the market as an ethnic space and made the Han fear their powerful neighbor and become aware of borders that cannot be trespassed. At this point, it is tempting to conclude that a new order was established and the market belonged to the Hui now.

However, as aforementioned, the Han are actually allowed to do business in the market, and the market gradually permitted many non-Islamic or Han elements to sneak in, such as liquor stores and blood tofu. The market drives Hui and Han, Islamic and non-Islamic into contact rather than dividing them up neatly. The new order in the market is not static or totally "Hui," but is layered and complicated.

## LIQUIDATED BY BLOOD AND ALCOHOL: "HUINESS" OF THE MARKET

In this section, I map some microlevel, quotidian but transgressive trading activities on the market, to question the "identity" of the market as a "Hui" Muslim market and problematize its orderliness. I start with three observations of market activities before analysis.

1. About 100 steps behind the entrance of the market, there is a liquor store, in front of which we find a human-sized statue, a male "bartender" wearing a cloak bowing to the street, with a bottle in his right hand and a cup in his left hand, inviting people for a shot.
2. Many a meat stall in the market with "halal" (i.e., prepared according to Islamic laws) signboards hanging on them sell blood tofu, a curd food made of animal blood instead of soybean milk.
3. On market days before the Lunar New Year, portraits of Chinese deities such as the God of Wealth and the Kitchen God are sold on the market. The portraits are marketed to the Han people who also frequent this market, as a Han tradition is to buy these portraits at the end of every lunar year pleading good luck for the coming year. But *akhonds* in the nearby mosque confirmed that some Hui would also purchase these gods' portraits, especially that of the God of Wealth and the Guanyin Buddha, also known as the Buddha of Mercy, who forgives sins. I have seen such portraits hanging in some Hui's shops too.

To appreciate these observations, one has to be aware that not only the consumption of, but also trade of spirits and blood are prohibited by the Islamic law; and toleration of portraits of deities could be considered as serious as suggesting a possibility of *shirk*, that is, practicing polytheism.

Here, I am not interested in the religious dead-end to which the concept of the "Hui" Muslim market is driven by the shot-inviting bartender statue, the blood tofu vendors, or the printed Chinese deities. Instead, I highlight them to problematize the Hui order on the market, because dealing in spirits, blood, and pictures of deities is not permitted by the Islamic law but is trickily allowed and incorporated as part of the everyday Hui market experience. Of course, there are voices against these practices, but the same dissenting voices perfectly represent the negotiability of the order established by Hui. The market cannot reductively be understood as a simple sum added up of individual's activities. Because there is always a tension among those activities and negotiation among individuals, any activity that is or is not tolerated in the market is a result of complex negotiations with the whole market.

No matter what are the negotiations, however, a conclusion could be drawn here that "Huiness" is liquidated in the market, not in a sense that it is fading away and will no longer exist in the future, because there are always people identifying themselves with Hui in one way or another, but that Huiness becomes fluid and coexists with elements that challenge it, such as liquor.[14] The marketplace is such "a liminal locale where the conventional reciprocities of life have been momentarily suspended in favor of a feverish process of negotiation" (Agnew 1986, 196), it has the potential to transform the whole world into an everlasting threshold phenomenon. This threshold of publicity and privacy, divine and mundane, halal and haram, human and nonhuman, us and other does not divide or separate, but connects and merges.

Therefore, if in the previous section I proved that after messy conflicts a new order (market) has been established by the Hui and thus new interethnic relationships, to bestow dialecticality and dialogicality on this orderliness, here I argue that the market order is forever being negotiated and reconstructed in different contexts. The market is always becoming but never concluding.

## THE MIGRATION OF THE MARKET

A stable position is the most noticeable sign for the market's orderliness. However, my market seems to observe no rules—not even its shape and position. On formal market days, it would trickily grow even more deformed by expanding to the highway. Since its establishment, its location has been under constant negotiation.

In this section I offer a map of the market's migration. I argue that the location of the market is never merely horizontal, vertical, or hierarchical nor can it be simply decided to be bottom up or imposed upside down, but there is always a balance achieved through a more complex system of intertwined networks.

### A New Three and Eight Market

According to the market chroniclers, the market was originally located in the western part of the village, or the West Village. Since its establishment, it occupied the street right in front of the West Mosque.[15] Local social ecologies however dramatically changed in the 1980s and 1990ss, after the construction of a highway passing the mouth of the East Village. A result is that many residents of downtown SW City (east of the village) started to come by the highway to purchase produce. People from the city found it difficult to drive into the West Village through its meandering paths, so they parked right at the entrance of the East Village. Besides, all the bus stops are located along the highway, even people taking buses would pass the East Village before they could reach the West Village.

As a result, villagers found it more profitable to do business at the entrance of the East Village, and gradually moved their gathering place to the East. The original Three and Eight Market in the West died out and was replaced by a new one in the East, leaving signs of long-passed prosperity along the streets of the West Village, such as signboards with their colors fading away. From the migration of the Three and Eight Market, it seems that my market is dialogic not only in terms of price (cf. Kapchan 1996, 43), but also in terms of power relations. In the market where exchange is a daily activity, different powers are mobilized to converge.

For instance, Mr. Rud cited a local idiom criticizing the functionaries of the West Village with a ridiculing laugh and said, "Economic of West H is doomed, the 3 & 8 Market is moved" (H xi jing ji mei kaifa, san ba daji ban le jia). This idiom is really an eloquent comment on the situation. It does not only present a fact, but also suggests a connection between the market, East and West Villages, local economics, and the government. Some villagers of the West Village told me that they had urged their functionaries to negotiate with the East Village, to see if the West Village could also join in administrating the new Great Market, but for some reason the functionaries who were in charge at that time were not interested. So gradually the market "officially" moved to the East Village.

Between the East and West Villages, the spatial struggle over the market, a concrete and also abstract space, is clearly observed. What is being contested here is also the right to run the market. Compared with the folktales relating the fight between Hui and Han over the market, villagers may sigh over the fact that this struggle happened again after a hundred years but this time among themselves, though in a less violent way. Now the East Village is winning, and the spatial becomes symbolic, representing the village's better position in a power relation. The east part of the village now has a priority in using the marketplace as its major tax resource and as a bargaining chip for possible negotiation with the government if an eminent domain right to the marketplace were claimed in the future. The spatial is also economic and political.

It seems that the change of market location is initiated from the bottom up. But the West Village functionaries' inertia, the East Village's support to its villagers, the government's construction of the highway, and the customers' choice all managed to influence the final position of the market on an economic or political plane. We can see a market order that is not realized in any single movement, but is the result of the interaction between multiple actants. Only about ten years after the market had moved, however, another "new market" came into being.

## A New Marketplace

To blame the local government and functionaries for inertia seems to be a little bit unfair, as they do manage to collect money from some vendors (though sometimes fail to do so).[16] They also burn the trash in the open air at the end of the day: normally at around four or five o'clock, strands of black smoke are seen billowing from piles of trash alongside the main street accompanied by a choking odor.

Beside those "efforts" to make the market organized, the local government also built a new market*place* at the end of the main street, right behind the spot where the market really flows. Although not having a cast iron pavilion as a "means of imposing order on the streets," as in the case of some European public markets (Tangires 2008, 22; see also Tangires 2002, 137), the marketplace provides decent facilities to offer a clean and organized space for trade. One cannot miss the huge blue signboard with golden characters that reads, "H Village Central Agricultural Produce Marketplace [*H Cun Zhongxin Nongmao Shichang*]" when passing by. The street is wide and straight, and there are spaces neatly divided for potential shops on both sides. According to many of my collaborators, this is a marketplace planned by the village government to run the current market in a better order.

Nonetheless, it seems that the market does not desire to move itself even one step into the space exclusively designated for it. It stops right at the threshold of the *official* marketplace, making the goals alleged by the slogans on the couplets under the signboard: "To bring prosperity to the market" and "To develop [local] economics" evaporate together with the local government's effort to organize it. The market still fixes its position at the mouth of the East Village looking over the flows of goods and people. So the officially designated marketplace is now deserted and appropriated for other uses.[17]

If one should judge this marketplace according to Helen Tangires's statement that "the public market, . . . remained the principal place where society could evaluate its success or failure at organizing urban life" (2002, 205), one can have an impression that the Three and Eight Market is a sign for a total failure of the local government.

A spatial struggle between the market itself and the local authority is obvious. We still recall that the market moved from the West Village to the East Village. In both cases of spatial struggle, we can say that spaces are not only struggled *over*, but could be struggled *out*: the West Village lost its positional advantages so the market moved *out*; and the local authorities of the East Village tried to force the market into the new spot designated for it, but the market refused and keeps *out* of the "officialdom."

With the market activities' hesitation, the official marketplace paused at the stage of planning and construction, but never realized the market as a "concrete abstraction" (Lefebvre 1991); in other words, no real market activities were carried out in the new market, because though authorities can construct buildings and streets, they cannot force any business to take place in them, at least not in this case: any space cannot be preset, but should be produced (Stanek 2008, 66). And no single party dominates the production of spaces, but all have to participate in negotiations. The order and disorder on the market are both relational. Less the endeavors of organization, there would have been no "messing up," and the market would not have had a desire to negotiate and transgress. As Peter Stallybrass and Allon White have argued: "Carnivals, fairs, popular games and festivals were very swiftly 'politicized' by the very attempt made on the part of local authorities to eliminate them" (1986, 16).

It seems safe to conclude by saying that in both cases of the market's migration or refusal of migration, the vendors and the market frequenters, both relatively "low" in social hierarchies,[18] have managed to negotiate the market order with those of relatively high status, the local authorities. However, with more details about the official marketplace unveiled by my collaborators, another layer of this negotiation appears. In spite of their lack of sociopolitical capital, the subaltern strategy is one invested in disruption—the disruption of high and low, of center and periphery, of official and personal.

In a recent discussion with my friend Mr. Jun who owns a shop in the market, however, he totally disrupted my understanding of the subaltern-versus-authoritarian relation by saying that the official marketplace is not official at all, but planned by an individual. He condemned with boldness that it was just the trick of a "local bastard" (*dangdi hunhun*). I was shocked by this rhetoric, as I had always been told by other collaborators that the place was constructed by the village authority. I had been framing the whole event through subaltern studies, imagining that the local vendors' and shop owners' strategies of refusing entrance to the new marketplace were passive, or bore the traits of negation and ambiguity similar to Ranajit Guha's findings on peasant insurgency in colonial India (in Chatterjee 2012, 55–56). Mr. Jun's information made me question my analytical framework and reoriented my understanding of the vendor-authority relationship to a more personal one.

Then I learned from Mr. Jun that the "bastard" in his words was his covillager Mr. Mo, who exploited other villagers' emotions and mobilized them ("low"-ranking villagers) to force the former head of the village to resign. Mo himself became the new village leader. After that, however, he started to abuse his power to benefit himself: one of his achievements was to build this new marketplace and try to drive people into it, under the name of the village officialdom, so he could collect more administrative fees. But the effort failed.

Jun's statement challenges my assumptions of the market's resistance against authority, and questions my efforts to discipline and defamiliarize an event that is a daily social reality to the local people. For some of the vendors, such as my friend Mr. Jun, local government is simply a "bastard," not a symbolical one, but a very concrete and touchable one: Mr. Mo. The new village leader, Mr. Mo, becomes an embodiment of the local authority, and vice versa. The government's endeavor to organize the market and vendors' refusal of this imposed order suddenly becomes all about relationship between real people. Boundaries between the political body, human body, and the market body are merged or, at least blurred. The "urban question" in this case (market planning), unlike what Lefebvre suggested (in Merrifield 2006, 67), appears to be less political, at least in the local vendors' eyes.

When authority is reduced to real people, there is certainly more than one way to negotiate to reach one's goal, especially in this marketplace in question, where personal connections are heavily relied on in business settings. It could be bribery for some, or a confrontation for others. Other strategies of disorder include "guerilla" vending and forming temporary small markets outside of the Great Three and Eight Market to avoid administration fees and also to lower the possibility of conflicts with other vendors who sell similar products.

To summarize the three previous sections, which respectively address the market as tolerating different orders in it and creating orders with other actants around it, the role of the market is thus bilateral: on the inside, it is both constructive and deconstructive, helping to create various networks but also merging boundaries between different people, objects, and ideas; on the outside, it becomes constructive, representing a wholeness. The image of the market as a body here is the best illustration of its role, because any living body is a dynamic and dialectical whole, which undertakes the processes of consumption and digestion inwardly, and those of expansion and development outwardly. The market, therefore, is not unlike a combination of the famous Rabelaisian carnival body or grotesque body (cf. Bakhtin

1984), Henri Lefebvre's dialectical human body that resembles a dialectical space (1991, 40), and Kapchan and Strong's "creole body" (1999, 241).

The market body, as the urban festival body described by Dorothy Noyes, "*attains wholeness* through a loss of boundaries, a massing with its fellows, and an unabashed indulgence in the senses" (1993, 142; emphasis added). Should we change "unabashed indulgence in the senses" to "constrained indulgence in transgression," the description perfectly fits my marketplace. But why "constrained?" I will explain in the following section.

## CELEBRATING TRANSGRESSION?

My discussion has been centered on the market as a boundary-merging or disturbing phenomena that winks to an argument loved by many researchers (including me) of markets, fairs, and festivals: that of the transgressive nature of this kind of phenomenon, which brings "a taste of life beyond the narrow horizon of the town or village" (Stallybrass and White 1986, 37). As suggested previously, transgression, whether on the level of macro-negotiations with the local authorities, of everyday market activities, or of the overlapping of these two, assumes an indispensable role in forming and transforming the market order and rendering it a dynamic and lively social organism and morphology. However, some transgressions are taboo and simply could not be brought to the table. For instance, dealing with pork has never been observed in this market, because this meat is so symbolically disputed and repulsed by the Hui, and abstinence from it is considered as *the* bottom line of being a Hui in many Chinese Hui communities. Transgression should also know its limits.

In this section I engage with the theory of transgression from the perspective of official planning. I clarify that transgression and disorder are not always celebrated in the market, but conditional and relational. I intend to layer the relationships between mess and order in the marketplace.

### National Highway, Municipality, and Market

Now I am returning to the highway beside the market, while going back in time to when it was constructed, to jump out of the box of the local and current, to perceive the market in a larger scale of society and in motion. The highway was called a "national highway" (*guo dao*), meaning that it is maintained by the Chinese government. Moreover, at around the time of the highway's construction, H Village and other villages around it, both Hui and Han villages, were all combined by the government under the name and the rule of "H Village Subdistrict Office" (*H cun jie dao ban shi chu*), officially making the market and the village's name a shared one between Hui and Han, thus forcefully changing the social settings of the villages. Should this be considered an imposed order on the market by a power that is even superior to the local authority, transgression and disorder have no power this time. Faced by the management of local space "on a grand scale" by the state (Lefebvre in Brenner and Elden 2009, 20), the city-level municipal reformation of administrative districts, and all the strong governmental willpower embedded in spatial planning "to impose *order* on the 'irrationality' of preexisting social spaces," (Wilson 2013, 370; emphasis added), the local market has limited choices. Its migration to the East Village is, as analyzed in previous sections, indeed a result of negotiation and a realization of market frequenters' and vendors' agency, but one has to admit that the space as originally inhabited by the local people conceded to the spatial construction as a representation of the state.

## CONCLUSION

February 6, 2015, the last market day before the Chinese New Year, I was talking to Imam Shir in the mosque. Akhond Na arrived, sighing, "Wow, the market is running messy (*luan tao le*), it went onto the highway!" My market still holds its right to become disordered. It probably will never become an "overarching symbol of government's commitment to a well-ordered public economy" (Tangires 2008, 25).

Admittedly, the market is not a Bakhtinian "center of all that is unofficial," nor does it "enjoy an extraterritoriality in a world of official order" (Bakhtin 1984, 153–54). However, neither is it completely wrapped in the authoritarian "urban fabric" (Lefebvre in Merrifield 2006, 82), be it national highway, municipal administration, or village authority. It is still, by being an ordered disorder, searching for a way to make known its struggles with powers-that-be and also struggles of the people attached to it.

Disorder is not simply chaos: it suggests an incompleteness, searching for balance and orderliness of always ongoing negotiations among various actants. The market's disorder does not simply tear the "urban fabric" apart, but re-patches it and sews it into a larger market fabric. This is a fabric woven with the networks of exchange and the circulation paths of not only goods but also ideas, relations, and so forth. The market enables people to negotiate with the state-sponsored "spatial practices (urban fabric)" and "representations of spaces (ideologies, logics behind infrastructures . . .)" using their own, lived, "representational space" or everyday life (See Lefebvre 1991, 38–39).

The market becomes a perfect concrete abstraction, which is nowhere but simultaneously everywhere, and wherever it realizes itself, an order emerges, but again, any order, even a governmentally imposed one, is open to disturbance and renegotiation. This dialectical relationship between order and disorder makes my market consonant with Lefebvre's "street," where "disorder lives," but it "generates another order" (in Merrifield 2006, 92).

## NOTES

The fieldwork was funded by the Mershon Center, The Ohio State University. The author's opinion does not necessarily represent that of The Chinese Academy of Social Sciences.

1. That means 3rd, 8th, 13th, 18th, 23rd, or 28th day of a month. This is a practice observed in many open-air markets—a market named "natural cycled market" by early geographic economists (Skinner 1964).

2. The village is divided into two parts, East H Village and West H Village. These two villages have strong connections, as almost all of their villagers are relatives.

3. I am using coded names for the village and city to protect my collaborators.

4. Islam prohibits the consumption of blood and alcohol.

5. The term "actant" is used here to avoid an overwrought application of the term "agency," which could suggest an arbitrary attribution of willingness to something that cannot generate willing itself, such as the market. However, the activities happening in and around the market did make it an "active body" (Lefebvre 1991) in many social relations, thus agentive in its behaviors. An actant, Latour reminds us, could be acting on its own, or be granted actions thus becomes a source of those actions (1996, 373).

6. One caveat is that we should *not* mistake the "market power" used here with the concept of market in economics, and by perceiving market as a power I have no intention of asserting that China supports a free-market economy. Market power in this chapter refers to the power of exchange, circulation, commoditization, liminalization, or negotiation.

7. Such as the folktale about how Lu Ban, a deified ancient Chinese carpenter and inventor warned the people of Dingling Village near Beijing to escape a fire by hawking chopsticks (kuai), jujubes (zao), peaches (tao), and large baked bread (da huoshao). The residents of Dingling then figured out that the names of the goods form a sentence: "kuai, zao, tao! dahuoshao!" Meaning: "Quickly, early, run! Big fire burning!" (see Xie 1988, 38–40).

8. A chain whip is a "soft" weapon made of connected metal segments.

9. Oiled ash wood batons of different lengths are traditional weapons used in martial arts in China.

10. A ghost market (*gui shi*) is a market runs from nighttime to sunrise. Fascinating stories are being told about ghosts doing business with living men in this sort of markets, but this is not the topic of this essay.

11. This is normally observed in narratives of the same event collected from different people as the narratives could be fictionalized experiences (in a folkloristic way: see Mullen 2000, 210), a construction or even secondhand construction of the past.

12. A "fourth master" is the lowest-ranked mosque clergy (*akhond*); he is in charge of slaughtering animals. So his kneeling down in front of a cow means, explained Mr. Rud, an apology to the animals he killed.

13. Those would be the Han's belief in karma and the Hui's Islamic faith, although the latter is not elaborated.

14. Huiness has always been fluid and negotiable, but my data in this chapter are only related to the current time and place.

15. Fieldnotes of February 24, 2015, according to Mr. Tsa and other people.

16. Five to ten yuan (RMB) (equals 1 to 2 dollars) per person per market day as administration fee.

17. In October 2015, Mr. Jun sent me a currently taken photo of this marketplace; it shows that even the slogans are not kept, they were all torn down by the strong autumn wind of North China.

18. To say frequenters are "low" in social hierarchy is based on a phenomenon that may contradict with Western readers' perception of farmers' market. In R. Black's work (2012), we consider product from farmers' marketplace as healthier than what is offered by the supermarkets, but in China supermarket is valued higher for its clean environment and convenient open hours. People of higher income normally prefer to go to stores rather than frequent farmer's markets. A new trend could also be observed recently, as people of higher income have private vehicles that make frequenting farmers' markets outside of the city easier, and some would take visits to farmers' markets as a folk, traditional tour. Either way, that the frequenters as a whole are placed lower than "government" is a fact.

# REFERENCES

Agnew, Jean-Christophe. 1986. *Worlds Apart: The Market and the Theater in Anglo-American Thought, 1550–1750*. Cambridge: Cambridge University Press.

Bakhtin, Mikhail. 1984. *Rabelais and His World*. Bloomington: Indiana University Press.

Bateson, Gregory. 1987. *Steps to an Ecology of Mind*. Northvale, NJ: Jason Aronson.

Bauman, Richard. 2004. "'What Shall We Give You?': Calibrations of Genre in a Mexican Market." In *A World of Others' Words: Cross-Cultural Perspectives on Intertextuality*, ed. Richard Bauman. Hoboken, NJ: Blackwell Publishing.

Black, Rachel. 2012. *Porta Palazzo: The Anthropology of an Italian Market*. Philadelphia: University of Pennsylvania Press.

Brenner, Neil, and Stuart Elden. 2009. "Introduction." In *State, Space, World: Selected Essays*, ed. Henri Lefebvre, Neil Brenner, and Stuart Elden. Minneapolis: University of Minnesota Press.

Chatterjee, Partha. 2012. "The Nation and Its Peasants." In *Mapping Subaltern Studies and the Postcolonial*, ed. Vinayak Chaturvedi. London: Verso Books.

Kapchan, Deborah A. 1996. *Gender on the Market: Moroccan Women and the Revoicing of Tradition*. Philadelphia: University of Pennsylvania Press.

Kapchan, Deborah A., and Pauline Turner Strong. 1999. "Theorizing the Hybrid." *Journal of American Folklore* 112 (445): 239–53.

Latour, Bruno. 1996. "On Actor-Network Theory: A Few Clarifications." *Soziale Welt*. 47 (4): 369–81.

Lefebvre, Henri. 1991. *The Production of Space*. Oxford, UK: Blackwell.

Lefebvre, Henri. 2014. *Critique of Everyday Life: The One-Volume Edition*. London: Verso Books.

Jordan, Jennifer. 2011. "In Search of the Elusive Heirloom Tomato: Farms and Farmers' Markets, Fields and Fieldwork." In *Food: Ethnographic Encounters*, ed. Leo Coleman. Oxford: Berg.

Li, Shujiang, and Karl W. Luckert. 1994. *Mythology and Folklore of the Hui: A Muslim Chinese People*. Albany: State University of New York Press.

Liu, Morgan Y. 2012. *Under Solomon's Throne: Uzbek Visions of Renewal in Osh*. Pittsburgh: University of Pittsburgh Press.

Merrifield, Andy. 2006. *Henri Lefebvre: A Critical Introduction*. New York: Routledge.

Mullen, Patrick B. 2000. "Collaborative Research Reconsidered." *Journal of Folklore Research* 37 (2/3), "Special Double Issue: Issues in Collaboration and Representation" (May–December 2000): 207–14.

Noyes, Dorothy. 1993. "Contesting the Body Politic: The Patum of Berga." In *Bodylore*, ed. Katharine Young. Publications of the American Folklore Society. Knoxville: University of Tennessee Press.

Pratt, Mary Louise. 1991. "Arts of the Contact Zone." *Profession*: 33–40.

Skinner, G. William. 1964. "Marketing and Social Structure in Rural China, Part I." *Journal of Asian Studies* 24 (1) (November 1964): 3–44.

Stallybrass, Peter, and Allon White. 1986. *The Politics and Poetics of Transgression*. Ithaca, NY: Cornell University Press.

Stanek, Lukasz. 2008. "Space as Concrete Abstraction: Hegel, Marx, and Modern Urbanism in Henri Lefebvre." In *Space, Difference, Everyday Life: Reading Henri Lefebvre*, ed. Henri Lefebvre and Kanishka Goonewardena. New York: Routledge.

Tangires, H. 2002. *Public Markets and Civic Culture in Nineteenth-Century America*. Baltimore: Johns Hopkins University Press.

Tangires, H. 2008. *Public Markets*. New York: W.W. Norton in association with Library of Congress.

Wilson, Japhy. 2013. "'The Devastating Conquest of the Lived by the Conceived': The Concept of Abstract Space in the Work of Henri Lefebvre." *Space and Culture* 16 (3): 364–80.

Xie, Mingjiang. 1988. "Dingling Da Huo Shao" (Dingling Tomb Burnt by Big Fire). In *Shi San Ling de Chuan Shuo* (Folktales of The Thirteen Tombs of Ming Dynasty), collected by Xie Mingjiang and edited by Yang Huilin. Beijing: Zhongguo Minjian Wenyi Chubanshe Press.

Yang, Mayfair. 2004. "Spatial Struggles: Postcolonial Complex, State Disenchantment, and Popular Reappropriation of Space in Rural Southeast China." *Journal of Asian Studies* 63 (3) (August). 719–55.

# 8

# Art/Work
*Precarious Encounters and Vernacular Economic Remedies*

Puja Batra-Wells

"ART," THEODOR ADORNO once wrote scathingly, is "permitted to survive only if it renounces the right to be different, and integrates itself into the omnipotent realm of the profane" (1983, 132). Relying on a Durkheimian binary, Adorno gestures to the long-standing antinomy between autonomous art as sacred and hallowed and its engagement with the market as imitative and impoverishing. This analysis documents the contours of this encounter with the profane, locating itself solidly in the middle world of artistic enterprise—that liminal space between stardom and penury, between abundance and scarcity. In the highly stratified artistic labor market, a few luminary artists in the top tier command multi-million-dollar prices. The tier below, considered "blue chip" artists, is represented by galleries, dealers, and auction houses and commands six-figure incomes. The third tier, constituting the focus of this research, represents the vast majority of visual artists, who often struggle to make a living from the sale of their work (McCarthy et al. 2005, xvi).

This expansive segment of visual arts labor disproportionately endures the impact of the prevailing neoliberal policy paradigm, typified in its experience of precarity.[1] This precariousness manifests in chronic economic insecurity, low pay, long hours, bulimic—often atomistic—patterns of work, along with profound feelings of anxiety and self-doubt about the capacities to finance work and studios and to make ends meet. Within this context, artists' self-directed encounters with the market necessarily retailor the long-standing disjunction between art and commerce. At once responsible for the production of innovative aesthetic output, these artists must simultaneously be agile in maneuvering market forces by virtue of imbuing

DOI: 10.7330/9781607327851.c008

an entrepreneurial sensibility, particularly in the absence of dealer relations, whilst being flexible in reskilling their labor in allied sectors.

In this chapter, I interrogate how practicing visual artists engage risk while deploying surplus-maximizing strategies in the context of unregulated markets. I am interested in unpacking the monetizing and nonmonetizing tactics brought to bear not only on the product(s) of artistic labor, but on the valuation of such labor that can and often does go unremunerated. While relaying the generalized forms of precarity experienced by artists, this work documents their responses, rationalities, resistances, and complicities. I rely heavily on the vernacular as a framework—where quotidian orders of economic sense-making are manifest and bring into focus the richness of practical repertoires that are locally grounded, responsive, and immediate (Bauman, qtd. in Noyes 2012, 33). This study is situated in Columbus, Ohio, and relies on in-depth interviews with forty-six visual artists.

Following a brief appraisal of the market ecologies within which informants work, I analyze the key assumptions that undergird the products of cultural labor based on the push and pull between artistic and entrepreneurial subjectivities using the lens of gift and commodity. After an enumeration of the varying typologies of risks along the economic and creative axes, the analysis concentrates on strategies of mitigation and their (productive and unproductive) outcomes.

## THE ECONOMIC TERRAIN

A profile of the contemporary labor market for artists based on the work of sociologist Pierre Menger reveals the following: as an occupational group, artists tend to be younger than the workforce; they are better educated and tend to live in urban metropoles. They have higher rates of unemployment and are chronically underemployed while also being more prone to holding multiple jobs (2006, 769). Compared to other workers in their occupational and educational category, they tend to earn less income and experience a great deal of income variability (769). Also, the market suffers from excessive supply of labor, inexhaustible differentiation in production, and reputational rents—which means that more-established artists command better prices based purely on recognition (766). Of significance, these earnings penalties do not disincentivize people from becoming artists, with more people aspiring to do so than the market is actually able to bear (776). Today, there are 2 million Americans within the umbrella category of "artist" with approximately 216,996 of those identifying as visual artists (working in the mediums of painting, sculpture, and photography) (Bradshaw

2008, 21). With a median age of forty-four, these artists are older than artists in most other specializations, but their median income of $30,600 is below the norm (Bradshaw 2008, 26). Recent NEA surveys show that arts-sales earnings constitute less than 20 percent of this total income—a fact mirrored in my fieldwork, as none of the informants I worked with were able to sustain themselves from art sales alone.[2] The median annual income for visual artists in Ohio is $28,330 (Bureau of Labor Statistics, 2015).

Compared with professions that require a similar level of training, artists receive lower income from the market but higher incomes from gifts in the form of grants, subsidies, and donations (Abbing 2002, 40). To understand art's economic exceptionalism, it is imperative to delineate between the two spheres that art operates in: the market sphere and the gift sphere (Abbing 2002, 41; Hyde 2009, 363). The interplay between these spheres congeals perceptions of art's autonomy from other segments of societal production—in that, while being traded in the marketplace, the field of art simultaneously engages in a full-throated disavowal of its economic constitution.

This disjuncture is made coherent through what Pierre Bourdieu terms as the "nomos" of the field (1996, 223). It is the nomos of any field that guards its normative order, its expectations, and rules as well as its boundaries (223). The rule at the center of art's exceptional economics is articulated by Bourdieu in pithy form as an "interest in disinterestedness" (1983b, 321). This disinterestedness indicates the field's autonomy from economic determinations because the field alone gets to define its criteria for production and evaluation (Johnson 1983, 15; Bourdieu1983, 115).[3]

Yet the nomos of the artistic field is not anticapitalist, because it functions with a particular economic logic—a "trade-off of immediate sacrifice for future gain" (Forkert 2012, 14). Most artists participate instead in what is referred to as the tournament model of success, which hypothesizes that "workers competing for the top level will accept relatively smaller wages in the short run in the hopes of someday winning the lottery and getting the balloon prize" (Plattner 1996, 13). Thus the idea of financial sacrifice and resulting poverty is understood as normative, with the economic insecurity borne by artists perceived as a form of choice (Forkert 2012, 14). This perception of choice negatively impacts the discourse about artists and economic inequality contributing to the naïve idea that artists don't suffer from "real poverty" (14).

I want to pause here momentarily to take up the idea of sacrifice—a word that finds its roots in the Latin *sacer*, which means to make holy or sacred. Sacrifice establishes a relationship between the sacred and the profane (Mauss, qtd. in Keenan 2005, 17). Actuated by the logic of the gift, it entails the destruction or privation of a good in the order of the Latin formula, "do ut des—or I give that you may give" (17). The artist's sacrifice follows this logic in dyadic form: as in a sacrifice *to* and a sacrifice *for* art. In the words of T. S. Elliot, "the progress of an artist is a continual self-sacrifice, a continual extinction of personality" (1921, 9). That is, the artist sacrifices himself, in the name of art. Simultaneously, he sacrifices for art any economic benefit that might sully the autonomy of his output.

This is the realm of the gift; exalted for its virtuosity, it animates an alternative system of values than the marketplace. The gift venerates the singularity of the individual where the marketplace is impersonal and indifferent (Abbing 2002, 44). The gift values the "indivisible qualities of art" whereas mechanisms of the market reduce these qualities to numeric values (45). The artist's sacrifice creates an obligation for support that relies on the principle of reciprocity based on the logic of the gift. This explains the vast asymmetry in incomes from market sphere versus the gift sphere. Here again, gifts infer a disavowal of self-interest in the short term so that benefits of deferral might be reaped in the long term.

As the nomos of any field is historically contingent, it is incumbent here that the vast reorganization of the cultural sphere under the aegis of neoliberalism be emphasized. The dominant modality under this regime is the creative economy that has upended many fundamental presumptions inhered by the principle of autonomy. The creative economy fetishizes the figure of the artist as an exemplary embodiment of individual talent and original "creativity" but releases the artist from the stigma from bourgeois enterprise, celebrating commercialism. In fact, once state and corporate institutions "recognized the value of avant-garde cultural practices as signifying innovation," their neoliberal impulses extended a rationality of competition and market-driven discipline deep into the cultural sphere (Forkert 2012, 27). This orientation then gives rise to a more explicitly entrepreneurial artist subject who in addition to creative production is also responsible for fund-raising, self-promotion in the form of "brand development," and networking as well as direct sales and the creation of alternative revenue streams. As postindustrial economies seek ways to diversify, the creative sector is seen as a resource for the growth of wealth. Thus, as Jen Harvie argues, artists are being "pressed to grow their industries and to be more business-like in the process" (2013, 65).

Under post-Fordist capitalism the generalization of "creative work" into all areas of economic life must be read as a palliative instrument in the face of increasingly flexible, mobile, and precarious employment (Hardt and Negri 2005, 112). Simultaneously, the manufacture of such precariousness requires individuals to "invent their own certainties," proliferating widespread "individualization" within society (N. Beck 1992, 14). That is, the risks and the responsibilities of participation are all borne by the individual alone, something that my artist-informants know a lot about.

## THE UNCERTAIN BUSINESS OF ART

As independent artists, most of my informants register an "entrepreneurial disposition." Since the eighteenth century (particularly after the demise of aristocratic patronage and the era of direct commission), artists in the West have engaged in practices to support their livelihoods in the form of self-promotion and distribution (via brokerage) (Forkert 2012, 16; Win 2014, 3). These activities functioned in line with the normative division of labor associated with an emphasis on autonomy. The difference today is marked by an emphasis on post-Fordist modes that echo neoliberal rationalities in the form of individualized flexible labor, entrepreneurial engagement, and risk management.

For informant and painter Nathalie Beck becoming "businesslike" was never part of the career equation. Like many informants, she voices a narrative of dissonant expectations between art school and art market: "I thought I'd learned everything I needed to, technique, process, how to talk about my work and to a certain degree, how to market yourself to galleries and shows. What I didn't expect was how hard it was going to be on the outside. It's like a bubble burst" (2015).

Such responses necessitate an examination of the economic assumptions made about the field prior to entry. The spectrum of belief regarding economic well-being spans from the "romantic" and "naive" to the more practiced, "not in it for the money" or "some things go beyond money" (informants Alden 2015; Espe 2015; Gazala 2015; Webber). The most salient feature of these responses is how they bifurcate along generational lines, with younger informants more eager to confess a dissonance than older artists—a reason for which could be the proximal distance in time with relation to art school. Additionally, older artists, tested by longevity in the profession, perhaps cleave more strongly to the illusion undergirding the field.

Part of the disdain, then, is tied to the art world's affectation of this indifference in the face of widespread malaise about the risk/rewards of higher education in the contemporary moment. As Madoff argues, the liberal ideology of the art school as a "laboratory free from the constraints of the world," while productive for the institution, is no longer tenable because it is accompanied by the perils of financial debt (2009, 274). A case in point is Michele Dean, a local sculptor whose debt is the result of the MFA boom of the past twenty years, which promised artists' recourse to academia as a failsafe against the vagaries of the market—a recourse, she feels, that left her with diminishing returns. In 2010, unable to afford her studio due to loan payments, she moved her practice home and is now financially supported by her spouse. Sculptor Walter Hermann (2015), abandoned his MFA midprogram, unable to "make wage" due to the employment restrictions imposed on graduate students, while artist Leah Martin (2015), a recent graduate from Columbus College of Art and Design—who racked up $50,000 in debt—conceded with some pessimism, "In the end, I have a general MFA and a certificate in college level instruction, which doesn't really mean anything anymore."

A corollary to the art school debt criticism is that informants feel largely underprepared by their educations to face the realities of the marketplace. The oversupply of labor is exacerbated by the proliferation of amateur content creators enabled by the Web 2.0 revolution. Significantly, this free or "cut price content" is a threat to the livelihoods of professional artists, "unable to compete with the commercial mining of these burgeoning, discount alternatives" (Ross 2007, 21). Informants are thus under strain to professionalize their identities via the entrepreneurial disposition to compete more efficaciously within an expanded field and, especially, in the absence of brokerage relations. Professionalization for them means self-branding, marketing, facilitating e-commerce, accounting and business tax preparation, agile exhibition schedules, and (social) networking in addition to maintaining a productive practice. It means fundraising, writing material or projects-based grants, self-publishing catalogue coffee table books, entering competitive shows, and exhibiting at least two to three times a year. Showing may include the juried or (for pay) art fair or state fair circuit (sometimes, for months at a time). It may also mean cultivating non-art-show venues where the work might be displayed in restaurants, beauty salons, bars, hotels, and coffee shops.

In conjunction with student loans, a number of informants carry substantive credit card debt to support themselves. Some, such as Mona Gazala, have taken loans and drained savings to finance projects, while others, such as sculptor Christina Smith (2015), have taken out second mortgages to defray the cost of familial obligations. These liabilities amplify the other risk that informants spoke most anxiously about, which was healthcare and unforeseen medical debt. Take, for example, the case of printmaking couple

Adam and Nora Nash (2015), who were driving back to Columbus from a vending fair in Cincinnati when wet road conditions led to an almost fatal accident. Adam bore the brunt of the accident with severe injuries to his left leg. The accident came three months after he made the jeopardous decision to quit a full-time teaching job with benefits to pursue printing professionally. Without health insurance, the couple had to bear the costs of traumatic surgery and recovery. While a quarter of my sample is on insurance through the Affordable Care Act, two admitted to being unable to afford the mandate at all.

As debt and health-care risks are now widely borne across an increasingly unequal economy, an examination of the class makeup of my sample is vital. These informants overwhelmingly identified themselves as middle class; an identification that was at times articulated as a taken-for-granted category or alternatively seen as onerous, in the form of "homogenous and suburban," or as an impairing mindset, "something to unlearn" (informants Brouillette 2015; Alden 2015).[4] There are two points in need of teasing out here within the wider context of visual arts labor and class. The first is that the middle-class character of my sample does not pertain solely to income levels, but also to a unique relationship to labor, indicating "an individual, self-directed relationship to production rather than administering and maximizing the profit produced by the labor of others (capitalist class) or by selling one's labor power (working class)" (Davis 2013, 28). As Ben Davis clarifies, this middle-class character is dual edged, as it is predicated on the professionalization of art as a means of support, while synchronically identifying "art" as a manifestation of creative individuality and self-expression (29). This duality makes palpable the strain between contradictory impulses that pit a kind of "embourgeoisment" against the long-standing tradition of bohemia (Rosler 2015).

Bohemianism institutionalizes art's exceptional autonomy via the politics of identity. The bohemian artist is unconventional: a rebel who casts off the safety net of middle-class comfort, for a life of penury, risk, and transgression (Wilson 2003, 12–13).[5] The bohemian stance authenticates the artist's occupational identity as a figure "whose role it is to explore marginal states of being and consciousness" (Seigel, qtd. in Wilson 2003, 13). The narration of this stance is captured by ideas about retirement and long-term financial planning, which some informants scoffed at. This is made lucid by sculptor Walter Hermann in the following way: "I have strong feelings about retirement. Honestly, if you're an artist and you're telling me that you are looking forward to retirement, I'm a little baffled by it. I personally want to be 135 and fall face flat dead in my studio working on a piece, without ever thinking about a 401K . . . I believe that retirement is an archaic twentieth-century term . . . besides, tomorrow is promised to no one."

Here the gaze refuses the gratifications of determined futurity in favor of present satisfactions, while simultaneously policing occupational identity. Other iterations of this speech genre include phrases such as "I'm already doing what I want to; why would I ever retire?" or the more presumptive "I think it is safe to say that most artists probably don't think about it" (informants Brouillette 2015; Espe 2015). The ideological commentary bucks the idea of work as alienating, projecting instead a view of work as the apotheosis of self-fulfillment.

Such renunciations do not, however, have universal appeal. In fact, bohemian discourse reveals itself as a distressed genre increasingly limited by informants' disenchantment with systemic economic pain on the one hand and middle-class aspiration on the other. Aging, emotional stress, and a desire for material comfort were the terms in which these limits were relayed. Artist Robert Read noted an attitudinal shift via the lens of growing older: "My retirement plan has always been to become a famous artist. That's stupid—wow, is that short-sighted. But, I didn't know that and now I'm staring at middle age. So as much as I've wanted them, I've created an environment where I can't support a child like I would want to."

His disappointment registers a denunciation of the "winner take all" orientation of the field that cost him the rewards of growing a family. The vast majority of informants also spoke about living with the vicissitudes of chronic financial uncertainty and the immense affective imprint it carries. Living paycheck to paycheck or what painter Cain Turner refers to as living "right now" comes with constantly "being down to the wire." For others, such chronic insecurity becomes the source of "long low periods" or "dark times" that existentially threaten the practice itself (informants Grant 2015; Thomas 2015). As informant Maureen Thomas (2015) elaborates, "It isn't romantic when you're choosing between buying canvas and car insurance." Economic calculations thus become tethered to material and often aesthetic calibrations. Finally, some informants made the case for material comfort, for being able to indulge in the dream of the "good life." Ceramist Susan Green, articulates this position by suggesting: "I want to be able to afford private school for my children because I live in the city. I want to be able to go on vacations with them and pay for college, and I want to retire comfortably when my arthritis gets bad and when I can't lift wet clay anymore—and I want to spend time with my husband. If that makes me bourgie, so be it."

## "MAKING DO" AND THE ECONOMIC VERNACULAR

I now focus in-depth on strategies of mitigation that offer a window into how informants engage with their local art economy. How they, in the words of Michel de Certeau, "make do," in their everyday engagements with adversarial conditions?[6] How are the contradictory juxtapositions between bohemian and bourgeois resolved in the field? An interrogation of these questions relies on the analysis of ineluctably local or situated forms of knowledge that circulate in the vernacular,[7] via practices of common sense, intuition, metaphor, and bricolage (Swann 2006, 57). These are economic literacies that have accreted through experience in the field and range from the formalist to the idiosyncratic. Here I elaborate on five such tactical forms,[8] in the guise of value recuperation, secondary work, alternative exhibitionary practices, credit incentivization, and the creation of communal capital.

### Recuperating [Economic] Value

Informants unanimously lament the issue of "value" in their encounter with the market. While they perceive their profession as universally esteemed, there is a coincidental sense of "devaluation" made manifest in chronic requests for free and donated work, a paucity in sales, and haggling over prices. An assessment of this situation is offered by artist Lisa McLymont (2015): "Because we are doing our artwork, we're doing what makes our hearts sing—it's perceived as easy and enjoyable, as 'you can blink your eyes and do that so why not just do it for me for free.'" Printer Adam Nash points to the changing and saturated dimensions of the visual arts labor market, suggesting that an already fraught system of a value is made worse when "everyone has a niece or an aunt who'll do that for free." Focusing the frame further, photographer Amanda Lewis spoke to the enemy within—the legions of artists who are willing to offer discounted services incentivized by the promise of greater "exposure." A comparative reading based on other "professions" further clarifies this vexing state: "Imagine asking a dentist to work on you for free" (informant Windham 2015).

While the gift economy encourages sacrifice and mutuality, for these informants, it also complicates relations with the marketplace. The gift sphere protects art's autonomy and its ineffable labors, making it resistant to the logic of simple exchange values. This resistance is married to the nature of time in artistic production—for, where work is waged by the hour, artistic labor "sets its own pace" (Hyde 2009, 87). Yet, in conjunction with the gift economy, informants also participate in the professionalized economy.

Here, artistic labor comes to be structured by the expectations of financialized entrepreneurialism in terms of wage labor, and the art object—the gift of these labors—takes on a commodity form. The realignment of artistic autonomy in line with market ideologies is not a source of alienation for informants. If anything, many spoke disdainfully about maintaining the veneer of a disinterested habitus, choosing instead to embrace unabashedly their monetizing agency. Sculptor Walter Hermann queries: "Have you ever met a starving artist? I feel it is a derogatory term that needs to stop being used, and we as artists need to stop perpetuating it. It allows people to devalue what we do, and to think that we shouldn't be allowed to make money off of it because we are supposed to have some form of struggle." Ceramist Charlie Sloan (2015) echoes this critique emphasizing that artists have "socialized the marketplace" in a way that permits economic devalorization by mystifying artistic production through discourses of inspiration, genius, and transcendent value.

The capacity to sell art is reported as the most significant, common-sense marker of validating an informant's status as a professional artist. Selling work is also a way to police professional boundaries between amateur producers and working artists (informant Parsons 2015). Notably, then, the commodity nature of the art object is not antagonistically framed, but positioned instead as the inevitable telos of the art-making process. Informants Claire Roberts (2015) and Michele Dean, for example, categorically refer to their work as "commodities" as a way to verify their full engagement with the market. For others, attending to the art object solely through the lens of commodity or exchange can to be too reductive. Instead, as informant Olivia Parsons concedes, the social life of the art object is neither fixed nor stable but manifests a processual ontology: "I sell work for people to experience, contemplate and enjoy. But once it leaves the studio, it could go anywhere and be anything and I'm okay with that."

The most compelling value-maximizing instrument at informants' disposal is their pricing strategy, which my research finds to be remarkably variant and unstandardized. These range from purely econometric calculi and comparative market analysis to esoteric enunciations of opportunity cost pricing based on a maker's bond with her art. Some use size as a measure, while others use square inches. Painter Adam Brouillette rejects the use of labor as an adequate matrix because it would discount "hundreds of hours I put into getting to this point and the hundreds of hours of education that I went through." Alternatively, there are informants who have tabulated per-hour labor by accounting for time, technical skill, and postgraduate training. Such wage labor prices ranged from twenty-two dollars an hour to thirty-five (informants Dean 2015; Windham 2015). Some add material cost to wage labor, while others include "business overhead costs" such as investment in technical assets (informants Gregg; Parsons).

For most informants art sales fail to be a sustaining source of income, however. Thus many rely on the sales of what Amanda Andrews metaphorically refers to as "bread and butter" pieces. These range from low-priced, quantity driven, child-directed lines for the Amanda and Mac Andrews (2014); to greeting cards and magnets for Michele Dean; tea towels, gift wrap, and monoprint demonstration sessions for Olivia Parsons; Christmas cards and short-run specialty vintage themed "gimmicks" for Claire Roberts; and hand-sewn rag dolls and polymer face-dolls for Alicia Noth. Social art practitioner Mona Gazala deconstructs her monumental "archaeological" installations to sell them in smaller pieces that incentivize appreciators to become buyers. Not as commonly, artists such as Adam Brouillette offer unsold catalogues on sale prices from time to time.[9] Compellingly, there are informants in my sample who speak very derisively of such explicitly commercial production by using "tchotchkes," "knickknacks," or other terms, arguing that artists would be better off spending their labor on improving their fine art than devaluing the field by proliferating craft production.

While the preceding analysis locates itself on the supply side of the market, informants have to deal with demand side resistances. One internal critique deals with aesthetic compromise, and the second with the fetishistic associations of art as commodity. Whereas in conventional markets the law of consumer sovereignty controls the success and failure of commodities, "art's commodification permits the artist to be a critical author" in spite (often regardless) of demand (Beech 2015, 14). This leads to high levels of "competition through unlimited differentiation" in artistic output (Menger 2014, 112). Thus some informants report undercutting others for projects as well as making explicitly commercial work, compromising the principle of autonomy. Such instances were relayed in tortured terms as in this circumstance narrated by Cain Turner (2015): "This woman in Mansfield saw something she liked and wanted it for her home. She would come to down to my studio from Mansfield and say, 'put this color over here, or I don't like this there, will you move this over here, I don't like black, I love black, um, I don't like red, I love red over here' . . . it was like this insanity. I wanted to say, you paint the damn thing, here's the brush because this is not even me."

The second thread of critique takes aim at buyer's perceptions of art ownership. The commodity form of the art-object congeals worth in the form of exchange value, which for Marx propagates a fetishistic relationship to the object (1992, 4). Such fetishistic relations are expressed in the heavily bloated prices that art can carry in elite markets.[10] Exaggerated prices lead to the categorization of art as a luxury good. Such associations of art as a speculative investment negatively impact buyers' willingness to spend money on art with ease. Informant Mona Gazala's perspective deserves full quotation here:

> Buyers and even the artists themselves market it [work] as a lifelong investment. People will buy a couch and throw it away after five years if they get tired of it. They feel like if they buy a piece of art, it's got to stay there forever. Even if it doesn't do something for them anymore. I think that's what holds people back—the permanence of the investment that doesn't cost more than their couch, which they are totally willing to pay for. But, they won't do it because they think it's like a child or a dog or something that you can't throw away and have to keep forever.

Thus, even when the art work's use value is expended for the buyer, a permanence is forged by its exchange value.[11] Gazala's proposition here is an appeal to buyers to relinquish the "auratic" and fetishistic qualities they confer to the art object—to acknowledge the mutability of the (object/owner) encounter and to permit its passage or "perishing."

## Secondary Work

The second tactic informants overwhelmingly report is secondary work. With none of my informants able to provision sustainable incomes from art alone, most resort to alternative forms of work to support their practices. Such work ranges from full-time corporate jobs and teaching to freelancing and part-time service and retail-based work. While informants overwhelmingly prefer alternative work in allied art fields—such as museums, galleries, or design—such work is often highly competitive and hard to come by in paid form. Many therefore work in fields in little congruence with their practices. Painter Mark Brown (2015) speaks of his full-time "day-job" at a pension fund with much gratitude, arguing that not having to worry about a steady income has a net positive impact on his art making, enabling greater creative risk and experimentation. In a similar vein, art-doll maker Alicia Noth (who works for a financial institution) appreciates the guarantee of benefits (retirement and particularly health care) that her job provides for her family.

Painter Adam Brouillette explains the ubiquity of secondary practice using art school as foil: "I boil this down and tell my students—a piece of paper is nothing. It might as well be toilet paper. The main thing you have to do is try to acquire as many skills because ultimately what you are going to be paid for in the real world is that." "Multiskilling," then, is a term I heard a lot in my fieldwork in conjunction with well-worn metaphors such as "wearing a lot of hats" and "juggling work" (informants DeRosa 2015; Read 2015). An outline of the contours of painter David DeRosa's practice gives shape to this state: "Being a working artist means being a code monkey, doing web development, web design, medical illustration, editorial illustration, cartoons [and] gallery work. I've even made my bread and butter doing old school portraiture." The governing logic of these occupational narratives emphasizes what Felix Warneken calls a "bricolage of activities" indicating the "combination of different forms of gainful employment to ensure survival" (qtd. in Koch 161). Such bricolage is celebrated in the creative economy as a form of adaptive fluidity, where individuals draw from their "means at hand" making use of opportunities at their disposal (Strauss 1966, 23). Multitasking connotes the flexibilization of labor that grounds the entrepreneurial disposition. It is the most destructive pathology of working under the aegis of late capitalism. Multitasking interrupts thought and action—it fragments consciousness and experience, seldom permitting an end to work.

## Alternative Exhibitionary Tactics

"Gallery representation is an interesting game," says Isaac Alden reflectively. "They represent you the artist, promote you but do they celebrate changes in your work and pitch such potential to collectors or are they just interested in selling? As an artist you have to be careful not to fall into the trap." Here, the "game" analytic offers insight into informants' anxieties about representation ethics in which "endogenously established rules may be disregarded when advantageous" (Palmer 2015, 39). The game also feels like a "set-up" for informants who cannot afford galleries' prohibitive sale commissions, which can range anywhere from 33.3 percent to 50 percent (Derosa 2015).

The most charged display circuit is the art fair, which is the primary way a number of informants encounter the market. Alongside the cost of entering some juried shows—which include high up-front costs in the form of application, vendor and booth fees—logistics are the hardest to manage. Packing and travel inevitably cause loss of work as does mercurial weather. Audience expectations for small and low-priced work are also a source of much aggravation. As artist Cain Turner states: "No one expects to come to an art fair and spend $3,000 on a painting when they're hot or it's raining.

Everyone there wants something for $50, and that was a wake-up call for me." Informants who refuse to do art fairs shared perspectives filled with much antipathy toward them. The "marketplace" setting was a source of particular distaste along with the concomitant shallow price points. Here informants rely on a spatialized logic to comment once again upon "art's devaluation"—for where a gallery or studio exhibition facilitates a "conversation" with or about art, the art fair, for them, is an exercise in obfuscation (Alden 2015; Gomez). In the words of photographer Bea Webber, "It looks like art, tastes like art, but isn't quite there" (2015). Commenting on the explicitly commercial nature of such work, Bea's critique seeks to disqualify it as categorically illegible as Art.

With a strain on available exhibition spaces, informants also rely on showing through alternative art spaces, for example, galleries set in private homes such as the Vanderelli Room in Franklinton and public spaces, for example, recreational halls and city halls. Many (mostly, younger) informants seek to show their work in private-service-sector businesses such as coffee shops, bars, restaurants and delis, salons, gyms, yoga studios, and even nurseries. Others report less-than-ideal experiences with work stolen from sites or having to engage with business owners who fail to pass along sales revenues. Informants who show work in alternative, nonart spaces also acknowledge a similar stigma (following the logic of the art fair) is attached to the practice but offer pushback through the lens of quality claiming the issue of location is irrelevant because the "work that sells" would do so regardless of where it is shown (Espe 2015).

## Credit Incentivization

While debt is one of the most burdensome risks that informants might take on, some choose to instrumentalize it to their advantage. Here, the entrepreneurial subject is herself or himself responsibilized by normative participation in debt culture, embodied by the figure of the creditor. Take the case of Mac and Amanda Andrews: Debt shaped their entrance to the field as they juggled credit cards, shifting balances based on interest for many years. Today, they use debt to monetize their catalogue by offering what Amanda calls her "good karma credit plan," a payment plan that allows buyers to pay for their art in installments of three, on credit (no debit cards allowed anymore). Karma credit recognizes the inelastic discretionary purses of postrecession art consumers and offers enough incentive that it counts for 20 percent of all their sales, particularly large and highly priced pieces. The plan's high rate of success is evinced by its attachment to a metaphysical comeuppance or, as Mac instructs, "karma always catches up with people."[12] Notably, creditworthiness is judged purely by "instinct and intuition," and buyers get to take possession immediately (Amanda Andrews). Amanda hasn't turned anyone down either, an indication of a continued willingness to incur a high degree of financial and material risk.

Without the assurances of credit-verifying services and capital at hand, informants often find themselves metaphorically "burned" by this practice. When artists enter into the creditor-debtor relationship, "one that makes up the subjective paradigm of modern-day capitalism," they enter into social relations based on power (Lazzarato 2011, 38). Where debt expresses a promise of payment, such payment is predicated on society's capacity to "engender a person capable of promising"—a power that mostly eludes my informants (30). Aside from the moral obligation to honor payment, buttressed by reactive precautions undertaken by artists, there is little recourse left to them (outside of civil court, which is prohibitive in cost).

### Communal Capital

One of the most consistent discourses I encountered in the field is about community and its significance in bolstering individual practices. Artists describe the local arts community as "open and not cliquish," "diverse and inclusive," "small yet vibrant" (Alden 2015; Gazala 2015; McLymont 2015; Sloan 2015). The term "community" is mobilized to relay the scene's "unique collaborative spirit," often in comparison to sister cities such as Cleveland and Detroit, which are positioned as "territorial" and "closed" (informants Gazala 2015; Lewis 2015). Artists speak of feeling part of a close-knit network, which is the source of much professional and financial support. As Cain Turner confesses: "Most art openings in the city are attended by other artists, not so much by common people." Additionally, artists tend to buy each other's work, even with limited purses (informants Halliday 2015; Lewis 2015). When money is restrained, barter economies and time swaps thrive.

The arts community supports a variety of independent arts organizations with varying emphases. These organizations function to bolster artist professionalization by providing members the benefits of mentorship, networking, exhibition, and public relations opportunities and workshops that enhance and support artists' practices. One of the most significant features of these organizations is that they run entirely on volunteer labor. Volunteer work is part of the cosmology of the gift economy (Hyde 2009, 157). Volunteering alleviates the isolation of individuated artwork and offers psychic and spiritual reimbursement while proliferating an ethos based on equitable participation and egalitarianism, though it is not without its problems. Fears proliferate about the exploitative edge of volunteering, which has caused some informants to veritably "burn out."

The final thread of critique points us to some of the limits of community that I want to explore through the lens of the overarching theme of this research—economic precarity. The term "precariat" is a "neologism that brings together meanings of precariousness and proletariat to signify the experience of exploitation and a (potential) new political subjectivity" (Gill and Pratt 2008, 27; Standing 2014, 13). This potential "class-in-the-making" for Guy Standing, has the potential to coalesce around the discontents of late modernity. Notably, this grouping suffers from deep internal segmentation, with some members being highly educated as knowledge or cultural workers and others (manufacturing laborers) who are less educated and reliant on more anachronistic skill-sets at a disjuncture from the needs of the global economy. My informants are members of this emergent coalition of flexibilized workers struggling under neoliberal market reforms. They uniformly express distress about their economic states in terms of marginality, uncertainty, and security. Within this context, I would invariably ask them if the collectivities they participate in could be harnessed to fortify their economic well-being, be it in the form of wage regulation, collective standards for unpaid work, or artist unions—in other words, what critical or political potentialities might these collectivities hold? Responses overwhelmingly stop short of finding merit in such "classed" mobilization. On the contrary, informants tend to communicate stakes and limitations in terms that reiterate their incorporation into an entrepreneurialized world order, specifically articulating a lack of time/labor as barriers to such radical restructuring.

## CONCLUSION: THINKING THROUGH PRECARITY AND ECONOMIC STABILITY

The preceding elaboration of a wide range of artist-informants' informal approaches toward pricing, the valuation of labor, the hierarchization of alternative employment, the politics of showing, and professional community-making helps delineate the daily orders that accompany the inhabitation of an entrepreneurial disposition. This disposition explicitly injects the market (the stigmatized and profane) into the autonomous zone of practice (sacred and valorized) and enables artists to compete more efficaciously in an increasingly competitive and saturated labor market.

It promises a degree of stability by mobilizing market-oriented rules of engagement but is also revealed as deeply unstable in its slide toward self-exploitation, its demands for flexibility, and its disruption of the gratifying rhythms of day. Simultaneously, the deterioration of bohemianism cannot be read as a complete evisceration, because artists continue to perform economic disinterest in public encounters. We can further distill that precarity doesn't always translate into instability and that it may be borne willingly in preferences to other possibilities, if, for example, it grants artists' more control over their practice.

## NOTES

1. The notion of precarity emerges at the turn of the twenty-first century as a mode of describing the condition of precariousness associated with short-term, insecure, flexible and often highly exploited forms of labor under neoliberal and post-Fordist regimes. The concept finds its inception in social movements in Italy and Spain that engaged the "crises of the welfare state, new contractual and working arrangements, migrant labor and mobility and gender" (Casas-Cortes 2014, 206).

2. In 2010, the NEA devoted less than 2 percent of its budget to direct grants to individual artists, while state arts agencies offered only 3 percent.

3. This disavowal is also celebrated in the lexicon of the avant-garde as "art for art's sake."

4. Of my sample, 94 percent was White; 50 percent was female; and 6 percent identified as gay.

5. Bohemia emerged at the same time as bourgeois society but predicated itself on the creation of differential identities deeply ambivalent about the social norms associated with mass production (Wilson 2003, 12).

6. Michel de Certeau argues that the often overlooked sphere of quotidian practice is replete with creative instances of resistance employed by the "common," "ordinary" masses that "make do" and "make over" cultural forms using "tactics" that pervert determining systems of domination (exerted in the form of strategies) (xii–xix).

7. For Noyes, the vernacular is located in "the immediate sphere of engagement in which actors negotiate between the tradition, professional and alternative discourses available to them, drawing on multiple resources to create a practical repertoire" (2012, 19). In the context of my study, these practical economic repertoires describe lay practices defined as vernacular economics by G. M. Swann. For Swann, the vernacular reveals a distinct performance of economic behavior, that while sharing some intellectual legacies with formalized practices, is the microeconomics of decentralized decision-makers (2006, 57).

8. I am relying here on de Certeau's conceptualization of tactics, which are the "art of the weak" and reflect quotidian enactments determined by an absence of power. That is, they expose operations within imposed sets of conditions, "manipulating events in order to turn them into opportunities" (2011, xix).

9. Many informants frown on discounting work because it impacts collectors' valuations of their work.

10. These trades are predicated on scarcity models.

11. Such commitment seems to foreclose changes in aesthetic sensibility.
12. The plan has a 3 percent default rate.

# REFERENCES

Abbing, Hans. 2002. *Why Are Artists Poor? (Waarom Zijn Kunstenaars Arm?)* Amsterdam: Amsterdam University Press.
Adorno, Theodor. 1983. *Prisms: Studies in Contemporary German Thought.* Cambridge, MA: MIT Press.
Alden, Isaac. 2015. Interview, September 19.
Andrews, Amanda. 2014. Interview, July 23.
Andrews, Mac. 2014. Interview, July 23.
Beck, Nathalie. 2015. Interview, September 21.
Beech, Dave. 2015. *Art and Value: Art's Economic Exceptionalism in Classical, Neoclassical and Marxist Economics.* Leiden, Netherlands: Brill Publishing.
Bourdieu, Pierre. 1993a. *The Field of Cultural Production: Essays on Art and Literature*, ed. Randal Johnson. New York: Columbia University Press.
Bourdieu, Pierre. 1983b. "The Field of Cultural Production or the Economic World Reversed." *Poetics* (12): 311–56.
Bourdieu, Pierre. 1996. *The Rules of Art: Genesis and Structure of the Literary Field.* Stanford, CA: Stanford University Press.
Bradshaw, Tom. 2008. "Artists in the Work Force: 1990–2005." National Endowment for the Arts. May. https://www.arts.gov/publications/artists-workforce-1990-2005. Accessed January 2016.
Brown, Mark. 2015. Interview, September 6.
Brouillette, Adam. 2015. Interview. August 17.
Bureau of Labor Statistics. 2015. "Occupational Employment Statistics: Fine Artists, including Painters, Sculptors and Illustrators." US Bureau of Labor Statistics. January 1, 2016. https://www.bls.gov/oes/current/oes271013.htm.
Casas-Cortes, Maribel. 2014. "A Genealogy of Precarity: A Toolbox for Rearticulating Fragmented Social Realities in and out of the Workplace." *Rethinking Marxism* 26 (2): 206–26.
Davis, Ben. 2013. *9.5 Theses on Art and Class.* Chicago: Haymarket Books.
Dean, Michele. 2014. Interview, July 17.
De Certeau, Michel. 1984. *The Practice of Everyday Life.* Berkeley: University of California Press.
Derosa, David. 2015. Interview, October 12.
Elliot, T. S. 1921. "Tradition and Individual Talent." *Bartleby*. Accessed January 2016. https://www.bartleby.com/200/sw4.html.
Espe, Marisa. 2015. Interview, November 15.
Forkert, Kirsten. 2012. *Artistic Lives: A Study of Creativity in Two European Cities.* Surrey, UK: Ashgate Publishing.
Gazala, Mona. 2015. Interview, October 3.
Gill, Rosaland, and Andy Pratt. 2008. "In the Social Factory." *Theory, Culture and Society* 25 (7–8): 1–30.
Gomez, Maria. 2015. Interview, October 4.
Grant, Todd. 2015. Interview, May 19.
Gregg, Melanie. 2015. Interview, August 24.
Halliday, Michael. 2015. Interview, October 1.
Harvie, Jen. 2013. *Fair Play: Art, Performance and Neoliberalism.* London: Palgrave MacMillan.

Hardt, Michael, and Antonio Negri. 2005. *Multitude: War and Democracy in the Age of Empire.* Westminster, UK: Penguin Publishing.
Hermann, Walter. 2015. Interview, October 25.
Hyde, Lewis. 2009. *The Gift: Creativity and the Artist in the Modern World.* New York: Knopf Doubleday Publishing Group.
Johnson, Randal. 1983. "Introduction." In *The Field of Cultural Production: Essays on Art and Literature.* New York: Columbia University Press.
Keenan, Dennis King. 2005. *The Question of Sacrifice.* Bloomington: Indiana University Press.
Koch, Gertraud. 2012. "Work and Professions." In *A Companion to Folklore*, ed. Regina Bendix and Galit Hasan-Rokem. West Sussex, UK: Blackwell Publishing.
Lazzarato, Maurizio. 2011. *The Making of the Indebted Man: An Essay on the Neoliberal Condition.* Los Angeles: Semiotext.
Lewis, Amanda. 2015. Interview, September 9.
Madoff, Steven Henry. 2009. *Art School: (Propositions for the 21st Century).* Cambridge: MIT Press.
Martin, Leah. 2015. Interview, October 19.
Marx, Karl. 1992. *Capital.* Vol. 1. London: Penguin Classics.
McCarthy, Kevin, Ondaatje, Elizabeth, Brooks, Arthur and András Szántó. 2005. *A Portrait of the Visual Arts: Meeting the Challenges of a New Era.* Arlington: Rand Research in the Arts.
McLymont, Lisa. 2015. Interview, October 2.
Menger, Pierre. 2006. "Artistic Labor Markets: Contingent Work, Excess Supply and Occupational Risk Management." In *Handbook of the Economics of Art and Culture.* Vol. 1, ed. Victor Ginsburgh and David Throsby. London: Elsevier.
Menger, Pierre. 2014. *The Economics of Creativity.* Cambridge: Harvard University Press.
Nash, Adam. 2015. Interview, July 27.
Nash, Nora. 2015. Interview, July 27.
Noth, Alicia. 2015. Interview, October 11.
Noyes, Dorothy. 2012. "The Social Base of Folklore." In *A Companion to Folklore*, ed. Regina Bendix and Galit Hasan-Rokem. Hoboken: John Wiley and Sons.
Palmer, Daniel. 2015. *Handbook of Research on Business Ethics and Corporate Research.* Hershey, PA: IGI Global.
Parsons, Olivia. 2015. Interview, May 12.
Plattner, Stuart. 1996. *High Art Down Home: An Economic Ethnography of a Local Art Market.* Chicago: University of Chicago Press.
Read, Robert. 2015. Interview, September 1.
Roberts, Claire. 2015. Interview, March 12.
Rosler, Martha. 2015. "School, Debt, Bohemia: On the Disciplining of Artists. Artanddebt." 4th ed. January 1, 2016. https://artanddebt.org/school-debt-bohemia-on-the-disciplining-of-artists/.
Ross, Andrew. 2007. "Mercurial Career of Creative Industries Policy." In *My Creativity Reader: A Critique of Creative Industries*, ed. Geert Lovink and Ned Rossiter. Amsterdam: Institute of Network Cultures. Accessed January 1, 2016. http://globalurbanhumanities.berkeley.edu/uploads/Mercurial_Creative_Indus_Ross.pdf.
Sloan, Charlie. 2015. Interview, October 10.
Smith, Christina. 2015. Interview, August 27.
Standing, Guy. 2014. *The Precariat: The New Dangerous Class.* London: Bloomsbury Academic.
Strauss, Levi. 1966. *The Savage Mind.* Chicago: University of Chicago Press.
Swann, G. 2006. *Putting Econometrics in Its Place: A New Direction in Applied Economics.* Edward Elgar Publishing.

Thomas, Maureen. 2015. Interview, March 24.
Turner, Cain. Interview, 2015. September 16.
Webber, Bea. Interview, 2015. December 12.
Wilson, Elizabeth. 2003. *Bohemians: The Glamorous Outcasts*. London: Tauris Parke Paperbacks.
Win, Thet Shein. 2014. "Marketing the Entrepreneurial Artist in the Innovation Age: Aesthetic Labor, Artistic Subjectivity and the Creative Industries." *Anthropology of Work Review* 35 (1): 2–13.
Windham, Hank. 2015. Interview, April 2.

# 9

## From Vision to Implementation
*Clashing Values of Economic Idealism and Solvency in Twin Oaks Community, 1967–1979*

Rahima Schwenkbeck

TWIN OAKS IS AN EGALITARIAN, income-sharing intentional community, founded in 1967 outside of Louisa, Virginia. The community developed a unique labor system that would create an egalitarian environment, allow for conflicting ideologies, and handle the distinctive challenges of operating a communally run business. Twin Oaks Hammocks became Twin Oaks' most successful business, supplying major retailers like L.L.Bean, REI, and Pier One with handmade hammocks. While Twin Oaks was ultimately successful, developing a communal economic system within a country heavily invested in neoliberal policies posed unique challenges. This case study utilizes a historical approach and relies on archival information to trace the early development of a communal society as it attempted to create a new socioeconomic system. It highlights the complex issues that arose as Twin Oaks navigated the complexities of developing its labor policy and means of financially supporting the community. The study emphasizes unexpected issues and gaps that emerged between an ideology and its implementation as Twin Oaks sought to gain stability after founding.

### THE DIVIDE BETWEEN IDEOLOGY AND IMPLEMENTATION

There are numerous literary, philosophical, and other ideological treatments of how utopia would look and function. Inspired by communal societies of the nineteenth century, B. F. Skinner, the famed psychologist behind behaviorism, wrote *Walden Two*, a fictional account of an idealized, egalitarian community of people living collectively and adhering to behaviorist principles (1979, 292). In the novel, members worked four hours a day and spent the rest of their time enjoying leisurely pursuits. Interested parties underwent a membership process but, once accepted, were free to leave at will. After publication, *Walden Two* languished on bookshelves for nearly two decades until the boom of the communal movement in the 1960s. Academic and countercultural readers alike were drawn to Skinner's work and began organizing to develop a *Walden Two* community.

In his address to the 1966 national convention of individuals looking to build a *Walden Two* community, Skinner expressed some uncertainty that *Walden Two* was the best model, but offered his full support to anyone willing to "try the experiment and come up with the real results" (1966, 2). People pursued *Walden Two* for a variety of reasons. Some were supporters of behaviorism and wanted to experiment with it on larger scale. Others felt *Walden Two* could lead to radical change in society. Some were dissatisfied with the progress of enacting President Johnson's Great Society and felt more could be done at the microlevel to improve the country (*Walden Pool* 1966, 1). The concept of *Walden Two* served as a vehicle for a diverse group of interests in hopes to build a new society for the benefit of all.

While there was a lot of enthusiasm for producing a *Walden Two* community, a split grew between various factions. Academics and psychologists wanted to cultivate more interest and secure grant funding before starting a community. "Nonacademic" participants wanted to build immediately, as the largest wave of communal development in the United States was well underway by then. One such group broke away to start Twin Oaks in 1967, which included an older married man who financed the community, a single mother and her child, a man in his early twenties, and a young couple. They faced a rocky start due to various ideological disagreements, personality conflicts, and a meager budget. *Walden Two* was a fictional utopia penned by Skinner, who had never had the experience of living in an intentional community. The novel was relatively short and focused on behaviorism instead of detailing the mundane practicalities of developing the community, such as how to fund it, or suggesting membership criteria, so the community scrambled to develop plans. Thus, as Twin Oaks grew, the ideology surrounding it began to change to account for limited space and labor resources, funding issues, local and state laws, and numerous other variables unaccounted for in *Walden Two*.

The biggest ideological difference that emerged between *Walden Two* and Twin Oaks was the move away from becoming a behaviorist community. Twin Oaks quickly realized they lacked the skilled experts and funds to properly set up as a behaviorist community, so their ideology shifted toward economic equality. The four-hour workday and communal living outlined in *Walden Two* became an end goal for Twin Oaks, which worked diligently to "create an egalitarian economic system" (Scott 1969). Twin Oaks saw themselves as "a radical alternative" to mainstream America (*Leaves* 1970, 8). They hoped to influence others with their practical attempt at bettering society by actively living "an economy of 'from each according to his ability, to each according to his need'" with the ultimate goal of creating "a classless society" (Scott 1969).

Twin Oaks' members wrote a great deal about their living experiment and shared it widely. A review in *Library Journal* found Kathleen Kinkade's book on the first five years of Twin Oaks to be, "an amazing well balanced account of one attempt at a new life style, and the reader comes away with the feeling that communal, rural living is a viable alternative for those who choose to learn a great deal about human interaction and simple agriculture as well" (Detlefsen 1973, 177). While there was a lot of interest in developing communes, particularly the guiding ideology, Twin Oaks sought to inform others about the gap between philosophy and actual implementation. Many members wrote about factors in selecting a physical location, how to incorporate, their struggles with membership, entrance fees, and more. Intentional communities offered a way to experiment with societal development. Twin Oaks actively sought to popularize the concept and offer their experiences for further reproduction and improvement, with the end goal of seeing numerous other communal societies develop across the United States to challenge capitalism as the status quo.

Twin Oaks' message was very appealing, and the community grew quickly through the mid-1970s. The community founded in 1967 with eight members, and by late 1969 it had approximately twenty members. A membership survey in 1970 revealed 15 males and 10 females, ranging in age between 17 to 39, with the average age being 22.5. Most members had at least one year of college. Among those who identified a religion, there were two atheists, five Catholics, and eleven Protestants. The average stay of a member was fourteen months. The membership was capped at twenty-five at the time, due to lack of room (*Leaves* 1970, 1). By 1975, Twin Oaks had more than doubled their population to sixty-two members, with a turnover rate around 25 percent. In 1976 Twin Oaks boasted approximately a dozen or so members who had lived there for five years, and twenty members had lived there for around two years. By 1977, the community had seventy-five members, ranging in age from newborn to 68, though more than 80 percent of its members were between 21 and 33 (*Leaves* 1977, 1). Currently, Twin Oaks typically has around 100 members, what their housing comfortably allows.

## CREATING AN EGALITARIAN LABOR SYSTEM

While dreaming of an ideal community is easy, getting people to perform the labor necessary to develop the community is another matter. Twin Oaks was looking to distance itself from the "anti-structure hippy approach" and did not want to allow members to simply do whatever they felt like, because it would leave universally undesirable tasks such as dishwashing forever undone (*Leaves* 1968a, 5). The need to properly manage membership and labor became especially apparent as their membership grew to the point at which they had a waiting list. To ensure members equally put in time developing the community, and that all essential activities were done—from washing dishes and balancing accounts to picking beans and shoveling manure—Twin Oaks began a system of labor credits and scheduled work. The system was modeled after *Walden Two*, in which a labor credit (LC) was "a means of exchange" or "unit of work" (Skinner 1976, 46).[1] Members were required to perform certain activities on specific days and earn a certain number of LCs to ensure the community's needs were met. Members of Twin Oaks signed up to complete specific tasks, such as auto maintenance, animal husbandry, weeding, and cleaning. Some jobs required proper training, such as accountancy, whereas others such as dishwashing were open to all.

The process of getting a skilled position at Twin Oaks was unique in that no prior experience was needed. Anyone interested could simply sign up to be interviewed for an open position. However, this also meant that someone could be trained in a new position only to give it up a week later. Some members flitted around jobs to see what they liked. It was their right to do so within the framework of the community, which encouraged people to express themselves fully, including through their labor, but it also meant that a lot of labor was wasted. Additionally, since several members might apply for the same task, sometimes the most skilled person was not assigned to the job they were best at, such as cooking. Some members found this rewarding since it allowed many people to experiment, but also wasteful. It arguably hindered the development of Twin Oaks and created what some members considered a culture lacking in responsibility ("Leaving Twin Oaks" 1977, 22–24).

Twin Oaks wanted to create a society in which labor was seen as nourishing to oneself and the community. This proved to be more complex than imagined, as meaningful work has multiple interpretations. It can be a personal fit, in which one does what one is passionate about, or a social fit, in that one does what one is best at in terms of contributing to the overall development of society (Michaelson 2011, 548–49). In such a system as

Twin Oaks, people are no longer removed from their means of production, all members had the opportunity to try a new position, and for the most part, all goods were shared.[2] As one member explained:

> The Labor Credit System is neither capitalistic nor equated with money. Nothing can be purchased for them, nor is any community member's share of food, clothing, luxuries or anything else based on them. The labor credit system is nothing more than a means of assuring that all the necessary work gets done and that some members do not get exploited by others who would rather sit back and slack their fair share of the work. We have a true communism here in that all property is owned in common and no personal fortune or position of supremacy can ever be attained by any one member of clique of "elite" members (Josh 1970).

The direct relationship drastically reduced the amount of alienation members felt between their labor and themselves; rather, members largely felt they were creating a new society and thus, no longer passively experiencing the world (Marx 2000, 177). Instead of material rewards, members benefited intrinsically from accomplishment and contribution to community development (Kuhlmann 2005, 112).

The labor credit system accomplished several things. It was pitched as the "trade-off between individual liberty to do certain things and individual freedom to enjoy certain other things." For example, the trade-off of getting up early to milk a cow was the freedom to enjoy a reliable supply of quality dairy products ("Labor" 1969–75, 4). Internally, it eased friction between members because it was assumed that everyone was doing their fair share as long as they met their labor quota. The labor credits system organized the community and coordinated several building, business, and other efforts to grow and stabilize. It also served as a handy accounting tool to determine how much labor each area of the community: farming, childcare, hammocks, automotive work, and so forth, was using (Kinkade 1987, 66).

The labor credit system was not without issue. Members were sometimes not as honest about the actual amount of work performed, which typically manifested in questionable record keeping. Sometimes members claimed they did work when they did not, others would double credit work—doing laundry while also working in the office, which only counted for one hour of labor, despite completing two activities. Other members would overcalculate, rounding 5.25 hours worked to 6, for example (Kinkade 2011, 183). Although members labored for the common good of Twin Oaks, people worked "harder for more direct personal benefit, and it would be dishonest to deny it" (Kinkade 1994, 47).

## THE IDEOLOGICAL PERILS AND ECONOMIC BENEFITS OF THE HAMMOCK BUSINESS

Although Twin Oaks worked toward self-sufficiency, they were not an isolationist community, nor could they produce all they needed. They required a cash income to pay for taxes, medical needs, construction materials, gas, and not-infrequent junk food splurges, among other needs. Initially, members took turns on "outside work" assignments, which often meant working as temps in construction work, office administration, and substitute teaching. Outside work was not reliable and disrupted the egalitarian sense of community Twin Oaks wanted to develop. For example, some firms would only hire women for secretarial work, and one employer refused to hire an African American member (they were sued for discrimination, and Twin Oaks won). Twin Oaks pursued a variety of entrepreneurial ideas in order to create a self-sustaining business so that members could work within the community and generate income.

Of all the businesses pursued, the most successful was Twin Oaks Hammocks. It was driven by one of the founding members, who explained how to weave the Carolina-style hammocks, designed the production equipment, and made sales contacts (Income Council). In fewer than three months, Twin Oaks had a solid hammock business ready for heavy production. Unfortunately, this was at the end of the summer, when hammock sales plummet. Hammocks are largely a seasonal good, and potential retailers did not want to waste space holding stock in hammocks over the winter. Twin Oaks found itself facing one of countless situations that questioned where they should funnel limited labor resources: to hammock making in preparation for sales the following year or to building efforts to house the growing community as winter approached. Twin Oaks tried to do both by selling their hammocks in the off-season. They appealed to subscribers of their community newsletter, *Leaves*, to make a purchase; had a salesperson visit Florida to sell hammocks to souvenir shops; and exhibited at sporting goods shows while members wove a stockpile of hammocks in hopes of large orders to come in the spring (*Leaves* 1967, 6). They needed income to grow, and members were willing to tough it out by sleeping in an unheated barn.

Hammocks were made in sizes small, medium and large. Depending on the size of the hammock and the skill of the hands, they took between four and six hours to complete (*Leaves* 1968a, 6). After the cost of materials, Twin Oaks earned roughly $1.50 per hour, which was "considerably better than any other way [they had] of bringing in cash income." Although selling directly to consumers was more profitable, Twin Oaks preferred to wholesale their goods, in part due to the belief that "Twin Oaks members are congenitally incapable of selling anything . . . There is something about selling that terrifies us" (*Leaves* 1968a, 7). Yet Twin Oaks was quite skilled at sales: a variety of retailers carried their products, including REI, L.L.Bean, Pier One, and other large retailers. However, the aversion to direct sales reflects the community's ambivalence about directly engaging with the capitalist system they were hoping to circumvent.

Twin Oaks was successful in part because the community continually improved the quality of its hammocks. For example, members initially used cotton rope, but switched to a synthetic material, polypropylene, which they found to be mildew-proof and lighter (which lowered shipping costs) and to retain original color longer (*Leaves* 1968b, 2). Later, in response to hearing some of the hammocks were wearing out, one member reported: "We now are putting plastic tubing through the stretcher to protect the harness. We are looking for a better method—it takes a long time to get the plastic through and it does not necessarily stay in place. But we are working on it. And from what I've heard . . . of our competition, we don't have any worth mentioning" (Christine 1969). This was not mindless boasting, but an accurate view of Twin Oaks' quickly rising position in the market.

Twin Oaks found the hammock business ideal in many ways. The capital investment was minimal, it was a scalable operation that easily grew along with the community, and it required little skill. Hammocks, as a nonessential item, allowed Twin Oaks, according to one member to "charge enough to cover our costs and provide some excess to build a community, without feeling like we are gouging the public" (Lenske and Wenig 1980, 5). Yet, some members struggled with "making a consumeristic luxury product" and "doing business heavily in the capitalistic grain" (ibid). Additionally, members were worried about Twin Oaks' heavy reliance on a single business. Yet, in a community where turnover was roughly 20 percent to 25 percent annually, it was difficult to find other ventures that relied on largely unskilled labor and with limited competition.

Instead of pursuing new business ideas, Twin Oaks made other furniture products that used hammock netting in their structure. Hammock making became such an integral part of the Twin Oaks income that the development of a hammock chair was touted as "the birth of a new industry" (*Leaves* 1976, 14). Twin Oaks also manufactured the "backpacking model," which was a woven net without a frame or stretchers. The community continually looked to develop other businesses, but its hammock industry continued to grow exponentially. Sales jumped from 1,900 in 1972 to over 2,500 in 1973. By mid-1974, sales were already over 3,000 units.

After test-marketing Twin Oaks hammocks, Pier One decided to add the hammocks to its general product list, resulting in a sale of 5,000+ hammocks in 1975. The community continued to defy sales and manufacturing expectations.

Twin Oaks faced a new, surprising issue: how to handle overwhelming sales. By 1974, the hammock industry was so strong that Twin Oaks members did not have to work outside jobs, as 3,000 hammocks brought in an annual net income in excess of $47,000 (Kinkade 1987, 87). While it would seem that the financial stability and self-reliance the hammock industry brought would be welcomed, it also meant that community members had to continuously make large loads of hammocks (Ken 1976). The repetitiveness of the work was a constant issue in the community, and a "periodic dump-hammocks-in-favor-of-something-less-bourgeois movement" appeared (Kinkade 1987, 87). Some members grumbled under the increasing weight of the orders, occasionally exacerbated by periodic large waves of member turnover. Remaining members had to retrain a largely new workforce, which slowed production because members were "putting a lot of energy into teaching new folks and even more energy into redoing their mistakes" (Kevin 1976). Further complicating things, some members opposed using ropes utilizing a petroleum derivative, so Twin Oaks expanded their product line to include a fabric-based hammock, which was not woven with ropes, but instead was composed of a large, single piece of cloth held between two stretchers. This was outside of Twin Oaks' specialty and sourcing, which led to further delays (Shea 1978, 13).

To lighten the load, hammock production was funneled out to other intentional communities. In true communal spirit, part of Twin Oaks' long-term goal was to develop "a business which helps support more than one community," so Twin Oaks worked with sister community, East Wind, to fulfill orders (Steven 1974, 3). The larger orders provided stability across multiple communities and supported both Twin Oaks and East Wind (Johnny 1975). In a hammock industry of approximately $13.5 million dollars in 1976, Twin Oaks had somewhere between 10 percent to 15 percent of the market share. Other major competitors included Pawley's Island, which sold approximately 75,000 units, and Klapat Mills, at 40,000 units. By comparison, Twin Oaks sold 8,569 hammocks in 1976 and was projected to sell 13,000 in 1977 (Shea 1978, 26). Twin Oaks produced the highest-quality hammock and was the price leader in the industry. As one October 1976 issue of *Money* noted, "one family . . . has enjoyed a hammock from a commune called the Twin Oaks Community in Louisa, Va. for seven years now, and it shows no signs of wearing out" (Tarrant 1976). The biggest detriment to business became the community itself, as it could only house so many people (Shea 1978, 14–15). Members simply could not produce enough hammocks to keep up with demand; even outsourcing to other communities did not alleviate the issue.

Production issues did not dampen demand. World Bazaar, a large gift store chain, contacted Twin Oaks to make 5,000 of the backpacker-style hammocks (Chip 1977b). In addition, L.L.Bean ordered over 1,000 hammocks. By June 1977, Twin Oaks' sales ran 70 percent above the previous year, and approximately 1,000 hammocks were on backorder. Production slowed as the "emergency production quotas" turned into the usual production needs to handle the incredible sales growth. The Hammock Manager pleaded with members to make more hammocks since they were losing accounts, commenting, "It's bad for Twin Oaks Hammocks reputation and business to not be a good supplier" (Chip 1977a).

## BALANCING COMMUNITY INCOME NEEDS AND LABOR IDEALS

Making hammocks was not difficult work, but it required attention to detail and a great deal of physical dexterity. Members weaved each hammock by hand; built wood stretchers; and stained, assembled, and packed each hammock. In addition, the hammock shop regularly needed "folks to help produce mores sales . . . to do fairs . . . put together mailings & help produce some simple, clean & effective art work . . . sales calls on the phone . . . type letters." But above all, the hammock manager needed, as one person put it, "folks who are not just into begrudgingly doing a few hammocks hours, I need people who feel what they are going to do is valuable, it would really help" (Gilbert n.d.).

As many members complained about the monotony of hammock production, occasionally notices would go around the community about the relationship of member and their labor. In one such public notice, "The Hammock Shop is More Than Just a Factory," one member wrote: "As industries go, this is one of great inter-connectedness. Each of the stations is in some way related to all of the others so that the final product is one of cooperative effort. The shuttle must be wound to a certain length so that the weaver does not have to weld at the end . . . so when we work in the hammock shop, let's remember how each process we do affects another worker and we can be proud of our successful communal effort." Members responded positively to this, finding it was "humanizing the industrial process," "far out," and simply, "yeah" (Carol Jo 1978).

The members of Twin Oaks continuously improved working conditions. The hammock rigs were built so that two people faced each other when constructing a hammock in order to make conversation easier and to develop a greater sense of communal good during its manufacture. One of the simplest things done to encourage people to congregate, and ideally work, in the hammock shop was to have food and drink items available, including pop, barbecued chicken, baked goods, and candy (Pomeranz 2007, 123). Labor credits were even given to encourage people to make delectable treats for the hammock shop. Live music, a high-quality sound system, book readings, and other activities were done to make the work more interesting. Finally, members could also choose to earn money toward their individual allowances or extra vacation time, or, for particularly communitarian-minded members, the incentive could be pooled to buy a larger amenity for the community, like a new sound system or film projector (Income Council n.d.). As the community struggled to keep up with orders that continually piled up, Twin Oaks began to offer financial incentives as a last-ditch effort to keep members' fingers furiously assembling hammocks.

Twin Oaks was not unmindful of the toll on community members and asked for input on how to budget the 700 hours that hammock production used weekly, as well as how the community would juggle prosperity with their overall goals and ideology (Sam 1977). Even contracting out more work to other communes such as North Mountain and Shannon Farm did not ease the burden. Twin Oaks toyed with the idea of not growing the hammock industry any more, since "demand for Twin Oaks Hammocks [in 1977] far exceeded [their] abilities and desires" (Larry 1977). Yet, members were asked to keep working extra hammock hours to help the community gain enough capital to start another venture so they would not have to keep making hammocks (Chip 1977a).

As part of the diversifying process, Twin Oaks evaluated their various ventures into their value per labor credit (LC). At the top of this list were hammock making, editing, lectures, and some of their construction efforts. Less-profitable activities, those making under $2.30/LC, included outside work, working for neighbors, and appliance repair. From this, evaluators identified the most likely sources of income. While lectures were profitable, they were not a reliable source of income. Editing was also profitable, but composed only 2 percent of their total income, since jobs were not guaranteed (George et al.). Twin Oaks' construction business, Glorious Mud, was run by skilled members and very profitable. However, Twin Oaks was reluctant to elevate it to a major business because of the costs of the machinery, advertising, and fear that skilled members would leave and shutter the business (Shea 1978, 15). After all, members could come and go as they pleased and take their valuable skills with them.

Twin Oaks had little in the way of promising new industries, but rather an odd assortment of ideas: contract jobs for assembling wood stoves, factory subcontracts, rope making, simple wood furniture, and hopes that one member's attempts to make solar-powered heaters would be successful and easy enough to reproduce for sale. The community largely resolved for itself that it did not care for retail sales, but was willing to manufacture items, which is somewhat curious since the main gripe of hammock making was that it was a repetitive task. What made divesture even more complicated was the relationship Twin Oaks had with East Wind Community, which became reliant on the fairly steady and significant income from hammock making.

Despite all the research, meetings, and planning, and the grumblings of members over hammock making, the status quo was easier to maintain. There was a big difference between ideals and needs when it came to floating Twin Oaks, and the community needed cash more than anything to stay afloat. Thus, in 1978, hammocks were 75 percent of the total income, with 45 percent from Pier One directly. Again, by the end of 1979, Twin Oaks claimed it was highly motivated to exit the hammock industry and hoped that by 1981, less than half of their income would come from hammocks, with Pier One contributing 15 percent or less to Twin Oaks' total income. To this end, Twin Oaks worked to become suppliers of various materials they used in the hammock industry, particularly rope. They also began to develop a line of rope chairs that could be used indoors and out and ideally would ease some of the seasonality of their sales (Chip 1979).

By 1980, Twin Oaks enjoyed a net income of $250,000, which broke down to a "modest $3,000 per capita" among seventy-five members. That year Twin Oaks made approximately 12,000 hammocks, accounting for two-thirds of their income (Lenske and Wenig 1980, 3). Of this small, niche industry, Twin Oaks became the second-largest and oldest manufacturer of rope hammocks, illustrating how badly the rocky economy of the 1970s impacted other hammock manufacturers. Twin Oaks prided itself as a worker-owned business, with the hammock shop serving as "a social center for T.O. for many years" (Lenske and Wenig 1980, 4).

## EXTERNAL DIFFICULTIES WITH THE HAMMOCK INDUSTRY

Developing a community-owned business presented several challenges. As *Walden Two* did not provide a blueprint for financing, members had to determine the best way to earn income while holding fast to community ideology. Internally, the repetitiveness of hammock making, and the community's overwhelming success in the market, provided physical and ideological challenges. Twin Oaks Hammocks also faced numerous external issues within the marketplace, including seasonality, delayed payment from vendors, clashes between idealism and ideal materials, and the competition that emerged between the community and past members as a result of an ease of entry into the market.

While Twin Oaks benefited immensely from sales with large accounts such as Pier One, there was a "considerable delay" between the point of order and payment (*Leaves* 1969, 2). Not only did the community have to wait for payment, they had to buy more materials in the meantime, which stretched their tight budget even further. It became demoralizing for Twin Oaks to be at the service of corporations. The unreliability of sales from large accounts such as Pier One, L.L.Bean, and REI meant Twin Oaks could not accurately forecast their finances. Pier One was notoriously unpredictable, but Twin Oaks continued to work with the company because it was a significant source of income, though the community was constantly oscillating between fears of Pier One severing their relationship to expecting an order of anywhere from 1 to 9,000 hammocks (Gilbert n.d.). For example, in 1980, Twin Oaks was thrown for a loop when Pier One issued an order for only 15 percent of their usual sales request, but the company quickly changed its mind and ended up placing the largest order Twin Oaks had ever received, which pulled the community from a financial into a labor panic (Komar 1989, 160; Pomeranz 2007, 112).

Despite how well Twin Oaks Hammocks was doing in terms of sales, the community continually struggled with cash flows because of the seasonality of the business and the rocky economic climate of the 1970s. The seasonality of the business meant that Twin Oaks relied on borrowing during winter months and then paid off debts during the boom of the summer months. The economy was feeling the punch of the second oil crisis that decade, and consistent stagflation resulted in an incredibly high interest rate, of 18 percent, from local banks. Twin Oaks expected to be $52,000 in debt by the end of February 1980. The Bank of Louisa agreed to lend the community $60,000; however, it was at an interest rate of 16.5 percent, which left the community asking, "if anybody has leads on rich friends who might be willing to lend us sums of a thousand dollars or more at lower interest rates" (Chip, Christopher, and Gini 1979). Twin Oaks did not want to mortgage their holdings and to put the community in jeopardy, especially since this was an annual issue they dealt with ("Proposed Econ Plan" 1978).

Sales and cash flow were only part of the business equation; labor was the other issue Twin Oaks faced. Working and living in the same space blurred the line between the two. While work left unfinished or poorly done for the community meant that members used a barely cleaned bathroom or ate a lackluster breakfast, it was not acceptable to send a half-assed hammock to a customer. As a result, Twin Oaks developed quality control regulations. First, they reminded members that above all, "this is an industry. The hammock shop provides the community with 65% of its annual income. In order that an industry be efficient we must strive for the highest level of dollars per hour. If we don't do this we are ripping ourselves off" (Ken 1975). Yet, collective responsibility meant that it was easier for some members to shirk work. By some estimates 25–50 percent of hammock hours were "fucked off," which meant that the community was often in financial straits and under considerable labor strain to make up those hours to fulfill orders. For one member who ran the shop, it became a serious issue of "when where and how do we share in the burdens of doing the work that is necessary and not what we want to do all the time . . . the labor credit system hides it to us at least temporarily what is going undone" (Koala 1976).

Twin Oaks faced competition from surprising sources. The hammock industry was chosen in part for its low barriers to entry, scalable cost, and ease of training. Particularly during the first few years of Twin Oaks, many visitors flocked to the community to see what communal living was about. The hammock business was a perfect way to capitalize on the mass of interested but temporary labor because the work was easy to learn. However, this meant that it was also easy for competitors to enter the industry. Business for Twin Oaks Hammocks was troubled as multiple ex-members began small hammock businesses, and the fellow communities Twin Oaks shared their workload with began to market their own brands of hammocks.

Twin Oaks met with one group of past members who began a hammock business nearby to see what their intent was. The former members claimed they were "not exactly sure" their plans were, but that they "enjoy[ed] making hammocks as a way to make income," believed there were "hammock orders in them thar hills, more than T.O. [Twin Oaks] will fill," and they wanted "to be a worker-owned business" but were "not interested in being in competition with T.O." at least "in the same way we would be in competition, with, say, Pawley's Island" (Sara 1977). They hoped to subcontract with Twin Oaks for filling orders, imagining it "could be worked out to . . . mutual benefit." The community of ex-members had plans for a three-point hammock and a rattan stretcher, but despite the noncompetition imagined, they finally admitted that they would also have to make traditional hammocks in order to have a product line that would appeal to buyers. Then, to dress it up, the ex-members hoped to establish a noncompetition agreement: "We could simply agree not to horn in on each other's sales. This is a minimum cooperation, but also minimum bureaucracy, sort of arrangement." They felt that their tiny community would not threaten major suppliers such as Pier One that Twin Oaks relied on, but failed to consider that Twin Oaks also desperately relied on small sales in order to keep afloat during the winter (Sara 1977). For example, when scrambling for accounts after it was believed Pier One was not going to place an order, Twin Oaks turned up Akron, a chain of California stores, but further digging found that this lucrative account had just been taken by East Wind (Planning Council 1979).

Advertising was a frequent site of contention. Once Twin Oaks allowed a trade journal to develop an ad for their hammocks. Unfortunately, the ad was "sexist, classist and slick in the worst definition of the word" (Lenske and Wenig 1980, 8). Twin Oaks decided to create their own ad, which they described as "definitely an amateur job" but as one that it did not rely on "the bathing beauty model in a piece of lawn furniture." Instead the ad featured some members of Twin Oaks in conventional, "gender appropriate" clothing. The community felt unhappy about the ad in the end; while the process allowed members to add input and respond to some stereotypical advertising troupes, members were concerned that working together in such a manner "doesn't always produce something that management thinks will be effective" (Lenske and Wenig 1980, 8). Additionally, some members were upset that they had to dress and appear conventionally, which was sharply in contrast to the gender fluid ideology of Twin Oaks.

The ideological and business needs of Twin Oaks were often at odds. Concerns over appealing to the business world created a bit of a rift between the hammock department and the rest of Twin Oaks, since, for some members, it created a sense of inequality between the business and the community (Lenske and Wenig 1980, 9). The hammock manager could order $20,000 of supplies without any concern, but did not order a new typewriter or phone system—even though one was badly needed—because it would look out of place with the rest of the community, which was largely populated by cast-off goods. Some members questioned the amount of resources going into attire, transportation, and materials for trade show booths and sales meetings, especially since the average Twin Oaks member wore old, typically out-of-fashion clothes, and hitchhiked or bused to most places. Not only were hammock managers under the extra stress of running an enterprise, but they had to do so while conforming to the ideological needs of Twin Oaks. One hammock manager reported being hassled over getting a $6 haircut to look presentable for a sales trip.

The desire to be environmentally conscious was another area of conflict. Twin Oaks used thousands of pounds of synthetic rope in their business, a nonrenewable fossil-fuel product. To compensate for this, they spent a great deal of time developing renewable energy sources for other aspects of hammock production (Lenske and Wenig 1980, 7). Twin Oaks experimented with various naturally sourced energy options, particularly passive solar heating, but as a result, projects cost more money and took longer to develop since members were typically not entirely familiar with these emerging types of energy sources. Twin Oaks successfully developed a solar-powered kiln to dry the sustainably harvested wood for the hammocks and continually sought ways to make their process more environmentally friendly.

## CONCLUSION

People joined Twin Oaks in order to experience a new social system, which included communal sharing of goods, labor, and experiences. The form of "non-monetary economy" developed by Twin Oaks offers one way to develop economic autonomy and a stronger cohesive base (Nelson and Timmerman 2011, 6). The name of this type of economy varies widely, but to Kinkade, Twin Oaks has a "classic utopian communism" form of economic and governing system. Other members have called it a "collectivized economy" ("Short Green" 1974, 22). People are free to do their chosen type of work, at the time they wish, unless the work dictates otherwise—for example, animals need to be tended to at specific times—and from that collective labor the community provides for all needs, from housing to dental care (Kinkade 2011, 184). Ultimately, they hoped their experience would lead to the development of numerous, similar communities. Yet, the community needed income in order to exist, which created some ideological rifts within the community. In particular, their booming hammock business remained a source of contention within the community. Despite the challenges of a communitarian business operating in a capitalistic world, Twin Oaks competed surprisingly well.

Exploring the concept of known and "unknown unknown" issues can help explain how the gap between ideology and implementation can emerge in organizations and some methods of addressing them. Twin Oaks, their labor system, and successful hammock industry offer an interesting case study that highlights the complex issues that arise when trying to create an alternative to capitalism, while thriving within it. Twin Oaks Hammocks was extremely successful, so members enjoyed the security and stability it brought to an otherwise often ephemeral type of community.... The hammock business was emblematic of the external struggle Twin Oaks had with how they fit into society as a realized alternative, but one that still had to function within the current structure. One hammock manager, Larry Lenske, found that there were two levels of the business: the intercommunity aspect in which Twin Oaks members had a say in their working conditions and their output and have ownership stake in it. On the other hand, according to Lenske, Twin Oaks had "to play enough by the rules of the dominant culture ... As in any business, a basic function of Twin Oaks Hammocks is to make money, but how we make money is just as important to folks here. That creates a basic tension between the hammock business and the community ... the hammock business has been a focal point for playing out a dance of balancing the ideals of community and the realities of running a business in capitalist America" (Lenske and Wenig 1980, 7).[3] The ultimate goal for Twin Oaks was to illustrate one way to become a "radical alternative to the competitive, consumer-oriented life" (Delano 1971). Yet there was always tension between the community's goals and the means to it by participating in capitalism.

The case of Twin Oaks sheds new light on issues of the commodification of craft. For example, Jane Becker's *Selling Tradition* focuses on the impact that selling regional handicrafts had on their makers through the interaction with the public and their expectations. In her work, Becker highlights writer James Agee's thoughts on the commodification of folk culture and its changes "that pandered to white, middle-class tastes" (11). For Twin Oaks, it is an interesting case of largely middle-class white people using Carolina folk craft methods to weave hammocks and support their community by selling to other middle-class whites at trade shows, where purchasers could experience the full transfer of the experience of buying from a hippie commune and all the mystique, excitement and bit of counterculture it offered to purchasers. Moving into a commune meant a member likely had enough resources and experience to be able to transition back into traditional society in case things likely fell through. During the 1970s, it was predominately middle-class, white, twenty-somethings who had the safety net available to catch them if their communal experience did not work out and thus whom the communal experience was largely composed of.

Twin Oaks largely avoided direct consumer sales, instead preferring to sell their goods to retailers for distribution. While participating in trade shows was a source of income for the community, it was dwarfed by wholesale revenue. Twin Oaks did modify their sales approach to mirror the expectations of the audience. For the most part, at craft shows members dressed as they normally would and used the venues to soft pedal communal living. The interaction, experience, and novelty of participating in the counterculture was packaged into the handcrafted hammocks they sold.

In contrast, when preparing for meetings with large retailers such as L.L.Bean and Pier One, Twin Oaks members would prepare by donning business attire and mold their presentation into what was expected in a traditional business meeting or conventional trade show. The members who agreed to manage the hammock operations also took on the task of acting as the front for the organization, thus allowing the rest of Twin Oaks members to exist as they would, outside the conventions of business and traditional social norms. For the business executives, it is not clear how much the aura of a commune played into their desire to purchase, or if it was all business. After all, Twin Oaks boasted of supplying goods of extremely high quality, long-term durability, and low prices afforded by their communal living. A business buyer would be foolish to go elsewhere. Twin Oaks took a great deal of pride in providing high-quality products, and regularly sent out their hammocks for comparison against other manufacturers. In one successful showdown with a competitor, judged by International Craftsman, Twin Oaks won. Of this news, one member wrote, "Communism strikes another blow against Capitalism!" (Tom 1975). Through their hammock business, some members felt their successful communal way of life was able remove resources from capitalist streams and divert them into supporting communal societies. The selling of handcrafted goods in the style of past Carolinian cultures to major retailers by a community looking to develop an income-sharing society is at first glance is easy to cast off as another tragedy of neoliberalism. However, as Becker reminds us, we must dig deeper and interrogate the structure of society: "Rather than concern ourselves with identifying the 'authentic' and the 'corrupted' or distinguishing between 'folk' and 'popular,' we must shift our attention to the very complex process of cultural change and the social and political relations that play such important roles in that process" (1988, 40).

As a brief epilogue, Twin Oaks is still weaving hammocks today, though they have since developed another industry to diversify their income and work: Twin Oaks Community Foods, a manufacturer of high-quality tofu. Yet, Twin Oaks has run into many of the same issues. Making tofu is very difficult and time intensive and creates a very hot environment—which becomes particularly unpleasant in the humid summers of Virginia. Additionally, food production is a costly and highly regulated business to enter. And of course, their high-quality goods means that sales and requests for order have already outstripped demand. Although developing a communal business is difficult, and carries many unique ideological issues within it, Twin Oaks has developed a successful model that has sustained the community for decades. However, the tension of a communal, income-sharing organization operating so well in a capitalist society remains.

## NOTES

1. The system of labor credits was initially thought of by Edward Bellamy in his work *Looking Backward* (1888) in which different work was given varying levels of credit to make certain jobs more appealing. It was believed that this would help even out the social and economic desirability of all jobs so that all roles of the community would be filled.

2. Each member had their own room in which anything they kept in that room was theirs alone. This meant that large goods—cars, bicycles, and so—were shared, but members had their own personal possessions. Each room is the private space of the member owning it, and no one can enter without receiving permission first.

3. It should be noted that some goods, particularly medical services, were gained through Twin Oaks' low individual income rate, which means that members qualify for low-cost or free health care from the government. Members had also paid for the medical needs of fellow members through paid blood donations, service bartering, and regular cash payments.

## REFERENCES

### Abbreviations

Twin Oaks archival holdings are held in the Albert and Shirley Small Special Collections Library of the University of Virginia in Charlottesville, Virginia. Materials from this collection use the following abbreviations.

AA: Additional Archives of the Twin Oaks Community
KK: Papers of Kathleen Kinkade, 1968–2008
TPTO: The Papers of Twin Oaks

Becker, Jane S. 1998. *Selling Tradition: Appalachia and the Construction of an American Folk, 1930–1940*. Chapel Hill: University of North Carolina Press.
Bellamy, Edward. 1888. *Looking Backward*. Boston: Ticknor.
Carol Jo. 1978. "The Hammock Ship Is More than Just a Factory." November 23. Box 3, 9840-Q, 1978–81 Income Council: Products Hammocks. TPTO.
Chip. 1977a. "HAMMOCKS NEEDS YOUR HELP." June 20. Box 3, No 9840-Q, Income Council: Products-Hammocks, 1971–77. TPTO.
Chip. 1977b. "News Flash—Polish Hammock Deal Is On" January 2. Box 3, No 9840-Q, Income Council: Products-Hammocks, 1971–77. TPTO.
Chip. 1979. "Where Do We Go From Here?" October 1. Box 4, 9840-Q, Planning Council: Community Planners—Business Meeting Notes 1979. TPTO.
Chip, Christopher, and Gini. 1979. "Planner Weekly" September 17. Box 4, 9840-Q, folder: 1969–81 Planning Council: Community Planners. TPTO.
Christine. 1969. Letter from Christine to Sherryl. July 22. Box 4, Additional Papers of the Twin Oaks Community. 9840–1. Correspondence of Twin Oaks Community, SC, 1966–69. TPTO.

Detlefsen, Ellen Gay. 1973. Review of the Walden Two Experiment in Library Journal. January 15. Box 2, No 9840-g, 1971–73, Business Papers of the Twin Oaks Community: Business Correspondence. TPTO.

Delano, Frank. 1971. "Facing the Future at Twin Oaks." *The Free Lance-Star Town and Country* (Fredericksburg, VA), November 27.

George, Joshua, Tamar George, and Vince George. n.d. "Income Activities at HOME." Box 1, MSS 9840-x, folder: 1976–80, n.d., Income Council New Industry Crew. TPTO.

Gilbert, Bob (Koala Bear). n.d. "All About Sales and Me Please Read." Box 3, 9840-Q, 1978–8,1 Income Council: Products Hammocks. TPTO.

Income Council. n.d. "Hammocks Incentive Program / Something Special / assorted incentive proposals." Box 3, No 9840-Q, 1977–79, Income Council: Products—Hammocks Production Incentive Program. TPTO.

Income Council. 1974. "Our Hammock Business." Box 3, No 9840-Q, Income Council: Products-Hammocks, 1971–77. TPTO.

Johnny. 1975. "Hammock Poop" March 26. Box 3, No 9840-Q, Income Council: Products-Hammocks, 1971–77. TPTO.

Josh. 1970. Letter from Josh to Binz, Boz, Kathy et al. January 2. Box 1, 9840-1, folders 1969–74, Defunct Groups. TPTO.

Ken. 1975. "A Please from the Hammock Production Manager" April 30. Box 3, No 9840-Q, Income Council: Products-Hammocks, 1971–77. TPTO.

Ken. 1976. "HAMMOCK SALES NEWS IN BRIEF." August 27. Box 3, No 9840-Q, Income Council: Products-Hammocks, 1971–77. TPTO.

Kevin. 1976. "Visitors and Hamx, or 1001 Ways to Make Me Lose My Mind!" December 15. Box 3, No 9840-Q, Income Council: Products-Hammocks, 1971–77. TPTO.

Kinkade, Kathleen, ed. 1987. *Leaves* 2 (Issues 16–30): 1972–74. Louisa, VA: Twin Oaks Community, Center for Communal Studies, University of Southern Indiana.

Kinkade, Kathleen. 1994. *Is It Utopia Yet?: An Insider's View of Twin Oaks Community in Its Twenty-Sixth Year.* Louisa, VA: Twin Oaks Publishing.

Kinkade, Kathleen. 2011. "Labour Credit—Twin Oaks Community." In *Life without Money: Building Fair and Sustainable Economies.* London: Pluto.

Koala. 1976. "$ this paper is entitled RED LETTER DAYS $." December 15 Box 1, 9840-P, 1976–79, Bulletin ("O&I") Board Notices. TPTO.

Komar, Ingrid. 1989. *Living the Dream: A Documentary Study of Twin Oaks Community.* Louisa, VA: Twin Oaks Community.

Kuhlmann, Hilke. 2005. *Living Walden Two: B. F. Skinner's Behaviorsity Utopia and Experimental Communities.* Urbana: University of Chicago Press.

"Labor." 1969–75. Box 5, 9840-j, Notes and Correspondence on Starting a Commune folder. TPTO.

Larry. 1977. "Question: WHAT IS HAPPENING WITH THE HAMMOCK INDUSTRY? Answer: A LOT." Box 3, No 9840-Q, Income Council: Products-Hammocks, 1971–77. TPTO.

*The Leaves of Twin Oaks.* 1967. No. 2, September. Twin Oaks Community. Center for Communal Studies. University of Southern Indiana.

*The Leaves of Twin Oaks.* 1968a. No. 8, December. Twin Oaks Community. Center for Communal Studies. University of Southern Indiana.

*The Leaves of Twin Oaks.* 1968b. No. 5, March. Twin Oaks Community. Center for Communal Studies. University of Southern Indiana.

*The Leaves of Twin Oaks.* 1969. No. 10, September. Twin Oaks Community. Center for Communal Studies. University of Southern Indiana.

*The Leaves of Twin Oaks.* 1970. Vol 12, May. Twin Oaks Community. Center for Communal Studies. University of Southern Indiana.

*The Leaves of Twin Oaks.* 1976. No. 41, August. Twin Oaks Community. Center for Communal Studies. University of Southern Indiana.

"Leaving Twin Oaks: A Conversation with Former Members." 1977. *Communities: Journal of Cooperative Living* (28) (September/October): 20–28.

Lenske, Larry, and Mikki Wenig. 1980. "It's the Community's Business." *Communities: Journal of Cooperative Living*, April/May: 3–10.

Marx, Leo. 2000. *The Machine in the Garden: Technology and the Pastoral Idea in America.* Oxford: Oxford University Press.

Michaelson, Christopher. 2011. "Whose Responsibility Is Meaningful Work?" *Journal of Management Development* 30 (6): 548–57.

Nelson, Anitra, and Frans Timmerman. 2011. "Use Value and Non-Market Socialism." In *Life without Money: Building Fair and Sustainable Economies.* London: Pluto.

Planning Council. 1979. "Update on Pier 1 1/7/79." Box 4, 9840-Q, Planning Council: Community Planners—Business Meeting Notes 1979. TPTO.

Pomeranz, Kelifern. 2007. "From Fiction to Reality: B. F. Skinner, 'Walden Two,' and the Twin Oaks Intentional Community's Attempted Realization of the Dream." PhD dissertation, Alliant International University, San Francisco Bay.

"Proposed Econ Plan." 1978. Bulletin ("O&I") Board Notices December 7. Box 1, 9840-P, 1976–79. TPTO.

Sam. 1977. "Your Input" August 15. Box 3, No 9840-Q, Income Council: Products-Hammocks, 1971–77. TPTO.

Sara. 1977. "Expatriates Hammocks, Inc?" Feb 15. Box 4, 9840-Q, Planning Council: Community Planners—Business Meeting Notes 1977. TPTO.

Scott. 1969. Letter from Scott to Kathleen Kinkade November 15. MSS 9841, Stacks 2105117-1001. KK.

Shea, Peter H. 1978. "Twin Oaks Community." Case study supervised by Bruce J. McLaren, University of Virginia Colgate Darden Grad School of Business Admin. Feb 24. Box 1, MSS 9840-x, 1977–78. Folder: Income Council. New Industry Crew Business Papers. TPTO.

"Short Green: A Rap on Communal Finances." 1974. *Communities: Journal of Cooperative Living* 10 (November): 22–24.

Skinner, B. F. 1966. "Recorded Greetings to Participants of the National Convention from B. F. Skinner." *Walden Pool* Newsletter Vol. 1, No. 6 (Atlanta, Georgia) September–October 1966. Box 6, 9840-h, 1966–67 Newsletters: Walden House and Walden Pool. AA.

Skinner, B. F. 1976. *Walden Two.* Indianapolis: Hackett Publishing Company.

Skinner, B. F. 1979. *The Shaping of a Behaviorist: Part Two of an Autobiography.* New York: New York University Press.

Steven. 1974. "Our Hammock Business." October. Box 3, No 9840-Q, Income Council: Products-Hammocks, 1971–77. TPTO.

Tarrant, Marguerite. 1976. Money article in October issue. Box 3, No 9840-Q, Income Council: Products-Hammocks, 1971–77. TPTO.

Tom. 1975. "Hammock Highs" Box 3, No 9840-Q, Income Council: Products-Hammocks, 1971–77. TPTO.

*Walden Pool.* 1966. "Social Reform Through Experimental Communities." Box 6, 9840-h, 1966–67 Newsletters: Walden House and Walden Pool. AA.

# 10

## "Why the Sea Is Salty"
*Folktales as Sources of Grassroots Economics*

Irene Sotiropoulou

THIS CHAPTER IS QUITE THE REVERSE of the theme of this volume: I am the economist meddling in the realm of folklore. I am here because I did not have many other places to look while searching to learn economics that is not taught in universities.

Moreover, as a feminist and anticapitalist economist I am treated sometimes like the folkloric element of economics, that is, an exotic Other who is stubborn enough not to have perished under tough modernization and impersonalization processes that everyone has to pass through during university studies. I consider myself as being also something like a folklorist in the realm of economics, seeing more old-fashioned injustice in the utilitarian universe than freedom for all and prosperity for everyone. If one explores mainstream (liberal and neoliberal) economic theory as a narrative of contemporary societies, or as part of the folklore of capitalist classes, then the discursive link between the pursuit of maximum utility and the realization of individual profits as the path to common welfare can be seen as one more form of storytelling, though economic reality makes it refer to the future and not to the past. "They lived happily ever after" is never the end comment about any economy that gets capitalized.

My basic position is that "folklore" is the term used initially by the middle classes and the state concerning the practices and arts of the people who were supposed to be tamed in the capitalized, modernized society and whom capitalism was so much in need of as producers during its expansion in eighteenth and nineteenth centuries. Thus, the construction of the notion of folklore has several connotations that obscure the lack of homogeneity of the "folk" and of their art, including the social struggles that were expressed through "folklore" but were understood as entertaining moments of a way of life in the process of fading out. Despite the critical approaches developed in folklore studies and in anthropology, these class-biased or even colonial constructions persist in views expressed in other disciplines, mass media, and the state authorities, who have a great share in the public representation of folklore and of the people who create it.

However, despite my reluctance to use the term "folklore" in my own research due to the general misuse of the term as described above, for the purposes of this chapter, I consider myself to be part of the "folk," and in practical terms I am. In more than one way, I bring my own folklore into this chapter and use my own experience of that folklore to take a critical stand toward both the economic discipline and the folktale tradition that form the central case study of this chapter. However, I also see folklore to be important in another way, from the other side of the looking glass, where the issues and debates that the folk raise are prioritized in the tales they tell, social struggles are not only transparent but materialize the folk as full of people and groups whose political and social understandings and aspirations go beyond the states' or powerful groups' agendas and constructions of them; and where the entertainment is not only a legitimate aspect of their practices but is part of the social issues that their folklore includes.

Therefore, this chapter is an attempt of seeing several aspects of the mainstream economy, namely, the capitalist economy, through the eyes of the people who created the cultures that are named folklore. My intention is to open a discussion about economics and its knowledge sources while contributing to the analysis of folktales as conscious collective comments about real life.

The next section explains how I came up with turning to folktales as a source of learning economics. Section 3 gives a summary of the Cretan folktale "Why the Sea Is salty" and some information about Crete and its economy. The fourth section presents my analysis on the major economic themes of the tale, and section 5 includes some general points about the entire folktale. Concluding remarks are presented in the last section.

## LEARNING GRASSROOTS ECONOMICS THROUGH FOLKLORE SOURCES

The chapter is part of a larger project of research that I started working on in 2012. While I was researching nonmainstream transaction modes in Greece during the years 2009–12, I had to engage with and counter the stereotypes about noncapitalist economic structures we are taught not only in economics but also in our everyday lives through mass media and public discourse.

One of the main tropes of picturing noncapitalist economies is the perception of their ignorance. The people who live in "traditional" communities are thought to be unknowledgeable and worse; they are pictured as conservative, stubborn, backward-thinking, and unable to understand the benefits they would have by getting integrated into the contemporary value chains;[1] and of course it is assumed that they never understand what capitalism is. Therefore, the mainstream and widespread view about "traditional" communities is that the economic activities, institutions, and structures people have in their communities are the results of this ignorance and backwardness because economic knowledge in universities is so advanced that we just need to disseminate it to the "villagers" for their own good (Mies 1988; Von Werlhof 1988). In the meantime, I had started doing collaborative research with a good friend and colleague from Turkey, Dr. Ferda Dönmez-Atbaşı (University of Ankara). We were discussing how economic scholarship is being constantly produced by mostly Western European and US institutions, and how the rest of the academic centers are required to conform with this knowledge. The first problem we faced is that this formal economic knowledge is historically and socially specific to the societies it has been produced in. The second problem has been that it is specific people—with specific class, gender, ethnic and educational backgrounds—who create or validate economic knowledge. So, we decided to look for this knowledge in spaces that are more informed by everyday communal life and/or social movements than established economic thinking and to use sources that are not placed in the economics or business or even in the political economy or geography section of the library. On the other hand, we are aware that everyday people and noncapitalist economic structures can also be exploitative, patriarchal, or unfair, and some research participants had already pointed out those issues.

In other words, my economic findings resonate with the debate concerning the role of folklore as a knowledge resource that informs us about social struggles that otherwise go unnoticed, or, worse, misrepresented and co-opted by the powerful. The emancipatory potential of everyday communal practices is not only a memory of past efforts against injustice but a blueprint or a message for us today bringing past social experience to contemporary debates. Exactly because the everyday practices and folklore as such can promote the political aims of one or another group, we need to be aware of the various roles of folklore and be attentive to the critical stance of the folk itself toward its own art. In that sense, I consider this chapter to be informed by the general context of debates in critical folklore studies (Briggs 2012; Gencarella 2009,

2010a, 2010b, 2011; Kousaleos 1999; Limón 1983, 1984, 2010; Lipsitz and Rodriguez 2012; Paredes 1963; Lopez Morin 2006; Scott 1985).

Folktales, therefore, are one among the many sources I use for learning and understanding grassroots economics. Just like other forms of folk literature and culture, they are tools or methods of the traditional educational system for transferring knowledge from generation to generation and from one person to another within a community. This traditional educational system runs parallel and/or in opposition to the formal networks of knowledge dissemination, particularly the formal education system of each country and it can show how a community differentiates itself from the prevailing social structures (Antoniou 2010). The work done by Jack Zipes (1993, 2001, 2006) for analyzing folk and fairy tales through historical materialist perspectives has been a major contribution to my effort, by giving me various methods and multiple examples of analysis.

Moreover, given that the folktales have many concrete incidents described in each story, one can gain an understanding about the economy without losing the social characteristics of the people involved in the economic activity. In a folktale you do not have an economic agent, or an economic man only,[2] but you do have the poor woodchopper, the rich trader, the bad king, the king's daughter, the old wise woman, and many other people or animals who clearly represent specific social groups or attitudes. Most important: class, gender and ethnicity, plus professional or educational backgrounds are clearly visible in a folktale.

On the other hand, the anonymity and the allegories within folktales, along with the indefinite time and space that are their hallmarks, provide chances for the storytellers to point out and criticize economic behaviors that otherwise might be dangerous to talk about. Folktales are not only an escape from obligatory economic situations but also the only route, because of their low cost and simple means of making them accessible to everyone, to disseminate ideas that in a formal capitalist setting would require volumes of capital and material means to be dispersed (Antoniou 2010).

The importance of folktales today lies also in their historicity. Of course, they are not historical narrations, and they are not supposed to be. Some of them have patterns that are quite old or ancient, and some have introduced features that refer clearly to a specific era—for example, the Venetian duke or the Ottoman pasha—but apart from that, they are not historical sources as such. However, we know for sure that they existed or were created or modified during the last centuries. Their transmission was coeval with the expansion of capitalist economic structures and the changes capitalism brought to not only economies but also to people's thinking. It would be absurd to say that folktales have not been informed or affected by capitalism before and after they have started to be transcribed or recorded by collectors.

It is also absurd to say that capitalist commodity production and money were not known to the storytellers just because the folktale does not use contemporary economic terminology, such as "commodity" or "wage labor." Quite the opposite: folktales, exactly because most important capitalist institutions (private property, the state, wage labor, the machine, the commodity, etc.) existed before capitalism, can also be a source of what everyday people thought of and did with the new articulation of economic structures into the capitalist mode (Zipes 2001, 160). Moreover, folktales contain information about economies that are noncapitalist, because people in small or rural communities had a very clear picture of the structure of their societies, even if they might not consciously constitute themselves as a class in the way this is expected by revolutionary theory (Meraklis 1984, 69–77; Meraklis 1988, 23–38; Taussig 1980, 60–67).

In other words, we need not use the survival of the folktales of noncapitalist societies as an argument to support the ahistorical view that noncapitalist communities have ever been static or unable to understand what was happening. Much less were they passive to the changes of the economy—the long story of revolts and riots proves that people understood very well what was happening. They just did not have access to academia and given that most of them were illiterate or with very limited education, they could not directly write their ideas and proposals about the economy as such. It is normal that people would express their views about the economy within social activities other than economics curricula (Beverley 2004; Meraklis 1988, 5–12; Zipes 2001, 29–38).

Far from my analysis is any thought of authenticity or eternal peasantry or working-class existence. Actually, this would be not only contradicting my critique of capitalism, but also it would mean that peasants are all the same; belonging to the same class, gender, or cultural backgrounds; and having all together the same class interests (Brass 2002, 2007). It would also mean that I follow the distinction between urban and rural communities common to some institutional histories, which I do not share. In capitalism, urban and rural areas are never separated (Harvey 2006, 373–445). In particular, Cretan society is constructed around a constant interaction of urban centers and rural areas where the same people live, work, transact, and interact in multiple spaces. After all, the folktales were stories for both rural and urban audiences (Meraklis 1988, 5), as the publication of the case study tale shows.

## THE ISLAND OF CRETE AND THE CASE STUDY FOLKTALE

To learn what people think of major economic issues that are also prominent in capitalist economies, I use as a case study a folktale from the island of Crete, Greece, titled "Why the sea is salty" (Γιατί ειν' η θάλασσα αλμυρά), or "The Little Handmill" (Το χερομυλάκι) as it is titled in other versions. The version I am using was collected by Yannis Mathioudakis and published in local Cretan dialect in his collection "Loulouda" in 1936 (1–5). I found it for the first time in Stamatis Apostolakis's (2014) paper concerning Mathioudakis's collections.

The real narrator of the tale is unclear. The collection is titled after a female name "Loulouda" that also appears in some of the other short stories published in the same collection, as a real person. Loulouda however, was also the nickname that Yannis Mathioudakis used to publish as a journalist in early twentieth-century Chania (Apostolakis 2014). The beginning of the tale has some typical folktale entrance phrases in which it is shown that the tale is narrated by a grandmother (lali-λάλη) or very old woman.

The story of the tale is as follows: The protagonists are two brothers, one of whom is very rich and the other very poor. The tale does not explain why two close relatives have such economic disparity. The rich considers his poor brother to be lazy because despite his poverty he does not go to "make a day wage" by working in his rich brother's fields. The poor brother prefers instead to play music with his lyra (a traditional string instrument) and sing as if he has no other worry than music. The rich brother is worried every day about how he will increase his wealth.

On Easter Eve, the poor brother is unable to provide for the festive dinner of his family and he continues to play his music. People from the village try to persuade the rich brother to give some food to his poor brother, but the rich brother refuses. After the villagers insist, he agrees, but he also says, "All right, let him have that lamb, curse it to be eaten by the Devil." The poor brother takes the lamb but having heard the curse, he travels by foot for an entire day to give the lamb to the Devil. Once he finds him, the Devil wants to give something back to the poor man who brought him a treat, and the poor man is persuaded to accept a little handmill as a gift.

The handmill is magic and can produce food depending on the way you turn it. So the poor brother takes it home and manages to put various types of food on the table. The family has a party, and the neighbors get curious and one by one visit the poor man. He shares with them his food and his secret about the little handmill that produces food without anyone needing to work for it. He also tells them the story about how the handmill was given to him by the Devil.

The rich brother is now jealous of his poor brother who continued as before playing the lyra and singing in his front yard. The rich brother thinks that this is very unfair, and he proposes to the poor brother to exchange the handmill for all his property (actually the fields and cattle in exchange for the handmill, the family house is exempted), and the poor brother accepts.

The rich brother now has the handmill and is afraid that his brother might realize the unfair deal. He tells his wife that they must go away. The rich couple takes the ship "to other worlds." During the sea trip, the couple get hungry, and the rich man uses the handmill to produce food. The food was not tasty, however, so he uses the handmill again to produce salt. But he does not know how to stop the handmill from producing salt, and the handmill produces so much salt that the table and then the ship get full of it. Due to the salt overload, the ship sinks into the deep. The handmill is still in the middle of the sea and still producing salt that the sea waves bring to the shores for the people to collect: "Since then the sea is salty and if you do not believe it, drink sea water and see."

I used this version of this folktale because it is very detailed in its main themes. The fact that it has been collected and transcribed in the early twentieth century (1936) makes this version especially informative in the sense that it mirrors exactly the time the Greek economy was capitalized (late nineteenth to early twentieth century). Moreover, the island of Crete was annexed to the Greek state in 1913. Therefore, the transcriber had some experience of the first integration of Crete into the economic policies of the central Greek state. However, Crete was never far from capitalist and protocapitalist structures due to its economy having a trade orientation. So, Cretan people had had a good picture of what capitalism is.

Moreover, that same period, the late nineteenth and early twentieth centuries, was the time that most local workshops and small factories had to face the pressures of industrially produced goods dumped into the Ottoman Empire (where Crete belonged as a region until 1898 and as an autonomous region until 1913) and into Greece by Western industries. Some industries could not survive or had to change or diversify their production to make sure they made a living (Rokou 2007).

It is beyond the scope of this chapter to analyze what happened at that time in the economy of the island. The important thing is that when this version of the folktale was transcribed, the local communities were struggling with capitalization.

The other important thing is that despite the era in which this folktale was narrated. it contains ideas about class differences and particularly about the use of technology that are not only progressive for their era but also progressive for our era, too. That means, that the storytellers of Crete were well informed and educated about those topics. We have good reason to believe that they would not have had formal economic training even if they had some education, since all of the economics departments in Greece were established long after 1936 and Istanbul University economics department was established in 1936.

Of course, no one can discard the hypothesis that people in nineteenth- and early twentieth-century Crete could have had some anticapitalist education through activism or newspapers, leaflets, or books with ideas originating in the Marxist, communist, or anarchist traditions. Illiteracy and ignorance are neither essential nor permanent features of peasants and workers (Meraklis 1988, 7–9, 20–21). Nor are illiteracy and ignorance necessarily linked or connected with a linear causal relation—one may be illiterate and highly informed or literate and ignorant (Willow Mullins, personal communication, May 2016). What is sure is that ecological critique to capitalist production as we know it today was not popular (or it was nonexistent) at that time worldwide, though it seems to be central in the folktale.

This advanced thinking, however, is the reason I turned to this folktale and to folktales in general. Moreover, it seems that critical thinking and grounded indigenous cosmologies that defy official ideologies (whether those come from the state or religion) are not uncommon in the island of Crete and the case study tale of this chapter is part of this general cultural practice. I would think of this folktale as one of the many "weapons of the weak," as James Scott (1985) means them, against injustice towards people and nature. The acute critique against the abuse of the mechanic production means and the irreversible environmental disaster this abuse brings are not something that should be unexpected but rather expected in a social context of critical thinking and long-lasting experiential encounters with various production modes (Herzfeld 1985, 2005; Scott 1985).

Concerning the limitations of this analysis: due to financial and other institutional constraints, I have not conducted field research concerning this folktale to explore whether people in Crete still know and narrate it and what and how they think of it. In addition, I have not conducted comparative analysis of other versions of the folktale along with versions in other neighboring countries. Neither was I able to check through field research the influence of the transcription and publication of this folktale in 1936, along with its print circulation, on other folktales that were transcribed in later decades. Much less was I able to investigate any previous influences on this folktale from other tales published earlier than 1936 (Bottigheimer 2009).

# WHAT WE LEARN FROM THE STORY OF THE LITTLE HANDMILL

For analytical purposes, I focus on the main themes of the folktale that can illustrate the economic knowledge this tale conveys.

### Poverty and Class Difference

The first thing that strikes one in the story is the acute economic difference between the two protagonists, despite their being brothers. Possibly, the storytellers preferred the protagonists in this version to be brothers instead of simple neighbors (as I have found in other versions), to show that not even close kinship was able to persuade the rich person to be generous. However, the most important problem of the story is that the economic disparity is not explained at all; it is taken as given.

Richness is specific: the rich person has fields and cattle and servants, which means that he has vast volumes of means of production and he employs other people to work for him. The word used for servants is *fameyos* (φαμέγιος), which usually referred to a very poor person who was living and working in a farm or manor since childhood. The person was considered a "member of the family" but of course it was one of the feudal contracts or roles for poor people, whose wage many times was meager or nonexistent. The rich brother has no children of his own, which also explains why he has many fameyos in the household to replace the missing children as a workforce (to the contrary, the kids of the poor brother are not made to work at all).

Poverty is specific too: the poor brother has no means of production, no fields, or no cattle; he can hire no servants; and he also is unable to secure income or even food for his family. The poor brother has kids, who, from the dialogue at the Easter dinner, seem to be at least three in number. The only thing belonging to the poor household is the house they stay in and the lyra of the father, which is a musical instrument he uses for amusement and not for income-generating purposes.

Women in this version of this folktale are almost nonexistent as characters, which is not common in Cretan folktales, in which women usually have protagonist roles in the tale plot. Neither are present any people from other ethnic groups that exist in other local folktales. So, in a sense this folktale is close to mainstream economic theory: women are absent, ethnic groups are absent, and class differences are perceived through men's activity and discourse.

There are more similarities with mainstream economics, though: First, no political structures or politically powerful people exist in the story. The only power that exists is economic power realized through possession, that is, private property over means of production. Moreover, the protagonists are free to reach agreements and contracts between each other. For example, the rich brother refers to the denial of his poor brother to become a wage laborer. And then, the two brothers agree to barter the handmill for the fields and cattle. Another important point of the story is that social checks and balances are not enough once the income disparities are so huge as between the two brothers.

The important political economic comment in the first part of the tale is the explanation the rich brother gives about his brother's poverty: it is because of his laziness, actually his denial to become a wage worker, that he is poor. The rich person considers the distribution of wealth absolutely natural, and he thinks that his brother remains poor because he is lazy. Therefore the rich acquits himself of any responsibility for his brother's poverty.

The laziness of the poor brother is also signified by the rich person through the artistic performance. Playing music and singing are considered added proof of his laziness and not a talent or an offering to the entire neighborhood, who could listen to his music and songs. The rich person points out that the lyra "will not give him to eat"; therefore art is deemed unproductive. Only wage labor is productive according to the rich person.

A final point about the description of class difference: the mood of the two brothers. The poor brother is always in good mood, while the rich brother is always in bad mood because he is so focused on making more money that he fights all the time with his wife and servants. In fact, the rich brother exercises psychological violence on his wife and servants because he is so stressed to make more money.

## Gifts, Redistribution, and the Devil

Easter festive days are on, and the two brothers need to make sure that they are able to have adequate food in their households. The poor brother is ready to have an empty table, though he says to his children that "God will send food" and continues to play his music, giving an example of portraying a social relationship between humans (the relationship of assuring that food is available to everyone) as a relationship of gifts between humans and metaphysical creatures (Meraklis 1984, 108–9).

The rich brother receives comments by the villagers telling him to give something to his brother. His response is reminiscent of the contemporary discourse about charity and social welfare in which poor people are pictured as unworthy of any provision because they are lazy and do not want to work. It also reminds one of many government programs in which unemployed people are put to work with less than legal minimum working conditions and wages in order to be entitled to some monetary income or unemployment benefit.

The rich brother, in order to get rid of the villagers, agrees to give his brother a lamb (traditional festive food for Easter in Greece) but he curses it to be eaten by the Devil. In Greece we say that the "named gift"—that is, the gift that is announced for someone—cannot be used or stolen or even regifted to anyone else. The bearer or keeper has an absolute obligation to give the gift to the final receiver.

As a result, the poor brother undertakes the task and labor of transporting the lamb to the Devil, acting as an unpaid servant to his rich brother, who considers him lazy. The rich brother does not care about this labor and does not offer any wage or reward for the bearer of the gift. The trip is long, and the poor brother finally finds the Devil in the evening. The Devil is happy to receive the gift, and he wants to reward the bearer who brought it to him.

The Devil therefore, is fairer than the rich man and he wants to reward the labor, not the gift itself. So, instead of sending back a gift to the rich brother, he gives a gift to the poor one. He also gives detailed instructions about the use of the handmill, and so the first conflict—whether the rich will distribute to the poor or not—is solved by a deus ex machina, which ironically is a nice and fair Devil.

The Devil here is more or less a trickster character. He is not evil; he harms no one. He is social and knows humans' customs. He is also the utmost irony of the tale: the poor person believes God will bring food, yet he finds a solution because of the politeness of the Devil. The comment is directly biting at Christian perceptions of charity and poverty, and, of course, it expresses folk beliefs about God: God permits such injustices as families being hungry at Easter and he will not send food himself, because he is nonexistent in the folktales. Humans have to find solutions themselves, based on how communal they are and how much solidarity they have (Zipes 2001, 183–86).

One would say that the poor brother himself is the God of the story who provides the food. To the surprise of the folktale audience and by the use of harsh irony, he becomes a god after acquiring the handmill.[3] He becomes god because of a machine and because he respects gift-giving rules, by being an honest, reliable, hardworking gift bearer, even if this means he has to serve a bad-hearted rich person and the Devil himself. The folk-story teller explicitly rejects "the other world" and ridicules religious beliefs, as the story ends with people dying with no further metaphysical implications. At the same time, it uses the religious symbols to depict effectively the class conflicts and struggles in the storyteller's community (Meraklis 1986, 133–35; Taussig 1980, 93–139, 235–54). It is beyond the scope of this study to analyze further the religious and cultural aspects of the metaphysical discourse used in the folktale. The only point I would make here is that the comparison between the rich brother and the Devil is clear cut: the former is worse.

The conflict is not actually resolved, however. The class difference still exists. The handmill after all does not produce anything apart from food.

## The Machine

The entire folktale is constructed around a machine. Of course, the idea that poor people or peasants do not know much about or are negative toward technology is a bourgeois perception. Indeed, they are often interested in and positive toward machines (Meraklis 1991, 206–22). Obviously, people can adopt a critical stance to challenge capitalist expansion or the use of technology.

There are many Greek folktales that include machines or robot-like animals or statues, which shows that people have knowledge and are interested in imagining automated machines and envision technological advances with impressive or magical potential. The folktale of the handmill is one of those narrations based on the idea of the automatic machine (Meraklis 1984, 103–6; 1991, 206–2).

The handmill is a small machine, very common in all households, even today, to grind spice, garlic, or salt. Therefore, it is kitchen technology. It can produce any food in any quantity. The only important thing about it is that you must know how to use it.

The centrality of the machine is not a coincidence. The poor brother lacks any means of production, and now he has one at his possession. Even his neighbors initially explain his ability to have enough food by his inventive mind. They explicitly gossip about him: "Do you see him, that we were laughing at him? He was not sitting in vain in the shade. He was torturing his mind to find a way for one to eat what he wants without working and labor to death. And here he is that he found it!" The villagers are down to earth and explain the new means of production by the inventiveness of the poor man. His staying at home, that is, away from the fields (that were owned by others), was productive. The poor brother was not lazy at all; he was just smarter and working for his own purposes.

The second aspect of the machine is how the poor brother uses it. He is not using it to make a fortune. He just covers his household needs and is generous enough to share food with neighbors and with his own brother. The poor man is continuing more or less like before, but now he and his family are not hungry. Moreover, his social life has improved; he can share with friends; he can give food gifts. He is continuing to have fun playing music and singing. Now, he has everything he needs.

However, the handmill is not perceived the same way by the rich brother. He is frustrated that his poor brother is not hungry anymore and that he achieved this without working. He still does not recognize the handmill as the result of labor and of the integrity of his brother. He is instead angry that his brother found this solution to acquire food without working. He is not pressured anymore by the other villagers to redistribute to the poor, but instead of being happy, he is frustrated probably because he cannot blackmail his brother anymore into becoming a wage laborer.

The machine is now what the rich man wants more than anything so that he does not need to work anymore. In this folktale, the only person who states that he does not want to work anymore is the rich brother. He never stopped considering his brother as lazy and he did not recognize, as the other villagers did, his brother's inventive work. He thinks that his poor brother has this machine in his possession without really deserving it.

As a consequence, the rich man barters with his brother to take the machine from him. He thinks that the machine is more productive than fields and cattle, because fields and cattle need vast amounts of human work to produce, while the handmill needs just to be turned one way or another. Therefore, their contract is an exchange of means of production.

The poor man accepts the deal with an "it is the same to me." At this point, the poor person exits the story. The tale follows the handmill and not the poor brother.

### The Abuse of the Machine

The rich man takes the handmill and arranges with his wife to leave the place quickly to avoid his poor brother understanding he has been tricked and asking for a reversal of the contract. The machine has been appropriated at low cost, and the new machine owner wants to make sure that the machine will not be reclaimed by the first owner or inventor.

Geographical distance is the best solution for the new machine owner. He will take the mechanical means of production away from the place it was invented and used. He will be rich while depriving the village and the poor brother from a mechanical means of producing food that was shared with everyone in the village. Eric Olin Wright (1994, 32–45) would comment that the rich brother is the capitalist who has serious motives to destroy the free food provision in his brother's household and in the village. If free food is available, people will not want to work in the rich man's fields to make a living or become fameyos, nor buy his food commodities.

Given that the narration follows the handmill and not the poor man, we do not know whether the poor brother will continue sharing. It is the rich man who does not share, neither when he has lands and cattle, nor when he has the handmill.

However, as the folktale informs us, the rich brother is so eager to take the handmill that he fails to ask for full instructions. He believes the machine is enough of a means of production without having full knowledge about its workings, which the inventor or the knowledgeable user has. I am not sure whether this is a hint about the fetish of the machine but it is clear that the mechanical means of production consists of two parts: one is the physical part, the machine as physical entity; the other is the knowledge underneath the machine, particularly the knowledge of its limitations and dangers. The second part is so much inalienable from the people who worked to create and design the machine that the rich person is finding his own punishment precisely because he attempts to appropriate the machine by cutting all geographical, legal, and social connections between the machine and the people who really know how to use it.

If the rich brother had stayed in the village, he would be able to avoid all this disaster and death. Of course, he would also have to recognize his dependency on the knowledge and expertise of the poor brother. And he would have to distribute food, and perhaps reverse the barter contract, in case his brother became aware of the bad deal. This fleeing is the symbolic breaking of the kinship, because one member of the kin wants more and more wealth. Such breaking of kinship structures for the sake of wealth is a process seen in several Greek communities during the last century or centuries (Meraklis 1984, 61–67).

Therefore, apart from "dead labor" embedded in the machine,[4] there is always need of social checks and balances and of live labor to make sure the machine is used properly without destructive effects. The checks cannot be performed except by the community and the machine's producer, whose origins are poor. The rich person cannot handle the machine alone and cannot control its negative effects.

The other central theme of this folktale, or perhaps *the* central theme, is the environmental disaster that happens at the end. The disaster brought by the rich brother's use of the machine is not only his death and of all the people on the ship; it is also the loss of the machine, as it stays forever in the deep sea and produces continuously vast amounts of salt.

The folktale belongs to the so-called justifying myths (αιτιολογικοί μύθοι), which construct a story as an explanatory narration for a physical or social phenomenon (Psaroulaki 2014). The sea does not have salt because of a sunken handmill; its salty taste is a phenomenon that goes beyond the human measures,[5] or metrics. If the salt comes from a misused machine, then the disaster is unlimited and huge, as well.

Moreover, the environmental disaster is irreversible. This is crucial, because the contract between the two brothers was reversible. Poverty was reversible, too. Even the bad relationship between the two brothers was reversible. What is not reversible in this tale is the destruction that the machine by the hand of the rich man brought to nature and to humans: chemical pollution and death. It is not a coincidence that the last part of the tale is similar to the version presented by Chourdakis (1999, 15–21), though the preceding parts are quite different—this ending must be the most important part of the tale.

Salt in the sea is not chemical pollution, of course, but the hint here is that before that "industrial accident" the sea consisted of fresh, drinkable water. Humans have to live with the environmental degradation forever. Because, even though the rich person has been physically destroyed as punishment, the machine cannot be physically destroyed. The magic of the folktale is not more powerful than that of the machine (Meraklis 1988, 26, 29).

## SOME ADDITIONAL OBSERVATIONS

The folktale does not directly deny basic inegalitarian (patriarchal, feudal, and capitalist) institutions such as private property or unequal wealth distribution. It seems possible that the previously poor brother just replaced his brother in the social structure of the village. This is very common in folk and fairy tales, that is, the expression of the desire not to smash unjust social arrangements but to bring the poor person into the place of the rich and powerful (Brass 2002, 2007; Meraklis 1988, 33–38; Zipes 2001, 29–37).

A counterargument would be that in times and in societies where direct critique to the powerful might bring harsh retaliation, a folktale such as "Why the Sea Is Salty" is the only way to talk about economic inequalities. The concept of justice in the folktale and the punishment of the greedy rich brother is something that could be revolutionary enough if it ever came true in real life (Moutzouris 2014b, 251–70; Psaroulaki 2014). Folktales provide routes for us to become crafters of history, but they do not decide our fates; their role is to make us rethink the way we live, and for this there is no need for an explicit call for revolution (Zipes 2001, 45; 2006, 6–8). Through the tale, the open-ended possibility for the poor brother and the entire village exists.

However, the storytellers do not seem happy with the socioeconomic structure of their community, because class structure is central in the evolution of the tale (Meraklis 1988, 34–35). Particularly concerning the difference in the use of technology between poor and rich people, this folktale makes clear that class is crucial in determining choices and the results of using the same technology.

It is also clear that technology belongs to the poor people, and it is appropriated, both institutionally and geographically, by the wealthy. Appropriation changes everything, from the purpose and social benefit that technology brings to the community to the death of people and environmental destruction. Therefore, the folktale gives clear practical warnings to everyone. The poor people need not say "it is same to me" whether they have technology or land, because at the end, the environmental destruction is also their problem.

Third, the stance of the folk-story teller is generally critical of certain modes of production and perceptions about economic activity and not of machines in general. This means that everyday people are not negative toward technology as such (Meraklis 1991, 206–22), but the seemingly magic nature of the handmill becomes the explanation of its retributive function (Kapsomenos and Papaderou 2014). They are, of course, suspicious, because technology might also come from the Devil, but they know very well that what matters most is who knows how to use the machines and who controls them. The use of the machine for more than what a community needs or for personal ends is what brings destruction.

Fourth, the folktale refuses to accept that some types of labor or human effort are not productive. This brings the folktale far beyond Marxist theory itself. The poor man is rewarded because he is working as much as is needed, and he obeys gift-giving rules that secure his own and his community's survival more than formal labor. Marxist theory is also challenged concerning the environmental aspect of the machine use: disaster is irreversible, which means that no human labor can bring the sea back to its preaccident state. The value of keeping nature intact or sustainable exceeds the "it is same to me" statement of the poor brother.

Finally, the folktale concentrates in a dense and short text (which embarrasses my chapter here) so much information concerning economic ideas and approaches. In economics, there is no way to model class, technology, environment, labor perceptions, and legal agreements in a single model like this one. In other Cretan folktales in which women have active roles, gender also runs through the entire text informing economic activity in ways that this folktale is missing.

The storyteller clearly shows that value has measurable and nonmeasurable parts. What the storyteller wants us to understand is the articulation, the full political economy of class, technology, private property, labor, and nature. In that sense, the method of modeling the economy followed by the folk storyteller has been very successful and gives us hints on how to invent better models for economics based on critical approaches (Beverley 2004).

## CONCLUSIONS

In this chapter, I explained how I began studying and analyzing folktales in order to learn economics as knowledge that everyday people have access to. The folktale "Why the Sea Is Salty" has been a very informative example about the views and perceptions of Cretan people in late nineteenth to early twentieth centuries concerning the use of technology and the class biases that affect it.

The analysis showed that the storytellers of Crete had a sharp understanding of emerging or expanding capitalism and its main features. This folktale is an example of how people educate themselves about the economy and provides clues as to how we can educate ourselves about the economy today.

Finally, I would like to mention that this analysis is not definitive, but an attempt to contribute to the discussion about noncapitalist economies and about folk culture that can be relevant today in many more ways than we could have imagined. Hopefully, more research in this direction will be done to reveal the relevance of folk cultures to contemporary societies.

## ACKNOWLEDGMENTS

I am grateful to Prof. Michalis Meraklis (Prof. Emeritus, University of Athens) for his encouragement and his precious advice on literature and analysis of folk culture. I would also like to thank Dr. Maria Hnaraki (Drexel University), for her encouragement to participate in this volume and her advice on Cretan culture; Dr. Ferda Dönmez Atbaşı (University of Ankara), for the inspiration and the common research on Bacilar/Grassroots economics project; Dr. Lisa Radinovsky, for her editing advice and insightful comments; and to the anonymous reviewers of this volume, who offered precious advice on literature and theoretical critique. I am also grateful to the editors of this volume, Willow Mullins (Washington University, St. Louis) and Puja-Batra Wells (The Ohio State University), for their hard work, advice, and support while I was preparing and improving this chapter, and I am particularly indebted to Dr. Mullins for her enlightening comments and editing advice, but mostly for her collegiality in advising on literature related to critical folklore studies. Finally, I am grateful to the librarians of the Municipal Library of Chania City for their generous assistance. All deficiencies of this chapter, however, are the sole responsibility of the author.

## NOTES

1. "Value chain" is a term meaning how value is created and increased from the so-called primary production (e.g., agriculture) to secondary/packaging and tertiary/services (transport and distribution), where the price of an apple is several times the wage the peasant earns for it.

2. That is the English translation of *homo economicus*, which is the human model or stereotype of mainstream economics. The economic man is a person who apart from being male and assumedly European-white, is supposed to seek his individual interest and maximum utility (profit) in the economy. That the phrase itself is gender specific, asocial, and ahistorical (particularly class- and race-unaware) is part of the problem mainstream economic theory has.

3. The story discusses the materialist connotations of metaphysical beliefs about food and distribution. "God will send food" or "god will help you" is very commonly used to appease people in distress even if the distress is caused by social structures and not random natural phenomena. That is, the audience of the folktale waits for a God to send food, and the tale narrator reverses the expectation by making the Devil a helper to the poor and the poor the possessor of technology. Reversal is a technique of narration. Therefore, the poor person is God here, the God that was expected to bring food and he literally becomes one when he starts sharing food with neighbors.

4. By "dead labor" I mean here the understanding stemming from Marxist analysis that the machines embody labor that has already been done when the machine is set in motion/function to produce through the use of more labor. In other words, the machine represents labor that has been performed in previous times and now cannot produce anything on its own the way a machine can but needs new labor or human effort to become productive. It is striking that death of human effort and machine are perceived as intertwined in this approach.

5. I was in dilemma which term to use, "human scale" or "human measures." In the end, I chose the latter, translating directly from Greek. When we say "human measures" in Greek, we speak about things that are within the "golden path," that is, something not too small not too big, nor something that is a *hybris*—something that makes humans behave like gods or compare with god(s). That salt in the sea goes beyond human "measures," then, means that we do not understand, we cannot even fully perceive what the scope of this much water with this much salt. This is why the destruction of the environment that is caused by the machine

is a hybris in itself. It creates a destruction that is beyond human measures, because humans played gods with the machine. They played gods because the rich wanted the machine for himself only and the poor said, "it is the same to me." Well, it is not the same for anyone, and both trespassed the "human measures." Even the humble peaceful acceptance of the abuse by the poor brother is trespassing the human measures. The human measures are both a complex individual and collective responsibility, as revealed in the tale.

# REFERENCES

Antoniou, A. A. 2010. "Economic Realities and Modern Greek Folk Literature" [in Greek]. *Historicals [Τα Ιστορικά]* 53 (December): 463–78.

Apostolakis, S. 2014. "The Folktales of Selino by Y. E. Mathioudakis" [in Greek]. In *The Cretan Folktale (tribute to Pavlos Vlastos)*, ed. K. Moutzouris. Conference Proceedings, Centre of Cretan Literature and Municipality of Minoa Pediadas, Herakleion.

Avdikos, E., ed. 2007. *Crete: Folk Civilisation—Localities: Resistances, Changes, Syntheses* [in Greek]. Athens: Taxideftis Publishing.

Bennholdt-Thomsen, V., M. Mies, and C. Von Werlhof. 1988. *Women: The Last Colony*. London: Zed Books.

Beverley, J. 2004. "The Subaltern and the Limits of Academic Knowledge" [in Spanish]. *Revista Aktuel Marx* 2 (August), trans. M. Beiza and S. Villalobos-Ruminott.

Bottigheimer, R. B. 2009. *Fairy Tales: A New History*. Albany: State University of New York.

Brass, T. 2002. "On Which Side of What Barricade? Subaltern Resistance in Latin America and Elsewhere." *Journal of Peasant Studies* 29 (3–4): 336–99.

Brass, T. 2007. "Subaltern Resistance and the ('Bad') Politics of Culture: A Response to John Beverley." *Journal of Peasant Studies* 33 (2): 304–44.

Briggs, C. L. 2012. "What We Should Have Learned from Américo Paredes: The Politics of Communicability and the Making of Folkloristics." *Journal of American Folklore* 125/495 (Winter): 91–110.

Chourdakis, A. 1999. *Cretan Folktales: The Folktales of Siteia* [in Greek]. Herakleion: Centre of Cretan Literature and Municipality of Minoa of Pediada.

Gencarella, S. O. 2009. "Constituting Folklore: A Case for Critical Folklore Studies." *Journal of American Folklore* 122 (484) (Spring): 172–96.

Gencarella, S. O. 2010a. "Gramsci, Good Sense and Critical Folklore Studies." *Journal of Folklore Studies* 47 (3): 221–52.

Gencarella, S. O. 2010b. "Gramsci, Good Sense and Critical Folklore Studies." *Journal of Folklore Studies* 47 (3): 259–64.

Gencarella, S. O. 2011. "Folk Criticism and the Art of Critical Folklore Studies." *Journal of American Folklore* 124 (494) (Fall): 251–71.

Harvey, D. [1982] 2006 *The Limits to Capital*. New York: Verso Books.

Herzfeld, M. 1985. *The Poetics of Manhood: Contest and Identity in a Cretan Mountain Village*. Princeton, NJ: Princeton University Press.

Herzfeld, M. 2005. *Cultural Intimacy: Social Poetics in the Nation-State*. 2nd ed. New York: Routledge.

Kapsomenos, E., and K. Papaderou. 2014. "Features of Cultural Localisation in Cretan Folktale" [in Greek]. In *The Cretan Folktale (Tribute to Pavlos Vlastos)*, ed. K. Moutzouris, 127–42. Conference Proceedings. Herakleion: Centre of Cretan Literature and Municipality of Minoa Pediadas.

Kousaleos, Nicole 1999. "Feminist Theory and Folklore." *Folklore Forum* 30 (1–2): 19–34.

Limón, J. E. 1983. "Western Marxism and Folklore: A Critical Introduction." *Journal of American Folklore* 96 (379) (January–March): 34–52.

Limón, J. E. 1984. "Western Marxism and Folklore: A Critical Reintroduction." *Journal of American Folklore* 97 (385) (July–September): 337–44.

Limón, J. E. 2010. "Breaking with Gramsci: Gencarella on Good Sense and Critical Folklore Studies." *Journal of Folklore Research* 47 (3) (September–December): 253–57.

Lipsitz, G., and R. Rodriguez. 2012. "Turning Hegemony on Its Head: The Insurgent Knowledge of Américo Paredes." *Journal of American Folklore* 125 (495) (Winter): 111–25.

Lopez Morin, J. R. 2006. *The Legacy of Américo Paredes*. College Station, Texas: Texas A&M University Press.

Mathioudakis Y. 1936. *Loulouda: Cretan Vignettes* [in Greek]. Chania: Observer Printing.

Meraklis, M. 1984. *Greek Folklore Ethnography: Social Formation* [in Greek]. Athens: Odysseas Publishing.

Meraklis, M. 1986. *Greek Folklore Ethnography: Mores and Customs* [in Greek]. Athens: Odysseas Publishing.

Meraklis, M. 1988. *What Is Folk Literature* [in Greek]. Athens: Centre of Marxist Studies and Modern Era Publishing.

Meraklis, M. 1991. *Our Folktales* [in Greek]. Thessaloniki, Greece: Constantinidis Publishing.

Mies, M. 1988. "Women's Work: The Blind Spot in the Critique of Political Economy." In *Women: The Last Colony*, ed. V. Bennholdt-Thomsen et al. London: Zed Books.

Moutzouris, K., ed. 2014a. *The Cretan Folktale* (Tribute to Pavlos Vlastos) [in Greek]. Conference Proceedings, Centre of Cretan Literature and Municipality of Minoa Pediadas, Herakleion.

Moutzouris, K. 2014b. "Injustice and Restitution of Justice in the Folktales of Western Crete" [in Greek]. In *The Cretan Folktale (Tribute to Pavlos Vlastos)*, ed. K. Moutzouris. Conference Proceedings, Centre of Cretan Literature and Municipality of Minoa Pediadas, Herakleion.

Paredes, A. 1963. "The North-American Cowboy in Folklore and Literature" [in Spanish]. *Cuadernos del Instituto Nacional de Antropología* 4 (Buenos Aires, Instituto Nacional de Antropología—Ministerio de Educación y Justicia): 227–40.

Psaroulaki, A. 2014. "Entrance and Exit in Cretan Folktale" [in Greek]. In *The Cretan Folktale (Tribute to Pavlos Vlastos)*, ed. K. Moutzouris. Conference Proceedings, Centre of Cretan Literature and Municipality of Minoa Pediadas, Herakleion.

Rokou, V. 2007. "The Tanneries of Chania: An Approach to Local Manufacturing Society" [in Greek]. In *Crete: Folk Civilisation: Localities: Resistances, Changes, Syntheses*, ed. E. Aydikos. Athens: Taxideftis Publishing.

Scott, J. 1985. *Weapons of the Weak: Everyday Forms of Peasant Resistance*. New Haven: Yale University Press.

Taussig, M. 1980. *The Devil and Commodity Fetishism in Latin America*. Chapel Hill: University of North Carolina Press.

Von Werlhof, C. 1988. "The Proletarian Is Dead: Long Live the Housewife!" In *Women: The Last Colony*, ed. V. Bennholdt-Thomsen et al. London: Zed Books.

Wright, E. O. 1994. *Interrogating Inequality: Essays in Class Analysis, Socialism and Marxism*. London: Verso Books.

Zipes, J. 1993. "Spinning with Fate: Rumpelstiltskin and the Decline of Female Productivity." *Western Folklore* 52 (1) (January): 43–60.

Zipes, J. 2001. *Breaking the Spell: Radical Theories of Folk and Fairy Tales [Romper el hechizo—Una visión política de los cuentos folklóricos y maravillosos]*, trans. V. Cuccaro. Buenos Aires: Grupo Editorial Lumen.

Zipes, J. 2006. *Fairy Tales and the Art of Subversion: The Classical Genre for Children and the Process of Civilization*. 2nd ed. New York: Routledge and Taylor and Francis Group.

# 11

## What Would Hermes Do?
### A Jungian Perspective on the Trickster and Business Ethics

William A. Ashton

THE TRICKSTER FIGURE IN MYTHOLOGY is often associated with markets and business (Combs and Holland 1996, 82). In Western myth Hermes, the Olympian Trickster figure, is the god of the marketplace. Hermes's name itself is evidence of his relationship to trade. In ancient Greece *herms*, stone markers, would mark the edge of a clan's territory. These herms would be the place of the earliest interclan "silent" trade, and then the place of interclan markets. Finally, when a centralized government regulated trade and the markets were brought into the city walls, the herms were moved into the cities to stand in the marketplaces (Brown [1947] 1990, 39–45). The Trickster is in business.

From a Jungian psychology perspective, the Trickster figure is an archetype (Rychlak 1981, 195) that has the ability to express itself both psychologically via symbols in dreams, actions, or creative activities (Rychlak 1981, 203–5). Thus, given the Trickster figure's association to business, we can use the Jungian perspective to aid us in analyzing current culture, especially current business culture. Researchers (Ho 2005, 2009; Maurer 2006; Miyazaki and Riles 2005) have recognized the importance of examining current business culture not as a unitary global phenomenon but as a culturally specific phenomenon. For example, Ho (2009, 178–80) recognizes the presence of "Western folk theories" propagated among businesspeople in what she describes as "corporate America" or "Wall Street" culture. For example, by examining three recent seminal events in Wall Street business culture we can see the utility of applying a Jungian-based Trickster archetypical analysis.

The 2008 economic crash initiated the worst economic downturn in eighty years (*The Economist* 2013). One of the many causes of this crash involved the pooled housing securities market. This market consisted of housing loans made to buyers with poor credit histories. The financial institutions then pooled together these high-risk loans and presented them as low-risk securities. Packaging high-risk securities together as low-risk securities is financially sound *as long as the individual loan risks in the package are not correlated*. Risks are uncorrelated when, for example, an economic downturn in Dallas will increase the number of housing loan defaults in Dallas, but this Dallas slump would not affect the ability of Seattle's homeowners' abilities to pay their mortgages. The financial institutions ignored an obvious problem with this plan: a regional or national economic downturn would cause homeowners in many cities to default on their home loans and violate the assumptions these low-risks securities were based upon. The scheme did not work, because these simple rules were not followed. This is very Trickster-like.

In mythology,[1] Tricksters often discover magical things that give them unlimited food or heightened abilities, but only if they follow the simple rules. When Tricksters do not follow the rules, they lose the magical thing and are worse off than when they began. For example, Coyote saw a man taking his eyes out of his head and throwing them on a cottonwood tree. After his eyes hung on the tree the man said, "eyes come back!" and they returned to his head. Coyote asked the man how to do the trick. At first the man was resistant, but after repeated begging from Coyote the man gave in. Before the man left Coyote, he warned Coyote not to do this trick more than four times in one day. "Of course not. Why would I do that?" Coyote replied. Coyote then did the trick, and he could see for miles and miles. After the fourth time he did this Coyote thought, "That man's rules are for his country. I don't think that applies here. This is my country." And so Coyote cast his eyes up into the tree for a fifth time, and they didn't return. Coyote stumbled around blind and crying (Hyde 1998, 3–4).

Volkswagen executives created a crafty plan to fool consumers. They heavily marketed diesel cars in the United States as a green alternative to other cars, based on the low emissions of the VW diesels. However, the cars were not low-emission vehicles. Volkswagen installed defeat devices in the cars. These inventions could detect when the cars were undergoing emissions testing and produce low emissions at the cost of poorer performance. When not being tested, the defeat device would direct the engines to produce high performance and high emissions. After discovery that Volkswagen had installed defeat devices in about 11 million cars, the company posted their first quarterly loss in fifteen years (a loss of $2.75 billion; Hotten 2015). Volkswagen got caught by their own invention.

Tricksters often invent traps, but in the end they are caught by their own inventions due to their own carelessness or hunger. For example, the Norse trickster Loki was hiding in the mountains (earlier he had angered the other gods). To avoid capture by the other gods, he builds a house with doors on all sides so no one can surprise him. Bored with hiding, Loki changes himself into a salmon and swims the mountains streams. Still thinking of avoiding capture, he further amuses himself by imagining how someone might catch him as a salmon. He invents the first fishing net as a model of his ideas. Then the gods approach. Loki burns his invention, changes into a salmon, and swims away. The gods find the ashes of the net, reconstruct the fishing net, and then use it to catch Loki (Hyde 1998, 18).

Today the largest hotel company is Airbnb, a hotel company that does not own any hotels. The largest taxi company is Uber, a taxi company that does not own any taxis. And Alibaba is the highest-valued retail company, a retailer that does not possess an inventory (Goodwin 2015). While this sounds contradictory it is part of a larger trend in business of focusing upon flexibility, feedback, and the taking advantage of the power of the market. Other examples of this general concept are strategic management, boundaryless organizations, and just-in-time logistics.

All of these elements, contradictoriness (of the web companies with no bricks-and-mortar components), "flexibility," "feedback," "boundary," and "just-in-time" are characteristics of the Trickster. In myth Tricksters usually have a few or no natural talents—or instincts—and can only mimic. The Trickster cannot fish like his brother, Kingfisher. This is why Carl Jung stated that the Trickster is "stupider than the animals" (Hyde 1998, 43). But in mimicking what they see Tricksters can learn new behaviors, make new things, and, thus, be flexible. As Hyde states: "If we [speaking of the Trickster] can imitate the spider and make a net, imitate the beaver and make a lake, imitate the heron's beak and make a spear, imitate the armadillo and wear armor, imitate the leopard and wear camouflage . . . then we become more versatile hunters, greater hunters" (1998, 43).

The above examples describe the Trickster's role in Western business and Western multinational corporations. The Trickster's influence on business is both positive, in developing new ways of thinking about business, and negative, in causing ethical misconduct and plain old foolish behavior. This chapter will examine the Trickster from a perspective of Jungian psychology, focusing upon business ethics and what the Trickster can tell us about conducting business ethically. In order to do so, we need to employ the Jungian concepts of primordial and divine trickster. Also, a Jungian approach will allow this chapter's analysis to connect to Jungian work on ethics and myth.

Before those concepts can be discussed, however, a brief overview of Jungian psychology is also necessary. First, to set the stage for the Trickster-oriented overview of Jungian psychology, a formal introduction to the trickster is provided. A trickster especially familiar to Jung, by way of Jung's analysis of alchemy (Rychlak 1981, 243), is Hermes (Combs and Holland 1996, 92).

# THE TRICKSTER

## A Starting Point: Hermes the Trickster

A very familiar version of the Trickster in business is presented in the *Homeric Hymn to Hermes*. In the *Hymn* (Hyde 1998, 317–33), Maia gives birth to her son Hermes, who was fathered by Zeus. Hermes quickly leaves his mother's cave, takes fifty of Apollo's cattle, and drives them backward from the meadow to confuse Apollo. Hermes kills and butchers two bulls and roasts their meat. Hermes then divides the meat into twelve portions and sets these portions aside, which was difficult to do because he is hungry. However, Hermes has bigger plans. Returning home, Hermes explains to his mother that he will not accept their life of living in a gloomy cave and will take from the gods what he needs.

At this point in the poem, Apollo discovers that some of his cattle are missing. Being a god, Apollo reads a sign and discovers that Hermes was the thief. Apollo, in a rage, goes to Maia's cave, confronts Hermes, and accuses him of stealing the cattle. Hermes responds by skillfully avoiding the accusation. Hermes replies, "Do I look like a cattle driver? What would the other gods think about your mental health, making accusations like this about a baby? Also, I'll swear an oath to Zeus that I didn't steal your cows, nor see anyone steal your cows. Whatever cows are." The combination of Hermes's boldfaced lying and skillful choice of words in his denial breaks Apollo's anger, and Apollo laughs at his stepbrother. The two brothers go to their father, Zeus, to resolve their dispute.

On Mount Olympus, the two brothers restate their cases to Zeus. Hermes repeats his boldfaced lies and prevarications about the cattle theft, which draws laughter from Zeus. Zeus ordered Hermes to return the cattle. At the barn in Pylos where Hermes stabled the remaining cattle, Apollo again becomes enraged at Hermes (most likely over the two dead bulls). Hermes begins playing his newly invented lyre, and the sound of the lyre is so beautiful that Apollo's anger at Hermes finally breaks. The two gods sit down and come to an agreement. Apollo pledges his love and friendship to Hermes, and Hermes pledges to never steal from Apollo.

## What Is the Trickster?

The term "trickster" first appeared in English usage in the eighteenth century to mean someone who deceives or cheats (Doty and Hynes 1993, 14–15). In the twentieth century, the word "trickster" was used to refer to characters in Native American and African folklore, and then the usage was later broadened to include similar figures in Western classical literature. By the end of the twentieth century, the study of the Trickster as a universal phenomenon was so well developed that different perspectives emerged regarding the phenomenon. One perspective—associated with Carl Jung, Karl Keréyi, and Paul Radin—holds that the Trickster myths reflect an archetypal phenomenon or a transcendent process of the human psyche. The other perspective, associated with Hynes and Doty, rejects the archetypal view and searches for causes of this universal similarity among Tricksters in comparative social functions, in psychological mechanisms, in literary traces, and in relationships to religious systems and rituals (Hynes and Doty 1993, 2).

Regardless of adherence to the archetypal or nonarchetypal perspective, most researchers can agree upon six defining characteristics of the Trickster (Hynes 1993, 34): (1) ambiguous/anomalous, (2) deceiver / trick player, (3) shape-shifter, (4) situation inverter, (5) messenger of the gods, (6) sacred/lewd tinkerer.

First, Tricksters are ambiguous and anomalous. Tricksters go from one extreme and then to the other, one moment acting wisely and the next moment acting foolishly. But this only captures part of the Trickster's ambiguity. As Hynes states, "He is not fully delimited by one side or the other side of a binary distinction, nor by both sides at once, nor by a series of oppositions" (1993, 34). This anomalous nature also is related to the Tricksters' boundary dwelling/crossing abilities and their general ability to break down existing boundaries and definitions. Hyde refers to the Trickster as "the lord of the in-between (Hyde 1998, 6)" because the Trickster is never home, but always passing through.

The second defining characteristic of Tricksters is that they are deceivers and trick players. Tricksters are smooth talkers who can twist words to their own benefit. Apollo addresses Hermes as a "messenger of shifty guile." Native American Trickster stories contain many examples of Tricksters playing tricks on other animals (which often end in those animals becoming the Trickster's dinner). These above examples have a dark tone, but remember Tricksters are ambiguous. This trick-playing characteristic of Tricksters is also related to playful fun and laughter (Doty and Hynes 1993, 28).

Third, Tricksters are shape-shifters. A common component to their trickery is the ability to change their appearance. Sometimes these changes are minor, as in a change of clothing, and other times these changes are true transformations of the Trickster's basic substance and nature. For example, Hermes changed into a mist in order to prevent being tracked by Apollo.

Fourth, Tricksters are situation inverters. One aspect of their trickery is the ability to transform a situation into its complete opposite. Powerful taboos are carelessly broken, the highest gods mocked, and the lowest and most profane acts exalted (Hynes 1993, 37). In the *Homeric Hymn to Hermes* we see Hermes place himself as an equal to the gods and then care so little about the gods that he tricks and deceives them. One aspect of this characteristic is the ability to turn success into failure and failure into success. For example, Coyote learned how to magically throw his eyes up into a tree, enabling him to see farther than normal. However, by not obeying simple instructions, he loses his eyes. Consequently, instead of having superior sight, Coyote is blind (Hyde 1998, 3–4). Tricksters are able to turn on its head any powerful person, situation, conclusion, or belief.

Fifth, Tricksters are messengers of the gods. Given their (often) half god / half human heritage and general traits of being anomalous (neither a god nor a human—the classification does not fit), Tricksters are a good choice to serve as the intermediary between the gods and humankind. Besides delivering messages to humans from the gods, this role also has Tricksters serving as psychopomps (the guide of souls in death), and cultural heroes who bring (steal? con?) gifts from the gods for humankind. In Greek mythology, Hermes filled all of these roles. He was the winged sandaled messenger of the gods, he guided the dead to the underworld (and guided a few out of the underworld; Otto 1978, 113), and brought gifts to humankind (Hynes 1993, 40).

Finally, the sixth defining characteristic of Tricksters is that they are sacred/lewd tinkerers. Tricksters are always inventing new things (which often end up gifted to humankind) or redesigning existing parts of things. These inventions are considered sacred when they end up as gifts to humankind. Some examples are the lyre, fire-sticks, sacrifice (Brown [1947] 1990, 67), and fishing hooks and nets (Hyde 1998, 18). However, when combined with Tricksters' shape-shifting abilities we often see the lewd side of their tinkering. Tricksters redesign their bodies, and these redesigns usually focus on their sexual or excretory organs. For example, Tricksters have made their intestines longer and shorter, detached their anus for guard duty, created monumental piles of excrement, or shorted and lengthened their penises (or losing it altogether; Hynes 1993, 42–44).

Thus, Tricksters are slippery characters. Tricksters are troublesome or downright dangerous to people, but they redeem themselves, in the eyes of humans at least, by the inventions they give to humanity and their intercession with the gods for humanity. This view of the Trickster, that they are sometimes helpful and sometimes harmful to humans, is not that helpful in answering the question "what would Hermes do in business?" Key to answering this question are the dual concepts of primordial and divine Trickster. In order to fully describe the primordial and divine Tricksters, a brief introduction to Jungian psychology is needed.

## JUNGIAN PSYCHOLOGY AND THE TRICKSTER

### Jungian Psychology

Carl Jung (1875–1961) was a Swiss psychiatrist credited with founding the Analytical School of Psychology (Rychlak 1981, 176). The Analytic School's main theme is of the psyche's growth based upon the reconciliation of opposite-valued thoughts. Normally, thoughts are split into polarities (e.g., "good" versus "bad") with one pole associated with our conscious sense of self, the ego, and the other pole associated with the unconscious alter ego, or shadow (Monte 1999, 439–41). These opposites are reconciled by the action of archetypes (Rychlak 1981, 205–8) and the transcendent function. The transcendent function is a naturally occurring drive for psychic wholeness. This wholeness is achieved via interpretation of symbolic material based upon different archetypes. Jung formally defined an archetype as an instinctual perception (Jung [1960] 2014d., 138–37) and conceptually located the archetypes in a transpersonal collective unconscious. Archetypes reconcile these opposites by expressing the opposites in symbolic form in the psyche or by a physical event, a synchronicity, which is connected symbolically to the archetype (Combs and Holland 1996, 65–67). Across the lifespan, this drive for wholeness and for the reconciliation of opposites is a major developmental task and is called individuation. While this may sound exceedingly within individual psychology and divorced from business and Wall Street corporations, authors (Neville 2003; Ketola 2012; Neville and Dalmau 2008; Rozuel 2010, 2013, 2015) have used Jungian psychology to develop theory, conducted experiments, and consult—all in business settings.

### Complexes of the Psyche

Subjectively, the most salient complex is the ego. To Jung, the ego is a complex in consciousness which is an agglutination of ideas associated with the feeling-tone of "me" (Jung [1969] 2014a, 323). But what happens to ideas associated with the feeling-tone of "not me"? There is a similar character which contains the ideas with the feeling-tone of "not me" called the alter ego or shadow (Jung [1969] 2014b, 266). The ego identifies the contents of the shadow as "not me" and wishes to ignore them. Jung calls this suppression (Jung [1967] 2014c, 57–59)—a conscious attempt to not be aware of an idea. Suppression, if done often enough will lead to repression, an unconscious attempt to not be aware of an idea (Rychlak 1981, 203).

The ego is our sense of self, of who we are, and the shadow is our negative sense of self. However, the ego is only our sense of *conscious* self. Who are we, actually? Just as our ego is the complex of conscious ideas associated with the feeling-tone of "me," the Self is the complex of *conscious and unconscious* ideas associated with the feeling-tone of "me" (Jung [1960] 2014d, 82). The Self is a complex that is shaped by the Self archetype (Jung [1969] 2014b, 267). The Self is the totality of our psyche, and the Self archetype is the concept of wholeness of the psyche. The ego thinks it is "me," but the Self is who we actually are in totality. The relationship between the ego and the Self is critical in psychological development across the lifespan (Edinger 1972, 37–38). However, since the Self has access to the unconscious ideas associated with "me," the ego is not aware of the Self. To Jung, complete psychological development depends upon the ego recognizing that it is not its own master, but that the ego serves a greater master, the Self. This greater master is unconscious and therefore unknowable and mysterious to the ego. If this sounds religious, it should. To a Jungian, religion is a symbolic expression of the relationship between the ego and the Self (see Edinger 1972). Again, while these concepts may appear distant from Wall Street, authors have applied these complexes to business (Neville and Dalmau 2008, 120; Rozuel 2010, 38).

The ego is balanced by the shadow. Jung places these two complexes in the personal conscious and personal unconscious, respectively. Jung states that the personal shadow is descendent from the Trickster archetype (Jung [1969] 2014b, 142) and that the Trickster is the archetypal parallel of the personal shadow (150). While Jung equates the Trickster with the shadow, he suggests that the Trickster archetype has more positive elements than the shadow (136). Jung seems to suggest (151) that the shadow stands at the beginning of the individuation process and that the Trickster archetype stands toward the end of the individuation process, usually after we understand the meaning of some disaster (probably created by the Trickster). How does the Trickster archetype aid in the individuation process? By the characteristics described by William Hynes (1993, 34). The Trickster archetype crosses and confuses boundaries (ambiguous/ anomalous); it deceives and tricks us; it takes every taboo, everything we base our world on, and turns it upside down (situation-inverter). The Trickster is doing this to guide us spiritually (messenger) to an amazing invention (sacred tinkerer), namely, individualization.

Jung believed that the psyche had a drive toward individualization, and it was facilitated when people attend to the psyche's symbolic activity (Miller 2004, 4). While the symbolism in dreams is one source of this transcendental material, Jung rejects relying on this source because dreams are pure products of the unconscious (Jung [1960] 2014b, 77). What is more useful is the active imagination. One form of the active imagination is paying attention to our moods and trying to create, though an imagination-based process, a conscious representation of the unconscious content that is causing that mood (Miller 2004, 23).

### Hermes from a Jungian Perspective

The image of the Trickster in *The Homeric Hymn to Hermes* is in some ways a one-sided view of the Trickster. Hermes is relatively unique among Tricksters in that he was able to *not* get caught in his own trap. Hermes's story diverges from other Trickster tales in which Hermes roasts the two slaughtered cows, smells the sweet smoke, and hungers. At this point, most Tricksters would be overwhelmed with their hunger and eat the meat (e.g., Hyde 1998, 33). But Hermes did not. By not eating the meat, Hermes left twelve equal portions of it. The symbolism of the twelve portions was that there was one portion for each of the Olympian gods—including Hermes. Thus, Hermes sets himself as an equal to the other Olympian gods (Brown [1947] 1990, 104–5; Hyde 1998, 58–59)!

In contrast to Hermes, many Tricksters are not able to control their basic desires, such as hunger, sexual desire, or trying to get more of any good thing. Coyote has the ability to see farther than normal, he ignores the rules because he wants to use this ability more, and he loses his eyesight. Coyote is about to resurrect his dead wife, but he cannot control his desire to embrace her for one more night, so he loses her and brings death into the world. Hyde (1998, 37) suggests that Trickster stories exist within a hierarchy between low (unable to control appetite) and high (able to control appetite).

Similarly, Jon Layton (1994), working from a Jungian perspective, suggests an archetypical distinction between a primordial and divine Trickster. The primordial Trickster's level of consciousness is at a basic childlike or animalistic level, and has not matured to the point of the use of concepts or judgment. At this stage, the primordial Trickster is motivated by desires for food and sex. This version of the Trickster seems mainly egoless and driven by impulses from the id. These drives create a Trickster figure who, out of ignorance, creates mischief and chaos. Thus, the primordial Trickster emphasizes the Trickster characteristics of ambiguous/anomalous, deceiver/trick-player, shape-shifter, and situation-inverter.

The more developed version of the Trickster, the divine Trickster, has a solidified consciousness and ego, is able to conceptualize, and is able to make judgments based upon his goals. The divine Trickster's goals are selfless and focused upon the betterment of humankind. Thus, the divine Trickster emphasizes the Trickster characteristics of messenger of the gods, psychopomp and tinkerer. This version of the Trickster is clearly seen in the *Homeric Hymn to Hermes*. Hermes is the god who is the friendliest to men, he brings gifts from the gods, invents gifts for humankind, and he is there to lead us at the time of our death. The divine Trickster tinkers with concepts in order to encourage humankind's cognitive and spiritual development. Divine Tricksters uses their other abilities—ambiguous/anomalous, deceiver/trick-player, shape-shifter, and situation-inverter—to force humans to break our conceptual ruts about ideas, our sense of self, and humankind's relationship to the gods.

An examination of *The Homeric Hymn to Hermes* (Hyde 1998, 317–33) makes it is clear that Hermes is a divine trickster. Hyde's main argument is that the Trickster transforms the world or makes a new world. This argument is supported in two ways: in Hyde's interpretation of the meaning of the cattle and in his interpretation of Zeus's and Apollo's reaction to Hermes's lies.

Hyde begins by noting that at the beginning of *The Homeric Hymn to Hermes* that Apollo's cattle are special cattle. These cattle are neither wild nor domesticated, and they neither are born nor die. They are immortal and unchanging (Hyde 1998, 58–80). Given this strange state, the cattle are of no use to people nor do the cattle have meaning. If the cattle cannot die, then they cannot be eaten. Thus, Hyde argues that Hermes, like other Tricksters, is a cultural hero. He is a hero because he transformed divine "pseudocattle" into edible cattle, and also created meaning by making these cattle fit the natural definition of cattle. Talk about divine tinkering!

Hermes's other great gift to humankind from this incident is the Trickster's lie. The trickster's lie is a transformative lie. It has the transformative ability to cancel any opposition to the lie (Hyde 1998, 70). However, the greatest gift of the Trickster's lie is its ability to move beyond the first-order/

zero-sum world of one party being correct and the other party lying, to the second-order world, a transcendence of which party is correct and which is lying. By doing so, the Trickster's lie goes on to build new truths.

The Trickster's lie cancels any opposition to the lie. Recall that in the *Hymn* (Hyde 1998) Hermes's lies charm Apollo out of his anger and into being amused at the skill at fabrication he has just witnessed. The skill at fabrication that so amused Apollo is partly in how well Hermes *truthfully* deflected Apollo's accusations. Never once did Hermes make a first-order lie. I can imagine Hermes looking around his mother's cave saying, "cows, cows; I don't see any cows, do you?" and perhaps lifting up a pillow and looking under it for a cow. The only problem is in Hermes's later comments, when he states that he could swear an oath about the cows. There are two ways out of this lie for Hermes. First, notice Hermes did not swear an oath about not stealing the cattle, but only said he *could* or *would* swear an oath. And second, Hermes could also swear that he did not steal Apollo's cattle, because perhaps the cattle did not ever belong to Apollo (Hyde 1998, 71–72).

Hermes is not playing a cheap word game. First, Hermes's goal is not to steal cattle, but to ensure his and his mother's standard of living and to make himself a god equal to the other gods (Hyde 1998, 322). Hermes's goal is to cause a change in the way goods and prestige are distributed among the Olympians. This change goes far beyond stealing a herd of cattle. Hermes wishes to question the order of things on Mount Olympus and is using the cattle as an example. Questioning the ownership of the cattle begs the questions: who decides these are Apollo's cattle, how did Apollo get these cattle in the first place, and should Apollo keep them all if they are only pseudo-cattle that cannot be eaten (Hyde 1998, 72)? Second, Hermes is proud of this cattle theft. In the end, he wants his theft to be noticed. Only with the theft noticed will Apollo and Zeus see his cleverness and ability and consider the greater questions Hermes wants Apollo and Zeus to consider.

If we stop to consider the language used in the above paragraph, we will notice that many terms that describe economics and business are used, such as standard of living, goods being distributed, and ownership. Hermes is all about business.

### The Divine Trickster in Business?

Hermes in the *Homeric Hymn to Hermes* was a divine trickster. If that is so, then how was he aiding humankind's cognitive and spiritual development? Hyde's analysis can be used to answer that question. Hermes transformed immortal cows so that they can be used by people, and Hermes introduced the

Trickster's lie, which created new meaning and new ways of understanding. Hermes in the *Hymn* was not stealing for the sake of stealing, nor was he stealing for the sake of his own belly. Hermes was stealing to transform the world for humankind. Why was this important for humankind? Or, more exactly, why was this important in Greek culture during the birth of mercantilism?

Norman Brown's ([1947] 1990) analysis of the cultural and historical context of the *Homeric Hymn to Hermes* suggests why Hermes's transformations are important. At the time of the writing of the *Hymn*, Brown describes a Greece undergoing significant social and economic change. Small local clans have been subsumed by a centralized aristocracy, and currency was now in widespread use. An important social change involved the growth in size, and political and social power of the economic classes of mercantile, craft, and itinerant tradespersons. Hermes, the god of the herms (the original market) and the god of the craftsperson (Hermes the inventor) is the god favored by these new classes. Brown states that the aristocracy resented or feared these new groups who favored Hermes, and this aristocratic negativity toward Hermes is reflected in the *Hymn* ([1947] 1990, 65). For example, Hermes ruthlessly attacks Apollo (the god favored by the aristocracy) and Hermes, who was not closely linked to thievery before, is now seen as a god of shifty guile and the god of thieves (Brown [1947] 1990, 22).

Seeing, as Brown does, Hermes's relationship to these economic classes and their struggle against the aristocracy, Hyde's view of Hermes's gifts in the *Homeric Hymn to Hermes* makes more sense. Hyde said that Hermes transformed immortal cows so that they can be used by people and that Hermes introduced the trickster's lie, which is a way of changing the status quo. So now, thanks to Hermes, cows are now available to "the people." That is, economic wealth is now available to all and not just the aristocracy. Hyde says that the Trickster's lie changes the status quo. Again, the people who pray to Hermes (mercantile, craft, and itinerate worker classes; Brown [1947] 1990, 84–85) want the status quo changed, and they want the wealth and power that they have earned by their hard work.

Hermes' actions in the Homeric Hymns to Hermes were symbolic of Hermes's divine Trickster-like action of transforming the way we think about ownership in a way to support the growing mercantile, craft, and itinerate worker classes. The appellation *Hermes the Thief* is mainly a name-calling attack against Hermes (see Brown's discussion of Hesiod's treatment of Hermes; Brown [1947] 1990, 50–60). Thus, Hermes was placed in charge of commerce because he has always been in charge of commerce and not because of some deeper association between business with prevarication and robbery.

The argument above does not remove the Trickster from business. The Trickster is in business and in the contradictions of business. The examples at the beginning of this essay—the 2008 financial crash, Volkswagen, Airbnb, Uber, and Alibaba—all suggest that the Trickster is involved in business. The distinction between the primordial and divine Trickster can be used to help understand how the Trickster is in business. Wall Street and Volkswagen were acting like primordial Tricksters. Wall Street got too greedy, ignored the rules, and killed the magic cow; Volkswagen devised a trap and then they ended up getting caught in their own trap. On the other hand, Airbnb, Uber, and Alibaba were acting like divine Tricksters. They changed the status quo, and by doing so they are creating new opportunities and new ways to enrich the people. Brown's Hermes—the champion of the mercantile, craft, and itinerate worker classes—would be pleased to know that Airbnb and Uber are allowing middle- and working-class people the opportunities to enrich their own lives both as wage earners and consumers.

The distinction between the primordial and divine Trickster can also help place the Trickster in a broader economic theory. The economic perspective of neoliberal capitalism underlies all of the examples of the Trickster in business in this essay. According to David Kotz (2009, 307), the main features of neoliberal capitalism include the deregulation of business to allow the "free market" to rule, a move away from fiscal policies designed to keep unemployment low, sharp reductions in governmental social spending, the reduction of taxes on the wealthy, and private and government attacks on trade unions. These features and their resulting policies contain the seeds, Kotz states, to economic expansion. Kotz also recognizes that these policies lead to growth in the inequality of wages and profits, the financial sector becoming absorbed in speculative activities and a series of asset bubbles crises.

In relation to the Trickster, neoliberalism's emphasis on markets has given rise to peer-to-peer businesses (e.g., Airbnb, Uber), also known as the sharing economy (Malhotra and Van Alstyne 2014, 24), which are placed within the neoliberalism paradigm (see Martin 2016; Schor 2014). The 2008 housing crash is an example of many of the negative outcomes of neoliberalism (e.g., speculation and bubbles).

A full discussion of the Trickster and neoliberalism is far beyond the scope of this chapter. However, in general, the Trickster would have a mixed relationship to neoliberalism. Using Hermes as an example, we can see that he would be positively inclined toward free markets (recall the root of Hermes's name). However, Hermes would balk at taxes that favor the wealthy, at attacks on trade unions, and at the redistribution of wealth away from lower classes (recall Hermes's innate dislike of the economic injustice between the gods living in Olympus and his disdain about his family living in a cave).

Applying the concept of the primordial versus divine Trickster has revealed several ways in which the Trickster is in business and how the Trickster can be used to inform business ethics. Similarly, several Jungian authors have specifically described a Jungian and archetypal foundation for business ethics.

### A Jungian Ethical Education

*A million zeros joined together do not, unfortunately, add up to one. Ultimately everything depends on the quality of the individual, but our fatally short-sighted age thinks only in terms of large numbers and mass organizations, though one would think that the world has seen more than enough of what a well-disciplined mob can do in the hands of a single madman.*
—Jung, *Collected Works of C.G. Jung, Vol.10: Civilization in Transition*

Cecile Rozuel identifies the roots of the 2008 financial crisis as the million zeros: individual workers keeping silent about their suspicions, shortsighted regulators, and entrepreneurs peddling unsustainable mass-consumption schemes (2015, 2). Jung's *million zeros* and Rozuel's analysis of the 2008 crisis all point to the work of the primal trickster in business.

What would be a Jungian solution to the primal Trickster in business? Authors such as Rozuel (2013, 2015) and Bernie Neville and Tim Dalmau (2008) offer different tracks of specific advice, which all revolve around what Rozuel (2015, 5–8) calls relearning the language of myths. These authors encourage businesspeople not just to learn the terminology of myth, but also to be encouraged to work with myth in active ways. While the idea of an education of myth may sound fantastic, Rozuel neatly identifies the first part of this education as already existing in the humanities. Specifically, she identifies ancient spiritual texts, children's literature, fairy tales, comic books, science fiction stories, contemporary fiction, and classic literature as teaching myth. Other formats have been used, such as movies, role-play, music, and other arts. Regardless of the material used, to enhance moral sensitivities Rozuel suggests that students should be encouraged to connect and identify with story characters, to empathize with the character's internal deliberations, to observe how this affects the psyche, and to observe other inner experiences. While reading stories are the starting point, Rozuel suggests that writing about the stories adds greater impact in that it forces individuals to make themselves vulnerable, which creates more situations to learn about their inner selves.

Finally, Rozuel introduces a uniquely Jungian element to her review of using the moral imagination in business ethics teaching, which allows for soul work. *Analyzing* literature, autobiographies, and works of art places the burden of work within the psyche on the ego and the student's consciousness. *Creative acts*, including creating writing, shift that burden away from the ego and conscious areas of the student's psyche to the unconscious areas of the student's psyche. The content of creative acts reveals parts of the student's soul, including moral values, goals, attitudes, and archetypal projections. This, in association with introducing to students basic Jungian concepts about the psyche (e.g., archetypes, ego, self, projection, shadow work, the need for opposites) and how to work with these concepts, will allow students to explore their morals and their ability to enact their morals.

## CONCLUSION: WHAT WOULD HERMES DO?

Neville (2003) critiques the one-sided overrepresentation of Hermes in business today in both preferred business ethics and business practices. It is the age of Hermes in business. In fact, Neville locates the age of Hermes in business as squarely in Western culture. The terms Neville uses to describe the age of Hermes—strategic management, just-in-time, managerial decentralization, devolution, deregulated environment—are very similar to the terms Karen Ho (2005) uses to describe Wall Street culture. Given this, myths about Hermes and other Tricksters would be a natural choice for inclusion in business education for both an ethical education and a value-added background in the tricks of the Trickster. A business education with a component on Hermes (and the other Olympian archetypes as suggested by Neville and Dalmau 2008) may provide a general value-added element to a business education. This value-added element would be derived from the often-discussed benefits of a humanities education for business people (Bennis and O'Toole 2005). Learning to distinguish between Hermes-style and Zeus-style organizations, for example, may give business people the cognitive frameworks to think more globally and inventively, that is, to meet the common business-speak exhortation to "think outside of the box," whatever that box might be.

Finally, this chapter began with several business examples. So specifically, what would Hermes do?

In the case of the 2008 crash, Hermes, the divine Trickster, would be aware that, given the Trickster's history, he would be likely to ignore the rules and try to cut off as much meat from the magic cow as possible. But doing so would only kill the cow. Hermes would be weakened by the sweet smell of quick profits, but his proud heart would stop him from killing the cow. This proud heart is his drive to earn a good place for himself and his family.

In the case of Volkswagen, Hermes—the god of the merchants, craftspersons, and itinerant workers—would think about whether this trick would transform business thinking in ways that would benefit people. The defeat device's deception would not be a lie to be proud of, would not delight those lied to, and would not focus attention on new ways of thinking about transportation and the environment.

Finally, in the case of Airbnb or Uber, Hermes was there. At some point businesspeople had to say to themselves, "I should start a taxi company without any taxis." Probably many businesspeople said to themselves, "I should start a taxi company without any taxis," or "I should start a hotel without rooms," and immediately rejected it because it was so contradictory. Perhaps Hermes was there when Brian Chesky and Joseph Gebbia said, maybe we can take this idea of helping people finding places to sleep during conferences and make it worldwide; and perhaps the Trickster was there when two internet entrepreneurs decided to start a cab company with no cabs. And Hermes said to them, "That makes no sense—let's play!"

## NOTE

1. While many of the examples of Tricksters come from anthropological and historical sources, there are many examples of current and Western Tricksters. These include Sherlock Holmes, Doctor Who (Charles 2013), and Ilan Cooperman-Segal (Cavaglion 2007, 248).

## REFERENCES

Bennis, Warren, G., and James O'Toole. 2005. "How Business Schools Lost Their Way." *Harvard Business Review Online*. Accessed January 27, 2016. http://www.uta.edu/faculty/richarme/BSAD%206310/Readings/Bennis%20OToole%20HBR%20How%20Business%20Schools.pdf.

Brown, Norman. O. [1947] 1990. *Hermes the Thief: The Evolution of a Myth*. Great Barrington, MA: Lindisfarne Press.

Cavaglion, Gabriel. 2007. "The Societal Construction of a Criminal as Cultural Hero: The Case of 'The Brinks Truck Theft.'" *Folklore* 118 (3): 245–60.

Charles, Alec. 2013. "Three Characters in Search of an Archetype: Aspects of the Trickster and the Flâneur in the Characterizations of Sherlock Holmes, Gregory House and Doctor Who." *Journal of Popular Television* 1 (1): 83–102.

Combs, Allan, and Mark Holland. 1996. *Synchronicity: Through the Eyes of Science, Myth, and the Trickster*. New York: Marlowe and Company.

Doty, William G., and William J. Hynes. 1993. "Historical Overview of the Theoretical Issues: The Problem of the Trickster." In *Mythical Trickster Figures: Contours, Contexts, and Criticisms*, ed. William. J. Hynes and William G. Doty, 13–32. Tuscaloosa: The University of Alabama Press.

*The Economist*. 2013. *The Origins of the Financial Crisis: Crash Course*. Accessed January 18, 2016. http://www.economist.com/news/schoolsbrief/21584534-effects-financial-crisis-are-still-being-felt-five-years-article on.

Edinger, Edward. 1972. *Ego and Archetype: Individuation and the Religious Function of the Psyche*. New York: Penguin Books.

Goodwin, Tony. 2015. "The Battle Is for the Customer Interface." Accessed March 3. http://techcrunch.com/2015/03/03/in-the-age-of-disintermediation-the-battle-is-all-for-the-customer-interface/#.aicvdtv:0sCd.

Ho, Karen. 2005. "Situating Global Capitalisms: A View from Wall Street Investment Banks." *Cultural Anthropology* 20 (1): 69–96.

Ho, Karen. 2009. "Disciplining Investment Bankers, Disciplining the Economy: Wall Street's Institutional Culture of Crisis and the Downsizing of 'Corporate America.'" *American Anthropologist* 111 (2): 177–89.

Hotten, Russell. 2015. Volkswagen: The Scandal Explained. *BBC World News*. Accessed December 10. http://www.bbc.com/news/business-34324772.

Hyde, Lewis. 1998. *The Trickster Makes This World: Mischief, Myth, and Art*. New York: Farrar, Straus and Giroux.

Hynes, William J. 1993. "Mapping the Characteristics of Mythic Tricksters: A Heuristic Guide." In *Mythical Trickster Figures: Contours, Contexts, and Criticisms*, ed. William. J. Hynes and William G. Doty, 33–45. Tuscaloosa: The University of Alabama Press.

Hynes, William J., and William G. Doty. 1993. "Introducing the Fascinating and Perplexing Trickster Figure." In *Mythical Trickster Figures: Contours, Contexts, and Criticisms*, ed. William. J. Hynes and William G. Doty, 1–12. Tuscaloosa: University of Alabama Press.

Jung, Carl G. [1969] 2014a. *Structure and Dynamics of the Psyche*. Vol. 8 of *The Collected Works of C. G. Jung*. Edited and translated by Gerhard Adler and Richard F. C. Hull. Princeton, NJ: Princeton University Press.

Jung, Carl G. [1969] 2014b. *Aion: Researches into the Phenomenology of the Self*. Vol. 9(2) of *The Collected Works of C. G. Jung*. Edited and translated by Gerhard Adler and Richard F. C. Hull. Princeton, NJ: Princeton University Press.

Jung, Carl G. [1967] 2014c. *Symbols of Transformation*. Vol. 5 of *The Collected Works of C. G. Jung*. Edited and translated by Gerhard Adler and Richard F. C. Hull. Princeton, NJ: Princeton University Press.

Jung, Carl G. [1960] 2014d. *Psychogenesis of Mental Disease*. Vol. 3 of *The Collected Works of C. G. Jung*. Edited and translated by Gerhard Adler and Richard F. C. Hull. Princeton, NJ: Princeton University Press.

Jung, Carl G. [1970] 2014e. *Civilization in Transition*. Vol.10 of *The Collected Works of C.G. Jung*. Edited and translated by Gerhard Adler and Richard F. C. Hull. Princeton, NJ: Princeton University Press.

Ketola, Tarja. 2012. "Losing Your Self: Managerial Persona and Shadow Pressures Killing Responsible Leadership." *Journal of Management Development* 31 (5): 470–87.

Kotz, David, M. 2009. "The Financial and Economic Crisis of 2008: A Systemic Crisis of Neoliberal Capitalism." *Review of Radical Political Economics* 41 (3): 305–17.

Layton, Jon. "Trickster and the Evolution of Consciousness." Unpublished manuscript, Antioch College, 1994.

Malhotra, Arvind, and Marshall Van Alstyne. 2014. "The Dark Side of the Sharing Economy . . . and How to Lighten It." *Communication of the ACM* 57 (11): 24–27.

Martin, Chris, J. 2016. "The Sharing Economy: A Pathway to Sustainability or a Nightmarish Form of Neoliberal Capitalism?" *Ecological Economics* 121 (January): 149–59.

Maurer, Bill. 2006. "The Anthropology of Money." *Annual Review of Anthropology* 35 (September):15–36.

Miller, Jeffrey C. 2004. *The Transcendent Function: Jung's Model of Psychological Growth through Dialogue with the Unconscious.* Albany: State University of New York Press.

Miyazaki, Hirokazu, and Annelise Riles. 2005. "Failure as Endpoint." In *Global Assemblages: Technology, Politics, and Ethics as Anthropological Problems,* ed. Aihwa Ong and Stephen J. Collier. Oxford: Blackwell.

Monte, Christopher. 1999. *Beneath the Mask: An Introduction to Theories of Personality.* New York: Harcourt Brace College Publishers.

Neville, Bernie. 2003. "Taking Care of Business in the Age of Hermes." *Trickster's Way, 2(1).* http://digitalcommons.trinity.edu/trickstersway/vol2/iss1/4.

Neville, Bernie, and Tim Dalmau. 2008. *Olympus INC: Intervening for Cultural Change in Organizations.* London, G. B: Karnac Books.

Otto, Walter. F. 1978. *The Homeric Gods: The Spiritual Significance of Greek Religion.* Trans. Moses Hadas. New York: Octagon Books.

Rozuel, Cecile. 2010. "Moral Tension in the Psyche: A Jungian Interpretation of Managers' Moral Experiences." *Electronic Journal of Business Ethics and Organization Studies* 15 (1): 36–43.

Rozuel, Cecile. 2013. "Calling to the Anima Mundi: On Restoring Soul within Organizations." *Journal of Management, Spirituality and Religion.* https:doi.org/10.1080/14766086.2013.801320.

Rozuel, Cecile. 2015. "Challenging the 'Million Zeros': The Importance of Imagination for Business Ethics Education." *Journal of Business Ethics.* Online Publication. https://doi.org/10.1007/s10551-015-2639-8.

Rychlak, Joseph. F. 1981. *Introduction to Personal and Psychotherapy: A Theory-Construction Approach.* 2nd ed. Hopewell, NJ: Houghton Mifflin Company.

Schor, Juliet. 2014. "Debating the Sharing Economy." http://greattransition.org/publication/debating-the-sharing-economy.

# 12

## Folk Economies and the Artisan Workshop

Amy Shuman

ON MY FIRST RESEARCH TRIP to study the marble-carvers of Pietrasanta, Italy, in 1982, I took the bus with two American artists to Pomezzana, a nearby mountain town, to visit the Milani toolmakers. After a half-hour walk through the village, we knew we had arrived when we heard the rapid tapping of an artisan pounding rows of teeth into a newly forged rasp. At the end of the path was the workshop, powered by a waterfall. The artists were there to purchase some tools, which they did, and when we sat down to talk, one of the Milani brothers pulled out a catalogue of artist tools from New York City, featuring the chisels, rasps, and other handmade sculpture tools made by the Milanis. The scene could have been a step back in time, except that it was contemporary, representing state of the artwork. The Milani family also sold their tools at a store in Pietrasanta, and even today their tools are in high demand and can be found in online catalogues.

The American artists and I were completely taken by the beautiful and seemingly premodern scene, but I soon learned that though the artisans of Pietrasanta have reverence for the making of a handmade tool, representing knowledge transmitted through generations of toolmakers, and though they lament the loss of some of that knowledge, they do not regard the Pomezzana water-powered toolmaking with nostalgia for a bygone era. Instead, they see their work as part of an ongoing enterprise, fully engaged in a global economy and employing skills that remain the most appropriate technologies for their work.

The artisan community of marble-carvers in Pietrasanta challenges many of our assumptions about artisan labor, knowledge, and modes of exchange. The Pietrasanta artisan community is not driven by nostalgia for earlier forms of technology but instead is an example of the coexistence of artisan and modern economies. Some artisan technologies, and marble-carving is an example, remain the most appropriate methods for the production of particular goods. Like other productions demanding very skilled workers, artisan marble-carving meets the needs of a contemporary marketplace. Understanding the marble-carving workshop in Pietrasanta requires foregoing some of the commonplace differentiations between art and craft, artist and artisan, traditional and modern, local and global cultural practice, and original and copy. It is not that these categories do not pertain but that the presumed differences between them can be misleading and can obscure our understanding of alternative economies of labor in the production of art. My goal is to identify the connections that matter and to describe the interdependencies, reciprocities, and circulations that constitute this artisan economy, especially, the elements of material (marble), tools, the processes of transmission of knowledge about stone-carving, histories of the community including histories of instruction, and the circulation of all of these.

In three decades of ethnographic and interview research, I observed how the relationships among tools, technologies, skill, and the production of works of art constitute a complex economy. In the case of the Pietrasanta artisans, this economy, though rooted in traditional embodied practices, has never been separate from global economies of exchange. Walter Benjamin's work provides a frame for considering the folk economies of reckoning with past and present technologies, marketplaces, and the transmission of skills. Further, his discussions of tradition are useful for understanding a reckoning with the past that refuses nostalgia.

Throughout this discussion, I am aware of the part I play in recovering a lost past even as I am observing present work. I arrived in Pietrasanta on the cusp of the decline of the practices I documented, an example of what Barbara Kirshenblatt-Gimblett calls the eleventh hour, "always with us, shifting its location with the imminence of the next disappearance" (1998, 300). Although I am more interested in the present than in a diminishing past, I remain nonetheless aware that I was present for a moment when the hold on the past was a self-conscious lament and when the knowledge I gleaned was presented to me as already fragmented. In this chapter, I resist the idea that folk economies necessarily invoke the past, and instead I address the way that the folk economy of the artisan community envelopes pastness in the present.

Folklorists studying individual artisans or artisan communities have often regarded them as pockets of anachronistic craft production, removed from the larger economy and separate from the manufacturing sector (cf. Briggs 1980; Glassie 1995; Jones 1995; Pocius 1997). Néstor García

Canclini writes, "It is said that artisan workshops correspond to a different mode of production, that they have long been replaced in the metropolises by manufacture, later by factories, and that unfavorable competition with capitalist enterprises relegates artisans to carry out repair work or other marginal tasks for which manual creativity still proves useful" (1993, 37). García Canclini critiques the opposition between tradition and modernity and the nostalgic regard often directed toward artisans as representatives of an earlier, sometimes premodern, period in which workers were not alienated from their labor and in which handmade production was valued. He describes the coexistence of ancient and modern ideological processes in Mexico, involving different sorts of reconciliation, whether through nostalgia for the handmade or the "before" or for tradition itself (2005, 42). Similarly, the long-standing global economies of the marble-carving artisans of Pietrasanta, Italy, challenge the idea that craft represents an anachronistic form of production. Their work integrates traditional and contemporary technologies, and their workplaces, or studios, follow principles of organization specific to the demands and value of the work, not always consistent with the expectations of a capitalist market economy.

The added value (Kirshenblatt-Gimblett 1998) of traditional knowledge is part of the economy of artisan labor; as a form of connoisseurship (Silverstein 2003), it is part of the metadiscourse about both the forms of production and the erosion of traditional cultural practices. In the contemporary Italian context, the term "artisan" can be applied to the work of skilled labor requiring years of apprenticeship or to ice-cream or other foods, signifying the handmade, local, and/or more highly valued, as opposed to commercially produced. Artisan labor and knowledge can also invoke the technological past and/or a nostalgic longing for an earlier mode of production. Although terms such as "local," "historical," and "handmade" are often conflated in this configuration of the artisanal, they are not equally applicable; nor are they necessarily equally valued. Several characteristics are potentially associated with artisan practices, including cooperative or family-run businesses, fair trade, informal learning practices, and small-scale production, but none of these is essential.

By describing artisan knowledge and production as a folk economy that exists alongside, in distinction from, and/or integrated with modern capitalist economies,[1] I suggest a reassessment of some of the categories imposed on artisan work. In Western cultures, the category of the artisan occupies a position variously described as in between art and craft/handicraft, between creativity and technology, between tradition and modernity, between farm and factory, and between the practical, or useful, and the (presumably not functional) work of art (Dickie and Frank 1996).[2] Each of these terms has complex histories, which further point to the ways that the category of the artisan negotiates other realms. I have divided my discussion into five areas. First, I chart the histories and cartographies of artisan production and export in Pietrasanta, including a discussion of the role of toolmaking and tool use as central to understanding how artisan technologies can be contemporary, rather than archaic. Second, to develop the idea of artisan material practices, I offer a historical account of the artisan workshop. Third, I examine the handmade as a poetics of practice that circulates with an embodied vocabulary. Fourth, I consider artisan stone-carving within the material of the environment, stone itself. Fifth, I discuss the organization of work in the relationship between artists and artisans. I propose the centrality of practice and the transmission of knowledge as central to understanding the marketplace of artisan production.

## ECONOMIES 1: HISTORICAL LEGACIES AND TECHNOLOGIES

Pietrasanta, Italy, today a town of about 35,000 residents, is located at the base of the Apuan mountain range, along the Mediterranean, at the northwestern corner of Tuscany. The Apuan mountains are made of marble, so Pietrasanta and nearby Carrara developed first as shipping ports for the quarries and later as artisan communities where the marble was made into architectural and artistic products for export.

The artisan workshop in Pietrasanta is part of an historical cartography that includes the marble quarries, the making of tools, the places for learning to carve, the making of sculpture, the related industries of bronze casting, and the global marketplaces for marble and marble sculpture. Pietrasanta became a site for the production of marble sculpture and architecture in the early 1800s, when artisans were enlisted to produce the altars, floors, and sculptures for the cathedrals of South America. (Many of the cathedrals were built in the 1500s, but the marble appointments were made centuries later.)[3] To respond to the market demand, studios in Pietrasanta and Carrara were created and employed hundreds of artisans. A school for artisans was created in 1842 in Pietrasanta; it became a state school for the study of art and architecture after World War II and no longer catered to the local population, but even in the 1980s, when I began my research, many of the artisans had studied there.

For the artisans, the cartography always begins with the quarries, the source of the marble, of course, but also the source of the consciousness of the region. Michelangelo famously (from the perspective of the locals) went to Pietrasanta to procure marble for the façade of the Church of San Lorenzo in Florence. He was called away to paint the Sistine Chapel, so the façade was never built; the marble was not quarried. However, this venture, a nonevent outside Pietrasanta, has remained a singular, founding moment with visible traces on the landscape. The road that was built to the quarry for the project still remains and is named Via Michelangelo. A plaque on a building in the central piazza of the city marks the place where he stayed. He was in Pietrasanta at the bidding of the Medici family, who owned the quarry in Pietrasanta and thus preferred that the marble be quarried there rather than from nearby Carrara. The Medici Palace, built to monitor various local interests, is now used as an art museum that includes a permanent exhibit of the cultural heritage of the area, a topic I will return to later. At that time, most of the flatlands extending to the sea were Malarial swamps; marble was not carved in Pietrasanta then, but Michelangelo is nonetheless claimed as part of the town's historical consciousness, part of its claim to a legacy of carving marble sculpture.

Other parts of the cartography are more rooted in practice. The marble quarries are the most visibly remarkable and majestic dimension of the landscape. Standing in a quarry, with its sheer rock face more than three stories tall, is like standing in a natural cathedral. The faces of the rock dwarf the enormous machinery and miles of diamond-encrusted cables crisscrossing the mountain that are used to cut the stone. Trucks carrying two-ton blocks of marble travel down the mountain all day; miles of stones, some from local quarries and some imported from other parts of the world, line the stretch of land near the railroad. The town itself has dozens of marble yards, small industrial plants where the marble is sliced into sheets used for architecture, and studios where the marble is carved.

The history of a community is rarely a straightforward chronology of facts about the significant changes shaping work and life. In my study of Pietrasanta, I expected technological innovations to be the dominant factor. However, the artisans did not describe major advances in technology as radically changing their work, and, instead, new technologies were incorporated into already-existing work practices. For example, when I asked the artisans about the introduction of pneumatic tools, they said that the tools were faster but required the same skillful use of the chisel. The newest technological innovation is the use of robots to do most of the carving, and it remains to be seen whether this technology will have a profound change on the structure of the workshop. There have always been new technologies, but technology alone is not responsible for change. Instead, the relationships between clients and artisans, regulations regarding apprenticeship, and other historical political factors have had even greater impact. In this discussion of historical perspectives on the artisan economies, I am interested not only in how contemporary events change historical discourses (White 1987), but also in how participants in the economy of the studio (artists, artisans, patrons, and others) deploy those histories differently in their understanding of how things work.

One way to understand the networks, material productions, and circulation of knowledge of the folk economy of artisan stone-carving is through tools, including toolmaking, the tools themselves, the circulation and marketing of tools, and the knowledge needed to make tools (Pursell 1985, 113). A focus on tools foregrounds techne, a particular kind of knowledge connected to craft. Craft here is the application of an art form; it refers "less to a class of objects than to the human ability to make and perform" (Shiner 2001, 19–20). On the one hand the discourse of tools refers to a relatively straightforward sense of know-how, and, on the other, know-how is anything but straightforward. Tools have histories, and knowing how to use them and how to make them can be the same as knowing everything about a culture, not only the explicit knowledge of what a tool can do but also the implicit knowledge that makes a tool part of the body.

In Pietrasanta, the story of tools often begins with the Milani family. Today, the Milani tool store in Pietrasanta caters to both locals and visiting artists, and the catalogue, available on line, offers tools to sculptors worldwide. In the 1980s, visiting sculptors, like the Americans who accompanied me on that first visit, made the trip to Pomezzana, and until about ten years ago, visiting the Milani shop was a sort of pilgrimage for artists. The tools are still made by hand, and the photographs on the web page document the forging process.

The association between modernity and technology doesn't fit the history of stone-carving in Pietrasanta, where Renaissance technologies used by Michelangelo often remain the most appropriate, and where new technologies do not always replace old ones but instead often exist side by side with them. Ledo Tartarelli, whose specialization was the ornamental dimensions of sculpture—including flowers, small animals, and other decorative elements—was a very accomplished bas-relief sculptor. He learned to carve using a manually driven drill. As a young apprentice, he would pull the rope that would drive the drill. This opportunity to observe the artisan closely was of course central to his learning. Tartarelli explained that though today one uses electric drills, and employing a child to pull the rope on a manual drill would be considered exploitive, the manual drill actually was preferable. "An electric drill has three speeds, but a boy can be trained to do about twelve different speeds." In many cases, new inventions do not necessarily improve the work.

## ECONOMIES 2: THE WORKSHOPS AS LOCAL AND GLOBAL ENTERPRISES

Probably the most visually obvious changes in the past two centuries of artisan work in Pietrasanta has been the size and economic structure of the workshop. The community's historical memory is preserved in turn-of-the-twentieth-century photographs of hundreds of men working in large studios that reproduced saints for Catholic churches and cemeteries, a practice that was interrupted by World Wars but that continued until labor laws in the 1950s and the decrees of Vatican II in 1962 resulted in their replacement by many small studios. When I arrived in Pietrasanta in 1982, dozens of studios occupied the lower floors of much of the historic district and beyond. Today, those studios, too, are gone. When people describe how Pietrasanta used to be, they usually refer to the sounds of the pneumatic chisels or the chink-chink of the hand tool, pervasive within the old part of the city. Today, the studios are gone, a few relocated to the outskirts of the city. The landmarks that remain don't acknowledge that they were ever there; instead, a sign documents Michelangelo's brief presence.

The workshops have changed in response to world wars, the Great Depression, changes in labor laws, and the rulings of Vatican II, which cut off the community's primary client, the Catholic Church,[4] and resulted in the closing of almost of the big workshops. Studios had closed before, especially during the two world wars and during the Depression, but after the early 1960s large studios never again opened.

Artisans responded to the closing of the workshops in several ways, the most repudiated of which was the initiation of small trinket making industries that made objects such as ashtrays and even telephones out of onyx. The artisans of Pietrasanta today still decry the use of their marble-carving skills for such (to them) demeaning ends. The market for funerary sculpture, including elaborate sculptured grave markers, continued, but the market for saints, that once sustained the community, was significantly diminished.

One of the most paradigm-shifting responses was initiated by the director of one of the large stone-carving studios, Henraux, created by a French company during the occupation of the area in the time of Napoleon (and still existing today). The director, Erminio Cidonio, invited many of the most prominent sculptors of the time—including Henry Moore, Hans Arp, Henri-Georges Adam, Isamu Noguchi, François Stahly, Émile Gilioli, Georges Vantongerloo, and Juan Miró—to bring models of their sculptures to Henraux, in the town of Querceta, near Pietrasanta to be carved in marble. The work required a complete paradigm shift for the artisans, trained to carve figurative sculpture and not necessarily appreciative of the abstract forms brought by the artists. Nonetheless, Cidonio's actions reinvigorated the area, and before long artists from all over the world were coming to Pietrasanta, both to learn how to carve their own work and to have their work carved by the artisans. A huge expatriate community developed and remains in the town to this day.

The Pietrasanta artisan community has been a global enterprise from the start, depending as it did on the cathedrals of Latin America. In a sense, the expatriate community of artists is a continuation of that global market. For more than a century, the region also dominated the production of marble-cutting equipment for industrial use. Today, as many local people observe, the market has shifted. Pietrasanta and Carrara often export raw marble rather than objects that have been locally produced. This is a source of tremendous concern and has been the focus of local protests.

## ECONOMIES 3: ARTISAN KNOWLEDGE AND THE HANDMADE

Positioned outside of the narratives of farm to factory or traditional to modern, the study of artisan technologies requires a reevaluation of some of the assumption that technology brings social change (Eglash 2006, 330). For folklorists, the dominant paradigm has been not so much the insistence on progress but the insistence on the value of the traditional, and especially, the handmade (Jones 1995). The distinction between handmade and machine-made isn't particularly relevant for the stone-carvers, since their work always includes both. Stone-carving is characterized by the idea Martin Heidegger described as "at handedness," the embodied know-how of people who work with their hands. Embodied knowledge is based on practice and experience and is not restricted to earlier technologies. Ethnographic research on the handmade reveals a more complex picture, one that recognizes the multiple dimensions of the handmade: if revered for intricacy and know-how, it can also be reviled as laborious, and, if nostalgically longed for, it is also quite present and ongoing. Generalized binary oppositions are inevitably blurred categories, whether between art and kitsch, craft and art, original and stylistic, or industrial and handmade.

For the stone-carvers of Pietrasanta, the handmade is part of an embodied practice of learning and working, in which tools are extensions of the body. Several scholars describe handmade work as personal, referring to a connection between the handmade work and the signature of the artisan. For example, Michael Herzfeld writes, "If selfhood is expressed through the production of objects, ideas about the relations among selves will presumably be reflected in ideas about originality, stylistic debt, and the force of convention. The distinctiveness of what an artisan produces perpetuates the performance of his selfhood, projecting it above crass commercialism" (2004, 153). In folk art discussions, a handmade object is often attributed to a particular maker; the named craftsperson gives the work additional value. However, this connection between signature and the handmade work is not a necessary one; it is part of particular cultural economies. For the Italian stone-carvers, the mark of the hand is important, but not as a signature. Today, much contemporary marble sculpture is polished, but figurative work done in Classical, Renaissance, or Romantic styles was not polished, and the chisel marks left on the surface were crucial to the effect. The textures created by the chisel could give the effect of skin or could differentiate among kinds of cloth or hair, and the artisans quickly recognize and differentiate the styles of, for example, early and late Renaissance silk. Thus, the hand leaves a mark, though not a signature. Some artisans nonetheless do leave personal marks. For example, Sergio, an artisan at Studio Sem, used a chisel with a missing tooth to create a particular effect on contemporary sculptures.[5]

The handmade is best understood as a poetics of practice and the circulation of an embodied vocabulary. That vocabulary can include discussions of attribution, signature, and ownership, invoking the politics and economics of power and appropriation. Discussions of poetics as practice, as an embodied vocabulary, also are implicated in political economic histories, but the stakes can include dimensions other than signature. This is one of the most perplexing dimensions of artisan economies. This is, I suggest, an area in which folklore research can intervene to counter views of the handmade as removed from the marketplace, as if it belongs to a timeless realm, sometimes including its value as a higher, more authentic kind of work.[6] In philosophical discussions from Plato to Heidegger, the hand-made has been exalted as an authentic form of work, granted the same aura as art.[7] Such arguments are often nostalgic, suggesting the loss of the authentic and its replacement with alienated or industrialized work. These issues are complex in Pietrasanta, where Michelangelo's *David* still does command reverence and where only the most skilled artisans attempt a life-size copy. A copy of the *David*, from a valuable three-meter-high block of rare statuario, the same marble used by Michelangelo, also exacts a high price, and, not surprisingly, the client is a museum or wealthy individual interested in displaying the work as a sign of its value.

Some artisans have worked for the same studio for decades. Before the EU, in the days of less formal financial accountability, pensioners were called back to work when needed and were paid in cash so that their earnings did not compromise their pensions. Today, although the labor market is still the same, with a limited number of highly skilled artisans, the cash economy has disappeared. An informal economy of favors exchanged and arrangements made plays as big a role as does the exchange of funds to compensate labor. Further complicating this scenario, and the folk economy of the artisan studio, the skilled artisan knows the value of his or her skills and does not impart them lightly. Only in rare cases can a less skilled artisan be employed to work alongside a more skilled artisan, who might offer guidance. To the contrary, all of the artisans describe learning by stealth, carefully watching an artisan complete a difficult task, practicing it, and then, perhaps, over time, earning the respect of the artisan, who might then offer advice. These dimensions of labor as embodied knowledge are more central to the working of the studios than are questions of the cost of producing a sculpture.

One way to describe the artisan economy of Pietrasanta is as discursive entanglements;[8] these are created by (1) the combination of traditional ways of working and the most contemporary technologies of diamond saws and pneumatic chisels; (2) the conjunction of the reproduction of traditional figurative work and the creation of contemporary abstract sculpture; and (3) the juxtaposition of the extraordinary larger-than-life proportions of the quarry and the ordinary, human-proportion of the handmade.

## ECONOMIES 4: THE ENVIRONMENT

The natural environment and artisan production in Pietrasanta are deeply mutually dependent. The studios, located at the base of the mountains, exist because of the quarries, and the quarries dominate the region not only literally but also in how the artisans understand their work (as a relationship with a living material) and in somewhat divisive politics today (Stigliano 2005, 16–17). The history of ownership and control of the quarries is as long and complex as the history of Western Europe. Recently, environmental activists have begun to intervene in what they see as wanton destruction of the mountains. The Salviamo le Apuane (Save the Apuan Alps) movement was initiated in 2009 (and has recently disbanded). The movement's webpage described the quarries as "the biggest European environmental disaster" in which "more than 800 quarries are impacting our delicate environment."[9] Until the past few decades, quarrying was part of a process that included the excavation of the stone, processing for architecture and sculpture, and the production of architectural slabs and of sculpture. Today, much of the marble is exported raw, without any production, and some is made into powder, sold as calcium carbonate. Environmentalists worry that since the calcium carbonate draws more profits, "there is no incentive to carefully carve out the blocks of marble" (Mistiaen and Briganti 2015). In 2011, part of the region was declared a UNESCO geopark, but even there, stone is still excavated from quarries. Protestors argue that the current practices are driven by short-term economic gains for the owners and a disregard for either the long-term well-being of the community or the environment. We can ask whether this is a continuation of old relationships or something new? Is it the same as the Medici ownership of the quarries that prompted Michelangelo's visit to Pietrasanta? That, too, was a situation that could be described as privileging outsider economic interests.

For many (not all) people in Pietrasanta, understanding current changes requires attention to the environmental dimension of the quarry, not only as a majestic, romantic source of the stone, but also as a site of crisis. As Lucy Lippard writes, "Nowhere are the ties between the people and land made clearer than when they are wounded together" (1997, 176). Lippard is writing about toxic places, but her comments apply to quarries and the like as well. The quarries are the source of the livelihood of the community, or they were. Environmentalists, concerned about the pulverization of stone to make calcium carbonate, are multiply concerned, both about the pollution, and about what they regard as the misuse of the mountain, and in particular the substitution of powder for carved marble.

Concern about the quarries is not new. A 1907 *Scientific American* article reports, "Few if any industries in the world have a greater percentage of waste than marble quarrying as it is done in Italy" (Willey), but few reports on the changing technologies in the quarry discuss environmental concerns, and even Willey's *Scientific American* article contextualizes technological choices as matters of economy, both the low pay of the quarriers and the choice of lower-cost methods, and does not consider environmental consequences.

## ECONOMIES 5: ARTISTS, ARTISANS, AND THE ORGANIZATION OF WORK

Until very recently, most studios organized work into specializations, including roughing out the form, carving hands, feet, faces, and breasts, carving the rest of the body, carving flowers, carving drapery or clothing, carving letters, and finishing. Historically, the specializations were designed to follow the order of work, and each specialization required different training. Learning to carve faces, breasts, hands, and feet required about ten years of apprenticeship. Each specialization also required slightly different tools.

Specialization is not new, and it has long been a fundamental dimension of the economy of craft, not only because specializations produced a status hierarchy but also because the organization of differentiated work was designed for greater production. For example, the expansion of trade leading to the exploration of the New World credits, among other things, the specialization of shipbuilders in Venice. Specialization in the artisan workplace differs in one profound respect from the modern assembly line, often characterized as producing workers alienated from the product of their labor. Unlike assembly-line workers, whose piecemeal work diminishes its value, the artisan specialists I interviewed all valued specialized skill. As Rockwell writes, "specialization can produce excellence by promoting expertise" (1993, 183). He reviews centuries of specialization in stonecarving and considers how more or less rigid organizations of the work might either afford efficiency or constrain creativity (182–83).

One of my primary interests in my research with the artisans was the question of how the specializations, designed for the production of figurative sculptures, translated into the production of abstract contemporary sculpture. I wondered whether the hierarchies that privileged the sculptor who could carve faces, breasts, and hands would still be relevant.

The Pietrasanta sculpture studios were set up to serve a patron-client arrangement. For most of the studios, until the 1960s, the Catholic Church was the patron, though individual patrons also commissioned sculptures for grave markers. Sculptors copied Classical, Renaissance, and Romantic sculptures, and, even today, it is not uncommon for a studio to be working on a life-size replica of Michelangelo's *David* or Canova's *Three Graces*. Copying or enlarging methods have always been part of the artisans' knowledge base. When, in the 1960s, contemporary artists began to bring plaster, wood, or bronze models to the artisans, who would enlarge them and carve them in marble, some of the same techniques were transferable to the new task. The artisans still used calipers and a three-pointed measuring tool to identify the places to carve on the block. However, most of the contemporary sculptors carved abstract forms rather than figures, and the artisan specializations, as mentioned above, were organized around the figure. The specialist who knew how to carve faces, breasts, and hands, remained the most skilled of the artisans, so some of the work organization still pertained. However, the specialist who carved cloth was almost irrelevant, as were the portrait carvers, some of whom also knew how to inlay colored stone, for example, to color the eyes, or other dimensions. I was particularly intrigued by what looked to me like a new role for the ornamentalist (ornatista), once relegated to minor tasks of carving a small animal held by a saint but now quite useful to the abstract sculptor, who appreciated a carver who could produce the three-dimensional detail found in bas-relief. I do not think that the hierarchical status of the specializations ever changed for the artisans themselves, but from my observation the skills of the ornamentalist were often well matched with the needs of the contemporary artists.

The relationship between the artists and artisans was not always easy. When the artists came in the 1960s, many of the artisans rejected the contemporary work, especially because it did not make use of the skills they most valued (Shuman and McMartin 2012, 76). A very few artisans, most notably Sem Ghelardini, did appreciate the contemporary work and took the opportunity to create studios to cater directly to them. Studio Sem, as it was called, became a cornerstone of the community.

## ECONOMIES 6: NETWORKS, TRANSACTIONS, EXCHANGE

My focus on the studio as a place of practice and the transmission and enactment of knowledge (skill), complements earlier folkloristic research on the folk economies of the marketplace (Kapchan 1993) as a meeting ground that disrupts any clear divide between traditional and modern practices. Some folklorists have focused attention on the circulation of knowledge, the practices of acquiring and transmitting skills. For example, Henry Glassie describes the rhythms of work and interdependence of the masters and apprentices in a Turkish blacksmith shop, among weavers, with a sled maker, and among others in Bursa (1995).[10] Glassie's account describes some of the last remaining artisans, an homage to a fading world of skills, which also has consequences for the circulation of goods and ideas.

The artisan economy of Pietrasanta accords value to social networks, a value that did not reside solely in commodities, the exchange of money for services, or the moral gift economies described by Mauss and Weiner.[11] The concept of folk economy introduces the possibility of many different kinds of exchange, whether exchanges of ideas, goods, people, or relationships. The primary dynamic of the folk economy of Pietrasanta is the relationship between artists and artisans. Probably most consumers of art are not aware that marble sculptures, especially large works, are often carved by artisans who enlarge clay or plaster models made by the artists. Artists depend upon the talents of the artisans, and, in this relationship, artisans are respected. The economy, then, includes both a monetary and a social exchange. Although he writes only about art, not about artisans, Lewis Hyde's distinction between market economies and gift economies, is helpful for understanding how these economies intersect. Hyde argues, "A work of art can survive without the market, but where there is no gift, there is no art" (1983, xi). His concept of gift encompasses, talent, inspiration, and the reception by the audience of a work of art, and he suggests that it offers an alternative to the more narrow, marketplace, idea of the compensation for labor and commerce as "traffic in merchandise" (xiv). Hyde's point is that art is about the movement of things, a kind of exchange best understood, he suggests, as a gift economy, though not a simple matter of givers and receivers.[12] Translated to the economy of the Pietrasanta stone-carvers, we can observe that the exchange is always more complex than payment for services, attribution of authorship, or ownership of objects. Additionally, the exchange relies on and creates dependencies. These are not a mere linear chain to be followed from the creation of the tool and the extraction of marble to the production of a marble sculpture.[13]

For the past decades, the economy of the stone-carvers has been in a state of flux. The area has become too expensive for the kind of international young artists who once flocked there. Some practices are ongoing; artists still bring their work to the artisans who do the carving. It's still possible to learn from the artisans, still in the same stealthy ways of observing and proving one's worth. At the same time, there are fewer workshops and fewer skilled artisans, and though marble is still available, some varieties are difficult or impossible to find. The clients change, sculpture itself changes, but so far anyway, what has been sustained through all of these changes is a way of working, a practice of knowing about marble, about the tools for carving, and about what counts as valuable work.

## CONCLUSION: TRANSMISSION, CIRCULATION, KEEPING THE CULTURE MOVING

The stone-carvers of Pietrasanta do not regard themselves as occupying a particularly noble position, and although they have great respect for their craft, like William Morris, they regard the relationship between the handmade and the machine-made as dynamic and connected (2000 [1883], 343). Perhaps because their work is not in any sense anachronistic, not reinvented to suit a contemporary longing for an earlier mode of work, they do not participate in a romantic labor discourse.[14] Also, as I discussed, if anything is romanticized in Pietrasanta, it is the marble quarries and the work of the quarries. Marble-carving does not compete with the dangerous challenges the quarriers face.

The artisan marble-carving workshops of Pietrasanta, Italy, encompass several mutually co-constitutive, interdependent, economies, including the organization of the workplace; relationships among artisans, artists, and clients; the larger historical context of global economies and their histories; the intergenerational transmission of skills in the context of changing technologies; and the relationship of the labor to the material, marble as an available, but limited resource, part of the history, the landscape, and the environment. In this chapter, I have described only a few of the particular interdependencies and intersections that have emerged in these co-constitutive economies. I offer them as an example of how the concept of folk economy might generally be considered to be comprised of mutually co-constitutive realms, an approach that, I suggest, provides a means for understanding the complexities of the artisan economy, including technological and social change, the intergenerational transmission of skills and knowledge, and relationships between local and global exchange.

The concept of folk economies combines the social networks of labor and the distribution of goods and resources with the systems of value that govern exchanges and assign them symbolic as well as practical meaning. Rather than disaggregate the value of things in terms of technology, labor, traditional cultural practices, or social networks, the concept of folk economies integrates these domains of cultural experience. The integration of these areas and, especially, the connections among changes in technology, the acquisition of skills, and the organization of the workplace has further consequences for understanding the larger political implications of the organization of labor and exchange (Appadurai 1986, 1990; García Canclini 2005).

Although part of global economies are certainly subject to changes in several global marketplaces—including the market for art, the market for marble sculpture, and the markets in which investment in art fluctuates—the artisan economy of Pietrasanta is also subject to local, culturally embedded assessments of worth and value. Worth is subtly evident in the ways that both artists and artisans who want to learn a skill must prove themselves worthy. Worth is also evident in the reverence for the material of marble and in the artisans' tools, coveted, and sometimes passed down to a worthy inheritor. These economies are not only not measurable, but the very idea of putting a price on them would miss their import.

In this chapter, I have argued that artisan economy of Italian marble-carvers combines a market economy of international exchange, a labor economy of regulations applied to a particular sector of worker, the environmental economy of marble, a local economy in which particular skills have both material and symbolic value and what might be best described as the economy of the studio, encompassing the transmission, performance, and exchange of knowledge. Historical, religious, technological, and political events have had significant impact on the community, but they are not sufficient for understanding how value is negotiated in an artisan community. Peter Rockwell writes that the methods of stoneworking "are based on ways of thinking that are alien to most of us. If we wish to understand the working of stone, we have to learn to understand and respect the thinking behind it"; "stoneworking is the product of training that leads to a method of thinking not simply a method of doing" (1993, 253). It is an example of an artisan economy that, among other things, trades in the stealthy appropriation of skills as a primary mode of learning, relies on an exchange of favors and loyalties, and thrives on respect and reputation. Artisan economies are probably not that different from other economies in their complexity. Other economies also depend on some relationship to technology, the environment, the history and politics of a region, global exchange, networks of favors and reputation, and embodied knowledge. What distinguishes the artisan economy is the ways in which it articulates these dimensions and configures interdependent relationships that extend beyond the market economy. What distinguishes the Pietrasanta marble-carving in particular is its unusual position between old and new technologies, local and global forms of exchange, and local, cultural sensibilities that are inextricably connected to work.

## NOTES

1. García Canclini writes, "It is common to regard arts and crafts as anachronistic objects" (1993, 37). See also Form 1987; Mishler 1992, 34.

2. It is beyond the scope of this chapter to describe the position of the artisan in the history of Western labor or to generalize about artisans beyond the particular group I describe here. However, several general points about artisan labor are relevant to understanding the Italian stone-carvers, and an understanding of the modes of acquiring and transmitting skills and modes of production of the Italian stone-carvers can contribute to our more general interest in folk economies. The politics of artisan labor has a long history, including the work of Thompson, who, in *The Making of the English Working Class,* described his project, "to rescue the stockinger, the Luddite cropper, the 'obsolete' hand-loom weaver, the 'utopian' artisan . . . from the enormous condescension of posterity" (1980, 12). See also Ranciere's discussion of the artisan and the politics of labor (1983).

3. The artisans of Pietrasanta populated the cathedrals of Latin America with marble and bronze sculptures. For a discussion of the production of wooden saints, see Glassie and

Shukla (2018). Their work similarly addresses questions of the circulation of artisan skills.

4. I discuss the history of the community in Shuman (2015) and the particular response to fascism in (Modan and Shuman 2011).

5. Also, see Marjorie Hunt's discussion of the personal marks left by the artisans who carved the National Cathedral in Washington, DC (1999).

6. See Bendix (2009) and Kirshenblatt-Gimblett (1998) for extensive critiques on this topic.

7. "For the Greeks, techne meant both the event of bringing something into the open, and the know-how required for accomplishing that disclosure . . . to 'pro-duce' something means to lead it forth . . . to release it so that it can manifest itself and linger in presence in its own way" (Zimmerman 1990, 230).

8. "Discursive entanglements" is physicist and feminist theorist Karen Barad's term to describe "highly specific configurations [that] change with each intra-action. In fact it is not so much that they change from one moment to the next or from one place to another, but that space, time, and matter do not exist prior to the intra-actions that reconstitute entanglements" (2007, 74). To some extent, Barad assumes the particular, if not the local and the ordinary. She is not rejecting history when she says that "space, time, and matter do not exist prior to the intra-actions that reconstitute entanglements."

9. The webpage includes Salviamo le Apuane, "Save the Apuan Alps English Page," http://www.salviamoleapuane.org/chi-siamo/english.html.

10. See also, Herzfeld's discussions of apprenticeship (2004, 117).

11. "Ownership of these possessions makes the authentification of difference rather than the balance of equivalence the fundamental feature of exchange" (Weiner 1992, 40).

12. See Carrier's essay "Exchange" (2006).

13. Vandenberghe (2002, 62) writes, "As Daniel Miller says: 'We do not think in terms of capitalist and socialist shoes' (1987, 115), and yet, if we want to understand the difference, if we do not simply want to follow the shoes themselves all the way from the consumer and the shoemaker to the tanner and the farmers who raise the cattle, but if we also want to understand the structural relations that form the content of the socio-technical network of cows, leather, tanners, shoestrings and shoemakers, we have to read and decode the artefacts as so many 'social hieroglyphics' (Marx 1976, 167)." Also see Žižek: "What is really a structural effect, an effect of the network of relations between elements, appears as an immediate property of one of the elements, as if this property also belongs to it outside its relation with other elements" (1989, 24).

14. See Herzfeld's discussion of the "glorification of the traditional" and the "rhetoric of nostalgia [as] a privilege of power, one that seeks to maintain the status quo by lamenting the disappearance of a suppositious ideal world of mutual respect that was in fact a rigid class structure" (2004, 31).

# REFERENCES

Appadurai, Arjun. 1986. "Introduction: Commodities and the Politics of Value." In *The Social Life of Things: Commodities in a Cultural Perspective*, ed. A. Appadurai. Cambridge: Cambridge University Press.

Appadurai, Arjun. 1990. "Disjuncture and Difference in the Global Cultural Economy." *Theory, Culture and Society* 7 (2): 295–310.

Barad, Karen. 2007. *Meeting the Universe Halfway: Quantum Physics and the Entanglement of Matter and Meaning*. Durham, NC: Duke University Press.

Bendix, Regina. 2009. *In Search of Authenticity: The Formation of Folklore Studies*. Madison: University of Wisconsin Press.

Briggs, Charles L. 1980. *The Wood Carvers of Córdova, New Mexico: Social Dimensions of an Artistic "Revival."* Knoxville: University of Tennessee Press.

Carrier, James G. "Exchange." In *Handbook of Material Culture*, ed. Chris Tilley, Webb Keane, Suanne Kuchler, Mike Rowlands, and Patricia Spyer, 373–83. London: Sage.

Dickie, Virginia Allen, and Gelya Frank. 1996. "Artisan Occupations in the Global Economy: A Conceptual Framework." *Journal of Occupational Science* 3 (2): 45–55.

Eglash, Ron. 2006. "Technology as Material Culture." In *Handbook of Material Culture*, ed. Chris Tilley, Webb Keane, Suanne Kuchler, Mike Rowlands, and Patricia Spyer, 329–40. London: Sage.

Form, William. 1987. "On the Degradation of Skills." *Annual Review of Sociology* 13: 29–47.

García Canclini, Néstor. 1993. *Transforming Modernity: Popular Culture in Mexico*. Austin: University of Texas Press.

García Canclini, Néstor. 2005. *Hybrid Cultures: Strategies for Entering and Leaving Modernity*. Minneapolis: University of Minnesota Press.

Glassie, Henry. 1995. "At Work in Bursa." In *Fields of Folklore: Essays in Honor of Kenneth S. Goldstein*, ed. Roger D. Abrahams. Bloomington, IN: Trickster Press.

Glassie, Henry, and Pravina Shukla. 2018. *Sacred Art: Catholic Saints and Candoble Gods in Modern Brazil*. Bloomington: Indiana University Press.

Hyde, Lewis. 1983. *The Gift: Imagination and the Erotic Life of Property*. New York: Vintage.

Jones, Michael Owen. 1995. "The 1995 Archer Taylor Memorial Lecture: Why Make (Folk) Art?." *Western Folklore* 54 (4): 253–76.

Herzfeld, Michael. 2004. *The Body Impolitic: Artisans and Artifice in the Global Hierarchy of Value*. Chicago: University of Chicago Press.

Hunt, Marjorie. 1999. *The Stone Carvers: Master Craftsmen of Washington National Cathedral*. Washington, DC: Smithsonian Institution Press.

Kapchan, Deborah A. 1993. "Hybridization and the Marketplace: Emerging Paradigms in Folkloristics." *Western Folklore* 52 (2/4): 303–26.

Kirshenblatt-Gimblett, Barbara. 1998. *Destination Culture: Tourism, Museums, and Heritage*. Berkeley: University of California Press.

Lippard, Lucy. 1997. *The Lure of the Local: Senses of Place in a Multicentered Society*. New York: New Press.

Marx, Karl. 1976. *Capital*, Vol. 1. Harmondsworth: Penguin.

Miller, Daniel. 1987. *Material Culture and Mass Consumption*. Oxford: Blackwell.

Mishler, Elliot G. 1992. "Work, Identity, and Narrative: An Artist-Craftsman's Story." In *Storied Lives*, ed. George C. Rosenwald and Richard L. Ochberg. New Haven, CT: Yale University Press.

Mistiaen, Veronique, and Chiara Briganti. 2015. "Michelangelo's Marble Is Being Sold Cheap by Industrialists" *Newsweek,* March 27. http://www.newsweek.com/2015/04/03/bin-ladens-and-tuscan-city-destroyed-marble-317224.html.

Modan, Gabriella, and Amy Shuman. 2011. "Positioning the Interviewer: Strategic Uses of Embedded Orientation in Interview Narratives." *Language in Society* 40 (1): 13–25.

Morris, William. 2000 [1883]. "The Revival of Handicraft." In *The Voice of Toil: Nineteenth-Century British Writings about Work*, ed. David J. Bradshaw and Suzanne Ozment. 340–47. Athens: Ohio University Press.

Pocius, Gerald L. 1997. "Material Culture Research: Authentic Things, Authentic Values." *Material Culture Review / Revue de la culture matérielle* 45 (1): 5–15.

Pursell, Carroll W., Jr. 1985. "The History of Technology and the Study of Material Culture." In *Material Culture: A Research Guide*, ed. Thomas J. Schlereth, 113–26. Lawrence: University Press of Kansas.

Rancière, Jacques. 1983. "The Myth of the Artisan: Critical Reflections on a Category of Social History." *International Labor and Working-Class History* 24 (Fall): 1–16.

Rockwell, Peter. 1993. *The Art of Stoneworking: A Reference Guide*. Cambridge: Cambridge University Press.

Shiner, Larry. 2001. *The Invention of Art: A Cultural History*. Chicago: University of Chicago.

Shuman, Amy. 2015. "Narrative and the Transmission of Traditions: Informal Learning among Italian Artisan Stone Carvers." In *International Handbook of Interpretation in Educational Research Methods*, ed. Marilyn Parsons and Michael Watts. London: Sage.

Shuman, Amy, and Keara McMartin. 2012. "The Artist-Artisan Collaboration in Pietrasanta, Italy." In *Studio Sem: The Artist-Artisan Collaboration in Pietrasanta, Italy*, ed. Pierangelo Ghelardini and Keara McMartin. Beeldengalerij: Het Depot.

Silverstein, Michael. 2003. "Indexical Order and the Dialectics of Sociolinguistic Life." *Language and Communication* 23 (3): 193–229.

Stigliano, Eric. 2005. *Michelangelo's Mountain: The Quest for Perfection in the Marble Quarries of Carrara*. New York: Free Press.

Thompson, E. P. 1963. *The Making of the English Working Class*. New York: Vintage.

Vandenberghe, F. 2002. "Reconstructing Humants: A Humanist Critique of Actant-Network Theory." *Theory, Culture & Society* 19(5–6): 51–67.

Weiner, Annette B. 1992. *Inalienable Possessions: The Paradox of Keeping-While-Giving*. Berkeley: University of California Press.

White, Hayden. 1987. *The Content of the Form: Narrative Discourse and Historical Representation*. Baltimore: Johns Hopkins University Press.

Willey, Day Allen. 1907. "The Marble Quarries of Carrara." *Scientific American*, November 16.

Zimmerman, Michael E. 1990. *Heidegger's Confrontation with Modernity: Technology, Politics, and Art*. Bloomington: Indiana University Press.

Žižek, S. 1989. *The Sublime Object of Ideology*. London: Verso.

# 13

# Consuming Authenticities
*An Economics of Folklorists*

Willow G. Mullins

> *Rather, the question is: who is mobilizing what in the articulation of the past, deploying what identities, identifications and representations, and in the name of what political vision and goals?*
>
> —Ella Shohat, "Notes on the 'Post-Colonial'"

WE ARE CULTURAL BEINGS. We are also economic beings. In capitalist economies, like the United States, "the marketplace" as folklorist Dorothy Noyes has said, "is the vitiated air we breathe" (1995, 473) but the marketplace, as behavioral economists such as Richard Thaler (2015) point out, is also a cultural space. Someone shopping for Central Asian textiles, for example, at the Santa Fe International Folk Art Market, may not be able to stop being influenced, consciously or not, by their awareness of US military actions in the Middle East and Central Asia, films such as *Borat* or other depictions of "the–stans" with their targeted and racialized humor, the images in *National Geographic*, or the catalogues from Fair Indigo that come through their door, or even their own awareness of their lack of knowledge about the region because it once was Soviet or is far away. Many studies of tourism, consumption, and commodity have explored these connections and influences between consumers of objects and the capitalist culture in which they consume (cf. Clifford 1988; Graburn 1976; Kirshenblatt-Gimblett 1998; Lau 2000b; Mullin 1995). Yet, thus far, few have looked at a group who consumes most actively, who seeks out that which they consume, and comes into the closest contact with the maker. This chapter focuses on the *folklorist* in the marketplace.[1]

Broadly speaking, folklorists began questioning how the collection and more particularly the presentation of folklore commodified culture beginning in the 1990s. Work at the intersection of folklore and the marketplace before then tended to focus on the commodification of folklore, or folklore put to use as an advertising tool (see Dégh 1994; Denby 1971; Dundes 1963; Mason 1954; Rohrich 1980). In the 1990s, however, the marketplace became a guiding metaphor in the field, with the folklorist positioned as the broker of folk culture (see Cantwell 1993; Korom 1999; Kurin 1997). In many ways, these texts moved the field forward by calling into question the economics and some of the politics of what folklorists do. They deeply explored the relationships and ellipses between those being represented and the audience, the consumer of the cultural performance, and how the folklorists made this exchange possible and comprehensible. They firmly situated the folklorist in the marketplace, but they also crafted for the folklorist a special niche, that of the middleman. I want to take this metaphor further and explore the middleman him- or herself.

The metaphor of the marketplace provides a way to expose some of the complexities and compromises of representing aspects of one culture to members of another. Folklorists, particularly in the United States, have engaged with the marketplace both as a metaphoric crucible for the creation of folklore and as a real commercial enterprise in which we act as brokers of culture. This position, however, can keep folklorists separate from and in control of culture as a commodity. Here, I rely on postcolonial discourse and fetish theory to interrogate the brokerage model of cultural representation. First, I hope to reveal how culture can become commoditized, particularly as a result of the prevalent, though frequently critiqued, multicultural model of representation, a process that lays cultural traditions bare for neocolonialist consumption by an empowered Western audience. Second, I propose a revaluation of cultural consumption in which authenticity becomes capital. The folklorist, then, acts not only as a middleman between producers and consumers but also as a consumer him or herself.

## THE BROKER AND THE OTHER

The concept of cultural brokerage helped to reveal the similarities between economic and cultural exchange. While a theory of cultural brokerage was originally developed in the 1950s, Christopher B. Steiner revisited it in his work *African Art in Transit* (1994) specifically in terms of the dealing of non-Western art to Westerners. If the broker moves between the sellers in one place or culture and the buyers in another, the culture broker represents, "sells," one culture, typically non-Western, to another, typically Western. The broker is more than a simple messenger, however, "who faithfully relates instructions and messages between two separate parties" (1994, 154–55). Instead, the broker translates, manipulates, and re-presents. As Steiner states, "rather than simply facilitate the relationship between two different groups separated by social, economic, or political distance, the broker actually constitutes, molds, and redefines the very nature of that relationship" (1994, 155).

The broker's influence is not without direction or moral mandate. Bringing cultural brokerage into folklore, Richard Kurin describes the job requirements of a culture broker as to "study, understand, and represent someone's culture (and sometimes their own) to nonspecialized others"—a process that includes negotiation, dialogue, and mediation (1997, 18–19). The broker for Kurin becomes a kind of cultural interpreter, whose knowledge base of two different cultures allows them to translate, a metaphor that still held currency in 2006 when it was revisited by Faye Ginsburg (2006, 492).[2] Kurin further contrasts this brokerage model of cultural representation with what he calls the "extractive model," on one hand, a kind of cultural theft performed while traveling among another people, and the "flea market" model, on the other, in which everyone is given access and widely divergent representations can exist side by side. The former is oft associated with an earlier era of folklore that sought to record and preserve the folklife of Others without necessarily referencing those who created it, an approach that led to particularly exploitative relationships and representations (see Graburn 1976; Kurin 1997; Mullin 1995). The latter, while seemingly more egalitarian, can cause important messages to be lost and create confusion.

The brokerage model is both useful and revealing. Whether building museum exhibits or festival presentations, writing ethnographies or teaching, many if not most folklorists broker culture for a living. Brokerage as a metaphor for what folklorists do is, in some ways, refreshingly honest. Its variety of meanings suggests the uneasy role that such scholars and cultural presenters fill by highlighting the positive potential of such brokerage without disregarding the more typically neutral and negative connotations of the name "broker." For example, while stockbrokers may be generally considered upstanding citizens, at least before the banking crises of the 2010s, pawnbrokers are often less favorably looked upon, and the term "broker" has historically included pimps and procurers of all kinds (*Oxford English Dictionary Online 2016*). Nonetheless, most folklorists seem to embrace the term's ambiguities while still invoking it positively.

As well they should. The cultural brokerage model offers the potential for more equal cross-cultural exchange than the typically unidirectional representations historically produced in American folklore and anthropology. The culture broker "is in a position to advocate a more balanced relationship, which could bridge the gap—at least theoretically—between the institution and the members of the community being represented" (Korom 1999, 260). And culture brokers have had some successes. To use an example from the Smithsonian's National Museum of the American Indian, during the planning of museum's exhibits, the conservation staff met with tribal representatives and exhibit curators to discuss how that tribe's objects would be presented, what conservation could or should be pursued, and what information was admissible or necessary for the general public (Heald 1997). Such consultations can be rare, underfunded, and divisive, but they can also provide moments of deep cultural connection. While brokerage can lead to rethinking representation, as a metaphor it also, perhaps unwittingly, uncovers some of the problems inherent in representation itself.

A tension exists in folklore between the histories and long-held received theories of the field and more recent critiques of those theories. In particular, this tension can be seen as the field has moved from seeking large-scale narratives that can be applied across cultures to answer the critiques that have demanded greater attention to specificity (cf. Dundes 2005; Haring 2018; Noyes 2016). Subsequently, folklorists and anthropologists have sought better ways to represent, yet always with an underlying belief that better understanding is born of more study, greater context, and ultimately more accurate representation. Edward Said, however, points to this attempt to solve gaps in culture with more knowledge as a central flaw within the social sciences. As Said points out, such study, like much of the folkloristic representation of other cultures, only allows for the depiction of certain kinds of cultural products (1979, 293). To draw from my own research in Kyrgyz art, much attention is given to the felt-making tradition as iconic and the quilting tradition as a point of universal connection, but not only do the painters and sculptors get overlooked by the West, so do artists who use felt as a medium for nontraditional objects.

Further, increased study may be the cause of tension rather than its solution, particularly for groups who have witnessed how studies by outsiders have been used as rationales for further subjugation (Smith 1999). As Hopi filmmaker Victor Masayesva has commented, the etic approach, long considered by scholars to increase objectivity, decreases accountability (Masayesva, qtd. in Leuthold 1998, 1). Folklore has certainly responded to such charges, resulting in much soul-searching and some changes in methodologies (see Lawless 1992). Still, many cultural displays continue to be plagued by unequal positions of power between researcher or broker and the people researched or represented. This disparity occurs in part because, despite claims that the goal of such brokerage is to bring two or more groups together, the success of the broker is often dependent on how they can maintain distance between those groups.

The culture broker's job security, ironically and often uncomfortably, relies in some ways on the two cultures never fully coming into contact. As Steiner notes, "the success of the middleman demands the separation of buyers from sellers" (1994, 130). This necessary separation challenges the conceit of broker as cultural advocate and cross-cultural presentations as offering "contact" and "understanding." The reason brokerage is requested is to bridge perceived cultural, economic, linguistic, or political differences (Steiner 1994, 130). The role of the broker as expert translator, however, becomes moot if people are able to cross this distance on their own. Cultural brokerage then offers an appealing model for a field predicated on the representation of others even while it reveals the uneasy relationships that such brokerage necessarily engenders. Yet casting cultural representation as brokerage draws attention not only to the sometimes contradictory and ambivalent role of the broker, but it also shows the economic value of culture itself.

## TO "CELEBRATE WHAT WE DESCRIBE": CULTURE AS COMMODITY

One of the difficulties with cultural representation is pragmatic. Generally speaking, most people would like to highlight the positive elements of their culture and to show off what they do best (see Baron 2010), and most people would prefer not to spend their leisure time attending cultural displays that make them feel uncomfortable. The broker, meanwhile, has an investment in making sure that both of these groups' desires are met and that funding institutions are happy. Yet another difficulty is that most folklorists honestly love what they do—they see value in the cultures and people with whom they work, and, like anyone who loves what they do, they wish to share that enthusiasm and value with others. At the beginning of the chapter, I quoted Dorothy Noyes's remark that "the marketplace is the vitiated air we breathe" and thus deserves study. She goes on, however, to express a valid concern with how folklorists approach that study, commenting that we tend to "celebrate what we describe" and thus may end up celebrating "the multinational," the global corporation, unintentionally, thereby undermining our investment in the local and particular (1995, 473).

Noyes's concerns are not unfounded. While folklorists might make conscious efforts to contextualize and provide spaces for multivocality, we must wonder what audiences and those representing or being represented take away. Further, we must be cognizant that the representations we help produce exist in a larger ecology of commodified culture that cannot but affect reception. It is a fairly short step from the celebration of multiple ethnic heritages in the kinds of multicultural festivals that are performed throughout the United States every year to a celebration of multinational corporations as working across ethnic and political boundaries, and the path between the two is often paved with the kinds of developmental rhetoric and good intentions that can blur the lines between commerce and philanthropy in complex ways.[3] Indeed, a glance through any recent *National Geographic* issue will provide multiple examples of multinationals using the language of development and multiculturalism to sell themselves, including IBM, ExxonMobile, and Toyota (November and December 2015).

Lying at the root of such celebration is the commodification of difference. This commodification fetishistically draws attention to some cultural differences while eliding others that evoke more difficult questions of race, class, or gender and histories of oppression. By shifting the focus onto seemingly more benign, dehistoricized differences, cultures perceived as minority groups are made safe for consumption by the majority (see Lowe 1996). In other words, multiculturalism. Much of what follows in this section has been hashed out before, more fully and complexly, in other places, but it bears repeating here because of how multiculturalism and capitalism work in concert to undermine the best intentions of culture brokers, cultural representatives, and audiences alike.

At least since the 1970s, multiculturalism has been promoted in the public forum in the United States as a way to celebrate difference and get beyond the conflicting histories that have existed between diverse groups. Celebratory multiculturalism optimistically seeks to acknowledge difference without distress, to elide the actual past through nostalgia for authentic culture. If the history of the United States is marked with racial division and cultural disunity, then multiculturalism is an effort at national unity and identity formation, based on the creation of what some folklorists refer to as a "usable past" (Brooks 1918, 337). The intentions of multicultural representations are generally perceived as positive—an attempt to redress the disunity of the past—but they might offer reconciliation without first examining truth.

This style of cultural commodification takes place through a process of detachment, flattening, and fetish. If folklorists are brokering culture, then culture itself becomes a commodity to be bought and sold, traded and consumed in the global marketplace. By selecting and detaching particular parts of a culture—whether it be material, dance, song, or traditional cure—the culture broker turns those elements into commodities. To change cultures into commodities, however, is to reduce and reify them, because they can only be consumable, especially by members of another culture, if they are remade into a familiar form—the ethnographic object.

By marking cultural forms as ethnographic objects,[4] they can then be further contained by categorizations familiar to Westerners. The process of dividing, cataloguing, and naming breaks down societies into consumable parts according to a Western ordering system and paradigm (Pratt 1992, 30), for example, as a Buddhist sculpture from Vietnam or a Inca knit hat from Peru. This kind of categorization bears uncomfortable similarities to colonial rhetoric, however. David Spurr describes this process as "classification," whereby "Western writing generates an ideologically charged meaning from its perceptions of non-Western cultures" (1993, 62). These meanings, however, are predicated on Western systems, which allow them to carry the ideological weight of fact by their association with larger Western philosophical structures, such as Science. The necessity for order as a way of reasserting Western power, however, results in a "cultural flattening that provides only the impression of particularities, thus extending the power of global capitalism" (Lau 2000a, 11). By reducing difference to a category loosely named ethnic, that is, not white middle-class American, multiculturalism sanitizes cultures for easy consumption and marketability, what Kimberly Lau refers to as "the reduction, fixing, and ultimately, containment of difference" (Lau 2000b, 71), and divorces it from its political implications (Rosaldo 1993, 64).

In order to maintain the celebratory stance, however, such flattening may be necessary even while it creates a view of culture that could not exist. The difficulty with this crystallization of culture lies both in how it reinscribes and elides institutional histories and how it may suppress the "organic growth" of cultures (Neil Bissoondath, qtd. in Golfman 1996, 176). As Diarmuid O'Giolláin asks: Do we, as folklorists, risk asking that cultures retain their traditions at the expense of their own economic progress? (2014). Taken to a cynical extreme, then, multiculturalism functions not dissimilarly from the line of multicultural Barbie dolls produced by Mattel, with each culture reduced to a new outfit for an otherwise generic Barbie, and the whole line aimed at sparking the fetishist's desire for owning one of each (Lau 2000b, 73).

Similarly, the multicultural stage can come to resemble a conveniently framed exhibit, a cultural zoo,[5] through which Westerners can come safely into contact with Others without contamination if they so wish but with the demarcation between self and Other clearly marked. In this way, the multicultural event becomes a sort of museum collection, with each culture providing a representative cuisine and cultural expression—dance, music, and so on—and each taxonomically labeled according to country of origin or region of the world. Such display may give consumers a sense of control over the rest of the world, building from what Andreas Huyssen has termed American society's "museumphilia" (Huyssen 1995, 27–30). In other words, the Western audience is able to fill their desire to fetishistically possess the Other.

The fetishist desires an object to help fulfill a perceived loss. In the case of the modern United States, where it can be difficult to convince college students in elective folklore classes that they have culture at all, that loss can be centered on visible cultural markers. The Western consumer is able to possess the Vietnamese statue and the Peruvian hat, for instance, and through them possess the perceived spirituality of the Vietnamese Buddhist and the artisanship of the Peruvian knitter. But the fetish operates one step further by invoking nostalgia for the authenticity of a romanticized agrarianism lost to modern technology (Lau 2000a, 7). A lifestyle Others are believed to still possess. As Susan Stewart argues, "the exotic offers an authenticity of experience tied up with notions of the primitive as child and the primitive as an earlier and purer stage of contemporary civilization" (1993, 146). While a return to agrarianism may not be possible, multiculturalism offers a chance to repossess at least a sense of authenticity through interaction with ethnic Others who presumably never lost it. Multiculturalism paradoxically celebrates those elements of human identity that we tend to believe nonquantifiable, such as culture, and categorizes and quantifies them.

Ironically, all of the essentialism associated with multiculturalism is driven, at least to some extent, by an impulse to celebrate the Other. However, the ways in which the cultures consumed have been made available, through dehistoricization and detachment, and specifically intended for enjoyment and celebration, assure that the hegemony they claim to challenge will remain in place. bell hooks has remarked that "to seek an encounter with the Other, does not require that one relinquish forever one's mainstream positionality" (1992, 183). Unfortunately, it is precisely this sense of the "playground," to use hooks's word for such encounters, that many culture brokers not only purposefully create but that many folklorists, perhaps unintentionally, construct in their desire to share their enthusiasm for culture. As stated before, cultural representations must appeal to their audiences, generally those who are already in a position of power, and make them feel as though their consumption is welcome. And the groups being represented or representing themselves often seek to share a culture of which they are justly proud. As a result, folklorists and other culture brokers have tended to highlight difference and offer it up for consumption at the same time that they admit the problems of multiculturalism.

Museum and festival representations of other cultures are a constant negotiation between multiple goals and interests, or as Kurin puts it, "institutional mission and scholarly/curatorially informed practice had to be weighed against the pragmatics of politics and economics" (1997, 38).[6] Yet the politics of such events are often dictated by the desire to create a feeling of temporary goodwill and by the economics of needing to increase audience numbers.[7] Too much catering to audience, however, can, at its worst, defang any real statement that such representation can make (see Behar 1993). And to insist that our representational goals are always what the audience departs understanding is to ignore a significant amount of cultural theory that would suggest otherwise (Clifford 1988, 52). Robert Cantwell has remarked on precisely this phenomenon at the Festival of American Folklife: "The conceptions to which such signs give rise in the Festival's environment of radical dislocation, the imaginary pictures of the whole people and ways of life for which the other has been made to stand, are essential to the feeling of goodwill, which is, in turn, socially essential; hence, the festival setting actually inspires us to form conceptions of others that are more or less developed versions of stereotypes" (1993, 151). For Cantwell, however, this repetition and formation of stereotypes do not seem too problematic, since they do succeed, he claims, in creating "goodwill." Nonetheless, one is left to wonder: in the cultural marketplace, what is the cost of such goodwill?

One way around such flattening may be to further examine and highlight in folkloristic representations the kind of networks and layering that folklorists have been committed to for years but have more recently gained institutional traction in the idea of intersectionality. Rather than probing sameness and difference through their uni-axis cultural manifestations, as multiculturalism often does, intersectionality begins by questioning the "vexed dynamics of difference and solidarities of sameness" (Cho, Crenshaw, and McCall 2013, 787). What intersectionality may offer folklore is a deep-rooted commitment to revealing institutionalized politics and oppressions within specific contexts, the contradictions that lie at the root of every person's identity. After all, who is only one ticked box of identity? Intersectionality may help lift the burden of ethnography from those deemed as Other and, with humble understanding of the power relations at work, move towards a coproduced conversation about culture rather than a consumption of it.

## AUTHENTICITY AS CAPITAL

If multiculturalism helps to describe what can happen when folklorists and other culture brokers "celebrate what we study," the questions remain *why* we are inclined to celebrate and what precisely it is that we are celebrating. The answers to both may lie in folklore's disciplinary history and, more particularly, in how the field creates and assigns value. In the marketplace for culturally marked objects and performances, the location of value is an ever-shifting target, dependent on the specific marketplace and market level and the context, the narrativization, of the consumptive act. In the philanthropic narrative through which goods from organization such as women's cooperatives or historically "folk" products are sold (cf. Littrell 2010; Whisnant 1983), value is based on a perception of how much good is done through the purchase: the object itself may or may not be construed as having intrinsic value, but it is valuable on the basis that it provides "help" to someone and a sense of moral worth to the consumer. For the aesthetic consumer looking for ethnic art, value resides in the object's nonconformity to the aesthetic legacy of Western art and therefore in its ability to reflect the good taste and connoisseurship of the consumer for recognizing it (see Graburn 1976; Price 1989; Steiner 1994). Folkloristic value, however, lies in authenticity.

Regina Bendix's intellectual history *In Search of Authenticity* details how the field of folklore has been predicated on an ongoing search for the authentic that has, from its earliest days, been tied closely to the commodification of culture valued as authentic. From the start, Bendix argues, folklore has been invested in authenticity both as a subject and as a way to advance itself as a social science: "Declaring something authentic legitimated the subject that was declared authentic, and the declaration in turn can legitimate the authenticator . . . Processes of authentication bring about material representations by elevating the authenticated into the category of the noteworthy" (1997, 7). Thus, beginning with German Romantic movement in the late 1700s and early 1800s, folklorists such as Johann von Herder and collectors such as the Grimms turned to the "folk" as a source of authenticity, sensuality, and poetry in the face of the modernizing and alienating forces of the early Industrial Revolution and the reason and logic of Classicism. The folk still possessed authenticity because they had not yet become modernized themselves, being largely rural, agrarian, and impoverished, what

Herder called the "old and wild people" (qtd. in Bendix 1997, 39). Yet this authenticity, fetishistically located in the folk, was also available for both consumption throughout the populace through "artifactualization," in the form of published collections aimed at middle- and upper-class audiences, and exploitation to nationalistic ends (Stewart, qtd. in Bendix 1997, 36).

As the nineteenth century continued, folklorists strove to legitimate their field of study in a growing culture of scientific inquiry. To do so, however, authenticity, as a romantic value, and cultural essentialism had to be redefined "as a scientifically verifiable entity" (Bendix 1997, 46). In other words, by defining the field of folklore in terms of authenticity, folklorists sidestepped overlapping too much with other cultural studies fields such as anthropology and found a common, quantifiable attribute that could be identified among wildly disparate texts from different genres and ethnic origins. In this way, the field claimed legitimacy by equating the search for authenticity with other scientific searches by distinguishing the real from the fake, folklore from "fakelore," according to prescribed formulae, for example, Vladimir Propp's—a legitimacy reliant on authenticity as a quantity that can be commodified in the products of folkloric collection and study. This definition of folklore as the search for authenticity would guide the field well into the twentieth century but, in doing so, turned authenticity into a fetish, located in Others and lost to the modern age (see Bauman and Briggs 2003).

Yet valuing authenticity leads to its own problems. Authenticity as capital conforms to economic models of scarcity. The authentic as a commodity is always in scarce supply, because with modernity and contact, it has always already disappeared, as Baudrillard has commented (qtd. in Bendix 1997, 9). The search for and consumption of authenticity are like opening and drinking an old cask of fine wine—it can only be consumed once. Authenticity, especially in the form of performance, can never be re-presented, since any such move will inherently change the context and thereby diminish the authenticity (Bausinger, qtd. in Bendix 1997, 9). Conversely, each performance can also be viewed as an authentic one—no more and no less authentic than any other. While salvage has largely been abandoned as a stated raison d'être in the field, it does not seem to have lost nearly as much traction in the audiences to whom cultural representations are presented. This perceived scarcity can be beneficial, since it can help bring in audiences who want to see the authentic performance while they still can. But this model does not exactly put the power of controlling representation into the hands of those folk groups offering performances of their culture.

In a classic middleman problem, the culture broker both helps unite providers and consumers who might not otherwise meet, but at a cost.

If authenticity is what is valued most, only the culture broker, positioned between the authentic performer and the audience, has the ability to confirm the authenticity of the performance. The performer relies on the culture broker to provide access to the audience; the audience relies on the culture broker to reassure them that the performance is authentic, that they are getting value for their time and money. Yet, by giving up that one-to-one encounter, the audience risks making the performance not about the folk group on stage but about the folklorist in the wings (see Percy 1975). The folklorist, as a culture broker and connoisseur, retains control of authenticity as a form of capital, even if they try not to, because of the value placed on authenticity and the institutional and capitalist structures of cultural exchange.

Folklorists have certainly discussed the problems inherent in privileging authenticity as capital and commodifying culture. Nonetheless, the power of the search for authenticity and its associated vocabulary to continue to direct the course of the field remain strong, both in how we study and how we represent. My own graduate experience serves as an example:

Early in my work on the marketing of Kyrgyz textiles to Western buyers, I was interested in exploring how Kyrgyz traditional felt making and felted objects have changed as they have gained greater attention in the global marketplace. As I began my preliminary research, however, a series of problems presented themselves. The first was an issue of anthropological conceit: to look at how something has changed with contact assumes that there was a distinct moment of contact, a before and after. It assumes that there is such a thing as a culture that is not always already in conversation with the cultures around it and, through them, with cultures even further away. Yet the Kyrgyz reside along one of the oldest and longest trading routes in the world: the Silk Road. The felt objects I wanted to study have already been adapted.

Second, I found it impossible to describe my project to anyone who worked in folklore studies without having to clarify that I was not interested in making an argument of greater or lesser authenticity. To describe a before and after in relation to tradition, I found, implied a value judgment in which the before, the authentic, was inherently positioned as superior to the after, the contaminated and inauthentic. Tellingly, it became apparent that folklore training itself created folklorists invested in authenticity, even a decade or more after we as a field have critiqued this investment.

To return again to Noyes comment that "we tend to celebrate what we study," we celebrate in part, then, because we ourselves have a stake in that celebration. Folklore as a field was built upon and continues to be held together by the search for and fetishization of authenticity. Authenticity is the capital we, as scholars and brokers, possess. As a field, we celebrate it perhaps because we always have, and as folklorists we are nothing if not drawn to tradition, and perhaps because it provides a common ground between the extremely disparate subjects of our work: foodways and folktales, place and patrimony, rugs and rape stories. As stakeholders, we often cannot afford, quite literally in the politics of either academia or public arts funding, not to be celebratory. However, to only celebrate, without self-reflection, diminishes the value of our subjects of study, our field, and ourselves. If Bendix's intellectual history of folklore shows us anything, it is that the search for authenticity as a driving force in folklore is itself a form of consumption,[8] a commodity fetish, and as such is not distinct from but rather part of the marketplace. For that reason, if for no other, we must study the marketplace and reposition ourselves not just as brokers but as consumers as well.

## FOLKLORIST AS CONSUMER

I want to describe briefly an event at an American Folklore Society Annual Meeting (AFS) held in Boise, Idaho, in 2009. This conference takes place at the end of each October in a different city each year. What occurred at and following the Boise conference is not isolated. I could have chosen any year that I have attended. Boise stood out only because of the clarity with which authenticity was invoked. As at many conferences, local organizers try to highlight some of the artistic and cultural specialties of the area. At AFS, the local draws tend to focus on local ethnic enclaves and regional histories. In 2009, being in Boise, a group of fellow folklorists and I chose to go to the local Basque pub, since Boise boasts a Basque community. We arrived during a late dinner rush, and once settled I began to look around. Almost all of the other patrons were folklorists attending the conference. Almost everyone who came in while we had our dinner was a folklorist. Our table, one of the small restaurant's larger ones, was taken over by another group of folklorists as we left. Something similar happened at an African restaurant when AFS was held in Milwaukee, and at the restaurants particularly noted for their New Mexican authenticity, either of cuisine or through their many years of operation, when AFS was in Santa Fe. No doubt, folklorists have a penchant for the ethnic and are ready to consume any that might be available. Call it professional interest. But the story does not end there.

I returned home from Boise early and so did not attend the Saturday night banquet. The banquet was catered by a Basque restaurant which served picon punch, a traditional Basque American drink. During the weeks following that banquet, Publore, the listserv dedicated to public-sector folklore, with over 600 members, hosted a lively discussion about the authenticity of that picon punch, complete with analysis about what was "wrong" with it and where one might find "the best" or most authentic picon punch in the American West. Thus, after spending the days of the conference listening to papers about the politics and problems of representation and cultural brokerage and debates in which the idea that authenticity was of questionable value was taken for granted, professional folklorists spent their nights consuming culture with abandon and showing off their connoisseurship of ethnic difference and its authenticity.

Regina Bendix stresses that folklore is about the *search* for authenticity, not the authentic object nor its location, but the *search* itself, which makes it a commodity fetish (1997). Because authentic experience has become a fetish in the field, it can also never fully be satisfied. Bendix compares it usefully to travel—the folklorist, like the traveler, must keep up the search, must continue to consume in order to maintain a sense of identity (1997, 17). Once the travelers stop traveling, they become something else: residents; once folklorists stop searching, they too become something else (culture studies scholars? Statisticians? Curator of popular antiquities?). This situation of always experiencing, always consuming, and always commodifying the experience becomes endlessly repeatable. Each experience, once had, no longer serves its fetishistic purpose, thereby serving to perpetuate folklore as a discipline in a way that pure location of authenticity cannot. The search for authenticity is forever shifting, for an authentic experience can always be around the corner, and any given experience can never be had more than once. Nowhere is this more apparent than in the theoretical move in folklore in the 1970s from collection to performance.

While earlier folklorists focused on studying folklore as reified texts, beginning in the second half of the twentieth century, linguists such as Dell Hymes (1975) and folklorists such as Dennis Tedlock (2012) began to question what we might miss when we record only the words of a folkloric performance. Certainly, the ethnographer could describe the surrounding context, or provide photographs, audio recordings, or, more recently, video, but none of these, even if taken all together, would give a later audience a sense of what it was to have been physically present. Around the same time, another group of folklorists began insisting folklore was less about product than process (Bauman 1978). This retraining of the lens of folklore from text to performance required a renegotiation of what was meant by the term "folklore" itself. Key to the newer definitions, however, is that what makes folklore folklore is that it is a performance. Yet a performance itself is an experience; one moreover that is unrepeatable, since, as Foley and others point out, the precise combination of context, performer, audience, timing, and so on cannot ever be repeated, nor can it ever be fully translated to someone who was not there (2002, 100). In other words, "you had to have been there" (Clifford 1988, 39).

This stance has positioned folklorists as connoisseur consumers of exclusive experience. Because a performance experience occurs only once, no one else can have had it. The folklorist as broker can attempt to re-create that experience for others through representation, but "ethnographies," James Clifford points out, "are fictions both of another cultural reality and their own mode of production" (1988, 81). The products of folklore, the ethnography, the festival, and the exhibit, provide a reference to the experience but like the shadows in Plato's cave, they are never complete; they never depict what is really there. The folklorist therefore retains the status of having *been there*; they alone gain the desired authenticity and as Bendix calls it "existential meaning" (1997, 17). This connoisseurship of experience could be seen in the Publore posts following the Boise conference, as folklorists began citing various bars around the West that served "authentic" picon punch. More interesting still was the low-level competition apparent in these posts, as each writer laid claim to greater levels of authentic experience, ultimately trumped with a reference to the Star in Elko, Nevada, and the (tongue-in-cheek?) suggestion that Boise's bartenders should learn how to make "real" picon punch from a YouTube video posted by the Western Folklife Center (Publore Archives 2009). But the turn to performance as the subject of study and the picon punch discussion on Publore reveal that it is not just authenticity that folklorists hope to gain from experience.

The question of where one might find "real" picon punch answered, the Publore discussion turned to the correct number of local specialty drinks it was acceptable for a folklorist to consume in the field. The discussion, I believe, was largely meant in jest, but as Alan Dundes has pointed out, our jokes say a lot about our beliefs and anxieties (1987). The goal of consuming the local alcohol was to prove interest in local traditions but, more important, to make connections by sharing an experience. That concept of the shared experience, the empathic moment when two or more people seem to truly understand one another, lies at the very center folklore. It is the thing I suspect many folklorists, consciously or not, most desire, whether it be in the individual interview, as a participant observer in a larger cultural group, or in a storytelling event. It is desired not because all folklorists are extroverts,[9] but because it is the moment when folklore flows most freely.

Amy Shuman states, "Storytelling promises to make meaning out of raw experiences: to transcend suffering; to offer warnings, advice, and other guidance; to provide a means for traveling beyond the personal; and to provide inspiration, entertainment, and new frames of reference to both tellers and listeners. I understand all of these possibilities as the promises . . . of storytelling" (2005, 1). Shuman is writing specifically of narratives, but her comments can be expanded to the field as a whole. Each performance offers us, folklorist and audience, the potential for empathy and true connection but only the potential. As novelist Russell Banks remarks, however, empathy itself is a kind of self-reflection, which begs the question if this search for empathy is really a search for self (2004, 327).

In Ireland, the word *craic* describes a particular sense of serendipitous communality. It is a difficult word to define for there is no real English equivalent. It is found most typically in answer to questions such as "how was your night out?" or, among musicians, "how was the session?" and in answers such as "it was great craic!" It encompasses the idea that the event was fun, but it involves more than that—there was laughter and the conversation flowed freely, with everyone enjoying themselves. More than anything, craic implies a sense of spontaneous fellowship, the feeling one gets that turns an ordinary party into a good one or a mundane conversation into something special. There can be craic among a large group or a small one. One cannot set out to have craic or plan it or re-create it; it simply happens or does not. Not every night out is great craic, and that is what makes craic special.

Folklorists are craic-heads. We, as a field, spend our careers seeking out and attempting to re-create, however palely, craic among people and the objects and words and gestures they leave in their wake. In doing so, we have become possibly some of the most adept consumers and commodity fetishists in the cultural marketplace, because what we consume, by its very nature, can never be consumed again. We must always keep traveling, in Bendix's metaphor, keep seeking out more craic, for only through its consumption can we continue to make the kinds of authoritative statements, about picon punch or anything else, that we do.

Folklorists, myself included, are consumers. We consume cultural knowledge, and we celebrate that consumption by insisting that it is really a form of empathy. Yet the empathy or the craic may be what most of us truly desire, and the knowledge, which points to but can never contain it, can serve as a fetish object to bolster us in a belief in our own legitimacy. As folklorists who have studied for years and become specialists in particular ethnic groups or genres, we may believe that we possess privileged knowledge, and with it we can cushion ourselves from the kinds of critiques we make of others and from charges of hegemony. Yet as brokers, we retain a power as the middleman who makes cultural exchange possible, bringing together groups who may not otherwise have met or might have met differently. We become translators, controlling both access and meaning. In this sense, we do reside in a position of power vis-à-vis the people we study and represent, and we do acknowledge that positionality. Together, these claimed privileges allow us to argue that better knowledge, better education, greater authenticity will right the wrongs of the past, will bring about cultural empathy, what Shuman claims is the promise of storytelling (2005, 1). But as consumers, our power is curtailed. To acknowledge our position as consumers is also to admit that our position of control and claims to superior understanding, knowledge, or empathy are partial fallacies. Instead, we reside in an unwieldy space, subject to distant and often incomprehensible market forces and the subject of our own critiques.

It may be precisely this sense of the marketplace's unmanageability that makes many folklorists so uncomfortable. We don't know to what ends our enthusiasm will be turned, how those cultural products we help commodify might be used or appropriated. And we often bear the weight of the deep nostalgia of our institutional forebears for the precapitalist, the agrarian, the village. The village, according to Clifford, allowed us to see our subjects and our position clearly: "Villages . . . offered a way to centralize a research practice, and at the same time it served as synecdoche, as a point of focus, or part, through which one could represent the culture as a whole" (1997, 21). Unlike the village, however, the marketplace in the age of online shopping often is not a real space. One may or may not be able to go there, and those places that can be visited are "messy" with multiple voices and interests and groups, as Deborah Kapchan (1996) and all who have written on the Festival of American Folklife have noted. To turn to the marketplace is to relinquish our position of control and to seek meaning in new ways and new places. It is an incredibly humbling move, for it requires us to reject what Bendix calls the "existential meaning" that our work provides. It makes us just like everyone else, subject to the same cultural and market forces, acting out the same cultural scripts. Bluntly put, positioning ourselves as consumers might call into question whether our centuries of collection and study have been worthwhile. I would argue that they have, but perhaps not in the ways or for the reasons we think. That analysis must be left to a later generation to decide. Yet to embrace our role as consumers and leave the village for the marketplace, or enter the marketplace of the village, also carries with it tremendous potential.

Like any human space, it has its inequalities and oppressions—the marketplace is no more fair than the village, but we have the chance at least to approach it with our eyes relatively open already to some of its injustices and its potential opportunities.

## NOTES

1. I use "we" and "us" to describe folklorists as a group throughout this chapter. I am writing from my own perspective as a folklorist with a particular positionality dually engaged in public and academic folklore in the United States. Certainly folklorists are a diverse bunch, and not all fit within the characterizations here described. But as Basso made clear in *Portraits of the White Man* (1979), it does not help to further our field to ignore that we, too, are objects of another's constructions. I use "we" because the actions of a few affect the work of all.

2. The idea of ethnography as translation has shown surprising longevity even after translation itself has been called into question in the face of semiotics.

3. Philanthropic marketing narratives are not the main topic here, but they do have some bearing. Many of the kinds of folkloristic productions I discuss here come with an implied message of helping other cultures, either to celebrate their culture or to find culturally based ways to more actively participate in capitalism (making traditional arts for sale, say). Thus, the step between the kinds of development-oriented capitalism of a craft cooperative—with its focus on cultural pride and economic development and the cross-cultural understanding that the sale of those crafts implies—and the folklore festival—with its focus on cross-cultural understanding and the development and cultural pride that it implies—is not as wide as we might think. Further, the multinational corporations who fund such events are banking on exactly such blurring by using a message of cross-cultural understanding, or even simply proximity to such messages, to sell their own products.

4. Kirshenblatt-Gimblett has stated: "Ethnographic objects . . . are artifacts created by ethnographers when they define, segment, detach, and carry them away" (1998, 2).

5. Cantwell notes that this connection was made by presenters in one American Folklife Festival when they were shuttled to and from the festival site on busses borrowed from the National Zoo, with the words ZOO BUS emblazoned on the sides (1993, 145).

6. Institutional missions can have an important impact on the kinds of representations seen in specific institutions. For example, the National Museum of the American Indian's mission states that the institution "is committed to advancing knowledge and understanding of the Native cultures . . . through partnership with Native people and others" (National Museum of the American Indian 2019). This last phrase has effectively meant that any representation must include the modern voices and the curatorial approval, on some level, of the people being represented. Contrast this to the Museum of International Folk Art's mission: "to enrich the human spirit by connecting people with the arts, traditions, and cultures of the world" (International Folk Art Museum 2019). This statement could be read as problematically eliding the people who actually produce the art. Yet, it must also be noted that these two museums, while both exhibiting Native art, do so for different audiences, in different contexts, and with different aims (footnote mine).

7. For example, one of the major questions on Missouri Arts Council grant applications is how the organization plans to increase audience numbers and reach out to new audiences.

8. For those preferring a psychoanalytic metaphor, in "On the Psychology of Collecting Folklore," Dundes makes a strong case for classifying folklorists as "anal retentive," sublimating desire into a compulsion to collect the "useless product of human activity" (2007, 416).

9. I, for one, am certainly not.

# REFERENCES

Banks, Russell. 2004. *The Darling*. New York: Harper Perennial.

Baron, Robert. 2010. "Sins of Objectification? Agency, Mediation, and Community Cultural Self-Determination in Public Folklore and Cultural Tourism Programming." *Journal of American Folklore* 123 (487): 63–91. https://doi.org/10.5406/jamerfolk.123.487.0063.

Basso, Keith. 1979. *Portraits of the White Man*. Cambridge: Cambridge University Press.

Bauman, Richard. 1978. *Verbal Art as Performance*. Prospect Heights, IL: Waveland.

Bauman, Richard, and Charles Briggs. 2003. *Voices of Modernity: Language Ideologies and the Politics of Inequality*. Cambridge: Cambridge University Press.

Bendix, Regina. 1997. *In Search of Authenticity: The Formation of Folklore Studies*. Madison: University of Wisconsin.

Brooks, Van Wyck. 2018. "On Creating a Usable Past." *Dial*, April 11, 337–41.

Cantwell, Robert. 1993. *Ethnomimesis: Folklife and the Representation of Culture*. Chapel Hill: University of North Carolina.

Cho, Sumi, Kimberlé Williams Crenshaw, and Leslie McCall. 2013. "Toward a Field of Intersectionality Studies: Theory, Applications, and Praxis." *Signs* 38(4): 785–810. doi:10.1086/669608.

Clifford, James. 1988. *The Predicament of Culture: Twentieth-Century Ethnography, Literature, and Art*. Cambridge, MA: Harvard University.

Dégh, Linda. 1994. *American Folklore and Mass Media*. Bloomington: Indiana University Press.

Denby, Priscilla. 1971. "Folklore in the Mass Media." *Folklore Forum* 4(5):113–25.

Dundes, Alan. 1963. "Advertising and Folklore." *New York Folklore Quarterly* 19: 143–51.

Dundes, Alan. 1987. *Cracking Jokes: Studies of Sick Humor Cycles and Stereotypes* Berkeley: Ten Speed Press.

Dundes, Alan. 2005. "Folkloristics in the Twenty-First Century." *Journal of American Folklore* 118 (470): 385–408.

Dundes, Alan. 2007. "On the Psychology of Collecting Folklore." In *The Meaning of Folklore: The Analytic Essays of Alan Dundes*, ed. Simon Bronner. Logan: Utah State University Press.

Foley, John Miles. 2002. *How to Read an Oral Poem*. Urbana: University of Illinois Press.

Ginsburg, Faye. 2006. "Ethnography and American Studies." *Cultural Anthropology* 21 (3): 487–95.

Golfman, Noreen. 1996. "Locating Difference: Ways of Reading Multiculturalism." *Mosaic: A Journal for the Interdisciplinary Study of Literature* 29 (3) (September): 175–85.

Graburn, Nelson H. H. 1976. *Ethnic and Tourist Arts: Cultural Expressions from the Fourth World*. Berkeley: University of California.

Haring, Lee. 2018. "Among the PALMs." *Humanities* 7 (2): 44. https://doi.org/10.3390/h7020044.

Heald, Susan. 1997. "Compensation/Restoration of a Tuscarora Beaded Cloth with Tuscarora Beadworkers." American Institute for Conservation, Textile Specialty Group Postprints of the 25th Annual Meeting, San Diego, 35–39.

hooks, bell. 1992. *Black Looks: Race and Representation*. Boston: South End Press.

Huyssen, Andreas. 1995. *Twilight Memories: Marking Time in a Culture of Amnesia*. New York: Routledge.
Hymes, Dell. 1975. "Breakthrough into Performance." In *Folklore: Performance and Communication*, ed. D. Ben-Amos and K. Goldstein, 11–74. The Hague: Mouton.
International Folk Art Museum. 2019. "Mission." Accessed July 10, 2019. http://www.internationalfolkart.org/about/mission-statement.html.
Kapchan, Deborah. 1996. *Gender on the Market: Moroccan Women and the Revoicing of Tradition*. Philadelphia: University of Pennsylvania.
Kirshenblatt-Gimblett, Barbara. 1998. *Destination Culture: Tourism, Museums, and Heritage*. Berkeley: University of California.
Korom, Frank. 1999. "Empowerment through Representation and Collaboration in Museum Exhibitions." *Journal of Folklore Research* 36(2–3): 235–41.
Kurin, Richard. 1997. *Reflections of a Culture Broker: A View from the Smithsonian*. Washington, DC: Smithsonian Institution.
Lau, Kimberly J. 2000a. *New Age Capitalism: Making Money East of Eden*. Philadelphia: University of Pennsylvania.
Lau, Kimberly J. 2000b. "Serial Logic: Folklore and Difference in the Age of Feel-Good Multiculturalism." *Journal of American Folklore* 113 (447) (Winter): 70–82.
Lawless, Elaine J. 1992. "'I was afraid someone like you . . . an outsider . . . would misunderstand.'" *Journal of American Folklore* 105 (417) (Summer): 302–14.
Leuthold, Steven. 1998. *Indigenous Aesthetics: Native Art, Media, and Identity*. Austin: University of Texas Press.
Littrell, Mary, and Marsha Dickson. 2010. *Artisans and Fair Trade: Crafting Development*. Sterling, VA: Kumarian.
Lowe, Lisa. 1996. *Immigrant Acts*. Raleigh: Duke University Press.
Mason, Julian. 1954. "Some Uses of Folklore in Advertising." *Tennessee Folklore Society Bulletin* 20: 58–61.
Mullin, Molly H. 1995. "The Patronage of Difference: Making Indian Art 'Art, Not Ethnology.'" In *The Traffic in Culture: Refiguring Art and Anthropology*, ed. George E. Marcus and Fred R. Myers. Berkeley: University of California.
National Museum of the American Indian. 2019. "Vision & Mission." Accessed July 10, 2019. https://americanindian.si.edu/about/vision-mission.
Noyes, Dorothy. 1995. "Group." *Journal of American Folklore* 108 (430), "Common Ground: Keywords for the Study of Expressive Culture" (Autumn): 449–78.
Noyes, Dorothy. 2016. *Humble Theory: Folklore's Grasp on Social Life*. Bloomington: Indiana University Press.
O'Giolláin, Diarmuid. 2014. "Narratives of Nation or of Progress? Genealogies of European Folklore Studies." *Narrative Culture* 1 (1), Article 5. http://digitalcommons.wayne.edu/narrative/vol1/iss1/5.
Oxford English Dictionary Online. 2016. Oxford: Oxford University.
Pratt, Mary Louise. 1992. *Imperial Eyes: Travel Writing and Transculturation*. New York: Routledge.
Percy, Walker. 1975. "The Loss of the Creature." In *The Message in the Bottle: How Queer Man Is, How Queer Language Is, and What One Has to Do with the Other*. New York: Farrar, Strauss, Giroux.
Price, Sally. 1989. *Primitive Art in Civilized Places*. Chicago: University of Chicago.
Propp, Vladimir. 1968. *Morphology of the Folktale*. Austin: University of Texas.
Publore Archives. 2009. publore@list.unm.edu.
Rohrich, Lutz. 1980. "Folklore and Advertising." In *Folklore Studies in the Twentieth Century: Proceedings of the Centenary Conference of the Folklore Society*, ed. Venetia J. Newall, 114–15. Totowa, NJ: Rowman and Littlefield.

Rosaldo, Renato. 1993. *Culture and Truth: The Remaking of Social Analysis.* Boston: Beacon Press.

Said, Edward. 1979. *Orientalism.* New York: Vintage Books.

Shohat, Ella. 1992. "Notes on the 'Post-Colonial.'" *Social Text*, no. 31/32, "Third World and Post-Colonial Issues," 99–113.

Shuman, Amy. 2005. *Other People's Stories: Entitlement Claims and the Critique of Empathy.* Urbana: University of Illinois.

Smith, Linda Tuhiwai. 1999. *Decolonizing Methodologies: Research and Indigenous Peoples.* London: Zed Books.

Spurr, David. 1993. *The Rhetoric of Empire: Colonial Discourse in Journalism, Travel Writing, and Imperial Administration.* Durham, NC: Duke University Press.

Steiner, Christopher B. 1994. *African Art in Transit.* Cambridge: Cambridge University.

Stewart, Susan. 1993. *On Longing: Narratives of the Miniature, the Gigantic, the Souvenir, and the Collection.* Durham, NC: Duke University Press.

Tedlock, Dennis. 1972. *Finding the Center: Narrative Poetry of the Zuni Indians.* New York: Dial.

Thaler, Richard. 2015. "Unless You Are Spock, Irrelevant Things Matter in Economic Behavior." *New York Times*, May 8, 2015.

Whisnant, David E. 1983. *All That Is Native and Fine.* Durham, NC: University of North Carolina Press.

# About the Authors

**William A. Ashton** is an associate professor of social psychology at York College, City University of New York. He has published in diverse outlets such as *The Journal of Personality and Social Psychology*, *Sex Roles*, *Fortean Times*, *Trickster's Way*, and *Lebowski 101*. Besides Jungian psychology, his research interests include fan culture (Big Lebowski achievers and Star Trek trekkies), and his lab-based research interests are focused on the attributions people make regarding rapists and women who have been raped. Ashton worked outside of academia for several years, during which time he led two nonprofit organizations and served as a business consultant.

**Puja Batra-Wells** is a scholar of American material cultures and folklore who studies informal economies and modes of cultural display and presentation. Her research is invested in the analytics of materiality and the intersections between economies of occupational practice, performance, and experience under conditions of endemic risk. She holds a master's degree in popular culture and a doctorate in comparative studies and a certification in public history. She is program manager for the Global Arts + Humanities Discovery Theme at The Ohio State University—an initiative that fosters cutting-edge cross-disciplinary research and collaboration in the integrated arts and humanities.

**Halle M. Butvin** is director of special projects at the Smithsonian Center for Folklife and Cultural Heritage. She leads the center's cultural sustainability work around the world, designing collaborative projects to support communities, safeguard their heritage, promote cultural expression, and elevate cultural practices to improve local economies. Prior to joining the Smithsonian, Halle spent ten years running One Mango Tree, a fair-trade textile and apparel business she started in Uganda, while also designing and implementing impact-driven international development programs in East Africa and Asia, ranging from democracy and governance to biodiversity conservation and economic growth. She holds a master's degree in city and regional planning from The Ohio State University.

**James I. Deutsch** is a curator and editor at the Smithsonian Institution's Center for Folklife and Cultural Heritage, where he has helped plan and develop public programs on California, China, Hungary, Peace Corps, Apollo Theater, Circus Arts, National Aeronautics and Space Administration, Mekong River, US Forest Service, World War II, Silk Road, and White House workers. In addition, he serves as an adjunct professor—teaching courses on American film history and folklore—in the American Studies Department at George Washington University. Deutsch has also taught American studies classes at universities in Armenia, Belarus, Bulgaria, Germany, Kyrgyzstan, Norway, Poland, and Turkey.

**Christofer Johnson** is a PhD candidate concentrating in folklore. He is primarily interested in the political agency of folklore and folksong in the Anglophone world, the cultural dimensions of power in the contemporary period, and the way that cultural artifacts impact and shape the development of national identity. His dissertation work centers on the idea of cultural resilience and the self-conscious ways that communities (especially communities of work) adapt (or don't), cope (or don't), and change (or don't) in the face of an increasingly globally integrated and connected world.

**Michael Lange** is an anthropologist, a folklorist, and a professor at Champlain College, in Burlington, Vermont, where he teaches a wide range of interdisciplinary classes. His ongoing research includes cultural identity and narrative, as well as cultural identity in academia, particularly the negotiation of academic and disciplinary identity in interdisciplinary spaces. He is the author of *Norwegian Scots* and *Meanings of Maple*. He has conducted ethnographic fieldwork in Scotland, Norway, Morocco, and the United States.

**John Laudun** is professor of English at the University of Louisiana, where his research focuses on how humans create their world with relatively simple resources, like words, or, in the case of his book *The Amazing Crawfish Boat*, how a diverse network of individuals can take pieces of metal and pieces of ideas and invent a traditional amphibious craft that transformed the economics of agriculture in a region. His work has appeared in a variety of academic journals and edited volumes, as well as been cited in newspapers and documentaries. He has been a Jacob K. Javits Fellow with the US Department of Education, a MacArthur Scholar, a fellow at the EVIA Digital Archive, a fellow with the NEH Institute on Network Studies in the Humanities, and a senior researcher in Culture Analytics at UCLA's Institute for Pure and Applied Mathematics. His work has been funded by the Grammy Foundation, the Louisiana Board of Regents, the Andrew Mellon Foundation, the National Endowment for the Humanities, and the National Science Foundation. For more information, please see http://johnlaudun.net/.

**Julie M-A LeBlanc** holds a PhD in folklore from Memorial University of Newfoundland and an MPhil in medieval history from Trinity College, Dublin, has taken cultural management courses at the École des hautes études commerciales (HEC) in Montreal, and is an accredited strategic performance management specialist from Rutgers University, New Jersey. In addition to holding policy, research, and parliamentary affairs roles, she is currently a senior analyst within the Government of Canada, working on Indigenous and international human rights issues, and is a part-time professor of Celtic studies at the University of Ottawa.

**Willow G. Mullins** teaches folklore through the American Culture Studies program at Washington University in St. Louis. Her published work has centered on textiles, in *Felt*, part of the Textiles That Changed the World series; articles on the unhomely and economy in the novels of Shirley Jackson and Tana French; and folklore theory, in *Implied Nowhere: Absence in Folklore Studies*. Her current research interests include the materiality of death and weatherlore in the era of climate change.

**Cassie Patterson** is assistant director of the Center for Folklore Studies and director of the Folklore Archives at The Ohio State University. Patterson's research interests include intersections of culture, economics, and the environment in relation to notions of place, space, and home; the politics of commemoration and public display; and the acts of travel and staying put. She is particularly interested in generational relationships in Appalachia and the ways in which Xennials and Millennials in the region (re)create a sense of place for themselves in a changing environment. Cassie is co-creator of the Ohio Field Schools initiative, an archival collection and service-learning course that teaches ethnographic methods through experiential learning. She also coordinates the Appalachian Studies Network@OSU.

**Rahima Schwenkbeck**, PhD, is an adjunct professor of American studies at George Washington University. She is also the owner of Time Machine Consulting, LLC.

**Amy Shuman** is professor of folklore in the Department of English at The Ohio State University. Her work for this volume was supported by a Guggenheim Fellowship. She is the author of *Storytelling Rights: The Uses of Oral and Written Texts among Urban Adolescents*, *Other People's Stories: Entitlement Claims and the Critique of Empathy*, and, with Carol Bohmer, *Rejecting Refugees: Political Asylum in the Twenty-First Century* and *Political Asylum Deceptions: The Culture of Suspicion*.

**Irene Sotiropoulou** is a heterodox economist currently based at the Energy and Environment Institute of the University of Hull. She specializes in ecological, feminist, solidarity, and noncapitalist economics; heterodox theories and practices about money and finance; and non-monetary economics and sharing modes. For analyzing everyday and folk culture with reference to grassroots economic knowledge, she has been awarded, along with Dr. Ferda Dönmez-Atbaşı (Ankara University), a Newton Mobility Grant by the British Academy. She is a fellow of the GEM-IWG/GEM-Europe and World Social Science Fellowship programs and a Fellow of the Monetary Research Center (UNWE) at Sofia.

**Zhao Yuanhao** holds a PhD from The Ohio State University, majoring in folkloristics and Near Eastern languages and cultures. He conducts fieldwork mainly among the Hui, a Muslim ethnic group living within the borders of China. Zhao's fields of interest are folk narratives, material culture, and anthropology of death. His other research projects include narratives about disgusting objects and dirt in folktales and traditional toys in Central China. He has published peer-reviewed journal articles and invited book chapters on various subjects in English and Chinese. He currently works with the Chinese Academy of Social Sciences.

# Index

Abrahams, Roger, 5–6, 13, 21
academia, 179, 218, 283
academic(s), 17, 21, 26, 93, 195, 216
Acheson, James, 112–114, 116
actant(s), 43, 156–157, 166–171
activism, 144, 221; activist(s), 145, 261
adaptation, 6, 15, 35, 48, 87, 90, 116, 182, 282
advertising, 30–31, 48, 53–54, 57, 64–67, 68, 203, 207, 272
aesthetic, 7, 79–83, 174, 181, 184, 280
African, 29, 44, 199, 238, 272
African American, 131, 135, 144–145, 147, 152
agrarian, 113, 119, 278, 280, 287
agriculture, 27–31, 34–39, 44–46, 79–83, 89, 98, 117–118, 135, 166, 196, 231
aid, 83–84
Airbnb, 236, 246
Alibaba, 236, 246
alienation, 5, 181, 183, 198, 254, 260, 263, 280
amateur(s), 110, 179, 183, 207
ambiguity, 167, 238, 273; ambiguous, 44, 101, 238, 242–243
American, 7, 10, 14, 20, 27, 29, 37, 44, 72, 80–86, 113, 199, 238, 277–278
anthropology, 43, 215, 274, 281; anthropologist, 48, 53, 156, 274
Appadurai, Arjun, 11–12, 266, 268
Appalachia, 15, 74, 130
apprenticeship, 79, 254, 257, 263, 268
appropriation, 4, 13, 47–48, 51, 166, 226, 229, 260, 267, 287
aquaculture, 29, 36, 124
archaeology, 118, 184
archetype(s), 20, 234, 238, 240–242, 248
architecture, 79, 255–256, 262
archives, 73–75, 145, 194
artifacts, 7, 10–11, 26–27, 28, 40, 44, 45, 73, 268, 288; artifactualization, 281
artisan(s), 18–20, 72–90, 122, 252–268, 278; artisanal, 27, 82, 254; artisanship, 38, 278
artist(s), 4, 11, 19, 40, 62, 73, 87, 89, 148–151, 174–190, 252–266, 274; artistic, 3, 13, 15, 27, 38, 79, 82–83, 149, 174–176, 182–184, 223, 283; artwork, 19, 149, 182, 188, 252

Asia(n), 96, 271
asset(s), 83, 130, 184, 246
Atlantic Ocean, 29, 109–113, 119–124
audience(s), 4, 8, 11–12, 17, 65, 79, 84, 90, 94, 134, 143, 210, 218, 224, 231, 265, 272, 276–288
authentic, 5, 10, 55, 85–88, 94, 105–106, 210, 260, 276, 280–282, 284–285; authentically, 96, 105–106; authenticate, 180, 269, 280
authenticity(ies), 21, 47, 83–87, 96–97, 104–106, 133, 218, 271–287
authorship, 148, 265
autonomy, 62, 176–184, 208

Bakhtin, Mikhail, 4, 13, 156, 168, 170; Bakhtinian, 19, 170
banking, 273, 288
barter(s), 188, 211, 223, 226–227
basket(s), 72, 74, 84–85
Bauman, Richard, 5, 11–12, 26, 118, 156, 175, 281, 284
bayou(s), 30, 45
Bendix, Regina, 6, 8–9, 12, 105, 268, 280–281, 283–287
biodiversity, 110, 123
bohemian, 19, 180–182, 190
border(s), 162
boundary(ies), 112, 126, 135, 160, 168–169, 176, 183, 236, 238, 242, 276
bourgeois, 6–7, 177, 180, 182, 190, 225
brand, 47–48, 59, 84–86, 95–96, 101, 177, 179, 206
Briggs, Charles, 11, 13, 21, 26, 109, 216, 253, 281
broker(s), 12, 21, 27, 272–287; brokerage, 12, 178–179, 272–275, 284
Buddhist, 161, 163, 277–278
buyer(s), 31, 73, 76, 83–87, 111, 184–188, 207, 210, 235, 272, 275, 282; buying, 14, 74–78, 83–84, 93–95, 104–107, 209

Canada, 47–51, 55, 62–66, 95, 97; Canadian, 29, 48, 51, 55, 59–60, 67
Cantwell, Robert, 11–12, 272, 279, 288

capital, 12, 125–127, 137, 167, 182, 188, 200, 203, 217, 272, 281–283; anticapitalist, 176, 214, 221; capitalism, 6, 9–13, 19–20, 112, 116, 177, 186–188, 196, 208–210, 214–220, 230, 246, 276–277, 288; capitalist, 5–8, 13–15, 20–21, 115, 126, 200, 209, 214–228, 254, 268, 271, 282; capitalistic, 198, 200, 208; noncapitalism, 216, 218, 230; precapitalist, 5–6, 287
carve(d), 130, 255–264, 268; carvers, 72, 79, 252, 260, 264, 266
celebration, 137, 275–283
chaos/chatoic, 19, 156, 159, 170, 243. *See also* disorder
China, 19, 96, 155–158, 169, 171; Chinese, 163, 169–171
Clifford, James, 8, 11, 18, 271, 279, 285, 287
collaboration, 34, 85, 145; collaborative, 147, 188
collector(s), 5, 186, 190, 218, 280; collection, 7, 10, 272, 278, 281, 284, 287
collective, 43, 68, 114, 126, 189, 195, 206, 208, 215, 240
colonial, 55, 62, 134, 167, 215, 277
commemoration, 131–143, 147, 151
commercial, 10, 35–39, 48, 58, 73, 77–81, 87, 89, 109–112, 162, 179, 184, 187, 254, 272; commercial fishing, 109–126; commercialism, 177, 260; commercialized, 48–49, 53–57
commodity(ies), 4–6, 9–13, 17–18, 21, 27, 33–34, 94–96, 99–100, 103–107, 175, 183–184, 218, 227, 264, 268, 271–272, 275–277, 281–286; commodification, 4, 10–19, 48, 78, 82, 94–95, 101, 104–106, 171, 184, 209, 272, 276, 280; commodified, 9–12, 17, 54–56, 95–96, 99, 104–107, 134, 272, 276, 281–287; commoditized, 11–12, 38, 97, 107, 272
communal, 114–115, 122, 133, 148, 194–213, 216, 224; communal capital, 182, 188–189
communism, 7, 198, 208, 210, 221
competition, 113, 177, 184, 200, 205–206, 254, 285
connoisseur, 282, 285; connoisseurship, 8, 254, 280, 284–285
conservation, 110, 113, 122, 126, 131, 274
consume, 3, 10, 26, 67, 95, 103, 159, 271–287; consumer(s), 4, 11, 13, 17, 21, 47–48, 50–59, 63–68, 73, 80–89, 95, 100–104, 107, 133, 184, 187, 199, 209, 235, 246, 264, 268, 271–272, 278, 280–287; consumption, 6, 11–13, 16–19, 31, 47, 66, 133, 163, 168, 171, 271–272, 276–286; consumptive, 38–39, 280

context, 6–7, 10–11, 13, 17, 27–29, 43, 58–59, 88, 100, 117–118, 152, 245, 262, 266, 274, 276, 280–281, 284–285
cooperative, 84, 117, 124, 202, 213, 254, 280, 288
corporate, 20, 67, 82–84, 97, 111, 115, 117, 121, 125, 135, 177, 185, 234; corporation, 3, 17, 81, 112, 205, 236, 240, 275–276, 288; corporations, 3, 112, 205, 236, 240, 276, 288
craft, 3, 21, 27, 38, 40, 49, 59, 67, 72–89, 184, 209–210, 245–246, 253–259, 263–267, 288
creativity, 12, 43–44, 79, 177, 254, 263
credit, 182, 187–188, 197–198, 203, 206, 235
customer, 56, 60, 84–92, 101–104, 129, 165, 206

debt, 59, 179–180, 187–188, 205, 260
design, 26, 54, 79, 83–87, 90, 97, 117, 126, 185, 239
devaluation, 182–184, 187
development: brand, 177; economic, 40–42, 45, 81–83, 130, 142, 276, 288; psychological, 241–244; societal/communal, 194–198, 208
devil, 48, 50, 59–62, 219, 223–225, 229, 231
dialogue, 81, 84, 86, 132–134, 141, 145, 147–151, 161, 273
disorder, 19, 155–160, 167–171. *See also* chaos
distribution, 8, 39–40, 59, 156, 159, 178, 209, 223, 228, 231, 266
diversify, 121, 177, 203, 210, 220
diversity, 15, 38, 64, 73, 132
donation(s), 135, 145, 148, 176, 182
Dorson, Richard, 7–8, 10, 14, 48
Dundes, Alan, 9, 48, 53, 68, 125, 272, 274, 285

earn, 79, 88–89, 175, 197, 199, 203, 205, 231, 245; earnings, 79, 82, 175–176, 261
economics, 26–28, 36, 39, 122, 125, 133, 137, 141, 151, 156, 165–166, 171, 176, 190, 194, 260, 272, 279; behavioral economics, 3, 271; discipline of, 3–21, 41–44, 57, 82–84, 88, 214–218, 221–222, 230–231, 244; economic advancement, 83; economic autonomy, 62, 208; economic meaning, 93–99, 104–107, 175–176; economic revitalization, 130, 136; economic viability, 96, 107, 110–112, 117, 123–125, 156, 178, 189; economist, 3–4, 16, 94, 156, 171, 214, 234, 271; insecurity, 174, 176; macroeconomics, 5, 13, 16; microeconomics, 4, 12, 16, 38–39, 190; *See also* development; socioeconomic

education, 76–77, 92, 148, 175, 178, 183, 216–218, 221, 247–248, 287
egalitarian, 20, 141, 189, 194, 196, 199, 273; inegalitarian, 228
employ, 3, 12, 82, 85, 123, 190, 199, 255, 261; employment, 21, 121, 177, 179, 186, 189. *See also* unemployment
enterprise, 80, 81, 85–86, 174, 177, 207, 252, 254, 258–259, 272
entrepreneurial, 115, 175–179, 183, 186–189, 199; entrepreneurs, 50, 149, 247
environmental, 20, 115, 221, 227–229, 261–262, 267; ecocultural, 122; ecology, 11–12, 44, 109–110, 116–117, 120, 123, 164, 175, 221, 276; ecosystem, 36, 109, 123
ethics, 12, 15, 19, 145, 186, 234–236, 247
ethnic, 9, 19, 56, 64, 66, 155, 160, 162, 216, 222, 276–278, 280–281, 283–284, 286; ethnicity, 158–159, 217
ethnography, 8, 11, 16, 19, 93, 253, 259, 273, 277, 279, 285, 288; ethnographer, 7, 11, 156, 284, 288
ethnology, 7, 28, 42, 55
Etsy, 3, 82
European, 5, 7, 18, 31, 44, 62, 67, 110, 121–124, 166, 216, 231, 261
exhibit, 135, 151, 179, 182, 186–188, 199, 256, 273–274, 277, 285, 288
exploitation, 8, 13, 47, 49, 55–56, 66, 81, 116–123, 168, 189–190, 198, 216, 273, 281
export, 55, 87–89, 96, 255, 259, 262

factory, 5, 26–27, 103–104, 202–204, 220, 254, 259
farmer, 27–28, 30–45, 97–98, 118–119, 122, 126–129, 198, 268
Festival of American Folklife/Smithsonain Folklife Festival (FAF), 18, 72–89, 279, 287–288
festival, 12, 18, 52, 167, 169, 273, 276, 279, 285, 288
fetish, 6, 13, 177, 184–185, 227, 272–284, 286
fieldwork, 48, 73, 93–94, 105, 115, 130, 152, 157, 171, 176, 186
financial, 14, 59, 85, 100, 105, 121, 136, 143, 176, 179–188, 195, 201–206, 221, 235, 246, 261; financial crisis (economic downturn), 14, 234–235, 246–247
folk, 3–21, 26–27, 54, 58, 63, 72–73, 77, 93, 125, 133, 152, 156, 158, 209–210, 214–217, 228–230, 234, 252–259, 271, 272, 280, 288; art, 4, 9, 11, 21, 77, 83, 260; folk economy, 38–39, 253–254, 257, 261, 264–266; group, 50, 52, 56–57, 281–282; knowledge, 53, 68
folklore, 5–15, 26, 28, 31–41, 47–60, 63–68, 76, 94, 107, 125, 133, 214–216, 231, 238, 260, 272–274, 278–285, 288; discipline of, folklore studies, 3–21, 26–27, 43–44; folkloristic(s), 48, 56–57, 60, 171, 264, 274, 279, 280, 288; folklorists, 3–17, 21, 26–28, 38, 40, 48, 53–58, 63, 77, 156, 214, 253, 259, 264, 271–288
folktale, 17, 20, 54, 157, 165, 171, 283. *See also* narrative; tale
French, 55, 60, 65, 133, 152, 258
funding, 52, 83, 111, 135–136, 148, 151, 171, 179, 195, 275, 283

gender, 80, 190, 207, 216–218, 230–231, 276
gift, 15, 40, 87, 175–177, 182–184, 188, 219, 223–226, 229, 239, 243–245, 264–265
Glassie, Henry, 11, 40–41, 253, 264, 267
global, 4, 13–18, 21, 51, 81–83, 87, 95–96, 110, 112, 115–117, 120, 123–124, 234, 253–255; corporation, 51, 259, 275; economy, 17–18, 27, 82, 133, 189, 252–254, 266–268, 275, 277, 282; marketplace, 17–18, 47, 52, 73, 81–83, 87, 89, 115, 255, 259
globalization, 4, 8–9, 14, 17, 21, 79–80, 110–112, 115, 122, 125
government, 19, 52, 57, 75, 93, 110–112, 116–118, 122–126, 139, 155, 165–170, 224, 234, 246; governmental, 15, 105, 170–171, 246
Graburn, Nelson, 11, 105, 271, 273, 280
graffiti, 131, 134, 148–149
grassroots, 5, 20, 80, 110–111, 136, 214, 217, 230
Greece, 49, 215, 219–221, 224, 245
greed, 33, 119, 228, 246

handcraft, 55, 72, 74, 80, 85, 88, 97, 209–210, 254. *See also* craft
handmade, 3, 11, 72, 81–83, 85, 86, 194, 252–261
harvest, 29, 31, 37, 45, 109, 112, 114, 208
hegemony, 6, 20, 139, 278, 287
heritage, 11, 19, 48, 50, 56–62, 72, 85, 88–89, 98, 106, 122, 125, 137–138, 151–152, 256, 276; hertiage tourism, 130, 132–133, 137, 151
heroes, 47, 50, 56–57, 62, 63, 68, 239
historical, 10, 29, 34, 50, 53, 57, 63, 66, 73, 88, 118, 133, 137–138, 140, 152, 160, 194, 216–218, 245, 254–258, 266–267

holistic, 5, 15–16, 122, 126
homogeny, 5, 41, 43, 82, 160, 180, 214

identity(ies), 3, 11, 17–18, 48–49, 50–51, 54–57, 66–68, 73, 79, 87, 94–96, 106–107, 114, 118–123, 132, 134, 162, 179–181, 190, 276–279, 284; identification, 17–18
ideology, 6–8, 20, 50, 57, 68, 156, 170, 178, 181, 183, 194–196, 203–208, 221, 254
image, 34, 50–56, 60–68, 95, 100–102, 130–131, 135, 137, 143–149, 152, 168, 242, 271; imagery, 66, 88, 97, 101, 115
incentive, 77, 187, 203, 262; incentivize, 182, 184, 187
indigenous, 9, 86, 134, 221
industrial, 5, 7, 43, 81, 103–104, 122, 202, 220, 228, 256, 259, 260, 280; industrialized, 5, 97, 117, 137, 260; postindustrial, 129, 131–132, 135, 138, 152, 177
inequality, 143, 145, 176, 207, 228, 246
injustice, 145, 214, 216, 221, 224, 247, 288
international, 34, 48–49, 54, 59–60, 62, 67, 81, 87, 89, 96, 116, 124, 265–266
interpretation, 47, 49, 56, 151, 240, 243
investment, 10–14, 21, 31–32, 83, 112, 126, 131, 184–185, 200, 266, 275, 282
Ireland, 49, 133–134, 286
Islam, 158, 162–163, 171
island(s), 18, 105–106, 110–113, 116, 118, 122, 125–126, 201, 206, 219–220

Kapchan, Deborah, 13, 156, 165, 169, 264, 287
Kirshenblatt-Gimblett, Barbara, 10–12, 18, 48, 104, 132–133, 253–254, 268, 271, 288
Kurin, Richard, 12, 74, 78, 272–273, 279

label(ing), 14, 17, 48–54, 57–68, 82, 93, 97, 100–102, 107, 152, 156, 278
laborer, 45, 189, 223, 226
Latin, 176–177, 259, 267
Latino, 65, 135
legend, 3, 28, 40, 48, 50–69, 158
liminal, 19, 164, 171, 174
Limón, Jose, 6–7, 9, 217
loan, 135, 179, 235
localized, 9, 17, 19; localness, 95–96
luxury, 185, 198, 200

machinery, 29, 31, 45, 203, 256
macrofolklore, 5, 9, 51
magic, 53, 219, 228–229, 246, 248

makers, 10–11, 20, 27, 35, 38–39, 41–42, 72, 82, 101, 209
management, 15, 111, 120, 123–124, 131, 170, 178, 207, 236, 248
manufacture, 27–28, 34, 41–42, 101, 135–136, 178, 189, 200–204, 210, 253–254
marginal, 180, 254; marginality, 189; marginalization, 146; marginalized, 13, 26, 81–83, 139
marine, 29, 110, 124–126
marketing, 3, 18, 47–68, 88, 92–96, 100, 102, 107, 162, 179, 257, 282, 288; marketable, 50, 60, 66, 277; marketed, 31, 49–50, 59, 66, 85, 96, 163, 235; marketers, 48, 53, 56, 65, 66
marketplace, 3–4, 10, 13–21, 26, 50, 73, 78–82, 86, 89, 107, 155–169, 176–179, 182–183, 187, 205, 234, 253, 255, 260, 264–266, 271–272, 275–283, 286–288. *See also* global
Marxism, 4–7, 221, 229
material, 4, 9–12, 20, 26–27, 37, 79, 82, 85–87, 100, 114, 135, 179, 181, 184, 188, 198, 200, 217, 240, 242, 247, 253–257, 261, 266–267, 277, 280; material culture, 4, 9–12, 21; materialist, 217, 231
mechanize, 31–32, 35–36, 45
media, 3–4, 21, 48, 53, 56, 63, 134, 142, 147–148, 152, 215–216
merchants, 121–122, 124
Mexico, 11, 132, 134, 254, 283
middleman, 79, 272, 275, 281, 287
minority, 155, 161, 276
modernity, 5, 44, 112, 189, 254, 257, 281; modernization, 214, 280
monetary, 10, 18–19, 175, 183, 187, 224, 265
moral, 19–20, 132, 134, 151, 157, 188, 247–248, 264, 273, 280
multicultural, 21, 272, 276–278; multiculturalism, 276–280
multinational, 17, 48, 51, 59, 236, 275–276, 288
museum, 12, 73–77, 83, 185, 256, 261, 273–274, 278–279
myth, 3, 20, 119, 228, 234, 236, 238, 247; mythology, 117, 234–235, 239

narrative, 10, 14, 28, 47–49, 60, 66, 68, 79, 93–98, 100–107, 120, 131–134, 138, 141, 152, 155–162, 178, 214, 259, 274, 280, 286, 288. *See also* folktale; tale
nationalism, 5, 50, 55–56, 281
Native American, 77, 131, 139–140, 238, 274, 288

National Endowment for the Arts (NEA), 176, 190
neocolonialism, 4, 13, 272
neoliberal, 8, 174, 177–178, 189–194, 210, 214, 246
network, 3, 9, 21, 26–45, 65, 113, 134, 147, 156–158, 162, 168–170, 188, 217, 264–268, 279; networking, 82, 177, 179, 188
nonprofit, 83, 86, 141, 143–144, 151
nostalgia, 5, 48, 137, 152, 159, 252–254, 260, 268, 276, 278, 287
Noyes, Dorothy, 12–14, 115–116, 125, 169, 175, 190, 271, 274–276, 282

object, 4, 9–11, 17–18, 27, 38, 40, 44, 62, 67, 73, 79, 103, 168, 183–185, 257–260, 271, 274, 277–288
occupation, 7, 9, 119, 123–126, 258; occupational, 7–8, 111, 114, 116–117, 126, 137, 175, 180–181, 186
ocean, 29, 114–115, 120. *See also* marine
orderliness, 156–157, 162, 164, 170. *See also* chaos; disorder
organization, 81, 144, 151, 157, 167, 188, 208, 210, 236, 247–248, 254–255, 263, 266, 280, 288; organizational, 8, 26, 43, 115, 130, 134
ownership, 11, 51, 111, 114–115, 124, 184, 209, 244–245, 260–262, 265, 268

Paredes, Américo, 6, 8–9, 11, 217
partner, 3, 85–86, 112, 123; partnership, 81, 84, 86, 112, 288
patron, 79, 86–87, 178, 257, 263, 283
pattern, 50, 63, 66, 87–88, 121, 174, 217
peasant, 5, 7, 55, 167
performance, 4, 6, 11, 13–15, 27, 56, 73–74, 104, 118, 156, 190, 223, 260, 267, 272, 280–286; performative, 13, 16
Peruvian, 73, 87, 96, 277–278
philanthropy, 130, 276, 280, 288
positionality, 11, 19, 167, 278, 287–288
postcolonial, 9, 13, 272
poverty, 80, 176, 219, 222–224, 228
Pratt, Mary Louise, 13–14, 156, 189, 277
precarious, 174, 177–178, 189–190; precarity, 8, 174–175, 189
preservation, 12, 19, 79, 85, 87, 89, 111, 112, 120–125, 258, 273. *See also* conservation
pricing, 45, 94, 183, 187, 189
primitive, 5, 111, 149, 278
privilege, 131, 262–263, 268, 282–287

production, 10, 32, 36, 39, 50, 59, 69, 85–86, 93–98, 102–104, 107, 111, 133, 136, 141, 152, 156, 167, 174–177, 180–184, 199–203, 208, 210, 220, 231, 253–267, 285, 288; craft, 72, 79–80, 83–84, 88, 184, 253; folk/vernacular production, 5, 11, 15; mass, 34, 80–81, 184, 190, 218, 221; means of, 7, 103, 198, 222–229; producer(s), 18, 38–39, 45, 52–58, 80–81, 84, 87, 122, 133, 183, 214, 227, 272
profession, 142, 176, 178, 182; professional, 79, 142, 179, 183, 188–190, 217, 283–284; professionalization, 179–182, 188
profit, 66, 76, 81, 98–100, 110, 120, 122, 125, 180, 214, 231, 246, 262; profitable, 31, 41–44, 99, 112, 165, 199, 203
proletariat, 7, 189
prosperity, 84, 158, 165–166, 203, 214
protectionism, 105, 106, 122
purchase, 17, 59–60, 72, 74, 79–81, 90, 102–103, 113–114, 163–164, 198–199, 210, 252, 280; purchasers, 112–113, 209

race/racial, 141, 143–145, 276, 231, 271, 276
regional, 47–48, 51, 54, 56–57, 116, 209, 235, 283
regulation, 27, 110, 115–125, 189, 206, 210, 234, 247, 257, 267
representation, 11–12, 17, 21, 49–50, 58, 60, 66–68, 129–151, 170, 186, 215, 242, 271–281, 284–288; representational, 51, 54–58, 95, 132, 141, 147–150, 170, 279; represented, 7, 12, 14, 49, 51, 54, 77, 81, 136–137, 143, 174, 272–276, 279–288
reproduction, 15, 47, 121, 133, 196, 204, 258, 261
reputation, 42, 105–106, 152, 175, 202, 267
resistance, 5–9, 17, 19–20, 113–116, 148, 168, 175, 182, 184, 190, 253
restoration, 44–45, 131, 141
retail, 80–89, 185, 204, 236; retailer, 81–100, 194, 199–200, 209–210, 236
revenue, 59–60, 86, 112, 121, 135, 177, 187, 209
revitalization, 129–131, 136, 143, 151–152
revolution, 43, 56, 81, 179, 218, 228–229, 280
risk, 33, 88, 109, 175, 178–180, 185–188, 235
rural, 7, 15, 28, 80, 82–83, 88, 118, 125, 133, 196, 218, 280

sacred, 88, 119, 174, 176, 189, 238–239, 242
scarcity, 3, 14, 89, 174, 190, 281

sculptor, 179–180, 183, 257, 259, 263–264, 274; sculpture, 175, 252, 255–267, 277
security, 33, 189, 209, 235, 275
selling, 18–19, 53–54, 59–60, 65–66, 78–80, 94, 160, 180, 183, 186, 199–200, 209–210; sellers, 272, 275
Shawnee, 131, 136, 139, 152
slave, 29, 131, 145–146
Smithsonian Folklife Festival. *See* Festival of American Folklife
Socialism, 7, 268
solidarity, 139, 143–144, 151, 224
souvenir, 81, 139, 199
Soviet, 6, 271
spending, 82, 184, 246
socioeconomic, 4, 7, 10, 14, 49, 50, 53, 194, 229
status, 4–6, 10, 135, 152, 167, 183, 263–264, 285
stereotype, 55, 65, 97, 207, 215, 231, 279
storyteller, 145, 217–218, 221–225, 229–230; storytelling, 72, 130, 214, 285–287
studio, 174, 179–187, 254–267
style, 66, 82, 88, 143–144, 196, 199, 202, 210, 259–260, 276
subaltern, 6, 161, 167
subjectivity, 175, 189
subsistence, 115–116
sustainability, 11–12, 17–18, 21, 73, 80–89, 110, 116–117, 120, 123–126; sustainable, 81–82, 86–89, 100, 119–112, 116, 119–126, 185, 208, 229; unsustainable, 124, 247

taboo, 113, 169, 239, 242
tactic, 50, 54, 182, 185–186, 190
tale, 3, 6, 10, 14, 20, 53–55, 215–231, 242, 247. *See also* folktale; narrative
talent, 40, 135, 177, 223, 246, 265
taste, 66–67, 96–97, 209, 280
technology, 4, 8, 14, 21, 32, 42–43, 45–46, 80, 83, 89, 92, 100, 108, 220, 225, 229–231, 252–262, 266–267, 278; technological, 99, 225, 254, 256, 262, 266–267
textile, 81–88, 271, 284
theft, 15, 237, 244–245, 273; stealing, 237, 239, 244–245
tools, 32, 34, 36, 45–46, 58, 73, 82–83, 89, 130, 152, 155, 198, 217, 252–260, 263–266, 272; toolmaking, 252, 255, 257
tourism, 11, 16–17, 19, 55, 81, 130–133, 137–138, 151, 271; tourist, 11, 18, 55, 77, 81, 88, 102–104, 117, 136–137, 140, 150–151; touristic, 11, 18; tours, 30–31, 130, 134

tradition, 3–6, 9, 13, 16–19, 21, 26–27, 34, 44, 48, 50, 52, 57–60, 64, 68, 72–80, 83–89, 94, 96, 100–101, 105, 109–126, 133–134, 163, 171, 180, 190, 207, 209–210, 215–221, 224, 253–254, 259, 261, 264–274, 277, 282–285, 288
training, 88, 176, 183, 197, 206, 221, 263, 267, 282
transaction, 9, 11, 13, 16, 215
transgression, 155–157, 162, 169–170, 180
transmission, 35, 48, 63, 217, 253, 255, 264–267
trends, 36–37, 42, 53–56, 66, 78, 84–86, 89, 101, 109, 236

unemployment, 175, 224, 246. *See also* employment
UNESCO, 13, 79–80, 82–83, 262
urban, 3, 7, 54, 79, 83, 125, 149, 166, 168–170, 175, 218
utopia, 19, 194–195, 208, 267

value, 6, 10, 13–21, 43, 45, 58, 66, 72, 79, 82–83, 87, 89, 93–94, 99–106, 122, 125, 132, 134, 137, 139, 151, 156, 177, 182–185, 203, 229–230, 236, 240, 248, 254, 259, 260–267, 275, 280–285; valuation, 19, 26, 44, 175, 189–190
vendors, 75–76, 78, 158, 160, 163, 166–168, 170, 180, 186, 205
vernacular, 11, 19–21, 133, 174–175, 182, 190
visitors, 18, 72, 74–79, 102–106, 130, 139, 142, 206

wealth, 21, 113, 163, 177, 219, 223, 227–228, 245–246
weave, 199, 202, 209; weaver, 40–41, 72–73, 84, 87, 202, 264, 267; weaving, 41, 86, 88, 210
website, 52, 100, 134, 143, 152
welfare, 190, 214, 223
Western, 20, 47, 83, 134, 220, 236, 248, 254, 267, 272–273, 277–280, 282, 285
wholesale, 3, 101, 200, 209
wholesalers, 27
worker, 6–8, 81, 83, 118–119, 121, 129, 137, 175–176, 202, 204, 206, 221, 223, 245–246, 253–254, 263, 267; workforce, 175, 201, 222
workplace, 8, 254, 263, 266
workshop, 17, 77, 88, 156, 188, 220, 252–268

Zipes, Jack, 6, 217–218, 224, 228–229

www.ingramcontent.com/pod-product-compliance
Lightning Source LLC
Chambersburg PA
CBHW020246030426
42336CB00010B/640